Jane Austen and Mozart

South Atlantic
Modern Language Association
Award Study

JANE AUSTEN AND MOZART

Classical Equilibrium in Fiction and Music

ROBERT K. WALLACE

The University of Georgia Press   Athens

Designed by Sandra Strother Hudson
Set in 10 on 12 Linotron 202 Baskerville
The paper in this book meets the guidelines for
permanence and durability of the Committee on
Production Guidelines for Book Longevity of the
Council on Library Resources.
Printed in the United States of America

Library of Congress Cataloging in Publication Data
Wallace, Robert K., 1944–
Jane Austen and Mozart.

(South Atlantic Modern Language Association
award study)
Includes index.
1. Austen, Jane, 1775–1817—Criticism and
interpretation. 2. Mozart, Wolfgang Amadeus,
1756–1791. 3. Music and literature. 4. Classicism in
music. 5. Neoclassicism (Literature) I. Title. II.
Series. PR4037.W32 1983   823′.7   83–1268
ISBN 0-8203-0671-1

TO JOAN FERRANTE WALLACE

The publication of this work was made possible in part through a grant from the National Endowment for the Humanities, a federal agency whose mission is to award grants to support education, scholarship, media programming, libraries, and museums in order to bring the results of cultural activities to the general public.

Contents

vii

Contents

Part Two
JANE AUSTEN AND MOZART

✍ Acknowledgments ✍

F OR HELP in pursuing the ideas presented here, I wish to thank the
students who have studied music and literature with me at Northern Kentucky University—especially that first brave bunch in 1974.
The university itself has encouraged the development of the ideas presented here in a variety of ways. In particular, I wish to thank the Fac-
ulty Benefits Committee and the successive chairmen of Literature and
Language, Joe Price, Frank Stallings, and Bill McKim. Also helpful was
a grant from the National Endowment for the Humanities which allowed me to participate in the summer seminar, "Studying English Literature in Connection with the Other Arts," led by Robert M. Adams at
U.C.L.A. in 1974.

Calvin S. Brown's *Music and Literature: A Comparison of the Arts* provided the primary written inspiration for an undertaking of this sort.
For his personal interest in the project and for his generous critique of
the entire manuscript, I am deeply grateful. I also wish to thank Karl
Kroeber, Jacques Barzun, Jean-Pierre Barricelli, Doris Brett, Ed Theo-
doru, and Barb McCroskey for their helpful responses to parts of the
manuscript. Among musicians, I am thankful to Jeffrey Siegel for a pianist's reading of several chapters of this book, to Charles Rosen for his
brilliant writing about the classical style, to Jonathan Kramer for opening his seminar in music theory to a carpetbagging littérateur, to Rosina
Lhevinne and Gladys Astor Philibert for introducing me to Mozart's piano
concertos, and to Phil Koplow for musical advice and inspiration. My
special thanks go to Ted Diaconoff and Gayle Sheard for bringing to life
musical scores I had discovered in Jane Austen's library at Chawton, and
to the Modern Language Association, the Kentucky Philological Association, and WGUC-FM (Cincinnati) for providing occasions where that
music could be shared.

For permission to study and make use of the music at Chawton I am
indebted to Sir Hugh Smiley and the Jane Austen Society; for personal

Acknowledgments

assistance during the actual research I wish to thank Mrs. Elizabeth Rose and Mrs. Patricia Burch. Henry Jenkyns most graciously allowed me to examine the Austen music books in his possession. The British Museum, the Library of Congress, and the Salzburg Mozarteum were particularly helpful in my musical research. For aiding my general research, I am grateful to the Cincinnati Public Library and to the libraries of the University of Cincinnati, the University of Wisconsin at Madison, and Northern Kentucky University. Among librarians, Pam Juengling at Northern Kentucky University has been particularly helpful.

Among the many individuals at the University of Georgia Press who have helped me transform a manuscript into a book, I wish to give special thanks to Paul Zimmer and Hilde Robinson. He insisted that I cut, but left the knife in my own hands; she taught me that a copy-editor can be a collaborator, in the best sense of the word. For help with the index, I am grateful to Barbara Rohrer.

Above all, I wish to thank my wife Joan, who, better than typing all these pages, inspires a larger life in which they have their place.

Introduction

COMPARISONS between or among the arts are often viewed with suspicion—and rightly so. However rewarding such comparisons may be in one's own mind, however successful they may be in the classroom, they are professionally hazardous for a variety of reasons. In a world of increasing specialization it is difficult enough to master one academic field without taking on another one as well. More than one reckless soul has embarked upon an extended interart comparison only to founder on the Scylla of dilettantism or the Charybdis of overspecialization.

Even so, there is growing recognition of the need for interdisciplinary knowledge, if only it can be given solid foundation. This book responds to that need by addressing audiences that have traditionally remained separate: admirers of Jane Austen and the English novel, admirers of Mozart and classical music; students of period styles, students of aesthetics. In addressing these separate audiences it aims to integrate them as well. Part of my rationale for wishing to do so is expressed by Leonard Meyer in *Explaining Music*:

> In a climate of disciplinary diversity and specialization such as the one we live in, the need for common unifying concepts—cross-disciplinary fields—is pressing. . . . In the social sciences and the humanities only the barest beginning has been made.
>
> But there is no real alternative. For most of us at least, the patent diversity of this world will not be made comprehensible by the transcendental visions of mysticism. Nor will it be united by trying to make the humanities more scientific, in the sense of striving for exhaustive systematization or exact quantification. . . . Different disciplines and diverse conceptual frameworks [must] be brought together through careful inquiry into problems and modes of organization which are really common and shared.[1]

Introduction

The present study strives to bring together for mutual illumination not only the artistic achievement of Mozart and of Austen but the disciplines of literary and of music criticism.

Working mainly in isolation from each other, literary historians and music historians have charted parallel shifts in style that occurred in each art roughly between 1770 and 1830. According to the conceptual framework of music history, the stylistic shift is from "classical" to Romantic. According to the framework of literary history, it is from "neoclassical" to Romantic. Although these two traditions (and the artists representative of them) often appear side by side in parallel time charts of the arts, such parallels are seldom examined or validated through rigorous comparison of individual artists (or even art works) from the separate traditions. The works of Austen and Mozart (especially in the context of their respective Romantic successors) provide an excellent opportunity for such comparison.

Many music historians define the classical style in Viennese music by reference to Mozart. Many literary historians define the neoclassical style in English fiction by reference to Austen. The works of each reveal an unexampled mastery of symmetry, balance, clarity, and restraint—even within their own classical and neoclassical traditions. In the textbooks and critical studies of their separate arts, each is often held up as the purest exemplar of the classical equilibrium that was soon to give way to Romantic subjectivity, vehemence, and fragmentation. In certain later works, Mozart and Austen even anticipate the world of Romanticism in similar ways. Yet no sustained attempt has ever been made to compare their artistic and stylistic achievements.

The lack of such an attempt perhaps owes more to the lack of a method than to the lack of a felt need. For, among literary critics at least, the basic impulse to compare Austen with Mozart has been strong. A bewildering array of critics has briefly compared these two artists for one reason or another. According to David Cecil, Austen's novels have a "Mozartean perfection."[2] Mark Schorer finds that Austen's prose "has analogies" with "the articulation of theme in a sonata by Mozart."[3] George Whalley sees Jane Austen as "a writer who is rather like Mozart, without the *Requiem*."[4] According to Richard Church, *Emma* is "so consummate purely as a story that again the hard-worn comparison with Mozart's symphonies must be made."[5] For A. Walton Litz the "sense of union of opposites" in *Pride and Prejudice* "prompts the common comparison with Mozart."[6] In Lionel Trilling's words, "one understands very easily why many readers are moved to explain their pleasures in [*Pride and Prejudice*] by reference to Mozart, especially *The Marriage of Figaro*."[7] Brigid Brophy compares Austen's novels not with *Figaro* but with *Così fan tutte* and *The Magic Flute.*[8] Louis Kronenberger compares readers "who think Jane Austen tea-tablish" with listeners "who think that Mozart tinkles."[9] For Margaret Kennedy, Austen and Mozart both provide us with "the first rate" to which "we can return again and again, in many moods, for many reasons, and find that it has never failed us."[10] Rebecca West finds Austen and Mozart to have similar "value," and Virginia Woolf briefly pairs Austen with Mozart in *A Room of One's Own.*[11] None of these writers, however, devotes more than a phrase, a sentence, or, at most, a paragraph, to the comparison.[12]

This study attempts to show that such widely held intuitions may lead not only to glancing strobelight asides but to rigorous and illuminating comparisons.[13] The task requires not so much madness, perhaps, as method.

In Part 1, this book compares the general stylistic achievement of Austen and Mozart through contrast with that of their representative Romantic successors in each art. In the process, a working definition of *classical equilibrium* is created that can be applied both to prose fiction and to instrumental music. Part 2 compares the specific artistic achievement of Austen and Mozart through the extended analysis of three pairs of works. Comparison of *Pride and Prejudice* with Mozart's Piano Concerto No. 9 (in E-flat major, K. 271) reveals the "classical equilibrium" of each artist at its most youthful and effervescent. Comparison of *Emma* with Piano Concerto No. 25 (in C major, K. 503) shows the "classical equilibrium" of each artist at its most massive and grave. Finally, comparison of *Persuasion* with Piano Concerto No. 27 (in B-flat major, K. 595) reveals in each artist a poignant pre-Romanticism. At the same time, a method is created for comparing the stylistic qualities, the aesthetic components, and the human significance of novels and of piano concertos.

Two appendixes describe and evaluate the piano music that Austen played and the songs that she sang—often from manuscripts copied out in her own immaculate hand. Her music is then related to the style and content of the fiction she wrote.

JUST AS HISTORIANS of music and literature have tended to work in isolation from each other, so have those critics in each field whose main concern is the close analysis of individual works. The two critical fields have opposing strengths and weaknesses. Stanley Cavell has argued that "music has, among the arts, the most, perhaps the only, systematic and precise vocabulary for the description and analysis of its objects." But this very ability to scientifically describe and analyze the musical "object" has paradoxically deterred many twentieth-century critics from practicing "humane criticism." Seconded by Joseph Kerman, Cavell argues that

3

if music criticism is to remain one of the humanities, ways must be found to address issues other than the application of advanced academic techniques to the internal dynamics of the accepted masterpieces of the musical canon.[14]

In literary criticism, too, the twentieth century has witnessed an increasing emphasis on the application of quasi-scientific analysis to the internal dynamics of the literary work per se. This trend first became prevalent under the hegemony of American New Criticism, which so confidently eschewed the pathetic fallacy, the intentional fallacy, and numerous other "fallacies" as well—so that the explicator could concentrate only on the internal dynamics of the text itself. The structuralist and semiotic methodologies that have since emanated primarily from France do not so often focus on the primacy of the individual text, but they certainly do stress the application of a quasi-scientific analysis. Even so, the literary critic in general (and the critic of fiction in particular) does not yet have purely analytic tools equivalent to those of the music critic, particularly with regard to the subtleties of structure and form.

Karl Kroeber has voiced the need for literary critics to develop more sophisticated tools for finding the "essential form" of a work of fiction. "We cannot significantly penetrate the secret of novelistic form through the mere analysis of words, syntax, imagery, character, setting, and so on, in themselves. We must devise methods for understanding the relations between these materials by which the novelist shapes his art."[15] Music criticism possesses such tools. To the extent that fictional and musical forms are comparable (of which more below), the discipline of music criticism can help the literary critic locate, identify, and articulate certain "essential forms" in fiction. Similarly, to the extent that the human concerns of fictional and musical works are comparable, the discipline of literary criticism can help the music critic achieve the "humane" criticism that often is lacking. By comparing individual Mozart concertos with individual Austen novels, I hope to show how each discipline's strengths can be applied to the material of the other. Such application, of course, requires caution.

LITERATURE and instrumental music are difficult to compare. The one art communicates with words. The other communicates without them. The difference is so obvious and profound that some critics in each field feel that the two arts are noncomparable—that the difference in artistic media precludes any comparability in what is communicated. Yet one function of all great art is to express human spirit in significant form. And one function of the criticism of great art is to be responsive both to the significance of the form and to the humanity of the spirit. This being

4

so, it is potentially possible to compare either the humanity of the spirit or the significance of the form even in media as different as prose fiction and instrumental music. In the case of Austen's novels and Mozart's concertos, both the human spirit and the significant form are in fact comparable.

Different though they are, prose fiction and instrumental music have some special similarities even as media.[16] Perhaps the strongest of these is that each is a temporal art. Sonatas and short stories, piano concertos and novels all unfold through time. This similarity often results in structures that are comparable—many of them intentionally so. It is well known that composers such as Berlioz and Liszt and novelists such as Joyce and Mann have structured works in whole or in part on models from the other art. Critics in both fields have naturally investigated such intentional parallels.[17] They have given little attention, however, to structural parallels not consciously intended by the artist, even though these too may be of value to the comparative critic.[18]

The fact that Austen did not consciously model her works on the structure of Mozart's does not necessarily detract from the similarities that may actually exist between the "essential forms" of his piano concertos and her novels. The existence of such similarities may in fact mean more when they are not premeditated. Comparison of Austen's use of the three-volume novel structure with Mozart's use of the three-movement concerto structure, for example, not only reveals similarities between the internal dynamics of works of art in two different media; it also provides highly specific examples of the structural dynamics through which a "classical equilibrium" tended to be expressed in each art.

As was suggested above, the music critic is generally able to analyze structure with more precision than the literary critic. Most music critics would agree that the first movement of Mozart's Concerto No. 9 (K. 271) is masterfully symmetrical in its structure and proportions. Most literary critics would acknowledge the same to be true of the first volume of Austen's *Pride and Prejudice*. Yet the music critic is able to be much more specific about the various components within the symmetrical structure—about the "essential form," to use Kroeber's term. Aided by the insights of musical analysis, Chapter 4 of this book reveals the degree to which the "essential form" of the first volume of *Pride and Prejudice* parallels that of the first movement of Mozart's K. 271. This analysis not only demonstrates a significant structural parallel between a musical movement and a fictional volume; it allows a more precise description of the fictional structure (and of the relations among its component parts) than literary analysis alone has provided.

The literary critic, on the other hand, is generally able to analyze the human and social content of a given work with more precision. Works of art consisting of words about people embody human experience more explicitly than those that consist of musical notes. The literary critic has relatively little difficulty analyzing the personality of Elizabeth Bennet in *Pride and Prejudice*, for example. But the music critic cannot so easily analyze the "personality" of the solo voice in a Mozart piano concerto—even though it is a truism of Mozart criticism that each concerto does have its own personality. Similarly, the literary critic can discuss Elizabeth's experience of maturity without fear of being misunderstood, whereas his musical counterpart cannot so easily discuss the "experience of maturity" of the solo voice. But Mozart's piano concertos, no less than Austen's novels, are social creations; the relations between the solo and orchestra in the concertos are often comparable to those between the heroine and society in the novels. For the extended comparisons in Part 2, I have selected three concertos and three novels whose respective solo voices and heroines are comparable in personality, in experience of maturity, and in their social relations with the orchestra or society at large. Demonstration of these similarities not only reveals comparable human experience in novels and piano concertos; it also makes possible a more detailed account of certain human and social dynamics in the concertos than music criticism alone has provided.

In Austen's and Mozart's greatest works, the essential human meaning is in fact inseparable from the "essential form." In *Greek Tragedy*, H. D. F. Kitto argues that the "meaning" of a Greek play is often found in its "form." According to Kitto, the meaning expressed by a play's form "is something more akin to the 'meaning' of a Rembrandt or of a Beethoven sonata" than it is to meaning of a purely philosophical or verbal sort.[19] The kind of meaning that Kitto has in mind is often the most difficult to put into words, yet it is also the most profound. It is the kind of meaning that Meyer attempts to explore in Mozart's work in his fine essay "Grammatical Simplicity and Relational Richness" and that Kroeber attempts to explore in Austen's work in his book *Styles in Fictional Structure*.[20] This book is designed to explore such meaning in both music and fiction. The juxtaposition and comparison not only of literary and musical works but also of literary and musical modes of analysis offers a method by which to explore such meaning with a depth and precision often difficult to obtain when viewing a single artist, art work, or artistic tradition through the lens of that single art's critical apparatus.

Toward the end of *Aspects of the Novel*, the novelist and critic E. M. Forster tries to bridge the gap between his own musical and literary experience. He is searching for an analogy in fiction to the experience he has of "the whole symphony" after hearing the final note of Beethoven's Fifth. He cannot find the analogy, yet he writes that "there may be one; in music fiction is likely to find its nearest parallel."[21] The kind of analogy he is looking for is one of the many that this book is designed to explore. I do not presume to decide whether fiction finds its *nearest* parallel in music; I will be satisfied if this study shows the parallel to be much nearer than is generally thought.

THIS STUDY of Austen's and Mozart's work focuses on stylistic and artistic comparisons as revealed in the art works themselves. Detailed speculation as to the biographical, psychological, social, or cultural causes for these similarities would be interesting, to be sure. But it must here remain secondary to a demonstration of actual similarities between Austen novels and Mozart concertos. Given the lack of any widely accepted methodology for comparing works of prose fiction and instrumental music, simply to locate, describe, and analyze tangible artistic and stylistic similarities between the two artists is a sufficient task for one book.[22] This is therefore a study of comparable art, not of the comparable influences that may have led to the creation of that art.

Nor is it a study of mutual influence. Mozart, of course, knew nothing of Austen. When he died in 1791 she was but fifteen years old. She knew Mozart's name, but seems to have known very little of his music, even though she was a dedicated amateur pianist (see Appendix 1). What Austen and Mozart have in common they developed in separate countries, in separate arts, and in separate decades. In one sense that separateness is a limitation of this study: there is no obvious academic necessity for its having been undertaken. But that same limitation is a strength and opportunity. True affinities that cross national, artistic, or academic boundaries are as valuable as those that do not. Migrations of the *Zeitgeist* aid our human attempts to track that monster as much as do its manifestations in a single time, place, or art. Even critics in a single discipline occasionally move to another time or place in order to do justice to their object of pursuit.[23]

Consider for a moment Austen's generally recognized position as the purest exemplar of neoclassical English fiction. Where does one turn in English-language fiction for a comparable achievement? Certainly not to any of Austen's novel-writing contemporaries, for her neoclassical novels, all of them published in the 1810s, were stylistically an anachronism. Among her predecessors, Fielding's novels are often termed neoclassical, but they are so much more robust and less constrained than hers that the juxtaposition inevitably invokes more contrasts than comparisons. Her style has been compared with the neoclassical poetry of Pope and prose of Samuel Johnson. But Pope's poems and Johnson's

7

essays do not parallel the aesthetic forms of Austen's novels in any tangible way, whereas Mozart's piano concertos do. Nor do their works embody the lively interaction between the one and the many (or the individual and society) that is found in Austen's novels—and in Mozart's piano concertos. Nor do Pope or Johnson or Fielding, each of whom lived in an earlier day and in a different way, show the transition toward a poignant pre-Romanticism that Austen's novels—and Mozart's concertos—do.

Mozart merits comparison with Austen, then, because his work contains exactly those qualities which help us to measure and celebrate the distinctive scope and quality, the distinctive spirit and individuality, of her own achievement. Literary critics have already recognized this truth collectively and intuitively, as it were, through the array of brief strobe-light comparisons cited above. Significantly, no composer other than Mozart has been similarly invoked for comparison with Austen—not even Haydn, who shares with him so many general stylistic qualities.

I have yet to discover, on the other hand, a music critic who has compared Mozart with Austen. And at first there would seem to be neither need nor justification. For Mozart in Viennese music, unlike Austen in English-language fiction, is far from being the sole pure exemplar of the classical style. The music of Haydn and of early Beethoven embodies the principles of that style as clearly as Mozart's does. Should we not then be content to compare Mozart with them—as has been done so well already—rather than with a novelist?

Haydn's work is stylistically close to Mozart, to be sure. But nowhere in Haydn's music does one find the consistently exquisite balance between the one and the many (or solo and orchestra) that in Mozart's piano concertos is one of the greatest legacies he has left to instrumental music. Haydn's own "classical" imagination simply did not function in that realm in a manner at all comparable to Mozart's—nor did that of Beethoven. No musician in the history of Western music has matched Mozart's achievement in this regard. Austen's novels do reveal a comparable imagination and achievement.

Consider also Mozart's special brand of pre-Romanticism. Haydn showed pre-Romantic tendencies during his *Sturm und Drang* period but gravitated back to a firmly classical aesthetic in the great symphonies that capped his career. Beethoven, like Mozart, moved from a classical aesthetic toward a Romantic one, but did so in a massively vehement way that can hardly be compared with Mozart's relatively poignant and understated path. To the same degree that Mozart's pre-Romantic tendencies demand contrast with those of Beethoven and Haydn, so do they compare with those of Austen, which they often parallel closely both in spirit and form. Austen's *Persuasion* merits comparison with

Mozart's Clarinet Quintet (K. 581) or his last piano concerto (K. 595) because in important ways that novel is closer to the spirit of these compositions than is the music of other composers in the Viennese tradition.

Certain believers in the *Zeitgeist* may well prefer to see more emphasis on the *causes* of the comparisons soon to be discussed than this book promises to deliver. Certainly the *Zeitgeist* had something to do with the similarities that exist between Austen's and Mozart's art. The Enlightenment was a contributing cause for the art of each, perhaps even a necessary cause. But it was not a sufficient cause. Had Austen not written the novels she did, today we would scarcely have a clear concept of the neoclassical English novel. Had Mozart not composed the piano concertos he did, we would scarcely have a clear concept of the classical Viennese piano concerto. As it happened, each did create works of art that in ways only briefly summarized here demand comparison with the work of the other as much as with the work of artists in their own separate fields. This is my justification for daring to compare them.

Concerning the genesis of great works of art, René Wellek argues that "causal explanation and even historical antecedents do not accomplish much. We must leave something to chance, to genius, to a constellation of circumstance. . . . Why not agree that we are faced here with some ultimate *data*? . . . The literary historian and the comparatist has done what he can do if he has accurately described, analyzed, characterized, and compared what he has seen and read."[24] In this book, Austen's novels and Mozart's piano concertos are the ultimate data whose mere existence is to be celebrated, not explained away. That they are in fact comparable on multiple levels of aesthetic, social, and spiritual meaning is the reality which I hope accurately to describe, analyze, and characterize.

FINALLY, in deference to the spirit of the eighteenth century, I wish to cite two passages that have often come to mind as cautions while working on this book. The first is Samuel Johnson's famous objection to the "metaphysical" wit of John Donne and other seventeenth-century poets on the grounds that "the most heterogeneous ideas are yoked by violence together."[25] The artistic worlds of Mozart and Austen are heterogeneous, to say the least. My constant goal has been to "yoke" them without doing violence to their separate natures.

Johnson wrote his famous comment in 1779, the year in which Jane Austen turned four years old. Although she was not able to publish *Pride and Prejudice* until 1813, she wrote much of it in the 1790s, and the novel sparkles with the kind of neoclassical wit of which Johnson was the recognized master. When Johnson himself joined the heterogeneous for the purposes of wit, he did so not with violence but with effortless ease. So did Austen. One celebrated example is the description of Miss Bingley as "all that was affectionate and insincere."[26]

Less celebrated, but more to my purpose, is the description of Mary Bennet as "deep in the study of thorough bass and human nature" (p. 55). "Thorough bass" and "human nature" are as heterogeneous as "affectionate" and "insincere." The one refers to music, the other to life; the one to technique, the other to spirit. The wit in their juxtaposition is governed by Mary's being the common denominator. As the phrase in its context shows, Mary is unable to discriminate; she approaches both music and life in the same overzealous and unimaginative way: "They found Mary, as usual, deep in the study of thorough bass and human nature; and had some new extracts to admire, and some new observations of thread-bare morality to listen to." The wit is not limited to the juxtaposition of the unlike. Austen might have written that Mary was "serious" in her study. Instead she wrote "deep." Applied to thorough bass, *deep* means low in the register of the instrument (as Austen, from her own keyboard experience, knew). Applied to human nature, *deep* means profound. The "depth" of Mary's study highlights the ironic portrayal of her insensitivity to the nuances of both subjects. The clarity of diction and of syntax contributes to the wit as much as does the juxtaposition of the heterogeneous.

The pages that follow risk not only duplicating Mary's mistake but compounding it: they juxtapose not only technique and spirit, not only art and human nature, but fiction and music. Such items are, of course, related. The trick, which Mary lacked, is to approach them in a discriminating spirit. Austen's artistic world is animated by just such a spirit. So is Mozart's. Each is a world in which apparent paradoxes and seemingly incongruous juxtapositions usually do turn out to be harmonious and revealing.

Part One

CLASSICAL EQUILIBRIUM IN FICTION AND MUSIC

FOR OBVIOUS REASONS, one cannot automatically equate the classical style of Mozart with the neoclassical style of Austen. The "neo-" is in the way, for one thing. But that prefix is a relatively minor obstacle compared with the difficulty of applying concepts of style across the boundaries of the separate arts. Critics such as Wellek and Robert Rosenblum have made abundantly clear that concepts of style can be slippery enough even when applied to a single art.[1] Even so, they and others recognize that terms such as *classical, neoclassical,* and *Romantic*—when used with care—are essential to critics and historians of the separate arts. Perhaps the most brilliant recent example of this truth is Charles Rosen's musical study, *The Classical Style.*[2] Rosen's analysis of Haydn, Mozart, and Beethoven demonstrates the degree to which period concepts can be essential not only when trying to understand and describe the general tendencies of an artistic style but also when trying to understand and describe the particular masterworks that contribute so much to our conception of—and definition of—style. Even so, a term such as *classical style* must be used with great care, even when applied to a single artistic work.

Taking an example from Rosen's subject—and from ours—consider Mozart's great G-minor Symphony (K. 550). It is generally celebrated as a definitive example of the classical style in music. Yet there are qualified music historians who would make a good case for its really being Romantic. Beethoven's "Appassionata" Sonata, on the other hand, is often viewed as a revolutionary Romantic work. But Rosen, and others, make an excellent case for its actually being classical. If there can be so much difficulty applying terms such as *classical* and *Romantic* to individual musical works, one might ask, how then can one even begin to compare such classifications across the boundaries of the separate arts?

The answer hinges on the fact that such concepts, highly debatable or even arbitrary when applied to a single artist or work, take on more solid meaning when viewed in relation to other artists or works. Nearly all music historians, no matter how they would classify them singly, would agree that Beethoven is *more* Romantic than Mozart—and that the "Appassionata" is *more* Romantic than the G-minor Symphony. In this sense, a term such as *classical equilibrium* would distinguish Mozart's achievement from Beethoven's more Romantic equilibrium. But it would also unite Mozart's and Beethoven's achievement when seen in the context of their more Romantic successors. Once this is understood, one can begin to explore the kind of classical equilibrium that Mozart achieved. It can then be compared, where justified, with the kind of classical equilibrium achieved by Austen in the literary realm.

It must always be remembered, however, that our perception of even such a quality as equilibrium is culturally conditioned. Consider again the G-minor Symphony. Robert Schumann, the great Romantic composer, found only Grecian simplicity and grace in the symphony. In the context of Mozart's own musical generation, however, the G-minor Symphony expressed just what Schumann felt it did not: "discontent, discomfort, worried anxiety."[3] The symphony itself contains both the qualities Schumann found in it *and* the ones he did not. But it has been much easier to perceive the grace and to overlook the "worried anxiety" for those generations, beginning with Schumann's, that have experienced Beethoven. Just as Beethoven's music has changed the perception of supposedly intrinsic qualities in Mozart's, so has music since then changed the perception of supposedly intrinsic qualities in Beethoven's.

For much of the nineteenth century, Beethoven was considered the apotheosis of vehement Romanticism. In 1972, however, Rosen persuasively includes him with Haydn and Mozart as an exemplar of the classical style. Rosen argues that Beethoven's music, so vehement and disturbing to musicians of his own generation and of many to follow, is essentially classical in the way it grounds its tensions within a structural and harmonic framework that provides . . . equilibrium. As much as we might like to think otherwise, our perception of the stylistic qualities of an artist or a given work of art is as much relative as it is intrinsic.[4] That is why the working definition of *classical equilibrium* developed below will consider Austen and Mozart in relation to their Romantic successors rather than in isolation.

As soon as the terms *classical* and *Romantic* are seen as tendencies on a continuum rather than either/or alternatives, much of the confusion in their use disappears. As Paul Henry Lang has pointed out with respect to music, "Romanticism should not be taken as the antithesis of classicism, nor was it a mere reaction to it, but rather a logical enhancement of certain elements which in classicism were inherent and active, but tamed and kept in equilibrium." The same "subjectivist tendencies," Lang continues, are present in both period styles. The essential difference is in the "vehemence" with which they are expressed.[5]

Few works show as clearly as Mozart's G-minor Symphony the extent to which the subjectivist tendencies soon to be given more vehement expression in the Romantic age could be tamed and kept in equilibrium by a classicist. Its agitated emotion is expressed in four separate, balanced, symmetrical movements. The nearly symmetrical opening theme expresses grace as much as it does "discontent, discomfort, and worried anxiety." Throughout the first movement the grace is as prominent as the anxiety—in the mirrorlike counterstatement of the opening theme, in the lyrical contrasting theme, in the exact repeat of the exposition, and in the return of the opening theme in its pristine clarity after the rigors of the development section.

By contrast, the first movement of Beethoven's "Appassionata" is vehemently Romantic. The asymmetrical first theme, the immediate separation of the second half of the theme from the whole, the sledgehammer chords that further fragment the theme in the counterstatement, the elimination of the repeat of the exposition, the heightened agitation with which the first theme returns after the development—each of these features serves to violate the classical equilibrium that can be said to prevail in the Mozart movement. Similarly, the *attaca allegro* that fuses the second and third movements of the "Appassionata" violates the classical equilibrium with which Mozart instinctively keeps his movements separate, no matter how imperative the emotion. Even so, the "Appassionata" *is* a work of classical equilibrium—when contrasted with Liszt's B-minor Sonata. Liszt's great one-movement masterpiece, composed in 1854, reveals the degree to which the "Appassionata," composed in 1805, strains the classical forms without actually breaking or supplanting them.

In English fiction there is no clearer example of neoclassical equilibrium than Austen's *Pride and Prejudice*, no more vehement embodiment of Romantic transformation than Emily Brontë's *Wuthering Heights*. *Pride and Prejudice* is widely acknowledged to be a neoclassical novel in its concern with universal truths clearly articulated, in its vision of individual freedom that is in harmony with societal surroundings, in its balanced and symmetrical structure, in its composed manners and language, and in its moderate pace leading to the daylight resolution of all major conflicts. *Wuthering Heights*, on the other hand, is widely acknowledged to be a searingly Romantic novel in its emphasis on the individual's isolation from and conflict with society rather than his integration with it, in its violent and vehement action and language, in its surface discontinuities of time and of structure, in its sputtering and irregular rhythm and pace, and in its emphasis on darkness and dreams and death as opposed to that which is "light, and bright, and sparkling" (to use Austen's aptly chosen words for *Pride and Prejudice*).

In spite of these and other dramatic differences between the two masterworks, there are Romantic elements in the former, classical ones in the latter. In literature as in music "Romanticism and Classicism represent two different but complementary modes of human existence." These words are from the *Short History of English Literature*, which goes on to argue that "Jane Austen, like . . . other convinced 'Classicists' of her period . . . was just as much a representative of the Romantic Revival as Wordsworth or Shelley or Keats."[6] This statement is particularly true of *Persuasion*, her last novel, as numerous critics have recently observed. Yet even in *Pride and Prejudice* many of the "subjectivist tendencies" found in Austen's later fiction are, to borrow Lang's words, "inherent and active, but tamed and kept in equilibrium."[7]

By the same token, *Wuthering Heights* supports the contention of the *Short History* that "classical restraint, harmony, proportion, and form . . . are just as much in evidence in the best of Romantic literature as in the best of the Classical." The structure of *Wuthering Heights*, so rough and discontinuous on the surface, ultimately embraces a harmony and equilibrium as satisfying as that of the "Appassionata." Even Heathcliff's visits to Catherine's grave, so full of Romantic sensationalism by comparison to Austen's novels, are presented with classical restraint by comparison to the stories of Poe.

To the extent that classical and Romantic modes are different in either music or literature, it is important to be able to distinguish between them. To the extent that they are complementary, it is important to recognize the elements they have in common, though the emphasis may be different. One of the most influential critical studies of the transition from neoclassical to Romantic in English poetic and critical thought is M. H. Abrams's *Mirror and the Lamp*. Abrams goes to great lengths to differentiate the kinds of vision implied by his two metaphors.[8] Even so, the mirror and the lamp both help one, each in its own way, to see.

One might differentiate the kind of vision achieved by Austen and by Mozart on the one hand and by Brontë and Beethoven on the other by suggesting that in *Pride and Prejudice* and the G-minor Symphony the balance of the parts, the clarity of articulation, and the elegance of the surface tend to be obvious to any attentive reader or listener immediately, whereas the intensity and depth of emotion tend to become fully clear only on subsequent encounters. In *Wuthering Heights* and the "Appassionata" the emotional intensity is obvious immediately, the formal balance and proportion only subsequently. This difference of emphasis is one measure of the "classical equilibrium" that distinguishes, though it does not absolutely separate, the style of Mozart and of Austen from that of their more Romantic successors.

In developing a working definition of classical equilibrium that can be applied to both music and fiction, Chapters 1, 2, and 3 present various terms, themes, and tendencies that are applicable to both arts and that can be related to the work of Austen and of Mozart in the context of representative Romantic successors. These chapters are a preparation for the extended comparisons of novels and piano concertos in Part 2. They also suggest in a general way the extent to which the transition from classical to Romantic in Viennese music is parallel to the one from neoclassical to Romantic in English-language fiction.

One final note. In the present context, the difference between classical and neoclassical is no obstacle to comparison. The classical equilibrium that Austen achieved is often prefaced by a "neo-" in order to distinguish her style from that of the ancient classical writers, for whom history has preserved no equivalent in music. As our working definition will show, Lang's concept of a classical equilibrium that tames and keeps in balance subjectivist tendencies to be given more vehement expression in the Romantic era applies as well to Austen's neoclassical literary style as it does to Mozart's classical musical style. As the above citations from the *Short History* reveal, the terms *classical* and *neoclassical* are often used interchangeably in literary criticism itself.[9]

Chapter One

COMPARABLE TERMS
IN FICTION AND MUSIC

THE APPLICATION of musical terminology to literary works, and vice versa, is tantalizing but fraught with danger. On a theoretical and highly conscious level, attempts have been made to show, for example, that themes in music correspond to subjects in a sentence, that harmony corresponds to adjectives, and rhythm to verbs. One can feel the potential force of the general analogy, yet there are great difficulties in giving it analytical precision or practical application.[1] In his Norton Poetry Lectures, Leonard Bernstein set out to apply Chomskian linguistics to musical "language." The open skepticism his attempt provoked from musicologists, linguists, and even journalists spotlights some of the difficulties inherent in such a comparison.[2] Predictably, semioticians, too, are beginning to investigate profounder-than-conscious parallels between verbal and musical communication systems.[3]

At the other end of the spectrum, a critic involved in the practical criticism of a work in one field sometimes invokes in passing the critical language of the other. Writing of *Pride and Prejudice*, Mary Alice Burgan points out that the "masterly orchestration of the episodes" emphasizes "the generosity of Elizabeth Bennet's wit." Later she refers to the "minuet of changing psychological postures" between Emma and Knightley in *Emma*.[4] *Orchestration* and *minuet* are here used in a general rather than a strictly literal sense. They are suggestive, as far as they go, without requiring further elaboration.

Similarly, a music critic may refer to a "paragraph" or a "sentence" or a "caesura" without specific elaboration as to what is meant. Consider Arthur Hutchings on the opening of the slow movement of Mozart's sonata, K. 332: "Here is the art of J. C. Bach made ethereal, the very opening paragraph having the general and subsidiary antitheses of the most polished Popian couplets."[5] One has a clear enough sense, perhaps, of what *paragraph* means in the above context (though one may

18

not be so clear about function of *ethereal* or its relation to *couplets*). Passing analogies of this kind can be satisfying, intriguing, or maddening, depending on their tone and purpose. But it would be wrong to think of them as either interdisciplinary or highly illuminating unless their implications are more fully worked out.

More ambitious analogies, it seems to me, do need elaboration. Take, for example, Trilling's comment that "one understands very easily why many readers are moved to explain their pleasure [in *Pride and Prejudice*] by reference to Mozart, especially *The Marriage of Figaro*." Or Church's comment that *Emma* "is so consummate purely as a story that again the hard-worn comparison with Mozart's symphonies must be made." Neither assertion is followed by another word as to the meaning of the musical analogy. Readers who are intimately acquainted with *Figaro* or the symphonies might agree or disagree intuitively with either assertion. But still they may have very little idea what is actually meant. Trilling says that "one understands very easily." If that is so, perhaps one understands too easily. Church speaks of the "hard-worn" comparison with Mozart's symphonies. But I have yet to see such a comparison actually tried on, much less worn out. If such comparisons are to be meaningful—and I believe they may be—the critic must communicate to the reader what actually is meant.

More frustrating still is literary criticism that uses a specific musical term in an ambitious way without showing sufficient sensitivity to its meaning or implications. A recent essay entitled "*Emma*: Point Counterpoint" begins with this sentence: "It is a rare pleasure to read a fugue, and *Emma* is the rare novel that provides that pleasure."[6] The essay contains many fine insights about *Emma*. But it unintentionally leaves the impression that the "pleasures of reading a fugue" are even rarer than the author meant to demonstrate. The definition of *fugue* is tucked away in a long footnote. The essay makes neither a sustained nor a precise attempt to apply either *fugue* or *counterpoint* to the novel itself. What discussion there is of "musical" form, while suggestive, is so general that it would apply almost as well to sonata-allegro form or to theme and variations as to the fugue. The impulse behind the essay is promising: to think about musical form can help us to think about *Emma*'s form. But the specific comparison delivers considerably less than it promises.

The use of terminology from one field to describe aspects of another is further complicated by what, in comparative languages, is the problem of false cognates. The term *theme* is quite precise in music criticism. It is defined in the *Harvard Brief Dictionary of Music* as "a melody which, by virtue of its characteristic design, prominent position, or special treatment becomes a basic element in the structure of a composition." In literary criticism, the term *theme* is not nearly so precise. It refers to a central or controlling idea or concern in a work, not to a finite element within its structure. In music criticism, *subject* is virtually indistinguishable from *theme*. In literary criticism, *subject* and *theme*, though related to each other, are absolutely distinct. *Tone* is related to *mood* in literature, but not in music. Other terms with different meanings in the two arts include *texture, accent, chromatic, harmony,* and *impressionism.*

On the other hand, many terms do—or may—have similar meanings in both music and fiction. This is particularly true of certain aesthetic concepts of the kind to be discussed below: equilibrium, balance, proportion, symmetry, restraint, vehemence of expression, clarity, ambiguity, wit. But even though such terms may have comparable meanings in the two arts, those meanings are derived from separate artistic traditions and modes of expression—a fact that successful comparative criticism must always keep in mind.

The discussion of comparable terms that follows is not designed to be exhaustive or definitive. Its immediate purpose is twofold: (1) to show that certain terms can be applied to instrumental music and prose fiction in such a way as to reveal similar qualities in works from either field; and (2) to show the degree to which the classical equilibrium achieved by Austen and Mozart in their separate fields comprises comparable aesthetic components. Whereas the comparable terms discussed in this chapter tend to emphasize the aesthetic components of the style of each artist, the comparable themes and tendencies to be discussed in Chapters 2 and 3 emphasize the social and spiritual components, respectively, of their comparable styles. All terms, themes, and tendencies discussed in a general way in this part of the book will receive precise elaboration and application in the detailed analysis and comparison of individual works in Part 2.

Equilibrium, Balance, Proportion, Symmetry

THE ABOVE TERMS, closely related to each other, are essential to an appreciation of the classical style in music. They are equally essential to an appreciation of Austen's fictional style. None of them belongs more to the criticism of the one field than the other.

The term *equilibrium* can be applied both to humans and to works of art. Applied to humans, equilibrium is less often achieved than aspired toward. A person or society that has achieved complete mental, emotional, or social equilibrium might best be thought of as dead. The same may be said of a novel or a sonata, though not so easily of a painting. On a canvas, formal equilibrium can exist visually. It can be perceived instantaneously, as it were. The same is true, to a limited degree, of architecture. Baroque Italian façades have been called "frozen music" because time is essentially frozen as the eye instantaneously perceives the stationary face of a building and the interrelations of its parts. Time is never frozen in this sense when one first experiences a novel or a sonata. Because fiction and music both unfold through time, the actual process of perceiving either art implies goal-directed motion rather than equilibrium per se.

In Austen's fiction, the novel in its form and the characters in their action tend to *aspire toward* equilibrium, which often seems to be achieved in the end. The same is true of the form and the musical materials of compositions in the classical style. Equilibrium is not so much a quality achieved in any given moment as a quality toward which the work may aspire. That quality ultimately exists, if it does, only at the end, when all of the parts can be experienced as a whole and in relation to each other. Equilibrium is perceived in music and in fiction, then, essentially through the use of memory.

As we attentively read a novel that aspires to the condition of equilibrium or as we listen to a musical work that does the same, we become aware of elements, large and small, that create the impression of balance, of proportion, of symmetry. In fiction the element may be as small and seemingly insignificant as a single phrase, such as Mr. Collins's mock-modest reference to his "humble abode" in *Pride and Prejudice*. First alluded to in chapter 14 of volume 1, his abode is painfully experienced in volume 2 and is blissfully irrelevant in volume 3. In music the repeated element may be as small and seemingly insignificant as a pair of thirty-second notes, those, for instance, in the ascending motif first announced in bar 7 of the second movement of Mozart's G-minor Symphony. Originally a part of the opening theme, this motif achieves independent status later in the movement and contributes significantly to its structural and emotional balance.

Like a phrase in fiction, a sentence can contribute to equilibrium: both in its local context and throughout the entire work. The celebrated opening sentence of *Pride and Prejudice* is a fine example: "It is a truth universally acknowledged that a single man in possession of a good fortune must be in want of a wife" (p. 5). The carefully ordered syntax creates a formal equilibrium to match the mental and social equilibrium conveyed—on the surface, at least—by the "truth" the sentence expresses. One measure of the equilibrium aspired to by the novel as a whole is the extent to which both its formal structure and its human actions extend the formal, mental, and societal equilibrium announced by the opening sentence.

A melody (or theme) in music may function in a similar way. In countless works by Mozart and his contemporaries, the opening theme of the opening movement achieves a comparable equilibrium both within itself (rhythmically, harmonically, and melodically) and in relation to its working out throughout the movement. This is true of the opening themes of all three Mozart concertos to be discussed at length in Part 2.

In large-scale works of music and fiction, of course, the ultimate equilibrium of form is generally achieved not only through the reiteration or reworking of the original material and the equilibrium which that material often implies, but also through the introduction of various threats to the original sense of equilibrium, threats which are subdued only after repeatedly being allowed to disrupt the sense of balance and proportion. Sometimes such threats are implied in the opening material itself (the ironies hidden in the first sentence of *Pride and Prejudice*, the overt opposition between piano and orchestra in the opening theme of K. 271). Threats may also result from the introduction of new and contrasting material (the presence of Mr. Wickham in *Pride and Prejudice*, the modulation to F minor in the development section of K. 271). Whatever the threats may be, the final result in music of the classical style or in an Austen novel is that the drive toward equilibrium tends to override the threats to the degree that balance and harmony are achieved in the end, a balance and harmony all the more to be appreciated for the various threats that have been overcome and, finally, incorporated into the overall pattern. Often one finds a balanced and symmetrical distribution not only of the harmonious forces but of the disruptive ones, as later analysis will show.

It is owing to similarities in the way both music and fiction unfold through time that musical form is of potential use in analyzing fictional form. As was stated above, form is easier to isolate in music than in fiction. And form in music can more directly be equated with style. Here, for example, is the formula from the *Pelican History of Music* for understanding the "classical" style:

> Ideally, we should concern ourselves only with the form each movement reveals—the particular way in which themes, rhythms, keys, etc. interact and are held in equilibrium.

It might seem rash, on the face of it, to apply such a formula to a novel. But one could surely do worse than to approach the study of style in *Pride and Prejudice* in this manner:

> Ideally, we should concern ourselves only with the form each volume reveals—the particular way in which characters, actions, locales, etc. interact and are held in equilibrium.

The *Pelican History* continues with words that apply verbatim to *Pride and Prejudice*: "In the classical style this sense of equilibrium is repeatedly threatened and disrupted, however subtly, but always renewed, reestablished."[7] Such dynamics are theoretically possible, of course, in music and fiction of many periods and styles. But they have seldom been achieved so subtly and so pervasively as in the style of Mozart or Austen.

As Rosen points out, the composer in the classical style is above all "concerned with reconciling the demands of expressiveness and proportion. Symmetry withheld and then finally granted is one of the basic satisfactions of eighteenth-century art" (pp. 49–50). *Symmetry, balance,* and *proportion,* like *equilibrium,* are general terms that do not have specific meanings limited to fiction or to music but whose presence in either art is subject to the conditions of that art. Symmetry is in each case a formal characteristic. Words, phrases, sentences, chapters, or volumes may be positioned in fiction so as to create symmetry through time. Notes, phrases, melodies, episodes, or movements may be so positioned in music. Balance, like equilibrium, is a term that can refer to qualities of form or to qualities of mind and emotion. Applied to the art of Mozart or Austen, it often refers to both. Proportion in both music and fiction is a term applicable to the balanced relation of the parts to the whole, a quality particularly important in comprehending the art of Mozart and Austen, but not, as might be thought, that of all artists.

In "Ligeia" (1838), for example, Edgar Allan Poe approvingly quotes Bacon's idea that "there is no exquisite beauty without some *strangeness* in the proportion" (emphasis Poe's).[8] The idea is applicable not only to "Ligeia" itself but to the rest of Poe's fiction. It is equally applicable to the music of Berlioz, Chopin, Liszt, and Schumann—the great composers of the decade of "Ligeia." Balance, symmetry, proportion, and equilibrium often do exist in their works, but frequently they are overtly violated in the service of a deeper expressiveness. In works by Austen or Mozart, the disruptive forces that threaten the equilibrium tend finally to be subordinated to the "truth" of an all-encompassing order. In words by Poe, Berlioz, Chopin, Schumann, and Liszt, the disruptive forces often tend to be elevated to the status of truth itself. Here, as in other ways, Beethoven and Emily Brontë might be said to straddle both tendencies. *Wuthering Heights,* like the "Appassionata," violates its own symmetry while preserving it.

Restraint vs. Vehemence of Expression

UNTIL RECENTLY, it was commonplace for critics in the two fields to assert that Mozart's art, on the one hand, and Austen's, on the other, lack feeling. During the last two decades it has finally been recognized that these two artists often express more variety of feeling than some of the Romantics with whom they have long been invidiously compared. The massive commercial promotion of Mozart's music announced by Time-Life records in 1979 would have been inconceivable even in the 1960s— as would have been the decision to launch that promotion with the late piano concertos. With Mozart's twenty-seven piano concertos now available in their full splendor both on disk and in concert, it is difficult to believe that throughout the nineteenth century and during half of the twentieth only one of them, the D-minor, No. 20 (K. 466), was much performed—and primarily because it "anticipated" Beethoven.

During that century and a half, Beethoven's expression of musical feeling had seemed so compelling that many listeners and commentators appeared unable to acknowledge feelings other than the kind he so eloquently and vehemently expressed. Grove's patronizing attitude toward Mozart and Haydn in his influential study *Beethoven and His Nine Symphonies* (1898) was in no way unusual for its time. Tovey could appreciate Beethoven without denigrating Mozart, but it was not until the 1940s that the English-language reader (in the work of Alfred Einstein and Cuthbert Girdlestone) could begin to encounter sustained appreciation of the wealth of emotion to be found in Mozart's purely instrumental music.[9] By the time of the excellent *Mozart Companion* (1956), appreciation of Mozart's great range of human feeling was becoming more widespread among specialists and performers, but even today there seems to be a great chunk of the audience-at-large for whom the music of Beethoven and his Romantic successors is felt to be preeminent in the expression of "feeling" and "passion."[10]

Similarly, if asked, "Who is more concerned with feelings, Jane Austen or the Brontës?" most readers of English fiction would unequivocally answer, "The Brontës." Feelings of rage or rebelliousness seem to be the ones most often meant when people write or speak of "feelings" in literature—or music. Such feelings are strong indeed in novels such as *Wuthering Heights* and *Jane Eyre*, and in music such as the "Appassionata." Much of Beethoven's music tends to swing between two polar opposites: strenuous rebellion and hymnic calm. Emily Brontë's fiction has much the same dualistic passional atmosphere; that is one reason David Cecil's distinction between the principles of "storm" and "calm" in *Wuthering Heights* has had meaning for many readers. One looks in vain to find these contrasting kinds of passion expressed more vehemently or more purely than they are in either the "Appassionata" or *Wuthering Heights*. But it is a precarious leap from this recognition to a conclusion that works of their kind are necessarily the ultimate in the expression of human feeling or even passion.

Feelings are as varied as is human experience, and so are passions.

Just as a person might have a passion for anguish, so might he or she have a passion for clarity, or honor, or delicacy, or decency. As Hume has pointed out, even reason may properly be thought of as a passion—and a strong one. "'What is commonly, and in a popular sense, called reason is nothing but a general and a calm passion which takes a comprehensive and distant view of its object'; and 'what we call *strength of mind*,' for example, is only 'the prevalence of the calm passions above the violent.'"[11] If the calmer passions often prevail over the more violent ones in the works of Austen and Mozart, that does not mean that the level of passion is low. Nor does it mean that the more violent passions are ignored. They tend only to be presented with more restraint.

A fine example occurs in chapter 13 of volume 2 of *Pride and Prejudice*. For an entire chapter we share Elizabeth's growing anguish as she reads Darcy's letter, rereads it, and realizes what it implies about her own perception and behavior. Hers is a very special kind of anguish, for it derives from her own character, at the same time that it helps to clarify that character. Not everyone would have reacted to Darcy's letter in the manner that Elizabeth does, and that is what makes her response so moving. In Charlotte Brontë's *Jane Eyre* the heroine is overcome with anguish when she discovers Rochester's wife in the attic. Almost anyone in her situation would be so overcome: the anguish results more from the situation itself than from her own character. That of Elizabeth, for those who feel it, is infinitely more moving and compelling—even though there is no shouting or screaming or pulling of hair. The reader first discovers that Elizabeth is deeply moved when the narrator informs us that "she read without comprehending, had to read again." Such an indication does not necessarily indicate that a character is greatly disturbed. Applied to Elizabeth, it does exactly that.

Two other examples of the restrained expression of violent emotion can be briefly cited from *Pride and Prejudice*. Elizabeth learns of Lydia's elopement when two letters arrive simultaneously from Jane. The first of the letters, the one containing the disturbing news, arrived late because it was "addressed ill." Knowing Jane Bennet's orderly ways as we do, that detail is all we need. Nothing more would have been gained by our seeing her bent over her table in a frenzy, scratching wildly with a quill pen on the clean and—unlike Lydia—pure white envelope. Darcy, too, though often condemned by readers and critics as cold, is capable of expressing strong emotion. A memorable example is the letter he writes to Elizabeth in volume 2—though its syntax is too formal to accord with Romantic expressive notions. That the "calm passions" prevail over the violent ones in most of the letter is owing entirely to Darcy's "strength of mind," not to any lack of violent or vehement feeling.

Similarly, anguish, alarm, and distress are among the great range of feelings and passions expressed in Mozart's music. Sometimes there is the equivalent of the entire chapter in Elizabeth's mind: the extended distress of the slow movement of K. 271, discussed below, is a good example. More often Mozart expresses disturbing emotions by incorporating a minor-key episode into the structure of a relatively spirited or jaunty rondo movement (the minor-key episodes in the finales of K. 488 and K. 503 are excellent examples). Only occasionally will an entire work be dominated by disturbing emotions; among the twenty-seven piano concertos, those in D minor and C minor (K. 466 and K. 491) are examples. But even in these cases Mozart tends to comply with his famous formulation to his father, quoted by Einstein, that "passions, whether violent or not, must never be expressed in such a way as to excite disgust" and that "music, even in the most terrible situations, must never offend the ear, but must please the listener, or in other words, must never cease to be *music*" (p. 385).

In both Mozart and Austen violent passions exist and are intense while present. But such passions take their place—and not necessarily the dominant one—among other passions of which the human being is capable. Nor is the fact that each artist tends to express such feelings with restraint rather than vehemence necessarily a drawback. Paradoxically, certain impressions and feelings—including those of the strongest kind—can be more strongly communicated through restraint than through vehemence, as our later comparison of specific novels and concertos will make clear. For now, suffice it to say that the frightening emotion that bursts forth during the second (and least "Beethovenesque") movement of Mozart's D-minor Concerto would lose much of its force if deprived of the extended limpid serenity in which the movement opens—and closes.

Although music and fiction are separate arts, their actual methods of expressing vehemence or restraint are in some ways comparable. In music added vehemence can be achieved by expanding the dynamic range between loud and soft. In nearly any pair of piano works by Mozart and Beethoven this difference is unmistakable. Parallel to stronger dynamic contrasts in music is the use of stronger diction to gain added vehemence in fiction. This can easily be seen by comparing the verbs, adverbs, and adjectives from nearly any page of *Wuthering Heights* with those found on any page of *Pride and Prejudice*.

Another reason Beethoven's music often seems more vehement than Mozart's is that he makes comparatively bold use of rhythmic irregularities and accents (syncopations, cross-rhythms, *sforzando*). Corresponding to rhythmic disruptions in music are rhetorical disruptions in fiction. On the first page of *Wuthering Heights* Heathcliff interrupts an involuted speech by Mr. Lockwood in midsentence. Such a breach of decorum never occurs in *Pride and Prejudice*—even when Mr. Collins is speaking.

Beethoven's music also tends to be more vehement than Mozart's because of its relatively abrupt harmonic modulations. Mozart's modulations were far from timid, but they were consistently well-prepared. When he wrote his father that "music must never offend the ear," the letter may well have been an attempt to justify what was, for him, an unusually bold modulation.[12] For Beethoven there were occasions in which music *must* offend. Harsh, unprepared modulations are one way in which his most vehement music undeniably does.

Comparable to abrupt harmonic change in music is abrupt contrast between the moods or locales of adjacent fictional episodes. Abrupt contrasts of this kind are comparatively rare in Austen's novels, which, on the surface, are as eager to please and loath to offend as Mozart's music. Austen's shifts in geographical locale—both short-range and long-range— are generally as seamless as Mozart's comparable shifts in harmony, as will be demonstrated at length below. In the fictional world of Emily Brontë, on the other hand, the mere movement from one room to another is often as dramatic and shocking as is the movement between adjacent bars (and harmonies) in Beethoven.

Brontë, like Beethoven, offends when necessary. Yet these two artists, so vehemently relative to Austen and Mozart, are in some ways models of restraint when compared with certain Romantic artists. We have already suggested a contrast between Emily Brontë's restrained handling of Heathcliff's visits to Catherine's grave and Poe's morbid necrophilia. One might similarly contrast Beethoven's containment of wrenching modulations within a strict tonal framework with the relatively unrestrained chromaticism often found in Schumann or Chopin. Ultimately, the overt vehemence of Beethoven and Emily Brontë tends to be powerful because of the underlying restraint with which it is expressed. With Mozart and Austen, the underlying depth of expression is made possible by the overt restraint with which human passions are presented.

Clarity vs. Ambiguity

MOST ART that means something to us has both clarity and ambiguity, however we define the terms. And the terms do not necessarily exclude each other. Consider El Greco's "Burial of Count Orgaz." Behind the crowd of earthly mourners are flames from torches. But are they flames? Could they not also be the feet of angels from the heavenly plane of the painting? They are, to the attentive eye, both torches and feet. This very ambiguity establishes a visual as well as a spiritual connection between earth and heaven. Clarity is achieved through ambiguity.

The torch-feet are a "local" ambiguity in that their color and shape allow them to be both foot and flame. A literary equivalent is the verbal pun than means more than one thing at the same time. One example we have already encountered is the phrase "deep in the study of thorough bass and human nature." The ambiguity of the word *deep* is made possible by the clarity of diction and of syntax. Emily Brontë's fiction, like Austen's, contains many such ambiguities. But hers tend to be more overt and longer lasting. Only the most careful reader will notice the ambiguities inherent in *deep* or in the opening sentence of *Pride and Prejudice*. But no reader of *Wuthering Heights* will miss the ambiguity of the triple name Lockwood encounters in the oak closet early in the novel: Catherine Earnshaw, Catherine Heathcliff, Catherine Linton. Though inexplicable on its first appearance, this "local" ambiguity is completely resolved—at least on the literal level—by the novel's end. In the works of Poe, many such ambiguities are never resolved. The notorious "ruby-colored" drops in "Ligeia" are an excellent example. The reader never learns whether they in fact existed.

A musical equivalent to the "torch-foot" is the individual note that has two meanings at once. Philip Barford points out that the Largo of Beethoven's "Hammerklavier" Sonata "begins with the note F natural. Coming immediately after the F-sharp-major chord of the Adagio sostenuto, it is bound to be heard as E-sharp, the leading-note of the key of that movement."[13] Here the clarity of the harmonic context makes the local ambiguity possible. Mozart's music is also full of such harmonic puns as the above. If in Beethoven such ambiguities are often more overt and longer lasting than in Mozart, they nevertheless tend to be resolved by the end of the movement in which they occur. In the music of both composers, the ultimate function of such local ambiguity is not so much to create a feeling of lasting uncertainty as to emphasize the strength of the tonic center in which the music is grounded. In the works of such Romantic composers as Chopin and Schumann, the ultimate function of such local ambiguities often *is* to create a feeling of lasting uncertainty.

El Greco's torch-foot is ambiguous not only in a short-range and local sense (is it a torch or a foot?) but also in a long-range and structural sense (does it belong to the earthly space or the heavenly space?). Mozart's music is filled with long-range structural ambiguities that create a seamless unity between form and content. There are magical moments in which the solo exposition of the sonata-allegro movement of a concerto merges so imperceptibly into the development that one cannot say exactly where the one ends and the other begins (the opening movements of both K. 271 and K. 503 are fine examples). There are minuet movements that create the illusion of continuous movement in spite of numerous breaks enforced by the repeat signs: each transition appears seamless because Mozart has designed the end of each section to flow not only into the beginning of the next but, during the repeats, into its own beginning. The E-flat String Quintet (K. 614) provides an excellent example.

Many of Mozart's most delicious structural ambiguities are apparent only to the trained listener. Buried in the unity and the seemingly seamless flow of the music, they are the art that has been concealed by art. Again, a letter from Mozart goes right to the point. He is writing his father about a newly composed group of piano concertos. "These concertos are a happy medium between what is too easy and too difficult; they are very brilliant, pleasing to the ear, and natural, without being vapid. There are passages here and there from which connoisseurs alone can derive satisfaction; but these passages are written in such a way that the less learned cannot fail to be pleased, though without knowing why."[14] Austen's art, too, satisfies the connoisseur at the same time that it pleases the "less learned." The connoisseur savors the buried implications of the opening sentence of *Pride and Prejudice* (realizing that a truth universally acknowledged is not always the whole—or the only—truth); the less learned reader agrees that "a man with money needs a wife" and connives with Mrs. Bennet to make the "universal" truth come true.

The large-scale structural ambiguities in Austen's fiction often pivot on the question of who is courting whom. In *Pride and Prejudice* the reader is teased by various pairings before the Elizabeth-Darcy love-match is openly declared in the middle of the novel. Even so, ever since the evening at Netherfield when Darcy eyes over his book the parading Miss Bingley and Elizabeth, the careful reader has known where the main energies of the book will be centered. There are similar long-range ambiguities in *Emma* concerning the love-matches between Emma and Knightley and between Frank Churchill and Jane Fairfax. But the central long-range ambiguity in that novel pivots upon the continuing incongruity between what Emma sees as happening (for example, between Mr. Elton and Harriet) and what is actually happening (in this case, between Mr. Elton and herself). All such ambiguities are resolved in the end, when Emma learns to see herself and others (including Mr. Knightley) more or less as they are.

The use of long-range structural ambiguity is nearly always at the service of clarity and ultimate unity in the works of Austen and Mozart.

And it often functions as a deft tool that is able to unite form with content seamlessly. Many such ambiguities in Beethoven and Brontë get resolved to a higher clarity too. Yet theirs are often more harsh than deft, stressing the struggle that is necessary if the seams are to be closed. One long-range structural ambiguity in the "Appassionata" pivots on the *attaca allegro* that shatters the second movement and launches the third. We are not so much thrown into doubt as to where the one movement ends and the other begins as we are thrown into doubt as to what a movement is—or means. This large-scale ambiguity has the effect of tearing at the very seams that hold the work together, whereas those in Mozart tend to disguise the seams. In *Wuthering Heights*, as in *Pride and Prejudice*, many of the structural ambiguities pivot on the question of who is courting whom. Yet even the confusion Lockwood experiences on this score in the opening chapters is more extreme than that experienced in Austen's fiction. By the end of the novel the various love-matches have been sorted out clearly enough, but the process has been far from deft. Cathy and Hareton achieve the kind of happy ending generally found in an Austen novel, but the love of Catherine and Heathcliff tears at the very seams of civilized love.

In the works of composers such as Schumann and Chopin and writers such as Poe, long-range structural ambiguities often become an end in themselves, and their implications are left purposely unresolved. A striking example from Chopin is the Presto of the "Funeral March" Sonata. Although it is the fourth movement of a sonata, it lasts little more than a minute. In harmony, rhythm, and melody, not to mention structure, it is more ambiguous than any sonata movement that had been written by that time (1839). One hears only a swirl of directionless motion, motion that is felt by many listeners to be a haunting musical expression of uncertainty as to where the soul will go after death. The pervasive ambiguities of this movement are not resolved into a higher harmony but instead are the means and the end at the same time. A similar effect is created in Poe's "Ligeia." At the end of the story we do not know whether Ligeia has returned to life through the death of Lady Rowena or whether the narrator has only imagined in madness that this has happened. The story gives no sure clues by which the ambiguity can be resolved. Quite as much as in *Pride and Prejudice* and *Wuthering Heights*, a major structural ambiguity pivots on the question of who is courting whom. Is the dead Ligeia courting the supersensitive narrator, the reader wonders, or is the mad narrator courting the dead Ligeia? Because the narrator is so "unreliable," we never learn the answer.

Ambiguity in Chopin and Poe—whether short-range and "local" or long-range and structural—is often both a means and an end of expression. In Mozart and Austen it is nearly always a means by which to achieve a higher clarity. In this way, as in many others, Beethoven and Brontë may be said to straddle both tendencies.

Wit

THE PLAYFULNESS with which both Austen and Mozart instinctively convert local ambiguities into a higher clarity contributes considerably to the wit for which each is justly celebrated. Near the beginning of this study, we found Mary Bennet "deep in the study of thorough bass and human nature." As was pointed out, this example of neoclassical literary wit is based on a clever juxtaposition of the heterogeneous, the delight of which is enhanced by the clarity of articulation and of diction. Such wit is not only highly characteristic of Austen and of many of her eighteenth-century literary models (Johnson, Pope, Addison, Steele); it is equally characteristic of the great composers who perfected the Viennese classical style in music (especially Haydn and Mozart, but not excluding Beethoven).

Rosen's description of the "genuinely autonomous musical wit" that developed in the second half of the eighteenth century reads like a description of Austen's characteristic verbal techniques. Although Rosen is describing the music of Mozart and Haydn, he could just as well be referring to the description of Miss Bingley as "all that was affectionate and insincere": "The incongruous seen as exactly right, the out-of-place suddenly turning out to be just where it ought to be—this is an essential part of wit" (p. 96). In addition to "clarity of articulation," Rosen points out, such musical wit requires a clearly defined harmonic context that makes it possible to recognize that which is out of place. The stable harmonic conventions utilized by Haydn and Mozart make possible the innumerable deviations (i.e., false notes, harmonic puns, deceptive modulations) recognizable as wit: "If wit can take the form of a surprising change of nonsense into sense, a classical modulation gives a splendid formula. . . . For a quick shift of context or a witty reinterpretation of a note, a dramatic and forceful modulation is indispensable" (p. 98). To the degree that stable harmonic conventions were eroded in the Romantic period, certain possibilities for wit were eroded as well. Wit does not cease to exist, but it often takes a different form (such as Berlioz's "yoking by violence together" the *Dies irae* and the "witches' sabbath" in the *Symphonie fantastique*). In much music by Schumann and Chopin, as Rosen points out, "even the classical harmonic pun—the violent fusion of two different harmonic contexts—is no longer possible, as the context no longer has sufficient clarity of definition" (p. 454).

Austen's neoclassical wit depends upon a similar clarity of definition. Clearly defined social boundaries in her novels make possible incongruous juxtapositions whenever characters cross the limits within which they by nature belong (Mr. Collins and Mrs. Elton are among the cruder examples). Similarly, the clarity of definition provided by the narrator's use of language establishes an implicit standard of speech and action by which each character may be judged. So pervasive is the tone set by the narrator in works such as *Pride and Prejudice* and *Emma* that it functions as does a stable sense of tonality in classical music: deviations from it, however slight, are noticeable and are potentially painful or comic. One of the most painful things in fiction is Mrs. Elton speaking: not so much because of what she says per se, but because of how tastelessly her every word departs from the tone of restraint and good breeding which has been established by the narrator and the "tonic" characters in the novel.

The sense of social, normative, and narrative stability so central to Austen's wit was substantially eroded in the work of many of her Romantic successors. Where this was the case (Charlotte Brontë and Edgar Allan Poe are good examples), the possibilities for—and the desirability of—Austen's type of wit tend to decline. Although wit does not cease to exist, it tends to be much less pervasive than in Austen's fiction. And the wit that does remain often tends to be softened toward sentimentality or sharpened toward scorn (both tendencies are particularly evident in Dickens's *Hard Times*).

With regard to wit, as in so many other ways, Beethoven and Emily Brontë may be said to straddle the possibilities outlined above. Not entirely lacking in wit, their work, in its vehemence, often transforms that wit into invective, sarcasm, or scorn. At the same time, each eschews the blatant sentimentality often indulged in by such Romantics as Dickens or Tchaikovsky. The transformation of wit into sarcasm and scorn, but stopping short of sentimentality, can be clearly traced within *Wuthering Heights* itself.

The wittiest moments in the novel occur in the opening chapters. When the citified Mr. Lockwood arrives at the Heights, his manners and diction are immediately juxtaposed with the realities of life there. The prolix ornateness of his speech is wittily juxtaposed with Heathcliff's blunt directness on the very first page of the novel. On the next page we find Lockwood entering the "penetralium" of the house. The pathetically cumbersome words he uses to describe the actions of the dog, which he inadvertently goads into attack by winking at it, are equally incongruous. Once the snow has covered the markers on the path between the Heights and the Grange in chapter 3, however, the tone of the novel changes. Such witty juxtapositions no longer have much place. Mixtures of the heterogeneous become increasingly passionate, painful, and intense. Wit gives way to unadulterated sarcasm and scorn as Isabella tells Nelly of the "joys" of her honeymoon, or Heathcliff addresses his own son as "God, what a beauty!" Toward the end of the novel this harsh and negative expression of human emotion is somewhat offset by the growth of love on two imaginative planes—Cathy and Hareton on the worldly plane, Heathcliff and Catherine on the spiritual plane. Yet in each case the temptations of a sentimental portrayal of redeeming love are sternly resisted.

The dynamics in *Wuthering Heights* briefly sketched above correspond in important ways to the successive "periods" in Beethoven's artistic development. In the present context it is sufficient to observe that in Beethoven's earlier works, which derive much of their surface character from the precedent of Haydn and Mozart, there is ample evidence of wit achieved by the playful juxtaposition of opposites. This playfulness becomes increasingly rough during the middle period, resulting often in violent "juxtaposition of the prosaic and the poetic."[15] Wit does persist into Beethoven's late period, partly because he continues to express himself within the confines of a stable system of tonality. But, like the wit toward the end of *Wuthering Heights*, it is often rougher—or even more mystical—than it is playful. Rosen's words are in need of some qualification, but in broad outline they are correct: "The civilized gaiety of the classical period, perhaps already somewhat coarsened, makes its last appearances in the Allegretto of Beethoven's Eighth Symphony, and in some of the movements of the last quartets. After [Beethoven], wit was swamped by sentiment" (p. 98). And, one might add, transformed into scorn.

The manner in which "classical" wit was later deflected into "Romantic" sentiment and scorn can be suggested by briefly comparing Schumann's *Carnaval* (1835) and Dickens's *Hard Times* (1854). More radically than in Beethoven's middle period, the aesthetic of each pivots on the "juxtaposition of the prosaic and the poetic." Indeed, both works, in effect, juxtapose a circus or a carnival with a middle class. Schumann's program helps the listener attach verbal meanings to the musical notes. Here, as in much of his most characteristic music (and journalism), Schumann expresses unmistakable sentiment for the sensitive individual and scorn for the society at large. The sentiment is expressed most obviously and beautifully, perhaps, in the "Chopin" section. The scorn is most baldly expressed in "David's March against the Philistines." In harmony and rhythm, the opposing moods and concepts that characterize the twenty separate sections of the *Carnaval* are "yoked by violence together" rather than being smoothly spun out within the context of a comfortably governing tonality or pulse.

In *Hard Times* Dickens expresses unadulterated contempt for Gradgrind and Bounderby, unabashed sentiment for Stephen Blackpool and the Slearys. The social and moral contrast between the forces of repression on the one hand and the laboring and circus people on the other is virtually unmediated by any common denominator. There is considerable wit and humor in Dickens's portrayal of Mrs. Sparsit, but this is swamped by the stronger polarities of sentiment and scorn.

Carnaval and *Hard Times* both reflect an erosion of the clarity and stability—in the one case harmonic, in the other social—upon which pervasive wit depends. In each case, the pleasures of "civilized gaiety" and of "classical" wit so central to the artistic style of Mozart and of Austen have been displaced by Romantic sentiment and scorn. This departure from wit as a touchstone of style—accompanied by a weakening of harmonic or social stability—is anticipated in late works by Austen and Mozart themselves, as shown in Chapter 6.

Conventional Language

GREAT ARTISTS often create their own conventions, some of which are rigidified only after the artist is gone. The sonata-allegro form perfected by Mozart and Haydn is one example. They created it as a living form, as an "organic" form in the later Romantic sense of the term—an organic form then rebelled against by many Romantics who could see only the rigidity they read into it and who ossified that form when not being self-consciously "organic" themselves. Every artistic medium has its own conventions, which pollinate, grow, flower, and eventually get pressed dry between the leaves of books. Some such conventions revive when exposed to gusts of air or warmth of touch (thereby becoming, in George Kubler's phrase, an "open sequence").[16] Others do not.

Conventional keyboard language in Bach's day included thorough bass, in Mozart's day Alberti bass, and in Chopin's day chromatic arpeggios. These keyboard conventions are comparable to the kinds of diction thought appropriate for poetry or prose in successive periods of literary history. Conventions in both music and literature come and go in response to changes in style, yet some remain relatively stable throughout periods of significant stylistic change. From Bach through early Schonberg well-tempered scales were as basic to most instrumental music as was "correct" narrative grammar to most fiction from Defoe until early

Mark Twain. Within the bounds of "correct" narrative grammar, of course, there were infinite ranges, from the prosaic (Defoe, Austen) to the poetic (Emily Brontë, Melville). Similarly, the use to which scales and arpeggios and conventional passagework were put ranged from the often purposefully prosaic manner of Mozart to the highly ornate manner of Chopin or Rachmaninoff. Only after Huck Finn's ungrammatical narrative voice and the shattered syntax of *Ulysses* came along could we realize some of the basic similarities between the prose styles of Austen and Brontë—just as Schonberg's twelve-tone scale made us more aware of the tonal continuity of music from Bach through Mahler than we would otherwise have been.

In both music and fiction, then, there are conventions and conventions and conventions, some of them changing with every artistic generation, some holding more or less stable for several centuries. Some artists tend to work comfortably within the accepted long-range and short-range conventions of their chosen art; others seem to have an almost compulsive need to challenge such conventions. Mozart and Austen tend in the former direction, Beethoven and Brontë in the latter, though to make either tendency into an absolute would be a severe error, as later analysis will show.

Artists respond not only to conventions within the language of their own artistic tradition but to conventions within the language of society itself. This is more obvious with fiction than with instrumental music, but it is true of both. A novelist may be more or less conventional in the manner of mirroring the actual or everyday language of society. The extremes may be suggested by contrasting the language of Austen and of Joyce. Austen's diction comprises words spoken by or easily available to the entire British upper and middle classes of her time; her characteristic language is very low in metaphors other than dead ones. Joyce's diction, of course, is idiosyncratic in the extreme, the terminus of this tendency being reached in *Finnegan's Wake*. Emily Brontë's diction is much more conventional than Joyce's, much less so than Austen's. Much of the meaning in *Wuthering Heights* is expressed in the conventional and prosaic language of Nelly and Mr. Lockwood, but much is also expressed through the idiosyncratic and poetic phrasing spoken by characters such as Catherine Earnshaw. This is not to say, however, that the prose of Austen, who eschews the poetically idiosyncratic, is any less artistic.

As E. H. Gombrich has shown so brilliantly with respect to painting, "art is illusion" even when it seems to be reflecting reality most directly.[17] There is plenty of individuality in the use Austen makes of conventional language. One outstanding example in *Emma* is Miss Bates, whose talk is so conventional, so lacking in individual inflection or shaping, that it becomes idiosyncratic and, in the context of the novel, highly revealing. Austen uses Miss Bates's mindless stream of chatter to bridge from one scene to another, to register the tensions buried in non sequiturs, to give us the lowest common denominator as a standard by which to judge the decency of the other characters in the novel (the standard by which Emma falls temporarily short, Mrs. Elton eternally). Mozart uses conventional scales and passagework in a similar way: to establish a feeling for tonality and for deviations from it, to provide guileless transitions from one "idea" to another, to register telling changes of mood by the slightest alteration in what has become familiar.

Mozart's often dramatic use of the simplest conventional material of the musical language of his day cannot be compared directly with the language of society itself because people do not speak in scales. But there is no doubt that the use Mozart made of certain musical conventions corresponded in some degree to the unwritten conventional expectations of his upper-class audience and patrons. Mozart's range of key signatures was extremely limited, even as compared to Haydn and Beethoven, not to mention later Romantics. He only once wrote a movement in the key of F-sharp major (the Adagio of K. 488) and for the most part he limited himself to works in a major key (in 25 of 27 piano concertos, 17 of 19 piano sonatas, 37 of 41 symphonies). Most serious students of his art feel that Mozart's great minor-key instrumental compositions (such as the D-minor Piano Concerto, the G-minor Quintet, or the G-minor Symphony) were expressions of personal emotion essentially out of keeping with the musical conventions within which he was normally content to work. Mozart's declaration to his father that music "must never offend the ear, but must please the listener" certainly reflects his own temperament to a degree; but it also reflects the expectations of the patrons for whom he composed, most of whom were interested in the preservation and beautification of the status quo that served them so well.

To some degree, the conventional expectations of the upper-class society for which Mozart composed are quite directly expressed even in his instrumental music: in the seeming simplicity and purity of form; in the tendency toward smoothness, seamlessness, and the harmonious resolution of conflict; in the reluctance to dwell overlong in painfully distant or difficult keys; and perhaps most of all in the relative absence of what in Beethoven's music is so undeniably present—stridently unpleasant sounds expressing the unpleasant anger of a soul smothered by a status quo that shows insufficient concern for the passionate aspirations of humanity at large. Such anger is at times expressed by Mozart. But it is seldom expressed so as to be "unpleasant" in the manner that

Beethoven often defiantly and dramatically desired to be. Musically and socially, *Figaro* and *Fidelio* are a telling contrast in this regard.

By the same token, no character in Austen ever breaks the unwritten rules of good breeding by speaking with the vehemence, the harshness, the irreverence of Heathcliff, who is a virtuoso of the unpleasant. This is not to say that Austen's world is necessarily less "unpleasant" than that of *Wuthering Heights*. Rather, its unpleasantness is often expressed in a conventional way by conventional characters; in the novels discussed below, Lady Catherine, Mrs. Elton, and Sir Walter Elliot are prime examples. One essential difference between their unpleasantness and that of Heathcliff is that they are not generally aware of it, whereas he is. Because in Austen and Mozart the full range of human emotion is for the most part embedded in the conventional, it can often be overlooked. Because in Beethoven and Brontë the strongest emotional effects are frequently expressed unconventionally, one cannot fail to be struck by them.

~~~ *Chapter Two* ~~~

COMPARABLE THEMES
IN FICTION AND MUSIC

C OMPARABLE THEMES, as well as terms, may be utilized for the purpose of interart criticism and understanding—if care is taken
and if distinctions are respected. I use *theme* here in its broad
literary meaning rather than its narrow musical one. Whereas a concerto or a sonata will have a finite number of themes (melodies), the
number of themes in a novel may be indeterminate. Whereas a musical
theme must be explicitly announced in order to serve its structural function in the composition, a literary theme is often not announced at all.
Instead, various themes take shape in the reader's mind as he or she
contemplates the entire work and its implications.

If one were to try to exhaust the themes from *Wuthering Heights*, for
example, one would have to frame statements, as various critics have,
on subjects as diverse as nature, love, social class, death, marriage, madness, demonism, elective affinities, individuality, mysticism, *ad infinitum*.
Because instrumental music per se consists of tones without words, it
cannot express in a literal way the kind of concepts or themes found in
a novel. It can, however, express such themes metaphorically. Advocates
of "pure" music, of course, deny that this is true. They argue that music
can have no meaning outside of music itself.

In *Philosophy in a New Key* (1941) Suzanne K. Langer addresses head
on the argument that music can have no nonmusical meaning. Allowing
that instrumental music is not capable of expressing ideas or emotions
directly, she explains how such music can, and does, create structures
analogous to our experience of ideas and emotions.[1] In 1927 J. W. N.
Sullivan anticipated the same argument in his fine book on Beethoven:
"Music, as an expressive art, evokes states of consciousness in the hearer
which are analogous to states that may be produced by extramusical
means."[2] In 1837 Hector Berlioz made a similar point in his discussion
of "emotional imitation" and "musical metaphor." Instrumental music,
according to Berlioz, can "arouse in us by means of sound the notion of

the several passions of the heart, and . . . awaken solely through the sense of hearing the impressions that human beings experience only through the other senses."[3]

The argument below compares the metaphorical expression of certain notions, impressions, and "themes" in music with their more literal expression in fiction. The musical themes of a Mozart concerto or a Beethoven sonata are finite and are generally agreed upon. The metaphorical themes of such works are as varied and as subject to interpretation as are those of *Wuthering Heights*. As Jacques Barzun recently put it, "The meaning of literature resides in the same motions of the spirit as those aroused by music; only the means differ."[4]

Individual and Society

JUST AS WORKS of fiction are capable of directly reproducing the conventional spoken language of a given society, so can they directly register the conflict between a given society and one or more individuals. Indeed, most novels openly explore such conflict. One major difference between the fiction of Jane Austen and that of Emily Brontë is the tendency of Austen's heroines to find their full individuality within the boundaries of taste and decorum that the society, at its best, allows.

Elizabeth Bennet is Austen's most striking example of full individuality achieved within the confines of society's implicit rules. Anne Elliot in *Persuasion* is her final example. In the case of Anne, it sometimes seems that society's conventions have become so bloodlessly ossified that true individuality will be entirely stifled. Yet "society" and the "conventional" are expanded by the addition of the Crofts and what they represent, and this allows Anne finally to find a home for herself without breaking abruptly or irrevocably from the world of her foolish father or her unconsciously audacious advisor, Lady Russell. The extent to which even Anne Elliot achieves her individuality within the context of society rather than in opposition to it is made strikingly clear by contrast with *Wuthering Heights*.

Heathcliff defines his identity against society. There is no room for him to express himself within its conventions, especially after he loses Catherine. Yet it might be said that Catherine Earnshaw embodies the irreconcilable conflict between individual and society even more searingly than he does. For Catherine feels the pull of the conventional, the pull of society, more strongly than he. She is literally made mad by her inability to choose between society's conventions (Edgar Linton) and her own deepest need (Heathcliff). *Wuthering Heights* does contain one heroine who, like Austen's heroines, is able to resolve the conflict between her own individuality and the conventions of society. Cathy Linton's courtship with Hareton ends the novel on an optimistic note similar to that in an Austen novel. It is not Cathy and Hareton, however, but Catherine and Heathcliff, who remain most strongly in the reader's mind and heart. Their tragic inability to resolve the conflict with society is one measure of the book's Romantic disequilibrium.

In the libretto of an opera, as opposed to instrumental music per se, the conflict between individual and society may be expressed as overtly as in a novel. Consider *The Marriage of Figaro*, the opera Lionel Trilling compares, in passing, to *Pride and Prejudice*. In plot alone there are significant parallels. In each case the conflicts between individual and society are resolved to the ultimate good of both parties. In each work that resolution is achieved by happy marriages that provide the occasion for all competing and conflicting individuals to be brought harmoniously together. Even so, one would have to analyze the music of *Figaro*, not its libretto, if one wished to explore at the deepest level its resolution of the tensions between the individual and the group.

To a degree perhaps unmatched by any other musician, Mozart was able to embody personality and character, human conflict and resolution, in tones. He did so not only in opera but also in the piano concerto, a musical genre in which he, in the history of music, remains peerless. The piano concerto is the pure instrumental form most conducive to expressing metaphorically the conflict between the individual and society. The concerto form lends itself to such expression because it pits a solo against an orchestra. The piano as an instrument lends itself to such expression because of its great range of register and expression; more than any other solo instrument, it can be heard as an equal to the orchestra itself. In addition, the solo piano in a piano concerto is generally the only piano. It therefore contrasts with the instrumental forces more sharply than does the solo in a flute, violin, cello, or horn concerto.

Mozart was himself a pianist, as were most of the composers who continued to write piano concertos into the nineteenth century. His achievement, even when measured against the collective achievement of his successors in the form, is astonishing both in quantity and quality. Particularly astonishing is the balance he instinctively achieves between the one and the many. His concertos typically begin with a "double" exposition. The first exposition always belongs to the orchestra, which establishes the tempo, themes, and rhythms that will dominate the first movement. In the solo exposition that follows, the piano begins to put its own personal stamp upon those materials. After this double exposition, the rest of the opening movement, plus the two movements that follow, develop within the framework thus established. Consistently noteworthy is the wealth of imagination with which Mozart instinctively allows the solo and orchestra to interact after the orchestra has established the essential boundaries of that interaction. Equally noteworthy is the inevitable goal of that interplay in each work: balance and harmony between the forces.

Mozart's artistic genius revelled in the kind of civilized interplay that, in his hands, came to characterize the piano concerto form. Such interplay did not fare well in the Romantic age, when the imperative of expressing individuality at the expense of society tended to disrupt the equal balance of forces. Beethoven's first three piano concertos each begin with an orchestral exposition on the model of Mozart's concertos. But none of them achieve the organic interplay between solo and orchestra that came so instinctively to Mozart. Beethoven's Fourth and Fifth concertos are magnificent creations, fully equal to Mozart's finest ventures in the form, but they depart from the Mozartean model both in spirit and in structure. Each begins with immediate interplay between solo and orchestra (in the "Emperor" Concerto the piano actually initiates the dialogue). In each concerto there is as much a sense of the solo taming or leading the orchestra as there is of the solo growing within the confines the orchestra establishes (which latter sense always prevails in Mozart's concertos, even in K. 271, a seeming exception, discussed in Chapter 4). In most concertos composed by Beethoven's Romantic successors, the emphasis tilts decidedly toward the solo, which sometimes even seems oblivious of the orchestra.

Concertos by Liszt, Tchaikovsky, and Rachmaninoff often seem to be grandiose wars that are won by the soloist. Those by Chopin and Schumann feature lyrical solo voices which often seem to avoid the engagement altogether. Chopin's E-minor Concerto, like those of Mozart, has an orchestral exposition. Yet that exposition, by Mozartean standards, is strange in its proportions (which is one reason it is often truncated in performance). The piano, when it finally enters, is mostly oblivious to what has come before. As Tovey complains, the "classical" orchestral exposition has, "for reasons impious to inquire," become "an ordinary symphonic exposition, prefaced to a sonata for a solo instrument with orchestral accompaniment."[5] From Chopin's E-minor Concerto (1830) it is but a short step to Schumann's Piano Sonata, Opus 14 (1835), subtitled "Concerto without Orchestra."

Not only the balance between the forces but the actual number of piano concertos (and masterpieces) declined into the Romantic period. Mozart composed twenty-seven piano concertos, of which a dozen are masterpieces. Of Beethoven's five piano concertos, two can without controversy be so designated. Among the nineteenth-century Romantics renowned for their piano concertos, the numerical output is decidedly slim: single concertos by Schumann and Grieg; two each by Chopin, Liszt, Brahms, and Tchaikovsky. Because Mozart's genius was best adapted to the variety of ways in which different solo "personages" could express themselves within the larger context which an orchestra could provide, his piano concertos are a much higher expression of his genius than are his nineteen solo sonatas. Beethoven's pianistic genius, on the other hand, found its highest expression in the thirty-two solo sonatas, not the five concertos. Composers such as Chopin, Schumann, and Liszt, too, achieved their most distinctive pianistic expression in their solo works (études, fantasies, preludes, sonatas).[6]

From Mozart through the nineteenth century, then, both the history of the piano concerto and the output of composer-pianists reflect an increasing emphasis on the solo (or individual) as opposed to the orchestra (or society). This changing emphasis parallels the change found in Emily Brontë's fiction as compared to Austen's. The increasing emphasis on the individual as opposed to the society in *Wuthering Heights* as compared to *Pride and Prejudice* is extended even further in a writer such as Poe, in whose fiction the obsessions and imperatives of the individual become so strong that the society often disappears altogether. In terms of the relation between individual and society, Poe's short stories are the verbal equilvalent of Schumann's "Concerto without Orchestra." In aesthetic form, they achieve a "unity of effect" similar to that of Chopin's highly charged études.

The heroines of Austen's novels and the solo voices of Mozart's piano concertos occupy very special positions in the history of their separate arts. They represent at its liveliest and its purest the ability of the individual to achieve full expression and individuality within the confines established by the many.

Indoors and Out

LIKE THE CONTRAST between individual and society, the contrast between indoors and outdoors is often explicit in fiction. Austen's fictional world is essentially an indoor one; Emily Brontë's is essentially outdoor.

The reader of *Pride and Prejudice* remembers scenes in Mr. Bennet's library, in Mr. Bingley's sitting room, in the Netherfield ball room, at Mr. Collins's "humble abode," at Lady Catherine's dinner table, inside the halls of Pemberly. Important episodes occur outdoors, yet each is more important for its contribution to the plot than as an expression of the intrinsic value of the outdoors per se. The outdoor world becomes somewhat more important in *Emma* as the setting for dramatic events, but still most episodes in that novel occur indoors, as is also the case in the almost claustrophobic *Mansfield Park*. Only in *Persuasion* does the outdoors exist as an intrinsic part of the value system of the book and as a shaping influence on the heroine's emotions. Yet even *Persuasion* unfolds for the most part in a variety of indoor settings: Sir Walter's Kellynch, with its ubiquitous mirrors; the two Musgrove houses at Uppercross; Harville's house at Lyme; and, at Bath, Camden Place, Mrs. Smith's room, the Octagon Room, the White Hart Inn, and the shop where Anne and Wentworth meet. Anne's autumn walk is important to her. So is the excursion to Lyme. The outdoors is indeed a sustaining presence in *Persuasion*, yet it is not quite what it often is in novels we tend to call Romantic: a refuge into which a character who is *entirely* stifled by society can escape in order to find his *only* sense of belonging.

In *Wuthering Heights* the outdoors has just such a function for Heathcliff and Catherine. As children, when they are not escaping out of doors by choice, they are being thrust out of doors in punishment. Catherine does voluntarily confine herself to an "indoor" world when she marries Edgar Linton, but in her terminal madness she strains to escape her "shattered prison" and find refuge in death—where Heathcliff finally joins her. Heathcliff's final visions of Catherine, his death at the open window, and his instructions to the sexton to remove adjacent panels from his and Catherine's graves all emphasize his yearning for the outdoors and the unbounded. The celebrated motifs of windows and imprisonment in *Wuthering Heights* emphasize the indoor-outdoor dichotomy almost obsessively: Cathy's ghost scraping at the window in Lockwood's dream; Cathy and Heathcliff looking in through the windows of Thrushcross Grange; Heathcliff being thrust out of the Grange and looking back in at Catherine being pampered; his running outdoors after hearing Catherine say she loves Edgar; her later following him into the storm; Isabella running outdoors to escape Heathcliff, her knife-pierced ear dripping blood; Heathcliff bashing his head against a tree when Catherine dies; his "visiting" her grave twice; his death indoors in the closet where Lockwood once dreamt of Catherine, but with the window open and his face washed by the elements.

The list could go on and on, yet one could compile an equal number of indoor scenes of great importance too: Lockwood's initial inspection of Wuthering Heights and its inhabitants; young Heathcliff's arrival and being inspected there; his and Catherine's "reception" inside Thrushcross Grange; Christmas Day at Wuthering Heights; Catherine's explanation to Nelly of why she loves Edgar; various encounters among

Heathcliff, Catherine, Edgar, and Isabella inside Thrushcross Grange between Catherine's marriage and her death; the long battle that leads to Isabella's flight from the Heights; the sickly Linton Heathcliff at Wuthering Heights; young Cathy's imprisonment and marriage to him there; Cathy and Hareton reading before the fire; and, of course, Nelly and Lockwood sitting indoors the whole length of the book, while she tells him and he tells us the story.

I list these scenes to emphasize the fact that while we generally think of *Wuthering Heights* as an outdoors book, perhaps half of the action, if not more, takes place indoors. As Margaret Homans has pointed out, the presence of nature in the novel often makes itself felt metaphorically, rather than literally.[7] We never actually see Catherine and Heathcliff together on the open moors, though we constantly imagine them there. Nor do we actually see Heathcliff striding alone across the bleak landscape, though our imagination pictures him so. Cathy Linton's and Linton Heathcliff's opposing views of paradise (riding a tree in the breeze vs. lying inert in the grass) are only metaphors spoken by Cathy, not conditions we actually see the characters enact. Catherine's characterization of Edgar and Heathcliff as being as different as "a moonbeam from lightning, or frost from fire" is made while speaking indoors with Nelly—as is her comparison of Edgar to the "foliage in the woods" and Heathcliff to "the enduring rocks beneath."

The presence and importance of nature in *Wuthering Heights*, then, is achieved as much metaphorically as it is literally, whereas the converse is true in Austen's world. Her novels tend to feel "indoors" not only because that is where most of the action takes place but because the diction of the novel is "indoors" too. As Mark Schorer has pointed out, the few metaphors that Austen uses tend to be those of the "counting house," the language of indoors business transactions.[8] Even when strong feelings are expressed, it is often through such proper and bloodless words as "mortification." Yet in Austen's world we often feel that such words, sensibly and discreetly used, are sufficient to convey the essentials of human experience.

In instrumental music, too, the contrast between indoors and out can be expressed both literally and metaphorically. In Beethoven's "Pastoral" Symphony, the bird call and the thunder are obvious imitations of sounds taken directly from nature (the kind of expression Berlioz calls musical "imitation" rather than musical "metaphor"). But its *metaphorical* expression of the *spirit* of nature is what makes the Sixth Symphony so much a work of the outdoors. As Beethoven himself insisted, the symphony is much less a transcription of the sounds of nature than it is an expression of feelings arising from encounters with nature. The essential "outdoors" reality of the "Pastoral" Symphony is a reality once re-moved—as is the metaphorical presentation of Cathy Linton's and Linton Heathcliff's outdoor paradises.

In this larger metaphorical sense, many of Beethoven's most powerful works express the spirit of nature and the outdoors as a primal force. The two symphonies which surround the "Pastoral," the Fifth and the Seventh, are magnificent examples. So are the two great piano sonatas of the same period: the "Waldstein" and the "Appassionata." In these works, as in *Wuthering Heights* at times, the outdoors is expressed not in literal sounds or scenes but in spirit. Beethoven's vehemence, like Brontë's, sometimes takes us "outdoors" simply by bursting the bounds of conven-tional expectations, producing an effect similar to that of breaking out of a room or a house in which we have been confined.

Similarly, the "indoor" character of Mozart's music is more often meta-phorical than literal. His tendency to stay within the boundaries, to work within limitations, to remain close to the "home" key compares with the tendency of Austen's characters to remain indoors, seldom venturing out—or far—for travel. Mozart's countless minuet movements are pat-terned on an indoor dance form (just as Schubert's and Mahler's *Ländler* are based on an outdoor dance form), but it is really the spirit of bal-ance, of propriety, of following the forms (the repeats, the trio, the *da capo* return) that gives most Mozart minuets their "indoor" quality. A few of his instrumental pieces do suggest the outdoors in quite a literal way: the "Hunt" Quartet, the various outdoor serenades that begin and end with marches by which the musicians enter and exit. But these are more strictly outdoors in occasion than in spirit; the Scherzo or finale of Beethoven's Seventh Symphony blow them right off the grounds, meta-phorically speaking.

Eric Blom notes that "open-air music, at which Haydn was such an adept, is not often thought of as one of Mozart's achievements." When Mozart does allow us to "breathe the warm air of a summer night out of doors," we are seldom, as with Haydn, "in the midst of a country land-scape." Rather, we are in the midst of "a very formal horticulture and topiary."[9] So it is with Austen. In the shrubbery at Rosings or Highbury, on the grounds at Pemberly or Donwell Abbey, we do "breathe the air of the out of doors." But we breathe it in the midst of "a very formal horticulture and topiary," not in the midst of the Yorkshire moors. The out of doors tends to exist in the works of Mozart and Austen for the sake of the human beings who have tamed it and who wish occasionally to occupy it. In Beethoven and Brontë it is a force larger than human lives to which humans must link themselves with feeling and spirit if they are to transcend a human society that is by definition belittling and stifling. With such high Romantics as Poe, Chopin, and Schumann, the outdoor-indoor distinction sometimes disappears altogether, leaving us in a psychological dreamworld devoid of spatial moorings.

Home and Away

THE CONTRAST between indoors and outdoors in fiction naturally extends itself to the contrast between home and away. Ever since Homer's *Odyssey* fictional characters have traveled away from home. Some, like Odysseus, come home again. From the fairy tale to the epic, from the romance to the novel, movement away from home and back again has been central to most stories of most ages. Few authors in any genre have written with a stronger sense of home than Austen, whose novels never leave her island or her era. Nor have many novelists used a sense of home so effectively as a structuring principle for their fiction. *Pride and Prejudice* is an excellent example.

The house at Longbourn, where the Bennets live, is the novel's home. The house itself is not described in any detail, yet the sense of home it provides is pervasive. Most of the action in volume 1 occurs at home at Longbourn. Most of the action in volume 2 occurs away at Rosings, during Elizabeth's extended visit to the Collinses. The action of volume 3, after the short visit to Pemberly, returns home to Longbourn. The pattern among the three volumes, then, is home-away-home. There is a similar pattern within each volume, as will be shown in some detail in Chapter 4. Much of the sense of equilibrium achieved by *Pride and Prejudice* comes from the stability and balance of its presentation of home. Much of its variety comes from its excursions to places away. The excursions away may be short or extended, but they are always well-prepared. And they are always presented in such a way that we never lose our sense of Longbourn as home.

The home-away-home pattern that Austen happens to use in *Pride and Prejudice* corresponds closely to Mozart's customary use of home-away-home harmonies. Much of the formal equilibrium of his Concerto No. 9 (K. 271), for example, results from his use of E-flat major as the tonal home. The first and last movements center on the home key as much as the first and last volumes of *Pride and Prejudice* center on Longbourn. The contrasting second movement centers on the related key of C minor, just as the second volume centers on the related (through the Collinses) locale of Rosings. The harmonic pattern of the concerto, like the geographic pattern of the novel, is home-away-home. (To call the tonic key in a Mozart work "home" and the contrasting key "away" is, of

46

course, to speak metaphorically. But one does so in good company. Even purists of the music-is-music-only school customarily refer to the tonic key of a classical composition as the home key.)

One reason that Mozart's piano concertos (and instrumental works in general) achieve such a complete sense of equilibrium is that he instinctively establishes the home key so unmistakably at the beginning of the work that any excursion from it is clearly felt—as is, of course, the inevitable return. The excursions may be brief and fleeting or extended and daring, but one thing is certain: we will always return home. Every Mozart piano concerto follows the home-away-home pattern *among* its three movements; in all the concertos but one the same pattern holds *within* each separate movement. This consistency, however, no more makes for redundancy than does Austen's treatment of fictional homes. As we will see in Part 2, Mozart's home-away-home harmonies in K. 271 contrast with those in K. 503 and K. 595 in much the same way that Austen's home-away-home locales in *Pride and Prejudice* contrast with those in *Emma* and *Persuasion*. Not only among but within their separate movements and volumes these two artists often use home-away-home harmonies and locales in extremely similar ways.

In *Wuthering Heights*, as in Austen's fiction, home and away can be literally equated with individual houses or estates. Here, however, in the place of a multiplicity of houses, there are only two. To judge by the title, Wuthering Heights would be "home" and Thrushcross Grange "away." But this depends very much upon point of view—and upon time. Wuthering Heights *is* home to Heathcliff—to the extent that the "gipsy-like" foundling ever has a home. But he never does have one in anything like the sense that Elizabeth Bennet does. Wuthering Heights is also home for Catherine Earnshaw, until she makes Thrushcross Grange her home by marrying Edgar Linton. But that new home soon becomes her "shattered prison." For Cathy Linton, Thrushcross Grange is home until she marries Linton Heathcliff, whereupon the Heights becomes home. When she marries Hareton, the Grange will again become her home—and a new one for him. Thrushcross Grange is home for Lockwood at the beginning of the novel. Wuthering Heights is shockingly away (especially in a psychological or emotional sense). Yet even at the Grange, which he is only renting, Lockwood is no more at home than the interpolated Heathcliff ever was at Wuthering Heights. The Grange *is* "home" in one sense: it is where Nelly and Lockwood sit as she tells him most of the story. The Grange, however, is not Nelly's home. She grew up mostly at the Heights. But that was not her original home, either.

In short, what is home from one point of view is away from another.

Apart from Joseph, for whom Wuthering Heights remains home during the entire novel, individual characters continually change their homes. The meaning of home or away is less stable than in Austen's fiction, but the contrast between them is much more obvious and brutal. Transitions from one to the other are much more abrupt. Geographically, the Heights and the Grange are only four miles apart; emotionally and psychologically the distance between them far exceeds what one finds in the physically more extensive world of *Pride and Prejudice*.

Beethoven's compositions, no less than Mozart's, generally follow home-away-home harmonies. But Beethoven's contrasts between home and away are generally starker. Much of the formal equilibrium of the "Appassionata" comes from the home-away-home pattern of its movements: the outer movements in F minor enclose the central one in D-flat major. Within this pattern, however, Beethoven creates harmonic conflict more brutal than in Mozart (even in the G-minor Symphony). The first movement modulates to A-flat major for the second subject, but this contrasting (or "away") material is quickly swept up into the storm of the home key. The second movement never leaves the key of D-flat major, whose harmonic stasis is complete—until it is shattered by the brutal attack of the third movement. In the raging F-minor finale, there is a brief, episodic second theme, but it is in C minor rather than in a major key, as expected. The harmonic contrast here is not only more brutal than in Mozart: it is different in kind.

In the "Appassionata," as in *Wuthering Heights*, home and away have come to resemble emotional states or philosophical abstractions. When the one principle is in power, the other seems hardly able to express itself. It is one of the paradoxes of Beethoven's music that both the vehemence and the formal equilibrium—both the violent expressiveness and the forged sense of organic form—are rooted in the firmness with which he establishes a home key so as to emphasize both deviations from it and the ultimate return. The same paradox governs Brontë's use of geographical locales in *Wuthering Heights*.

Composers and authors of many historical periods, of course, have made use of some kind of harmonic or geographic contrast. But few have used the various home-away-home possibilities with the stark brutality of Beethoven and Brontë—or with the clarity and ease of Mozart and Austen. Many Romantic artists made strong inroads on the pervasive sense of home central to the art of all four. In music, the future of such harmonic stability was anticipated by the name given to a work composed for the solo piano in 1822: the "Wanderer" Fantasy. The sobriquet attached to Schubert's work was not intended to indicate its harmonic destiny, but it does accurately do so.

Though numerous Romantic compositions (especially those in sonata form) continue to follow the basic home-away-home pattern typical of the classical style, many make radical departures. Composers such as Schumann, Schubert, Chopin, Liszt, and Wagner often delay the establishment of a home key to lengths that Mozart or Beethoven would have found excruciating. More important, even after a tonal home is finally established, their modulations often wander so far away that there is no return. The Romantic music that was most exploratory in form tended to convert the home-away-home pattern into home-away. The inevitable return home began to seem not only anticlimactic but even false. The "Wanderer" Fantasy and the Presto from Chopin's "Funeral March" Sonata are two of the earliest Romantic works that wander far beyond the harmonic boundaries within which not only Mozart but Beethoven instinctively remained. The harmonic instability and rampant chromaticism of the Presto are so severe that "harmonically," as Alan Walker notes, "the movement is poised on the brink of atonality—an astonishing achievement for a 29-year-old in 1839."[10]

In English-language fiction the work of Poe offers an excellent mid-nineteenth-century parallel to the propensity of the home key to wander. In "Ligeia" we never learn where home is. The narrator thinks he met Ligeia in "some large, old, decaying city near the Rhine," but he is not sure. As to his own home, no mention is made of it at all. In "The Masque of the Red Death" Prince Prospero's castle is home for the story, but it is located in an unmoored never-never land. In "The Fall of the House of Usher" the narrator is only a visitor to the house of the title, whose location is unspecified. The story ends not with a return to a home but with the destruction of one, from which the narrator flees. Poe's one novel, *The Narrative of Arthur Gordon Pym* (1838), is a "wanderer's fantasy" from the point of view of a stable home. So is Melville's *Moby-Dick*. Home in each work is only the shore from which to launch out into the open seas. Each work ends far from its forgotten home, with a boat sinking or disappearing into the middle of the ocean.

In both the fiction and the music of the Romantic period, the stability of the opening home is often vulnerable to a high degree. The subsequent wandering to places and harmonies far away is often prolonged to the degree that "away" actually comes to prevail over "home," not only geographically or harmonically, but emotionally and psychologically.

Sanity and Madness

SANITY AND MADNESS, like most of the "themes" discussed above, are conditions that can be expressed literally in fiction but only metaphori-

49

cally in music, apart from opera or program music. Austen's world is eminently sane: the only characters who could actually be called *in*sane are insanely conventional (I am thinking here of such individuals as Lady Catherine, Mrs. Elton, and Sir Walter Elliot). In *Wuthering Heights*, on the other hand, Catherine Earnshaw becomes literally mad. Yet her madness reveals important psychological truths, as do dreams in the novel—both her dreams and those of other characters. Heathcliff, too, becomes technically mad just before he dies. He suffers from a "monomania" which causes him to see Catherine's eyes everywhere he looks. There are hints of madness even in the most sane characters: Lockwood, for example, dreams of rubbing a ghost's hand against the glass so that it bleeds. Yet *Wuthering Heights* can also be called a sane book, for its irrational elements are presented to us by Nelly through Lockwood and are therefore contained in a frame that helps us understand them.

In Poe's world, madness generally is not so framed and contained. Instead of the episode of Catherine's madness we have entire stories whose relation to social or everyday reality is not at all clear: "Ligeia," "The Fall of the House of Usher," "The Masque of the Red Death," even the *Narrative of Arthur Gordon Pym*. Madness in these and other stories by Poe often seems not so much a condition into which a sensitive person can be driven by the pressures of society or psyche but instead the very essence of a person's life or condition. Unlike *Wuthering Heights*, which often uses dreams to reveal psychological truths about a character we see moving in a recognizable external world, Poe's stories themselves often seem to be continuous dreams whose relation to external reality is unclear.

Mozart's music, like Austen's fiction, can be called eminently sane. Where madness occurs, it is often a conventional madness. From the major operas, I think of the chilling and obsessional madness of the Queen of the Night in *The Magic Flute*, a madness expressed, for the most part, in virtuoso but conventional coloratura scales. From the instrumental music, there is the "madness" of *A Musical Joke*. Its melodies and musical forms are essentially those of Mozart's "sane" music. But here those materials are unshaped by taste or restraint. They are allowed to ramble inconsequently, creating a conventional madness that seems to have been as abhorrent to Mozart's ear as were the words and actions of Mrs. Elton or Mr. Collins to Austen.

If one chooses to define sanity by such concepts as harmony, equilibrium, and concord, then one certainly can find its metaphorical equivalent in certain kinds of instrumental music. But as the above examples make clear, it would be as wrong to equate "sanity" in Mozart's music with the following of harmonious conventions as it would be to do the same for Austen's novels. In both artists' work equilibrium, harmony, and concord are not givens but rather conditions to be aspired toward. The highest "sanity," concord or completeness, is the kind that can incorporate significant disturbing elements without balance or equilibrium being lost. The "madness" of Lady Catherine or Sir Walter, of the Queen of the Night or *A Musical Joke* is that their worlds are too conventionally self-enclosed: there is no room for the assimilation of experiences or feelings that do not conform to predefined rules or forms. The characters in Austen's fiction who achieve the most admirable equilibrium are those who allow their balance to be disturbed by feelings and insights they had not before experienced, and who can incorporate such new experience into their continuing life.

One example in *Pride and Prejudice* is the shock Elizabeth feels upon receiving Darcy's letter. For a long while she is unable to read the words, to focus her thoughts. Such a condition is unprecedented in the life of this eminently rational young woman. But this same vulnerability enables her to grow emotionally. After she does assimilate the import and implications of the letter, she attains a new equilibrium more mature than she had known before.

Emma undergoes a similar experience after realizing what Mr. Elton is really up to. On the evening following the carriage-ride in the snow, she loses her steel-trap hold on reality for a considerable time—as she does again during other revelations later in the novel. Emma's vulnerability to experience, her ability to assimilate events outside of her expectations, allows her, too, to grow. The equilibrium she attains by the end of the novel is at once more vulnerable and more stable, richer and more varied, than the complacent balance she had shown in the opening chapters.

Anne Elliot is emotionally the most vulnerable of Austen's heroines, and emotionally the richest. The equilibrium she experiences at the beginning of the novel is neither Elizabeth's high-spirited assurance nor Emma's high-minded arrogance. It is more of a high-strung limbo. Anne's is an equilibrium vulnerable to the slightest touch. In chapter 9, when the Musgrove child is clinging to her back, she becomes aware that someone—and not only someone, but Wentworth!—has lifted him off. This seemingly trivial event causes her to "lose her mind" and become more "disturbed" than has any other Austen heroine:

> Her sensations on the discovery made her perfectly speechless. She could not even thank him. She could only hang over little Charles, with most disordered feelings. His kindness in stepping foward to her relief—the manner—the silence in which it had passed—the little particulars of the

circumstance—with the conviction soon forced on her, by the noise he was studiously making with the child, that he meant to avoid hearing her thanks, and rather sought to testify that her conversation was the last of his wants, produced such a confusion of varying, but very painful agitation, as she could not recover from, till enabled by the entrance of Mary and the Miss Musgroves to make over her little patient to their cares, and leave the room. She could not stay.[11]

Her inability to speak, her "most disordered feelings," her need to leave the room—all indicate deep disturbance in a nature such as Anne's. They also indicate the vulnerability that allows her to incorporate a wide variety of experience into the "equilibrium" and "sanity" she finally achieves. The long broken fourth sentence, followed by the short fifth ("She could not stay"), is at once a measure of her vulnerability and awareness. But Anne, sensitive though she is, is never shown in touch with such irrational things as dreams. In Austen's fiction, dreams are left to a three-word sentence (and paragraph) uttered by the inconsequential Miss Bates in *Emma*: "Extraordinary dream indeed!"

The equilibrium achieved in Mozart's instrumental music is harmonic, rhythmic, melodic, and structural. His music attains to equilibrium not because these elements are stable throughout but rather because they are vulnerable and changing—because the final stability is achieved through the assimilation of so many threats. That the threats to stability are not often so vehement and fiercely discordant as those in the music of Beethoven and many of his Romantic successors does not mean that "disturbing" elements and tendencies are lacking. They are, to return to Lang's words, "inherent and active, but tamed and kept in equilibrium." As with Austen, such elements pervade Mozart's later works more than his early ones. Among the piano concertos, K. 466, K. 488, K. 491, and K. 595 are particularly fine examples. Even in these works, however, deeply disturbing elements are generally expressed within an overall pattern of equilibrium and restraint.

A moment similar to Anne Elliot's "disturbance" in chapter 9 occurs in the slow movement of K. 466. The piano opens the movement with a bright, sunny, beautifully disposed melody and is accompanied spaciously by the orchestra. Then, in a moment nearly unprecedented in Mozart, this slow, harmonious movement is violated by a vehement, violent episode in G minor that blows away the equilibrium of the opening. Composure is gradually reestablished during a masterful transition back to the opening material, which, sounding the same, is also different and never will be the same.[12] The equilibrium at the end of the movement is ostensibly the same as at the beginning, but the feeling is infinitely richer—much as it is when Anne finally regains her composure: "She was ashamed of herself, quite ashamed of being so nervous, so overcome by such a trifle, but so it was; and it required a long application of solitude and reflection to recover her." Anne's heightened burst of feeling, like that in the concerto, would be impossible without the context of suspended surface equilibrium in which it occurs. Romantic artists, to the extent that they wandered outside the boundaries of classical equilibrium and restraint, lost the possibility of creating precisely this kind of irrational outburst, though they found their own telling varieties, to be sure.

In both Mozart and Austen, episodes of madness, disturbance, and discord tend to be temporary.[13] In Beethoven and Brontë, invasions of the irrational tend to be more massive and lasting. Although a kind of equilibrium is attained at the end of *Wuthering Heights*, the disturbing or irrational elements have not been entirely assimilated—as attested by the merging bodies under the earth and the wandering spirits above it. Both Catherine and Heathcliff do achieve a vision of equilibrium before they die, but the equilibrium each anticipates is not a richer version of what she or he has known before. It is, rather, an equilibrium altogether different in kind. Each feels that she or he is passing from a "shattered prison" into an unworldly world of peace unknown to other mortals.

In works from Beethoven's early and middle periods, strong passions (often embodied in obsessive rhythms) batter at the classical forms even while being contained by them. In Beethoven's late period they occasionally shatter those forms altogether, entering a mystical world in many ways similar to that aspired to by Catherine and Heathcliff. Harsh contrasts in harmony, violent contrasts of dynamics, madly but sometimes blissfully syncopated rhythms, obsessions with individual motifs, a tendency to divide the musical world into torrents of motion and islands of calm, a yearning for unity that converts the most disparate melodies and even movements into one—all these elements indicate tendencies toward disturbance and even madness in late Beethoven that have parallels in *Wuthering Heights*. (The late quartets and the last piano sonata, Opus 111, are fine examples.) Both artists, however, generally manage to contain such irrational forces within the framework of accepted artistic forms, broadly defined (the novel of matrimony, the music of stable tonality). The final effect of their works is not so much of madness breaking through to shatter the forms altogether as of madness being incorporated within the firm, though highly precarious, bounds of sanity and balance.

Among certain post-Beethoven Romantics we have the equivalent of Poe's short stories, where the disturbance or madness is not so much contained within the expanded clutch of the recognized forms but rather seems to forge new forms of its own. A convenient comparison is between Poe's "Ligeia" and Berlioz's *Symphonie fantastique*: convenient because the program for the symphony compares with the plot of the story. Each is about a man driven to the use of opium because of his obsessive memories of the woman he loves—a man who is definably mad. In Poe's story, the madman himself is the narrator. We are lost in a sea of ambiguity. Did the ruby red drops exist or did he only imagine them? Did Lady Rowena exist? Or even Ligeia? The story provides no context by which such questions can be resolved.

Berlioz's symphony (subtitled "An Episode in the Life of the Artist") is in five movements rather than the customary four. The obsession with the beloved is so strong that the *idée fixe* invades all five movements. The delightful delirium of the waltz (the second movement) suggests the bizarre dancing in Poe's "The Masque of the Red Death"; the grotesque beheading of the *idée fixe* (and of the "narrator") in the fourth movement suggests the morbid mutilations found throughout Poe's fiction; the scathingly ironic juxtaposition of the witches' sabbath and *Dies irae* in the fifth movement parallels Poe's implicit parody of biblical language in the last paragraph of the "Red Death." Like "Ligeia," the symphony ends in discord, confusion, and ambiguity. According to Berlioz's program, the last two movements are a two-part dream in which madness prevails. Musically, they are sonata-allegro structures deeply ambiguous in form.[14]

To find the equivalent of Poe's structuring of a complete work around madness or obsession, however, it is not necessary to draw upon Berlioz's *Symphonie fantastique* and what might seem an unfair reliance upon its program and therefore its nonmusical content. One need only consider Robert Schumann's music, especially his most individual and interesting works for solo piano—the *Symphonic Études*, *Carnaval*, *Kreisleriana*, etc. It is by no means fanciful to label such works schizophrenic in tendency. The split in Schumann's literary persona between Eusebius and Florestan is reflected in the divided character of his lyrical pieces just as it was embodied in his last years of literal madness. Schumann's personality seems to have been divided much as was Catherine Earnshaw's. He despised the philistines while wanting success by their standards; he loved the subjective and the idiosyncratic while being afraid of it too. His best and most personal music achieves a creative balance and tension between these two forces, but its equilibrium is of a totally different kind than was achieved by Mozart. Whereas Mozart's music generally begins by creating a sense of equilibrium into which disturbing elements enter, finally to be resolved, Schumann's often begins in discord and seeming madness. Often no clear home key is provided early enough to measure with precision the deviations from it. Structurally, many of Schumann's episodic works alternate between contrasting materials or principles that are not so much resolved as bravely juxtaposed.

In short, there are elements of "sanity" and "madness" in the music of Mozart, Beethoven, Berlioz, and Schumann, just as there are in the fiction of Austen, Emily Brontë, and Poe. The "madness" in Austen and Mozart tends to take the form of temporary deviations from the "sanity" by which it is measured and into which it finally becomes incorporated.[15] In Brontë and Beethoven the deviations are more massive and threatening. While the disturbances are often contained by the "sanity" of a large structural form, they at the same time call into question the adequacy of such forms as vehicles for the true expression of that which is truly irrational and subjective. In certain works by Poe, Berlioz, and Schumann, madness can be said to triumph over sanity as it has conventionally been understood. Such madness expresses itself in forms which by previous standards are ambiguous and unresolved—while at the same time achieving a unity of effect and execution that is, paradoxically, the unity of the unresolved or the unreliable.

Growth and Transformation

IN FICTION, a static character is one who does not essentially change in the course of the work. Examples from *Pride and Prejudice* include Mr. and Mrs. Bennet, their daughters Jane, Mary, Kitty, and Lydia, Mr. Collins, Charlotte, Sir William Lucas, Lady Catherine, Mr. Bingley, Miss Bingley, Wickham, and the Gardiners. In short, nearly everyone in the novel is static except Elizabeth and Darcy, each of whom develops and grows. Elizabeth overcomes her pride enough to admit her love for Darcy and to accept his second proposal. Darcy overcomes his prejudice enough to propose twice to Elizabeth—and to agree to unite his name and fortune with her family.

In *Wuthering Heights* there are fewer static characters. Joseph is one character who does not essentially change. Linton Heathcliff is perhaps another. But consider Catherine, Heathcliff, Edgar, Isabella, Cathy Linton, Hareton, Nelly, even Lockwood. All of these characters change in the course of the novel, some of them much more dramatically than either Elizabeth Bennet or Fitzwilliam Darcy. A brief comparison of the developing characters from each novel will clarify the distinction I wish to make between character growth and character transformation.

Both Heathcliff and Catherine are dramatic examples of character transformation. The transformation Catherine undergoes is revealed most starkly in her terminal madness, making overt a split in her personality that had occurred much earlier.

> But, supposing at twelve years old, I had been wrenched from the Heights, and every early association, and my all in all, as Heathcliff was at that time, and had been converted at a stroke into Mrs. Linton, the lady of Thrushcross Grange, and the wife of a stranger; an exile, and outcast, thenceforth, from what had been my world. . . . I wish I were a girl again, half savage, and hardy, and free; and laughing at injuries, not maddening under them! Why am I so changed? why does my blood rush into a hell of tumult at a few words? I'm sure I should be myself were I once among the heather on those hills. Open the window again wide, fasten it open! Quick, why don't you move?[16]

The changes Elizabeth Bennet undergoes are tame, to say the least, by comparison. Likewise, the transformations experienced by Heathcliff make Fitzwilliam Darcy look almost static by comparison: he is changed from a foundling into an unwanted Earnshaw, into Catherine's soul mate, into a boy consumed with revenge, into a man still in love with Catherine, into a man consumed with revenge, into a man obsessed by a ghost, into a man utterly beyond revenge. Even Lockwood, one could argue, changes as much as Darcy does.

For all their growth in *Pride and Prejudice*, then, Elizabeth and Darcy are almost static when contrasted with Catherine and Heathcliff. They each grow, but they are not recognizably different in character at the end of the novel than they were at the beginning. In essence Elizabeth is the same bright, agile, sympathetic creature she was from the first, the only difference being that her experience (and her ability to adapt) has deepened and polished the good qualities she already possessed. The same is true of Darcy. He remains the rather proud and formal man he first appeared; the only difference is that the experience he has gone through has brought out the best of those qualities and has allowed Elizabeth (and the reader) to view them in a much more favorable light. Yet, lest the growth achieved by Elizabeth and Darcy be undervalued, they only need to be compared with their amatory foils—Jane and Bingley.

In Austen's other novels, too, characters tend to be introduced to the reader full-blown, with their essential traits already developed (even though they may originally be misperceived or misinterpreted, as in the case of Darcy or Wickham). Those characters who do change—and they are numerically few—tend to grow through experience that deepens, rather than transforms, qualities originally present. So it is, in general, with Mozart's treatment of musical themes. Without insisting that musical themes are directly analogous to fictional characters, one can compare the manner in which each are treated. Just as *Pride and Prejudice* and *Wuthering Heights* illustrate the growth and transformation, respectively, of characters, so do the opening movements of Mozart's G-minor Symphony and Beethoven's "Appassionata" illustrate the growth and transformation, respectively, of musical themes.

The opening theme of the G-minor Symphony is announced, repeated, and counterstated in the first twenty-seven bars. Because it is announced in unison by the violins only, and because the theme itself consists of repeated motifs, its character and shape are undeniably clear even before the exact repeat of the entire exposition stamps its character still more indelibly upon the ear. With respect to the growth or transformation of this theme, the exact repeat of the exposition can without doubt be labeled static. The opening theme does grow in the development section, of course, where it undergoes considerable modulation and melodic alteration (including inversion). Even so, its shape remains recognizably that of the theme as announced in the exposition. The return "home" at the recapitulation brings the theme back in all its pristine clarity, for it is stated and repeated essentially as it was when first announced, the only change being a subtle accompaniment added by the bassoon.

The opening theme of the movement, then, grows in much the same way as does Elizabeth Bennet. Clearly delineated at the very beginning, it returns with even more clarity at the end. It has grown and deepened through the experience it has undergone in the development, but it has not been transformed into something different in its essentials from what it was. Yet, lest its growth through time be underestimated, it can be compared with the contrasting second theme of the same movement. Like Jane and Bingley, this theme is announced with great clarity—and some drama—in the exposition. But it does not even appear in the development section. Like Jane and Bingley late in the novel, it returns calmly in the recapitulation in its original form, its melody unchanged in shape, its harmony transposed to the tonic. It has changed its key, just as Jane and Bingley have been modulated into happiness, but it has not grown in the sense that the opening theme has. Melodically, it is as static as are most of the individuals in *Pride and Prejudice*.

The general pattern outlined here holds for most of Mozart's movements in sonata-allegro form. Themes are generally announced and contrasted with great clarity in the exposition. As a rule, one of the themes—usually but not always the first—is allowed to grow during the development section. The recapitulation is almost always announced by a return of the opening theme in its original shape and harmony; it is followed by the other themes in forms that are equally recognizable.

Even the theme that grew in the development—if one did—is allowed to return in its original shape. It may be deeper in experience and therefore richer in meaning, yet it remains essentially what it was.

Beethoven wrote many works throughout his career that treat their thematic material in the manner of Mozart: works whose themes grow without being transformed. The first movement of the "Pathétique" Sonata, Opus 13, is a typical example. But the "Appassionata" embodies another tendency in Beethoven, one that was to have a great influence upon his Romantic successors. The principle of thematic transformation is as central to the first movement of Opus 57 as character transformation is to *Wuthering Heights*.

The opening theme of the "Appassionata" has two parts. As soon as the theme is announced and repeated in sequence, its second half— including the trill—is detached from its first half. It is then separated from itself by the "fate" motif. When the entire opening theme tries to return in the counterstatement, it is brutally smashed by sledge-hammer chords. Like Heathcliff, this musical theme is composed of contrary components. Like Heathcliff, it is subjected to strong external threats before it can discover and begin to celebrate its own shape. Even in the beginning of the exposition it has undergone pressures that begin to transform it into something new. The process of transformation is so intrinsic here that Beethoven omits the traditional repeat of the exposition.

The process of transformation is further intensified in the development section, where the opening theme is not only subjected to strong modulation but is again stripped of its second half. At the recapitulation, where we expect to find a return of the opening theme in its original shape and pristine clarity, the new pulsations that are added in the bass have an ominous effect that transforms the original nature of the theme as thoroughly as Heathcliff's conversion to revenge transforms his character. In the subsequent counterstatement, the sledge-hammer attacks are as severe as they were in the exposition; in the coda the original theme returns once more, this time stripped entirely and irremediably of its second half (including trill). As severely as Heathcliff or Catherine, this theme has been transformed, not merely changed or deepened, by the experience it has undergone.

The process of thematic transformation developed by Beethoven was taken even further in the Romantic age. In Liszt's B-minor Sonata the thematic material is transformed again and again throughout the single movement masterpiece. In Berlioz's *Symphonie fantastique* the *idée fixe* is transformed each time it appears—most dramatically *among* the five movements, culminating with its grotesque caricature during the witches' sabbath, but also *within* a single movement, such as the first, where from exposition to development to recapitulation it is altered dramatically. Almost any history of the Romantic age in music will stress the importance of thematic transformation—just as almost any history of the Romantic age in literature will stress the importance of character transformation (in poetry as well as in fiction).

The transition from character growth toward character transformation is as clear in American fiction as it is in British. Washington Irving's Rip van Winkle and Ichabod Crane (like Austen's heroines and Mozart's themes) change but are not transformed. Hawthorne's Wakefield, Dimmesdale, and Ethan Brand; Poe's Usher, Ligeia, and William Wilson; Melville's Babo, Ahab, and Pierre—all of these characters are transformed as radically as are Heathcliff and Catherine and the musical themes of the "Appassionata" and the *Symphonie fantastique*.

Life and Death

THE ULTIMATE transformation in human life is death. In both fiction and music death becomes epidemic in the Romantic age. Among the writers discussed above, the affliction is as clear as one would ever want to see. In 1842 Poe begins a story with these words:

> The "Red Death" had long devastated the country. No pestilence had ever been so fatal, or so hideous. Blood was its Avatar and its seal—the redness and the horror of blood. There were sharp pains, and sudden dizziness, and then profuse bleeding at the pores, with dissolution. The scarlet stains upon the body and especially upon the face of the victim, were the pest ban which shut him out from the aid and from the sympathy of his fellowmen. And the whole seizure, progress and termination of the disease, were the incidents of half an hour.[17]

Although Austen lived and wrote until 1817, well into the nineteenth century, her fiction escaped the affliction. It was, in effect, quarantined—and more lastingly than Prince Prospero's castellated abbey.

In Emily Brontë's one novel there are many more deaths than in Austen's six taken together. It is difficult to remember an important character's ever dying in an Austen novel; it is felt to be a great event when Louisa Musgrove falls on the Cobb and is temporarily unconscious. There *is* one death in *Emma*: the narrator curtly informs us that "the great Mrs. Churchill was no more. It was felt as such things must be felt. Every body had a degree of gravity and sorrow; tenderness towards the departed, solicitude for the surviving friends; and, in a reasonable time, curiosity to know where she would be buried."[18] Death not only occurs seldom in the novels, it is seldom mentioned—one painful exception being Mrs. Musgrove's "large, fat sighings" over her long-departed Dick. One wonders whether the careful avoidance of death in Austen's novels contributes to the ubiquitous presence of "mortification," not as applied to the flesh but to the feelings. Death does inhabit Austen's novels, but it is emotional, social, and sometimes spiritual death, rather than corporeal.

Wuthering Heights, while not overlooking emotional, social, and spiritual death, attends in a virtuoso way to that of the body and the organism entire. Not only are the deaths numerous, they are infinitely varied: the calm exit of Mr. Earnshaw, surrounded by his family in a parlor tableau; the rapid departure of Mr. and Mrs. Linton, in the middle of a subordinate clause; Frances's abrupt translation to realms inanimate; Catherine's protracted delivery and release; Isabella's offstage demise; her brother Edgar's melting away; Hindley's unnatural end; poor Linton's sickly expiration; Heathcliff's ghastly calm. Not only are the actual descriptions of death varied but so are their aftermaths and ramifications: from the "heavenly" discussion young Heathcliff and Catherine have following Mr. Earnshaw's death to the "morbid" visits Heathcliff thrice pays to Catherine's grave, twice in life and finally in postdeath decomposition.

Poe's work has even more death per paragraph-inch than Emily Brontë's. Even without descending to such depths as "The Pit and the Pendulum," we can call a familiar roll: Usher and his sister Madeline (do the doctor and the servant perish too?), Fortunato, Prince Prospero and his revellers, Mme and Mlle L'Espanaye (in the Rue Morgue apartment), Ligeia and Lady Rowena, Pym's shipboard companions, the man with the hideous eye. Poe's dead remain with us because they are interrelated, not only in the psychologically incestuous dream-world they inhabit, but in the morbidity with which their departures are rendered.

In *Wuthering Heights* the cruelty of Lockwood rubbing the ghost-girl's hand against the broken glass or the morbidity of Heathcliff's undertaking arrangements can be connected to social or psychological truths in the daylight world of the novel. The cruelties and morbidities in Poe often seem calculated primarily to satisfy a craving for the bizarre. One virtuoso example occurs in chapter 12 of *Pym*, when the narrator's ship approaches a wandering brig that is covered with decomposing bodies. One man seems still to be alive.

> We saw the tall stout figure still leaning on the bulwark, and still nodding his head to and fro, but his face was now turned from us so that we could

not behold it. His arms were extended over the rail, and the palms of his hands fell outward. His knees were lodged upon a stout rope, tightly stretched, and reaching from the heel of the bowsprit to a cathead. On his back, from which a portion of the shirt had been torn leaving it bare, there sat a huge seagull, busily gorging itself with the horrible flesh, its bill and talons deep buried, and its white plumage spattered all over with blood. As the brig moved further round so as to bring us close in view, the bird, with much apparent difficulty, drew out its crimsoned head, and, after eyeing us for a moment as if stupefied, arose lazily from the body upon which it had been feasting, and, flying directly above our deck, hovered there a while with a portion of clotted and liver-like substance in its beak. The horrid morsel dropped at length with a sullen splash immediately at the feet of Parker. May God forgive me, but now, for the first time, there flashed through my mind a thought, a thought which I will not mention, and I felt myself making a step towards the ensanguined spot.[19]

In chapter 12, where the cannibalism anticipated here actually takes place, it occurs, in one of Poe's most morbid yet appropriate puns, "piecemeal."

Published in 1837, two decades after Austen's death and one decade before *Wuthering Heights*, the above passage takes a morbid fascination with death about as far as it can go. Both *Pym* and *Wuthering Heights* measure in a dramatic way the distance many Romantic writers traveled from Austen's deathless world. So do the novels of mid-nineteenth-century writers as diverse as Dickens, Balzac, Hawthorne, Melville, and George Eliot.

In music, the Romantic obsession with death is most easily measured in opera and program music. With opera it is necessary only to match the essentially deathless worlds of *The Marriage of Figaro*, *Così fan tutte*, and *The Magic Flute* against the afflicted worlds of *La Traviata*, *Otello*, *Macbeth*, *La Bohème*, *Tosca*, *Tristan und Isolde*, and *Pelléas et Mélisande*. Mozart's artistic world, of course, is not as deathless as Austen's—as the *Requiem*, *Idomeneo*, and *Don Giovanni* attest. But even in *Don Giovanni*, where death is sharp and dramatic, it is not prolonged to the extremes often found in Romantic opera (the last arias of Isolde or Violetta) or fiction (Dickens's Little Nell). Indeed, Don Giovanni's abrupt death at the end of the opera perfectly balances his abrupt murder of Donna Anna's father at its beginning. Its impact is structural as much as it is emotional.

With program music, the *Symphonie fantastique* is an obvious example of emphasis on death. But equally obvious among more strictly instrumental music in the Romantic Age is the popularity of "funeral march" movements from Beethoven through Mahler. Beethoven's first full funeral march is in the piano sonata Opus 26, which was soon followed by the slow movement of the "Eroica" Symphony. In each case, the funereal mood is evoked by instrumental means alone (as is also the case in Berlioz's march to the scaffold). The "Funeral March" movement of the B-flat-minor Sonata is the best-known depiction of death in Chopin's music, yet it is far from the only one: the postdeath Presto which concludes the same sonata is at least as interesting in this regard. The Adagio of Bruckner's magnificent Seventh Symphony, written in homage to Wagner, is another famous funeral march. So is the gruesome-gay slow movement of Mahler's First Symphony, to mention only one of the earliest and most obvious examples of the theme in Mahler's compositions, nearly all of which are implicitly (and often explicitly) concerned with death, as are, to a slightly lesser degree perhaps, the fictional works of his near contemporary, Thomas Mann.

Happy and Unhappy Endings

AUSTEN'S NOVELS are famous, and to some notorious, for their happy endings. Not only do Elizabeth and Darcy marry but so do Jane and Bingley; even such ogres as Lady Catherine and fools as Mr. Collins have their place in the "perfect" ending that weaves all the strands of the action into a faultless garland topped with a silken eighteenth-century bow. Not only does *Pride and Prejudice* end in such a manner but so do *Sense and Sensibility*, *Mansfield Park*, *Emma*, and *Northanger Abbey*. Only in *Persuasion* is the happy ending slightly qualified. The long awaited and much deserved marriage of Anne and Wentworth is clouded over by the fact that he belongs to the Royal Navy as well as to her. The clear implication of the last paragraph is that their incipient attainment of sweetness and light might some day be endangered.

The happy ending is a convention of the comic tradition in which Austen chose to write; she deepens this convention without actually transgressing it in the last chapter of *Persuasion*. A similar comic tradition governed the *opera buffa* style which influenced and shaped not only *The Marriage of Figaro* and *Così fan tutte* (with their perfect endings in which everything is resolved) but also Mozart's multimovement instrumental forms (sonatas, concertos, symphonies, and chamber music). Just as the overwhelming proportion of Mozart's multimovement works are in the major key, so can the overwhelming proportion of them be said to end happily. To some modern ears, Mozart's charming, often frisky finales are as disappointing as are Austen's "perfect" endings. Yet those finales—even apart from the few minor-key works—are far from uniformly "happy." Several of the later piano concertos conclude in much the same way *Persuasion* does, with a happy ending that is somewhat qualified. This is particularly true of K. 488 and K. 595, both of whose final movements are colored with hues of the first two, resulting in works whose sunny/sad, agitated/resigned contrasts run from beginning to end.

Whereas Austen's most ambiguous ending, that of *Persuasion*, is still an assertively happy one, the ending of *Wuthering Heights* is both happy and not. Brontë's novel has at least two endings: the conventional happy ending that features Cathy and Hareton's marriage in life coexisting with the unconventional ending that features Catherine and Heathcliff's marriage in death. Lockwood reports both endings at the end of the book; he does not choose between them. Readers often do. Those for whom the marriage of Cathy and Hareton is the "true" ending tend to argue that if Catherine and Heathcliff had not been so "excessive" in their passion, they, too, might have turned out all right. Readers for whom the Cathy-Hareton union is a weak, vapid evasion of the issue tend to feel that life is meaningless unless one is able to harness and express the magnificent passions of a Catherine or Heathcliff. Even those in the latter group, however, divide sharply as to the nature of Catherine and Heathcliff's end, the "sad" advocates stressing the pain they suffered in the mundane world that could never appreciate them, the "happy" advocates stressing their ultimate union of souls and even cells.

In many of Beethoven's greatest works it is equally difficult to determine whether the ending is happy or not. Take the "Eroica" Symphony, for example. Some listeners consider its ending to be uplifting because the massive codas of the first and last movements reaffirm the home key and all of the stability it represents, thereby grounding the enormous tensions of the work (the phrase is Rosen's) in such a way that they are resolved. Other listeners, who feel the tragedy of the second movement and of the development sections of the first and last movements, find that the strained equilibrium attained at the end serves not to resolve the tragedy but rather to anchor the structure that expresses it. So it is with the "Appassionata." The work is either a muscular classical framework that admits vehement passions into its outer movements only to show how boldly it can contain them, or it is an anguished cry from the soul so piercing that one can have no eye or ear for the structure that supports it. With Opus 111 the problem is somewhat different. The ending, if felt to be happy, is often felt to be so in some mystical or transcendental way; listeners who are not transported in this manner tend to feel that there is no ending at all and that the work is unhappily without shape or resolution of any kind. Indeed, during the most of the nineteenth century Opus 111 was thought to be an unfinished sonata.

The above doubts about the nature and meaning of the ending of a work occur throughout Beethoven's career in ways analogous to the doubts and possibilities raised by the ending of *Wuthering Heights*—and any number of other Romantic literary works. In American fiction, for example, *The Scarlet Letter* provides a comparably ambiguous ending, teeming with multiple meanings. Dimmesdale's tragic death coincides with the victory of truth, ending the novel not only with Hester's bereavement but with Pearl's redemption and release.

With writers such as Poe and composers such as Chopin, the ambiguous or double ending of the kind produced by Brontë and Beethoven often (though by no means always) gives way to a terminal world that is conventionally melancholy. Nearly all of Poe's stories are unhappy by any traditional definition of the term. So, it might be said, are Chopin's sonatas and concertos for piano, all five of which happen to be in a minor key. Although music in a minor key is not necessarily unhappy (as many Baroque compositions attest), the minor-key music composed by Chopin and many of his contemporaries usually is. Even in his celebrated short forms Chopin writes in a minor key as often as in a major one. This trend in his music—and his era—is a significant departure from the music of Mozart, Haydn, and even Beethoven, whose overriding practice was to start and to finish the great majority of their works in a major key.

In short, Mozart and Austen generally wrote in a classical (or neoclassical) style in which the comic or happy ending was conventional. Poe and Chopin both wrote in Romantic styles within which the unhappy ending was itself becoming a convention. In this way, as in others, the works of Emily Brontë and Beethoven can be said to straddle both tendencies.

Chapter Three

COMPARABLE TENDENCIES
IN FICTION AND MUSIC

I N APPLYING certain terms, and then themes, to both music and fiction, our discussion has become increasingly metaphorical. A consideration of tendencies demands even greater care. Much of what we feel, and even know, about a work of fiction or music is not easily expressed in the critical terminology of either field. The tendencies of a great artist's character or soul are difficult to analyze precisely. They are the critic's most elusive, most essential game.

Consider, for example, Melville's *Billy Budd*. Some critics consider it Melville's "testament of acceptance." Others find it an ironic, unsparing indictment of the claims of civilization. Similar disputes have raged as to the ultimate meaning of Milton's Satan, Mozart's Don Giovanni, Brontë's Heathcliff. The most important questions are the hardest to answer. Resolving them requires equal attention to the form and the spirit of the artistic work. Even then, answers are seldom absolute, and critics of goodwill will disagree.

Even if one did allow, for example, that *Billy Budd* attests to a greater acceptance of fate than most of Melville's earlier works, with a writer such as Melville the idea of acceptance is always less than absolute. In *Billy Budd* he asks: "Who in the rainbow can show the line where the violet tint ends and the orange tint begins? Distinctly we see the difference of the colors, but when exactly does the one first blendingly enter into the other?"[1]

The Tendency toward Classical or Romantic

EACH OF THE TERMS and themes discussed above—and listed below—suggests a polarity to which a musical or fictional work may tend.

Equilibrium and Balance	vs.	Imbalance
Symmetry and Proportion	vs.	Irregularity of Form

Restraint	vs.	Vehemence of Expression
Clarity	vs.	Ambiguity
Ambiguity as a Means	vs.	Ambiguity as an End
Wit	vs.	Sentiment
Wit	vs.	Scorn
Conventional Language	vs.	The Unconventional
Individuality within Society	vs.	Individuality Apart from Society
Indoors	vs.	Outdoors
Home	vs.	Away
Sanity	vs.	Madness
Growth	vs.	Transformation
Life	vs.	Death
Happy Ending	vs.	Unhappy Ending

Combining these polarities and applying them to individual works of music and fiction produces a useful working definition of the opposing tendencies toward classical or Romantic expression from the late eighteenth century to the mid-nineteenth century. A work may be called classical to the extent that it tends toward the categories on the left, Romantic to the extent that it tends toward those on the right. (To feel the boundaries of this working definition, one should scan from top to bottom on each side, as well as line by line.)

By the standard presented here, most of Mozart's and Austen's great masterpieces are decidedly classical, those of Poe, Chopin, and Berlioz tend to be Romantic, and those of Beethoven and Emily Brontë tend to straddle the "vs." Such labeling helps to flesh out the comparable stylistic shift from classical to Romantic that historians of music and of fiction have traced carefully in their separate fields but have seldom yoked together—by violence or any other means. History aside, it points to individual works in the two fields that have exciting aesthetic similarities, as Part 2 is designed to show in the case of Austen and Mozart.

Still, it must always be remembered that we are speaking of tendencies, not absolutes. Classical artists such as Mozart and Austen, for example, have no monopoly on a quality such as equilibrium. Romantic works may achieve equilibrium too—it simply tends to be a different kind. "The perfection of Romanticism," Jacques Barzun has written,

is to bring into a tense equilibrium many radical diversities. It consequently produces work that shows rough texture, discontinuities, distortions—antitheses of structure as well as of substance. From the classical point of view these are flaws; but they are consented to by the Romanticist—even sought after—for the sake of drama; they are not oversights on the artist's part but planned concessions to the medium and the aim it subserves—as in engineering one finds gaps, vents, or holes to balance the effects of expansion by heat or stress of vibration. So, far from lacking a sense of form or neglecting its claims, the Romanticist abandons the ready-made formula because its excessive generality gives it too loose a fit.... The result is characteristic distortion or asymmetry.[2]

The kind of tense Romantic equilibrium described here is found not only in Berlioz's *Symphonie fantastique* but in Balzac's *Père Goriot*, not only in the *Carnaval* but in *Hard Times*, not only in the "Funeral March" Sonata but in *Pym*, not only in Liszt's B-minor Sonata but in *Moby-Dick*. These examples of Romantic equilibrium—not to mention those of Beethoven and Emily Brontë—help us to define and appreciate the kind of classical equilibrium Mozart and Austen achieved.

Ultimately, the similarities between Mozart's and Austen's achievement are of interest not so much because each can be said to be the purest exemplar of "classical equilibrium" in his or her separate tradition, but rather because their greatest works express comparable spirit. The human meaning of their works is comparable—and that meaning often finds expression in comparable forms. The same holds true for many of the Romantics briefly alluded to above. Of interest to the musical and the literary taxonomist, the affinities of such artists are I think more deeply significant to the human aesthetician; that is, to the critic who wishes to trace manifestations of the human spirit in those art works which explore the timeless questions of society and of psyche in a mutually illuminating manner.

When comparing Mozart concertos with Austen novels in Part 2, I am in each case trying to probe truths and realities that are social and psychological as well as aesthetic. What in the old bold days was called the *Zeitgeist* contributes to some of these similarities.[3] So, I believe, do accidents of birth and status, quirks of evolution and revolution, patterns of repression and regression, joys of the sublime and sublimation. An artist's tendency to be either classical or Romantic as I have employed those terms often carries with it several concomitant tendencies, each of which will be discussed briefly before the detailed comparison of individual works begins.

The Tendency to Preserve the Fabric or Burst Its Form

THE TENDENCY of both Austen and Mozart to preserve the fabric is for me one of the deepest affinities of their art. So is the shared tendency of Beethoven and Brontë to burst the fabric while preserving it at the same time. Often the tendency of Romantics such as Poe, Berlioz, or Chopin is either to burst the fabric altogether—thereby creating the "gaps, vents, or holes" Barzun writes of—or to reduce it in size. In many distinctively Romantic products, the lack of traditional shapeliness is compensated for by bursts of iridescent color.

My use of the word *fabric* is meant to suggest clothing, even tailoring, a concern that preoccupied people of Austen's and Mozart's time and station more than it does most of us today. The artistic fabrics created by Austen and Mozart are among the best-woven we know: each thread added to the pattern blends with what is there and leads to the shape, color, and texture to come. Seamless from start to finish, their best works embody a shapely ideal, tailored to adjust with pliant ease to every inclination of the body and spirit within. Their best products stretch but never rend, and are as durable as anything mankind makes may be.

I speak here metaphorically of the impeccable shape of Austen's and Mozart's best works, of the ease and elegance with which form fits content, but the idea of not rending the fabric has applications beyond the haberdashistic. The fabric of society is never openly rent in their artistic worlds, even when such a fate might seem deserved. The human and spiritual imperfections of such characters as Mrs. Bennet or Lady Catherine, of Miss Bates or Mrs. Elton, even of Sir Walter Elliot, serious as they are, are not sufficient to destroy the social fabric or to make it unfit for even the most discriminating. In Mozart's operas, the preservation of the social fabric, even if imperfect, is most clear in *Figaro*, where the Count, for one, deserves rougher treatment than he gets, but in the end is forgiven, as is the differently undeserving Papageno in *The Magic Flute*. In Mozart's instrumental works, too, the conventional, while transcended, is never ruptured in the process, as the piano concertos so vividly demonstrate.

Not only in art but in life Mozart and Austen tended to operate within the fabric—or the restraints, if you will—of society at large. Mozart chafed under the traditional role of the musician as servant to the wealthy, but he neither shed his livery nor terminally ruptured his relations with the prominent. He remained, too, a dutiful son and husband, finding more peace, joy, and meaning in his relations with his father and wife, in particular, than many modern commentators have been willing to approve of. He broke with the Archbishop of Salzburg, yes, but in doing so he did not oppose in principle the assumption that the musician was to serve the powers that be. Rather, he proudly trotted off to Vienna to be better appreciated—for a time. It remained for Beethoven to burst the tight-knit social forms that made a musician an extension of the ornate silken fabrics that graced Vienna's intimate salons and curtained her theaters.

Even more did Austen operate within the conventional possibilities that society held out to her. Having eschewed the "felicity of matrimony," she was seemingly content to be a loving daughter, sister, and aunt. One natural extension of this role was to read her literary entertainments (such as "First Impressions," the first version of *Pride and Prejudice*) to the family circle. Becoming a professional novelist at Chawton does not seem to have much altered her familial role. When visitors were announced by the "creaking door," she apparently put her writing out of sight and became sociable. She played music every morning before breakfast on her rectangular pianoforte, but seldom admitted to family or friends how deeply she loved and felt that music, allowing them to think she practiced only to be able to play for the pleasure of others at dances (see the Appendixes).

Austen in her life and novels, like Mozart in his letters and librettos, took no particular notice of the French Revolution, as commentators on Austen in particular never tire of pointing out. (Mozart lived until 1791, long enough for the omission to appear significant to several students of his life and art.) Yet each has been called revolutionary by some, even though operating in life and art within the fabric of what society and its conventions held dear.

Beethoven's attitude toward the French Revolution and the need for sweeping social change, his implacable assault upon aristocratic assumptions in both his life and art, are too well known to require comment in the present context. Nor is there any doubt that the vehemence of his social beliefs strongly influenced the shape of his music. Some of his early works stretch Mozart's artistic forms out of recognizable feel, if not shape; some middle-period works burst those forms to the seams; and his later works occasionally transcend those forms, when not casting them aside altogether. The force of his music, like the comparative ease of Mozart's, is a partial metaphor for his experience of the social fabric itself.

Emily Brontë's attitude toward the social fabric, on the other hand, is so obscured from us that even speculation is difficult. Like Austen, she was deeply committed to being a sister and daughter—which in her family included the right, even the duty, of being an amateur artist. But we know almost nothing about her attitudes toward the day-to-day life of society at large. The paucity of information is such that critics have often been driven to extrapolate her social attitudes from *Wuthering Heights* itself. Some speculate that her strong identification with Heathcliff, whether conscious or not, reveals a strong tendency to burst the social fabric altogether. Given the shape of the novel, however, and the function of Nelly and Lockwood as narrators, one could just as well argue that Brontë's novel, no less than Beethoven's music, reveals a concomitant respect for the value of form and of forms, if imbued with passionate human spirit.

If neither Beethoven nor Brontë slipped into society's fabric with the artistic ease of a Mozart or an Austen, neither was that fabric ever as irrelevant to them and to their artistic purposes as it would sometimes seem for artists such as Poe, Chopin, and Schumann. Beethoven and Brontë both wrestled against the confines of the social fabric. To the degree that they burst its seams or cast it aside or transcended it, to that same extent did they also know it and feel its importance. Their distinctive products are as rough-hewn as they are well-tailored, but they are still social products intended for all humanity to wear, if they dare.

The tendency to preserve the fabric or to burst its form has psychological as well as aesthetic and social ramifications. Preserving the psychological fabric can be associated with the tendency toward equilibrium, balance, and sanity in the works of Austen and Mozart, as opposed to the tendency toward disturbance, irregularity, and madness in the works of Brontë, Beethoven, and some of the other Romantics discussed above. The presence or absence of such tendencies in artistic works, while to some degree a result of artistic traditions and social possibilities, inevitably relates to the "psychological fabric" of the artist, though to imply a one-to-one relationship here would be foolhardy. Berlioz did not have to be psychologically mad to write the *Symphonie fantastique*, nor was Mozart necessarily in a state of exquisite equilibrium when he wrote *Eine kleine Nachtmusik*. Yet Berlioz once took a dose of poison along with him when expecting an amatory crisis, something it is difficult to imagine Mozart doing, even if overwrought.

The psychological fault-line that sears each sentence of the *Heiligenstadt Testament* yet is kept from breaking by Beethoven's immense will, corresponds in the deepest way to qualities found again and again in his music. Whereas much of Beethoven's music hovers over that psychological fault, works by Berlioz, Schumann, and Poe sometimes seem to emanate from down in the chasm, while those of Mozart and Austen tend to be comparatively faultless, earthbound, and entire. Severe obsessions, regressions, and sublimations often seem more dramatically to shape the surface fabric of Romantic-tending than of classical-tending works, as can be authenticated in some cases, merely felt in others. It may well be, for example, that much of the pent-up energy that strains the fabric of Beethoven's and Brontë's works is repressed sexual energy, that Chopin's and Poe's putative search for surrogate mothers contributes to the small-scale and sometimes claustrophobic, yet often caressing intimacy of some of their most distinctive works, and that the complex fabric of feeling and form developed and preserved by Mozart and Austen corresponds in some way to the psychological and emotional texture of the social and familial lives they led.

Such speculation, of course, is outside the central focus of this study, whose primary concern is to show that the art of Austen and Mozart actually is comparable. Accomplishing this feat with precision is demanding enough, even without trying to explain all the possible whys and wherefores. But such exploration would be of interest. In addition to monitoring migrations of the *Zeitgeist*, one would have to untangle the organic filaments of each artist's social, psychological, and cultural lives—and then rejoin them.

The Tendency toward Clarity of Form or Urgency of Feeling

MANNERS are essential in Mozart and Austen. It is impossible in the work of either to distinguish what is expressed from how it is expressed. The feeling results from the form as much as the form results from the feeling. An identical expression of urgent feeling may be exquisite or laughable, depending on the context of place and timing. There is a time and a place, for example, for an orchestral tutti to be eloquent in a grandiose way—as in the opening bars of Mozart's Piano Concerto in E-flat Major (K. 482). But later, when the orchestra interrupts the exquisite delicacy of the solo's entrance by repeating its own opening statement unaltered, the grandiose has become pompous. (This quality is brought out nicely in the Barenboim recording with the English Chamber Orchestra.) Comparable to the unmannerly orchestral interruption in K. 482 is the characteristic behavior of Mr. Weston in *Emma*. His effusion of feeling is always genuine, but it can be warm or tasteless depending on the circumstances. As Mr. Weston has no proper sense of place or timing, he thinks himself always warm.

In Beethoven and Brontë, on the other hand, genuine feeling tends to be an absolute good. Heathcliff gnashes his teeth and bashes his head in grief over Catherine. These actions are acceptable, though physically repugnant, because they are genuine, whereas a mother's "large, fat sighings" in Austen's *Persuasion* are unacceptable, though genuine, because they are physically repugnant. Many of Beethoven's musical excesses were as shocking to his contemporaries as Heathcliff's were to Brontë's. In the context of Mozart's or Austen's art, they might have

71

been not only painful but laughable. But in the art of Beethoven and Brontë they are truth—the mighty truth of the heart that must express itself without regard for pleasantries or manners. Early reviewers found the works of each to be "coarse" and "crude." They were so by choice, as their art tells us again and again. Each was so under the imperative force of urgent emotion.

In the world of Poe or Berlioz one often feels that strong and morbid expressions are more shocking than urgent. The opening chords of Beethoven's "Pathétique" Sonata were as shocking to his audience as the juxtaposition of the witches' sabbath with the *Dies irae* was to that of Berlioz. Yet, more than in Beethoven, many of the striking effects in the *Symphony fantastique* seem to be as much the result of cool calculation as of urgent feeling. Likewise with Poe. His fiction, like Emily Brontë's, is filled with the gnashing and bashing of bodies and with raids on graves. Yet in Poe these more often seem to be the result of shrewd manipulation. The mixture between calculated charlatanism and genuine if obsessive working out of psychological compulsions is impossible to fix with precision in Poe; perhaps Lowell's "three-fifths of him genius and two-fifths sheer fudge" comes near the mark. I always suspect some fudge in the cauldron of Berlioz's witches' sabbath, too, even when stirred by it.

Poe does excell, however, in expressing a single emotion with maximum intensity. The celebrated "unity of effect" in his short stories derives from the calculated manner in which a predesigned emotional effect has been executed. Many of Chopin's études and preludes, too, are based upon one prevailing mood or emotion: the single-minded emotional content allows a unity of effect similar to that achieved by Poe. Many short works by both artists are structurally as perfect in their way as are much longer works by Mozart or Austen. But neither Chopin nor Poe was able to master the blending of various feelings and forms in large-scale works with the exquisite consistency of either Mozart or Austen.

Beethoven and Brontë did achieve such mastery, but in a different way. In their greatest works one often feels that genuine emotion is forging its own form, rather than expressing itself within one. *Wuthering Heights* is a forceful and compelling aesthetic whole, but its unity derives from structuring principles that are worlds apart from those of Austen's novels. Its unity seems to be the organic product of irrepressible feelings that shape an entirely idiosyncratic but satisfying form. So it is with the "Appassionata." The proportions of the parts to the whole are as balanced as in Mozart's best works, but the unity seems to have been generated by the feeling. The "Appassionata" strives for the kind of unity of effect that Chopin was later to achieve on a much smaller scale (in the "Octave" Étude, for example), yet manages at the same time to satisfy the large-scale formal proportions that Mozart harnessed for a much different kind of expression, an expression that even when painfully anguished, as it is in the G-minor Symphony, continually reveals the clarity of its form as sharply as the urgency of its feeling.

The Tendency toward Accommodation or Struggle

WITH A GREAT ARTIST or individual it is often impossible to determine whether his or her ultimate tendency is in the direction of acceptance and resignation or of challenge and rupture. In which direction did Goya tend? Or Gandhi? Or Christ? Each tended in both directions—at different times and in different ways. So it is with Mozart and Austen, and with Beethoven and Brontë. Superficially, one might say that the former pair, more "classical-tending," leans more strongly in the direction of accommodation, whereas the latter pair, more "Romantic-tending," leans more toward struggle. Essentially as well as superficially this may be true. But the issue is difficult. And interesting.

Mozart's tendency toward accommodation is evident throughout his life and his art. A letter written when he was fourteen urges his mother to be calm if an ailing relative should happen to die: "I hope with God's help she will soon get well again, but if not, one must not grieve too much, for God's will is always best and God doubtless knows best whether it is better to be in this world or in the other." The famous 1787 letter to his father expresses a comparable attitude toward his own life (Mozart was then thirty-one):

> Since death, when we come to consider it, is seen to be the true goal of our life, I have made acquaintance during these last few years with this best and truest friend of mankind, so that his image not only no longer has any terrors for me, but suggests, on the contrary, much that is reassuring and consoling! And I thank my God for blessing me with the opportunity (you understand me) of coming to recognize Him as the key to our true blessedness. —I never lie down upon my bed without reflecting that—young as I am—I may perhaps never see another day—and yet not one of those who know me can say that I am morose or sad among my fellows! For this blessing I daily thank my Creator and wish with all my heart that my fellow-men may share it.[4]

In contrast to this attitude is the indelible image (whether apocryphal or not) of Beethoven on his deathbed, shaking a clenched fist at the storming heavens.

Ready accommodation is also shown in Mozart's life by the alacrity with which, having been rejected by the captivating Aloysia Weber, he settled for her sister Constanza. He even accommodated himself to the Archbishop of Salzburg for many years, breaking away only after being ejected from the potentate's office by a lackey's boot in his pants. Accommodation is also shown by the pattern of his compositions. Throughout his career he wrote essentially what was commissioned; he was the craftsman who did what was assigned. Even his few personal, more private works show, if not accommodation, resignation. And even those works that express resignation most strongly (such as the G-minor Symphony, the G-minor Quintet, and the C-minor Piano Concerto) tend to experience and accept that condition rather than overcome it, as it is often overcome in the finales of Beethoven's characteristic minor-key works. Resignation, of course, in no way dominates his music as a whole; it is difficult to think of an artist who matches Mozart in consistently rich and joyous celebration.

In life as in sound, Beethoven often seems the epitome of struggle, the antithesis of accommodation. "Prince, what you are you are by the accident of birth; what I am, I am of myself. There are and there will be thousands of princes. There is only one Beethoven."[5] In life he struggled against the prerogatives of princes, against the onset of deafness, against the paltriness of human beings. In music he struggled against the boundaries of Haydn's and Mozart's forms until he forged them into his own. But his struggle in life and in art led, too, to moments of supreme accommodation and even resignation: "Es muss sein!" (It must be!). The peace he achieved and expressed while writing certain movements of his late quartets and sonatas is as serene and tranquil as that of Mozart at his most blissful.

Overtly, Austen's works are full of accommodation, of the reverse of struggle. Every novel has its memorable examples: Charlotte Lucas accommodating herself to a life (an entire life!) with Mr. Collins; Emma resigning herself to an eternity of Miss Bates's empty chatter; Anne Elliot accommodating herself to a life without Wentworth, and without anyone else either, until fortune smiles on her and returns to her her bloom. Austen knew such conditions in her own life. In her twenties, despairing of ever having a worthy suitor, she even accepted the proposal of a real-life equivalent of Mr. Collins, only to think better of it the next morning and resign herself to a life as an "old maid." When Charlotte accepts Mr. Collins's proposal in *Pride and Prejudice*, her brothers are "relieved from their apprehensions of Charlotte's dying an old maid." As for Charlotte herself, she

was tolerably composed. . . . Her reflections were in general satisfactory. Mr. Collins to be sure was neither sensible nor agreeable; his society was irksome, and his attachment to her must be imaginary. But still he would be her husband. Without thinking highly either of men or of matrimony, marriage had always been her object; it was the only honourable provision for well-educated young women of small fortune, and however uncertain of giving happiness, must be their pleasantest preservative from want. This preservative she had now obtained; and at the age of twenty-seven, without having ever been handsome, she felt all the good luck of it. (p. 107)

That the author of this passage came close to acquiring such a "preservative" herself shows a decided tendency toward accommodation in her own character.

But the above passage also shows that Austen, like Mozart, possessed a subversive streak in addition to a resigned one. Its major outlet was irony. The irony in her novels is often so scathing that D. W. Harding has described it as "regulated hatred." And the novels are tame compared to some of her letters (Mozart's letters, too, could be decidedly cruel). Even so, Austen's art and life are characterized by strong elements of accommodation throughout their evolution. She stayed within the bounds of what she knew well: the English gentry, the domestic novel, conversations in which there is always at least one woman present. She remained within these bounds as instinctively as her heroines remain within the circle of familial homes, but she made that world of small compass entirely her own. She once described that world as "the little bit (two Inches wide) of Ivory on which I work with so fine a Brush."[6] She was as content to operate within its confines as Mozart was within his five octaves of ivory—a restriction in the register of the piano that Beethoven struggled to transcend.

Paul Henry Lang's description of Mozart's essential artistic character in this respect applies equally well to Austen:

> It may be said that there are composers who develop by constantly stepping out of their frame and following a new direction. Because they continually uproot themselves they grow erratically and may perhaps fail to attain their full stature. Others circle their domain with their first steps; every circle brings them to known territory, yet every circling results in new discoveries and conquests.
>
> Mozart was of the second type; he was always faithful to himself. Even in his early works most of the "themes" of his music are already present, and it is fascinating to watch how these "themes" reappear in successive works, always deepened and enriched. Such a composer does not constantly seek the new, trying to "advance"; he holds his ground ever more firmly, becomes stronger; every new work means more than the previous one precisely because he is content to follow his natural growth. To change, and to proceed into new territories, is always an adventure; [but] for the creative

artist the only sure progress is into the depths of his own soul. And this is
the most difficult and most exciting road.[7]

The manner in which both Mozart and Austen instinctively circle and
recircle their original domain is one of their most significant affinities,
as Part 2 will show.

How Emily Brontë might have developed as a writer of fiction is impossible to say. There was one novel and she was dead. In that one novel
there are strong tendencies toward both accommodation and struggle.
Struggle is most striking in the lives of Heathcliff and Catherine, though
hardly a single character with the possible exeption of Joseph is exempt.
Accommodation is also most striking in Heathcliff and Catherine—in
their deaths, not their lives. When Catherine speaks of escaping "this
shattered prison," she is referring to the shattered fabric of her body,
about to die biologically, to that of her marriage, long dead spiritually,
and to Thrushcross Grange itself, which refuge Heathcliff's mere return
had shattered for her. She looks forward to death as her "best friend,"
much as Mozart does in the letter to his father—though her anticipation
is vehement, whereas his is resigned. Heathcliff, too, embraces death as
it approaches. He not only resigns himself to it, but courts it as earnestly
as he had courted Catherine during his years of struggle.

Knowing so little of Emily Brontë's actual life and thought, it is all but
impossible to evaluate her own tendencies in the direction of either accommodation or struggle. Of one thing, however, there can be no doubt.
She was a "creative artist" whose "only sure progress" was "into the depths
of her own soul." There she explored the various tendencies of the human soul about as strongly as had ever been done between the covers of
a book. Her sister Charlotte tells us that when Emily became terminally
ill she was pitiless toward her own body and made no attempt to postpone the inevitable. Whether that courageous fact should be interpreted
as a tendency toward accommodation or struggle seems to me impossible to say.

Part Two

JANE AUSTEN AND MOZART

THE DEGREE TO WHICH both Austen and Mozart may be said to have "circled their domain with their first steps" is illustrated by the brilliant achievements of *Pride and Prejudice* and Piano Concerto No. 9 (K. 271).[1] Mozart was only twenty when he composed his first great keyboard concerto. He still lived in Salzburg, his childhood home. Austen was only twenty when she began her most famous novel. She still lived in Steventon, her childhood home. Although K. 271 was followed in the next fourteen years by eighteen piano concertos of considerable to exceeding merit, it is surpassed by none of them—just as none of the novels Austen wrote in the wake of *Pride and Prejudice* surpasses it.

Mozart's Piano Concerto No. 9 (as we number them today) was composed in 1777 for one Mlle Jeunehomme, a French virtuosa who visited Salzburg. Widely performed today, the "Jeunehomme" Concerto is regarded by some as Mozart's first undeniable masterpiece in any instrumental form. It is the starting point for Rosen's analysis in *The Classical Style*. But for more than a century and a half it was seldom performed. Mozart was unable to publish it during his lifetime. After his death, this early work was particularly slow to emerge from the long neglect suffered by Mozart's concertos in general. Even Girdlestone's pioneering study of the concertos in the 1940s considerably underrates it. Einstein's *Mozart*, however, written in the same decade, gives the concerto its due, comparing it with "similar bold ventures, full of both youth and maturity, in the works of other great masters: the wedding panel by Titian known as 'Sacred and Profane Love,' Goethe's *Werther*, Beethoven's 'Eroica'" (p. 294). Similarly bold, youthful, and mature is *Pride and Prejudice*.

Unlike Mozart's K. 271, *Pride and Prejudice* has been highly appreciated for more than a century and a half. Yet it, too, suffered some early neglect. Begun in 1796, its first version (entitled "First Impressions")

79

was completed the following year. Like K. 271, it failed to find a publisher. The novel as we know it today was rewritten at Chawton. Finally published in 1813, it has been the favorite of most Austenites ever since. Yet as Austen's novels, like Mozart's concertos, have come to be more fully appreciated and understood, *Pride and Prejudice* has increasingly had to share the spotlight with the other five novels—*Sense and Sensibility, Mansfield Park, Emma, Persuasion,* even *Northanger Abbey*. Critics now argue quite vehemently over which is the best of the six, and there is not a single one without its advocates. This is as it should be. Each of the six, while remaining within the domain of the domestic comedy of marriage, has its own tone, its own flavor, its own personality, if you will.

With Mozart's piano concertos, as with Austen's novels, the question will perhaps never be settled as to which is the best. With at least a dozen of the great concertos, it is the criterion applied rather than the splendor of Mozart's achievement that makes preference among them possible. Given such multiple riches from which to choose, I have selected the three novels and the three concertos with the most significant affinities of both spirit and structure. As noted in the Introduction, I have also selected a sequence that reveals the stylistic and spiritual development of each artist over time—a sequence that takes us from the youthful classical equilibrium of *Pride and Prejudice* and K. 271 through the mature classical equilibrium of *Emma* and K. 503 to the poignant pre-Romanticism of *Persuasion* and K. 595. As much as the two later pairs of works differ from the earlier pair, so do they resemble them—as each artist, circling the original domain, enriched and deepened the themes of the earlier achievement and progressed further into the depths of the soul.

Although the method of comparison will vary somewhat for each successive pair of works, all three comparisons proceed movement by movement and volume by volume. In the words of the *Pelican History,* this will allow the "form each movement reveals" ("the particular way in which themes, rhythms, keys, etc. interact and are held in equilibrium") to be compared with the form each volume reveals (the particular way in which characters, actions, locales, etc. interact and are held in equilibrium). Within this framework, considerations of form will naturally lead to those of spirit.

Before proceeding with the specific comparisons, I wish to comment briefly on the interpretation, in words, of piano concertos. As indicated in Part 1, I shall be discussing metaphorical human "themes" as well as literal musical ones. I shall be comparing the interplay between solo and orchestra in a concerto with that between individual and society in a novel. In his great essay "The Classical Concerto," Tovey directly addresses the question of whether a piano concerto can have the kind of meaning I would attribute to it. His answer to devotees of "absolute music" is characteristically argumentative and discursive. But it so clearly expresses two of the premises upon which the following analysis is based that I wish to quote it at some length.

> The primary fact that distinguishes all works that have in them the character of the concerto style, is that their form is adapted to make the best effect expressible by opposed and unequal masses of instruments or voices. . . . Nothing in human life and history is much more thrilling or of more ancient and universal experience than the antithesis of the individual and the crowd; an antithesis which is familiar in every degree, from flat opposition to harmonious reconciliation, and with every contrast and blending of emotion, and which has been of no less universal prominence in works of art than in life. Now the concerto forms express this antithesis with all possible force and delicacy. If there are devotees of "absolute music" who believe that this is the very reason why these forms are objectionable, as appealing to something outside music, we may first answer that, if this were so, then neither Brahms, Beethoven, Bach, Mozart, Haydn, nor any person of so much calibre as Clementi, ever was an "absolute musician," or had anything to do with such a mysterious abstraction. And secondly we may reply that this dramatic or human element is *not* outside the music, but most obviously inherent in the instruments that play the concerto; and that, so far as such a feebly metaphysical term as "absolute music" has a meaning, it can only mean "music that owes its form, contrasts, and details solely to its own musical resources." As long as musical instruments and voices exist, there will always be the obvious possibility of setting one instrument or voice against many; and the fact that this opposition exists also in human affairs is no reason why music should cease to be "absolute" or self-supporting—unless we are likewise to reason that man ceases to be human in so far as his five senses are shared by lower animals.[2]

As long as concertos and novels exist, there will always be the possibility (which I hope to make obvious) of comparing the manner in which each sets the one instrument or person against the many.

Mozart's piano concertos exploit the range of possible expression between the one and the many more fully than does the music of any composer before or since. Consciously or not, critics often personify the piano when describing the dynamics of his concertos. Here is Einstein on the manner in which equilibrium is always threatened, but finally regained, in a Mozart concerto: "The symphonic element creates for itself a protagonist, the piano; it thus creates a dualism that endangers its unity; and it then conquers this danger" (p. 288). Girdlestone entitles an early chapter "Relations between Piano and Orchestra." He formu-

81

lates the problem (and the solution) of the concerto form in this way: "to combine solo and orchestra without, on the one hand, the orchestra being treated as a simple accompanist, or, on the other, the solo losing its personality by blending too intimately with the mass of instruments. Balance of the two forces, struggle without triumph, collaboration without blending: such is the ideal of every concerto worthy of its name" (p. 67). Such, at least, is the ideal of every classical concerto worthy of its name. As Tovey, Einstein, Girdlestone, and Rosen are all quick to point out, this ideal did not last long into the Romantic age, whose piano concertos tend to be dominated by the solo instrument.

One final historical note. When Mozart took up the concerto form it was one of the least "serious" of instrumental forms, a form designed primarily to entertain. He gave that form a dignity and a seriousness of purpose at the same time that he preserved and perfected its playful spirit. As Einstein writes, "Mozart's piano concerto never seems to overstep the bounds of society music. . . . And yet it always leaves the door open to the expression of the darkest and the brightest, the most serious, the gayest, the deepest feelings" (pp. 288–89). Austen's achievement with the domestic novel is comparable. The author of *Pride and Prejudice* indicated her seriousness of purpose in a narrative aside in *Northanger Abbey*, the novel she turned to next. Noting "almost a general wish of decrying the capacity and undervaluing the labour of the novelist, and of slighting the performances that have only genius, wit, and taste to recommend them," she defines the best kind of novel as a "work in which the greatest powers of the mind are displayed, in which the most thorough knowledge of human nature, the happiest delineation of its varieties, the liveliest effusions of wit and humour are conveyed to the world in the best chosen language."[3] This definition does not apply to all great novels, but it does apply to the greatest of Austen's. It does not apply to all great piano concertos, but it does to the greatest of Mozart's.

Einstein concluded the passage quoted above with the assertion that "listeners who can really appreciate Mozart's piano concertos are the best audience there is." Similar assertions are often made about those who can really appreciate Austen's novels. They are made for similar reasons, as I hope to show.

Chapter Four

PRIDE AND PREJUDICE AND PIANO CONCERTO NO. 9 (K. 271)

P RIDE AND PREJUDICE consists of three volumes of nearly equal length—23, 19, and 19 chapters. Geographically, the first volume is centered at Longbourn, the second at Rosings, the third at Longbourn again.

K. 271 consists of three movements of nearly equal duration—10, 12, and 10 minutes (in the Kipnis-Marriner performance). Harmonically, the first movement is centered in E-flat major, the second in C minor, the third in E-flat major again.

The action of volume 1 of *Pride and Prejudice* is intense and playful, complex and quick-paced. Volume 2 is slower in pace and deeper in emotion. Volume 3 returns to the quick-paced action of volume 1 but is more relaxed in structure.

The first movement of K. 271 is an intensely playful and quick-paced Allegro. The second movement is slower in tempo and deeper in emotion. The third movement returns to the high spirits and quick tempo of the opening movement but is more relaxed in structure, including a "surprise" minuet.

For the comparisons made so far, many Mozart concertos would have served about as well as K. 271. Its form, to the degree indicated above, is the form of them all. All of Mozart's great concertos have three movements of more or less equal length; all of them are home-away-home in harmony; all of them are fast-slow-fast in tempo. The fact that most Mozart concertos parallel the broad formal outlines of *Pride and Prejudice* is itself of interest, especially since that novel is regarded by many as the most structurally perfect that Austen wrote (there are some holdouts for *Emma*).

K. 271 has even more affinities with *Pride and Prejudice* than most Mozart concertos do. Those affinities are emotional and spiritual as well as structural. Broadly speaking, the mood of each work is happy-sad-happy in the successive volumes or movements. Most of Mozart's piano concertos follow such an emotional progression, but in few of the others is the contrast among successive movements so complete. There is also more emotional contrast among the successive volumes of *Pride and Prejudice* than has generally been appreciated. The emotional progression in each work helps to reveal the comparable "personalities" of Elizabeth Bennet, on the one hand, and the solo voice of K. 271, on the other. Each "personality" serves to unite the three volumes or movements over which it comes to preside.

Each of Austen's heroines is the central unifying element of the novel in which she appears. But Elizabeth Bennet's personality and the novel it pervades are unique. She is the wittiest and most vivacious of Austen's heroines, the most pert and even impertinent. She dominates *Pride and Prejudice* from the first chapter, where she does not appear but already is mentioned as her father's favorite, until the last, in which she marries Fitzwilliam Darcy. She is not only the most brilliant personality in the novel but also the one with the greatest emotional range—a fact that is highlighted by the variety of roles in which we come to know her. One reason the novel ends when it does is that the development of Elizabeth's character has, in essence, ended. She has shown us her full emotional range as she has become complete. Writing to her sister Cassandra, Austen "confessed" to thinking Elizabeth Bennet "as delightful a creature as ever appeared in print." In describing the novel itself as "light, and bright, and sparkling," she was describing its heroine as well.[1]

Each of Mozart's piano concertos is unified by the presence and "personality" of the solo voice in all three movements. Among a family of varied and striking personalities, the solo voice of K. 271 is sharply individual and distinct. As Girdlestone points out, it is "proud and self-assured" from the opening bars (p. 93); the piano's relation to the orchestra is marked throughout by "wit and ease" (p. 96). Rosen finds the solo voice "impertinent" in the opening bars (p. 60); later he refers to its "witty insouciance" (p. 198). Other Mozartean solo voices are as individual and distinct, to be sure. But perhaps none is as witty and bright as that of this early concerto. Nor are many capable of the deep, regal grief found in the slow movement. Likewise, few are able to follow feeling and grief with wit and playfulness as energetically as this solo does in the third movement. H. C. Robbins Landon refers to its "saucy elegance" in the Rondo.[2]

Elizabeth in the first volume and the solo voice in the first movement each establish themselves as witty, agile, and elastic. They display comparable "personalities" not only through these intrinsic qualities but through the manner in which each relates to the larger group (Elizabeth to the society, the solo to the orchestra). In the second volume and movement each undergoes an "experience of maturity" brought about through the imaginative assimilation of grief. In each case this experience deepens and refines the innate qualities that sparkle so brightly not only in the opening volume and movement but again in the third. As much as does Elizabeth, the solo voice of K. 271 shows that it can assimilate sorrow without losing its ease, that it can age without losing its youthfulness, that it can become all the more itself for its reliance on others, all the freer for its admission of need. Other solo voices embody such qualities in Mozart concertos, as do other heroines in Austen novels. But in none of the others is the presiding personality as "light, and bright, and sparkling" as in these two youthful masterpieces.

Balanced Opposition

THE "pride and self-assurance" of the solo voice of K. 271 express themselves in an entrance that is unprecedented—and, what is more, unsubsequented—in Mozart's piano concertos. The solo enters in the second bar, before the orchestra has concluded its opening phrase (Figure 1).

Figure 1

Neither in the eight piano concertos that precede K. 271 nor in the eighteen that follow does Mozart allow the solo to enter before the orchestra has completed its entire exposition.

This "premature" entry shows impertinence—a willingness to violate the forms. It also shows wit and ease. The piano not only interrupts the orchestra's opening statement; it also answers and completes it. Like Elizabeth Bennet, the solo voice of K. 271 does things which, if they were done by others, would be offensive, yet does them in such a way that the result is not only individual but charming. As Rosen has shown, the charm resides in the wit and the symmetry of the phrasing.

> This is an astonishing and delightful opening, surprising not only for its use of the soloist at the very outset, but also for the wit with which he enters, as he replies to the orchestral fanfare. For this wit, the exquisite balance of the phrase is essential: the orchestra falls an octave and rises a fifth, the piano then rises an octave and falls a fifth within an equal length of time. We are not by any means intended to hear this as an inversion, as would be the case with a theme inverted in a fugue. That is the last thing the style requires, and the most ruinous of effect. The symmetry is concealed, delicate, and full of charm. (p. 60)

The kind of concealment that Mozart achieves here is exactly the kind that delights "connoisseurs" at the same time that "the less learned cannot fail to be pleased, though without knowing why." Austen achieves the same kind of concealment in the opening sentence of *Pride and Prejudice*: its implied ironies and inversions are no more intended to be "heard" on first reading than is the concealed inversion described by Rosen.

No less than the first theme of the concerto, the first sentence of the novel is witty, charming, and clearly articulated: "It is a truth universally acknowledged that a single man in possession of a good fortune must be in want of a wife." But as Dorothy van Ghent points out,

> The sentence ironically turns itself inside out, thus: a single woman must be in want of a man with a good fortune. In this doubling of the inverse meaning over the surface meaning, a very modest-looking statement sums up the chief conflicting forces in the book: a decorous convention of love (which holds the man to be the pursuer) embraces a savage economic compulsion (the compulsion of the insolvent female to run down male "property"), and in the verbal embrace they appear as a unit. The ironic mode here is a mode of simultaneous opposition and union: civilized convention and economic primitivism unite in the sentence as they do in the action, where "feelings" and "fortune," initially in conflict, are reconciled in the socially creative union of marriage.[3]

The conflict implied by the opening sentence is not fully resolved in the action of the novel until the marriage of Elizabeth and Darcy that concludes volume 3. Nor is the "simultaneous opposition and union" between piano and orchestra in the opening bars of K. 271 fully resolved until the end of the third movement—as will be shown.

In spite of the concealed subtleties, the opening "statement" of each work is announced with remarkable concision and directness. The opening theme of the concerto consists of three bars of music containing seventeen (melodic) notes. The opening sentence of the novel consists of twenty-three words. The articulation of the musical theme is unusually clear in melody (unison phrasing), harmony (tonic-dominant stability), and rhythm (emphatic rests). The fictional sentence is equally clear in diction, syntax, and emphasis (it is set off as a separate paragraph). To further clarify the musical theme, Mozart repeats it immediately: bars 4–6 duplicate bars 1–3. To further clarify the fictional sentence, Austen mirrors it in the action of chapter 1. The mere arrival of Mr. Bingley at nearby Netherfield suggests that the opening statement will soon be embodied in action. But the connection becomes explicit when Mrs. Bennet responds to her husband's question as to the marital status of the newcomer. "Oh! single, my dear, to be sure! A single man, of large fortune; four or five thousand a year. What a fine thing for our girls!" (p. 6). Already Mrs. Bennet has gleefully particularized the universal truth: Mr. Bingley must be in want of a Miss Bennet.

Because of the wit and clarity of its first appearance, the opening theme of K. 271 is able to serve as a clear structural guidepost throughout the rest of the movement. This function is further clarified by the fact that Mozart introduces each new section of the first movement with an emphatic return of the opening theme. The Allegro of K. 271, like the first movement of most Mozart concertos, consists of an orchestral exposition, a solo exposition, a development, a recapitulation, and a coda. At the opening of the solo exposition (bar 63),[4] the opening theme is announced as it was at the beginning: the first phrase by the orchestra, the second by the piano, both phrases repeated. The same pattern holds at the beginning of the development section (bar 156). It is reversed, however, at the beginning of the recapitulation (bar 196). There the piano introduces the first phrase, leaving the second to the orchestra, which, during the repeat, takes its own phrase again. At the beginning of the coda (bar 282) the orchestra and piano once more give out the opening theme just as they did in the opening bars. By this point, the piano's intrusion into the orchestra's statement sounds almost conventional, so often has it been heard.

Fictional sentences seldom serve as structural guideposts in the way that musical themes often do, but the opening sentence of *Pride and Prejudice* is articulated and positioned in such a way that it does have a somewhat comparable function. In volume 1 Mr. Bingley and Mr. Collins are the single men of good fortune most visibly in want of a wife. Jane Bennet, Miss Bingley, and Charlotte Lucas are the single women most obviously in want of a man of good fortune. During the opening six chapters at Longbourn, the main focus is on the way in which Jane and Bingley respond to the "truth universally acknowledged." In the next six chapters at Netherfield they remain the ostensible center of attention, though Darcy and Miss Bingley and (by extension) Elizabeth become important too. The arrival of Mr. Collins in chapters 13 and 14 brings a new embodiment of the opening statement, as do the excursions to Meryton in chapters 15 and 16, where Elizabeth and her younger sisters combined with Wickham and his fellow officers become the center of attention. The announcement of the Netherfield ball in chapter 17 and the ball itself in chapter 18 return the emphasis again to Jane and Bingley. Collins's proposal to Elizabeth in chapter 19 is a new application of the opening "truth," an application that Collins willingly transfers to Charlotte Lucas in chapter 22 when finally convinced that Elizabeth will not have him.

Whereas the opening words of *Pride and Prejudice* have an unusually strong structural function in the first volume of the novel (of which more below), the opening notes of K. 271 have an unusually strong metaphorical function in introducing the conflicting principles (as well as principals) that will animate the rest of the movement. Rosen writes of the first theme that "the stately is opposed to the impertinent, and balanced perfectly by it" (p. 60). This characterization applies not only to the theme itself but to each restatement of it by the two principals throughout the movement. It also applies more generally to the character of the two principals (the orchestra and the solo voice) themselves.

Nothing could be more stately than the orchestra's opening phrase, *forte* and in unison, based on the tonic triad. Perhaps that is what prompts the solo to interrupt with impertinence. Yet, as we have seen, the intervention is as charming as it is bold. As the first movement continues, the solo voice is unusually content to restrict itself to the material given out by the orchestra. In most Mozart concertos, the orchestra gives out many themes from which the solo selects several for its own use. In addition, the solo usually introduces one or two themes of its own during its own exposition. But here, in the words of Girdlestone, "no theme is reserved for the solo. On the contrary, the piano takes a mischievous delight in sneaking all its subjects from the enemy and using them to its own ends" (p. 96).

One reason this solo voice needs no separate theme of its own is that the orchestra presents such a wealth of ideas in its own exposition. Rosen's detailed analysis of the concerto enumerates no fewer than ten "themes" in the orchestral exposition, though several of these are derived from each other (p. 210). For the analysis that follows, two major themes must be singled out: the opening theme, which has already been discussed at length, and the second, or contrasting theme, which is lyrical and mellow rather than agile and forceful. This theme consists of two related melodies (Figures 2a and 2b) that are always presented in the same or-

Figure 2a

Figure 2b

der. This extended two-part theme is not present in the development at all. Its central purpose in the movement is to contrast with the springy, busy first theme. The way in which the piano handles its softer, sweeter challenge brings out a different part of the solo's "personality."

The solo voice, though conservative in its adherence to the thematic material of the orchestral exposition, is notably free in its use of that material—and not only in the opening bars. At the end of the orchestral exposition, the piano does not wait for the cadence and pause that traditionally announces its "official" entry. Instead, it sneaks in before the cadence with a trill. As in the opening bars, it is showing considerable freedom, but not so much as to seem more bold than charming. After patiently sharing out the opening theme again with the orchestra, the piano then begins its exposition by running off with the first part of the theme—just as it will do, even more dramatically, at the beginning of the development and of the recapitulation.

Whereas the solo's treatment of the opening theme that it always shares with the orchestra shows off its agility and its individuality, its sounding of the orchestra's long, mellow second theme shows its ability to follow and to support in a subdued but imaginative way. In both the solo exposition and the recapitulation, the piano plays both parts of this theme essentially as they had been "exposed" by the orchestra. In each case the oboes respond to the solo's sounding of the second melody by repeating it exactly. In the recapitulation the horns join in to play the first melody in unison. Because both melodies of the second theme (like that of the opening theme) are unchanging in shape, each return of this material serves to emphasize the changing relations among the solo and orchestra as the movement unfolds.

The paradox outlined above—by which the solo voice is extremely brilliant and individual at the same time that it introduces no new material of its own—is analogous to the kind of individuality embodied by Elizabeth Bennet in the first volume of *Pride and Prejudice*. She is the most prominent presence in volume 1, yet she initiates very little of the action herself. Essentially, she responds to the actions, hopes, and wishes of others. The main action centers on Jane's interest in Bingley at the beginning of the volume and on Collins's interest in Jane, then Elizabeth, then Charlotte at the end. Elizabeth's infatuation with Wickham seems only a brief interlude, and her passing encounters with Darcy seem only to be bridges to more important episodes involving others. Elizabeth's liveliness throughout, the wit, agility, and grace with which she enters into whatever is happening, is comparable to the manner in which the solo voice of K. 271 responds to the opening theme it always shares with the orchestra. Her gentle and abiding care for Jane and her support of Jane's love for Bingley are comparable to the manner in which the solo embraces the mellow second theme in an intimate rather than challenging way.

Elizabeth's intrinsic qualities and her mode of relating to others give obvious cohesion to volume 1—as is the case with the solo voice in K. 271's first movement. But the opening volume, no less than the opening movement, also gains cohesion by the deft and symmetrical manner in which its major structural units are related. With Austen as with Mozart, the meaning of a work derives from its structure as much as from the human and musical materials themselves. Both the first movement of K. 271 and the first volume of *Pride and Prejudice* are composed of five major structural units whose proportions, "locale," and function are profoundly comparable.

As OUTLINED ABOVE (and as recognized by most students of the concerto), the first movement of K. 271 consists of five major structural units, each one introduced by the opening theme shared by the orchestra and the piano. Their relative proportions are balanced and symmetrical, as can be indicated by their inclusive bar numbers: orchestral exposition (1–62), solo exposition (63–155), development (156–95), recapitulation (196–281), and coda (282–360). Here, as in other Mozart concertos, there is some room for debate as to exactly where the solo exposition or the development begins, though in either case the debate would be over no more than a few bars. Fortunately, Mozart's employment of the opening theme at every important structural juncture makes the schema enumerated above one to which most musicologists could give their assent.

There is no such consensus as to the major structural divisions of the first volume of *Pride and Prejudice*. Although it is widely acknowledged as one of the most symmetrical and beautifully organized novels in the English language, although many critics have attempted briefly to trace its structure, and although many critics have noted that the germ of much of the action is contained in the opening sentence, there is no discussion of the novel as a whole or of the first volume as an entity which attempts to analyze its structure with even the precision of the widely accepted, bare-bone outline summarized above for the first movement of K. 271. Some would argue, of course, that fictional structures cannot with success be analyzed in such a manner—even structures as "perfect" as that of *Pride and Prejudice* is universally acknowledged to be. I am prepared to argue otherwise.

Simply put, the first movement of K. 271 provides an excellent model for perceiving the structure of the first volume of *Pride and Prejudice*. The novel volume, like the concerto movement, contains five structural units that are largely symmetrical. They are: chapters 1–6, chapters 7–12, chapters 13–16, chapters 17–18, and chapters 19–23. For convenience of comparison, these units may be labeled the Longbourn exposition, the Netherfield exposition, the Collins-Meryton development, the Longbourn-Netherfield recapitulation, and the Collins coda. The fact that I have named them so as to parallel the musical divisions may appear suspicious. But the purpose of the structural analysis of any complex artistic work is to help us experience and understand its shape and flow. I would not be so rash as to claim that the analysis that follows is the only possible perspective from which to view the structure of volume 1. But I do claim that the musical parallel does help us to experience and understand how this particular fictional volume works. It has the additional value of demonstrating some precise similarities between musical and fictional forms.

The idea that the first six chapters form a unit will not appear farfetched to readers who have given any thought to the structure of the novel. Nor will the idea that the next six chapters form a similar and related unit. These opening two units of the novel are comparable to the double exposition of K. 271 in several ways. The first unit, which I have labeled the Longbourn exposition, presents the main thematic subject of the volume, the major characters who will embody it, the first ball, which allows those characters to interact with some complexity, and the extended verbal aftermath of the ball. This is similar to the function of the orchestral exposition in introducing the musical themes, the instrumental alignments, and the rhythms that will be heard throughout the movement.[5] In addition, the first six chapters establish Longbourn as the "home" of the novel as thoroughly as the orchestral exposition of K. 271 establishes E-flat major as the home key.

In the concerto, the first two notes are bold E-flats one octave apart. By the beginning of the fourth bar the key of E-flat major has been firmly established. There are slight digressions from that key during the rest of the orchestral exposition, but there is no modulation to any other key. Likewise, the opening discussion between Mr. and Mrs. Bennet establishes Longbourn as "home." The first six chapters are all presented from its point of view, even during the few moments when the action, technically, goes somewhere else. Chapter 3 features the ball (or assembly) during which the Bennet girls meet Darcy and Bingley in public for the first time. The ball is not at Longbourn, but it is not anywhere else either. Its locale is presented as an extension of the Bennet domain and has no separate existence of its own. Likewise, among the conversations that are reported in chapter 6 is one that takes place at Lucas Lodge, where Charlotte lives. The location is acknowledged, for accuracy, but not in such a way as to emphasize Lucas Lodge as a "felt" locale. In what I have called the Longbourn exposition, places such as Netherfield Park, Lucas Lodge, and the unspecified ball room do exist. But they are treated as an extension of Longbourn, just as in the orchestral exposition of K. 271 all of the notes outside the E-flat major scale are touched upon, but always so briefly and fleetingly that the harmony remains securely in its E-flat-major home.

Chapters 7–12 are as firmly centered at Netherfield as the opening six were at Longbourn. Yet the major "themes" and participants remain those of the first six chapters. The same is true of the solo exposition of the concerto movement. The harmonic "locale" modulates from E-flat major, the home key, to B-flat major, the dominant. But the thematic material remains what it was in the orchestral exposition. Both the solo exposition and the Netherfield "exposition" retain the material of the opening structural unit at the same time that they vary the "locale" of the action and the spirit in which the leading "themes" and participants are treated.

The opening sentence of chapter 7 begins a new section of the first volume as clearly as bar 63 begins a new section of the concerto movement. In bar 63, the solo exposition begins in earnest with the restatement of the concerto's opening theme—still in the home key. Chapter 7 begins with an amplification of the novel's opening sentence—as it applies to the Bennet home: "Mr. Bennet's property consisted almost entirely in an estate of two thousand a year, which, unfortunately for his daughters, was entailed in default of heirs male, on a distant relation; their mother's fortune, though ample for her situation in life, could but ill supply the deficiency of his" (p. 25). It is not surprising that a chapter that begins with this sentence would soon "modulate" to a nearby estate that could help to compensate for the "deficiency" in Mr. Bennet's situation. By the middle of chapter 7, Jane has ventured to Netherfield by horse. By the end of the chapter, Elizabeth has followed her there on foot. The action does not then leave Netherfield until the two daughters return home together at the end of chapter 12.

The shift in locale from Longbourn to Netherfield that occurs in chapter 7 is different in kind from the seamless transitions to other places (the ball, Lucas Lodge) in the first six chapters. It is given much stronger emphasis. The letter of invitation arrives from Miss Bingley. Mrs. Bennet intimates the pleasure she would derive from Jane's getting wet in the rain and therefore being stranded with Mr. Bingley at Netherfield. Jane takes the horse. She then writes from Netherfield of her illness. Elizabeth walks there through the rain. Mr. Darcy is surprised by "the brilliancy which exercise had given to her complexion." And Miss Bingley is surprised by the sight of petticoats "six inches deep in mud." All of this action—in the context of *Pride and Prejudice*—serves to emphasize in a memorable way the transition from the one locale to the other.

The shift to a new key in the solo exposition of the concerto is given comparable emphasis. Just as the opening sentence about the Bennets' property prepares for the departure to Netherfield, so does the restatement of the opening theme in the home key prepare for the modulation to the dominant key. The piano begins the modulation when it briefly "develops" the orchestral half of the opening theme. It then reinforces the modulation with brilliant scales and passagework that also serve as a transition toward the second theme. The pianistic virtuosity here is both "mechanical and conventional," as Rosen points out. "The brilliance is used to set the modulation into relief, and less conventional material would not do." The musical transition is heightened by "the inexpressive nature of the music here, its banality" (p. 204).

After the piano has established the new key of B-flat major, it introduces the mellow second theme, which had belonged only to the orchestra in the opening exposition. The fact that the solo is this time leading us through material of the "other" corresponds to the enlarged role of Elizabeth in the Netherfield "exposition" as opposed to the Longbourn one. Technically, Elizabeth is no more the center of attention than before, her role remaining subordinate to Jane and Bingley. But Elizabeth is in fact central from the moment she arrives at Netherfield, just as the piano is from the moment it brilliantly modulates to B-flat major before introducing the orchestra's second theme. She becomes central not only for the reader but for Darcy, whose engagement with Elizabeth's wit at the expense of Miss Bingley is the subplot of this section of the novel. Many of their conversations occur in the proximity of the Bingley's pianoforte, which figures separately in chapters 8, 10, and 11 (the intervening chapter 9 being devoted to the embarrassing visit by the rest of the Bennet family). At its best, the civilized banter between Elizabeth and Darcy is as exquisitely matched and perfectly balanced as is the oboe's answer to the piano's statement of the mellow second theme. But neither the Netherfield exposition nor the solo exposition is the place for meaningful dialogue to be extended at great length.

Chapter 11 ends with the abrupt termination of the dialogue between Elizabeth and Darcy about pride and vanity (itself a variation on Elizabeth's and Charlotte's discussion of the same subject in chapter 5). Elizabeth responds to Darcy by saying:

> "And *your* defect is a propensity to hate everybody."
>
> "And yours," he replied with a smile, "is willfully to misunderstand them."
>
> "Do let us have a little music," cried Miss Bingley, tired of a conversation in which she had no share. "Louisa, you will not mind my waking Mr. Hurst."
>
> Her sister made not the smallest objection, and the pianoforte was opened, and Darcy, after a few moments recollection, was not sorry for it. He began to feel the danger of paying Elizabeth too much attention. (p. 51)

This chapter ending perfectly complements the end of chapter 6 (and of the Longbourn exposition). The "material" or "subject" is the same—Darcy's interest in Elizabeth. The participants are the same—Darcy, Miss Bingley, and Elizabeth. But the treatment has changed. In chapter 6, Darcy's praise of Elizabeth's eyes had caused a catty Miss Bingley to gleefully project for him a future of close attachment to the Bennet family.

> "You will have a charming mother-in-law, indeed, and of course she will be always at Pemberly with you."
>
> He listened to her with perfect indifference, while she chose to entertain herself in this manner, and as his composure convinced her that all was safe, her wit flowed long. (p. 25)

By the end of chapter 11 Darcy's indifference is no longer perfect, though Miss Bingley's wit remains unchanged.

By the time Elizabeth and Jane return to Longbourn in chapter 12, Elizabeth's central position in the action has been consolidated and spotlighted even though she has taken no real initiative of her own, but rather has continued to respond—albeit imaginatively and with feeling—to the initiatives of others. The same is true of the solo by the end of the solo exposition of K. 271. It has introduced no new material of its own, yet has responded within the boundaries laid out by the orchestral exposition in such a way as to draw considerable attention to its own brilliance and adaptability.

The Netherfield exposition of volume 1 ends with the return to Longbourn at the end of chapter 12. The next structural unit, the Collins-Meryton development, begins with the arrival of Mr. Collins's letter and his person in chapters 13 and 14. Just as the development section of the concerto begins with another restatement of the opening theme, so does the arrival of Collins embody anew the opening statement of the novel. No less than Mr. Bingley is Mr. Collins "a single man in possession of a good fortune" and "in want of a wife." Furthermore, the fortune he possesses is the Bennet fortune; he is the "distant relation" alluded to in the opening sentence of chapter 7. Whereas the first two chapters devoted to Mr. Collins are still set at Longbourn, the next two chapters take him (and the Bennet daughters) to Meryton, "modulating" to a more distant locale than has so far been visited. Meryton is only one mile from Longbourn, whereas Netherfield is three. But socially, emotionally, and psychologically, it is much more distant.

This transition, like the earlier one to Netherfield, has been carefully prepared. Just as Collins was alluded to in the opening sentence of chapter 7, so was Meryton alluded to in the second sentence of chapter 7: Mrs. Bennet's "father had been an attorney in Meryton, and had left her four thousand pounds." Later in chapter 7 Lydia and Kitty had accompanied Elizabeth as far as Meryton during her walk to Netherfield in the rain. But it is not until chapters 15 and 16 that the reader actually enters the world of the officers, of the Philipses, and of Mrs. Bennet's "roots." Similarly, it is not until the development section of the first movement that the dissonant harmonies only alluded to at the beginning of the solo exposition (when the piano had briefly "developed" part of the opening theme before modulating to the dominant) are finally explored in earnest.[6]

The world of Meryton is exhilarating and free but it is also slippery and precarious—as are Mozart's development sections in general and that of the first movement of K. 271 in particular. Elizabeth's infatuation with Mr. Wickham displays a new and impulsive side of her personality. Her freedom with him corresponds to that of the piano as it takes the familiar opening theme an octave higher and into new keys at the beginning of the development section, into regions where it can be followed only by the winds. Yet, like the heightened exchange between the piano and oboe, which modulates to a disquieting F minor, her colloquy with Wickham proves unsettling. When he delivers his damaging account of Mr. Bingley's friend Mr. Darcy, Elizabeth, in spite of her excitement, is eager to return to the safer confines of Longbourn, where she can share her new-found exhilaration (and information) with Jane. Before returning home, however, she must give due attention to the Philipses' table and to her conversely clamorous companions, Collins and Lydia. In K. 271 there is a similar feeling of emotional suspension when the dangerous, exhilarating part of the development section (derived from the opening theme) is succeeded by less expressive material (derived from a less memorable theme) that forestalls the inevitable and reassuring return home.

One of the clearest measures of the "development-like" quality of chapters 13–16 in *Pride and Prejudice* is the "recapitulation-like" quality of the chapters immediately following. In K. 271 the minor-key excursions of the development section end when the opening theme returns in the home key to begin the recapitulation. At the end of chapter 16 the excursion to Meryton ends with an equally emphatic return home to Longbourn. Indeed, the last paragraph of that chapter is a verbal equivalent of the delicious retransitions by which Mozart so often eases the listener from the complications of a development section to the security and stability of the recapitulation. That paragraph begins with Elizabeth, amidst "the noise of Mrs. Philips' supper party," thinking of Wickham. It ends with Elizabeth, in a carriage, surrounded by Collins and Lydia.

> Elizabeth went away with her head full of him. She could think of nothing but Mr. Wickham, and of what he had told her, all the way home; but there was not time for her even to mention his name as they went, for neither Lydia nor Mr. Collins were once silent. Lydia talked incessantly of lottery tickets, of the fish she had lost and the fish she had won; and Mr. Collins . . . had more to say than he could well manage before the carriage stopped at Longbourn House. (p. 74)

The words *Longbourn House* bring us home as emphatically as does the piano's bold E-flat, *forte*, that announces the return of the opening theme at the beginning of the recapitulation. The two words gain emphasis by their placement at the end of a chapter. They gain added force by the fact that the phrase *Longbourn House* is here used for the first time in the novel.

At the very beginning of chapter 17, Elizabeth speaks with Jane and is able to relieve some of the pent-up excitement of her encounter with Wickham. Here Elizabeth is finally the one to initiate an important conversation, just as the solo finally takes the initiative by introducing the first half of the opening theme at the beginning of the recapitulation. Just as Elizabeth's conversation with Jane briefly re-creates the ambience of the Meryton development, so does the piano's brief development of the second half of the opening theme (immediately after exchanging that theme with the orchestra) briefly reawaken the modulatory and motivic energy of the concerto's development section. Elizabeth's and Jane's intense discussion, however, is soon interrupted by the arrival of the invitation to the Netherfield ball. Once the invitation is received, chapter 17 reverts to the primary concern of the Longbourn and Netherfield expositions: the match between Jane and Bingley as it is tastelessly pursued by Mrs. Bennet and tastefully supported by Elizabeth. The ball itself in chapter 18 (by far the longest chapter in the volume) returns the action to the locale and ambience of the Netherfield exposition (chapters 7–12). Together, chapters 17 and 18 recapitulate the major themes, locales, and personages of the first twelve chapters, though in somewhat different combinations.

Similarly, the recapitulation of K. 271 returns directly to the primary musical material as it had been doubly exposed at the beginning of the concerto. Although the melodic treatment of the themes is closer to that of the solo exposition (the brief development of the opening theme, the oboe's extension of the second melody of the second theme), the harmonic treatment is this time closer to that of the orchestral exposition; the home key again prevails. The solo voice, which was prominent in the second exposition, and the orchestra, which was prominent in the first, now blend together in a more intimate collaboration. Even more than before is "the stately opposed to the impertinent, and balanced perfectly by it." The balanced opposition of the first theme is livelier than before owing to the sudden reversal of roles: after the solo steals the first part of the orchestral theme, the orchestra, having played the second part, steals it back. The balanced sharing of the second theme is mellower than before, owing to the added warmth of the horns. In Girdlestone's words, the recapitulation of a Mozart concerto movement is "the meeting place of the sometimes very diverse elements that had made up the two expositions, and it is delightful to speculate concerning the manner in which this meeting will be managed" (p. 34). There could be no better description of the function of chapters 17 and 18 of *Pride and Prejudice* with respect to the Longbourn and Netherfield "expositions."

At the beginning of the Netherfield ball, Elizabeth and Darcy spar with each other as briskly as do the piano and orchestra over the opening theme in the recapitulation—with Elizabeth this time taking the initiative by alluding to her acquaintance with Mr. Wickham. When Mr. Collins intrudes, Elizabeth no longer has "any interests of her own to pursue," so she turns "her attention almost entirely on her sister and Bingley." At the Netherfield ball, Jane and Bingley are now blending in full harmony. Elizabeth foresees "all the felicity which a marriage of true affection could bestow" (p. 86). This pleases her so deeply that she is largely able to overlook the manner in which not only Collins but also the rest of the Bennet family seems to have conspired to "expose themselves as much as they could during the evening" (p. 89). Their display of folly recalls the manner in which the Bennet family had earlier exposed itself, in chapter 9 of the Netherfield exposition.

Elizabeth's joy at the prospect of Jane's imminent happiness even allows her to endure Collins's inexplicable persistence in wishing to have every dance with her. Unlike her mother, Elizabeth does not yet foresee the proposal that is soon to come. She is happy as the family returns home from Netherfield, but not as happy as Mrs. Bennet, to whom the last paragraph of chapter 18 is devoted.

> Mrs. Bennet was perfectly satisfied; and quitted the house under the delightful persuasion that, allowing for the necessary preparations of settlements, new carriages and wedding clothes, she should undoubtedly see her daughter settled at Netherfield in the course of three or four months. Of having another daughter married to Mr. Collins, she thought with equal certainty, and with considerable, though not equal, pleasure. Elizabeth was the least dear to her of all her children; and though the man and the match were quite good enough for *her*, the worth of each was eclipsed by Mr. Bingley and Netherfield. (pp. 90–91)

At Mrs. Bennet's level, both the first paragraph of chapter 1 and the first paragraph of chapter 7 find their perfect resolution in the last paragraph of chapter 18.

The fictional cadence that cements in Mrs. Bennet's mind the union of Longbourn and Netherfield is followed immediately by the Collins "coda." Just as in K. 271 the return yet again of the opening theme in the home key announces that the recapitulation has ended and the coda begun, so does the opening sentence of chapter 19 make a similar announcement: "The next day opened a new scene at Longbourn" (p. 91). This "new scene" begins immediately with Collins's proposal to Elizabeth. It continues with her spirited refusal, his rapid turn to Charlotte, her ready acceptance, and the Bennet family's reaction. Collins's pompous, mechanical proposal embodies the opening "subject" of the novel in its crudest possible form: it assumes, as does the conspiring Mrs. Bennet, that Elizabeth will allow Collins to possess *her* simply because he possesses a fortune. When Collins disbelieves her reiterated refusal, thinking her merely coy, she is driven to speak with more sincerity and force than anywhere in volume 1: "Can I speak plainer? Do not consider me now as an elegant female intending to plague you, but as a rational creature speaking the truth from her heart" (p. 95). Her deflection and rejection of Collins's offer of marriage is the fullest example in volume 1 of Elizabeth's dignity, freedom, and grace.

The eloquence of her response to Collins near the end of the first volume corresponds to the eloquence of the solo cadenza near the end of the first movement. As soon as the return of the shared opening theme announces the beginning of the coda, the orchestra, *forte* and in unison, makes a statement of the kind that demands an answer (bars 288–93). The answer is the cadenza. First the solo mimics the orchestra's imperious demand, taking it delightfully higher. The solo then asserts itself with forceful octaves in the bass and with chromatic passagework that creates dramatic expectations. After an emphatic pause, the piano speaks in a voice whose rhythm and inflection are the most individual sound that has been heard in the movement (bars 309–12). The material is not new; it is the first half of the second melody of the second theme (see Figure 2b). But the solo has created a context in which this melodic fragment sounds entirely personal and individual. Its two six-note phrases are melodically similar and rhythmically identical. Their "speech rhythm" resembles that of a simple, reiterated six-syllable declaration in words. After the piano briefly "develops" this material by freely reasserting its last two notes (an ascending minor second), suitably expressive passagework leads back to the coda per se.

As Girdlestone points out, this cadenza contains "no pure virtuosity." Nor does it have any "superfluous adornment" (p. 97). The effect is of unembellished communication straight from the heart. In this sense, it corresponds to Elizabeth's "I am a rational creature" speech. After the eloquent and individual voice of the cadenza, the orchestra returns in weighty unison. Its *forte* sound now contrasts with the sound of the solo more than ever. The piano enlivens the concluding strains of the movement, not by following the lead of the group, but by playing a trill that breaks into brilliant downfalling arpeggios. The balanced opposition between stateliness and impertinence is as lively at the end of the movement as it was at the beginning.

A comparable opposition has animated Elizabeth's encounter with Collins. He, of course, believes his proposal to have been stately and her rejection of it impertinent. In reality, it is he who has been impertinent and she, in the best sense, stately, in the manner in which she dismisses him. Her tactful but firm rejection of his proposal shows that she, while aware of the universal truths her society acknowledges, is able to improvise within the boundaries of those truths. The cadenza reveals the solo's ability to improvise within the boundaries established earlier by the orchestra. It is in this sense a compression and crystallization of the function of the solo exposition itself.[7]

Even though Collins's proposal is structurally an appendage to the Jane-Bingley plot line of volume 1, Elizabeth's stately deflection of her impertinent wooer is a crystallization of what is best in the volume itself. Charlotte's subsequent acceptance of Collins throws Elizabeth's refusal into high relief: it also perfectly puts into practice the attitude toward matrimony that Charlotte had first exposed in chapter 6, at the end of the Longbourn exposition. Just as the coda to the concerto movement is centered in the home key that has prevailed since the beginning of the recapitulation, so is the "coda" of the first volume centered at Longbourn. As earlier, some of the action occurs at Lucas Lodge. But here, as in the Longbourn exposition, that locale is presented as an extension of the Bennet domain rather than as a "felt" locale of its own.

The wrapping up of the Collins "coda" is interspersed with news of the Bingley party's departure for London—which hints at the sorrow and uncertainty that will prevail in much of the volume to come. But this volume ends as it began, with Mrs. Bennet complaining to her blithely indifferent husband. She is in "an agony of ill humour" over the thought that Charlotte Lucas will one day be mistress of Longbourn. Her voice dominates the last page of the volume, as does the orchestral voice the last page of the movement, while the solo voice, its attention elsewhere, holds a trill that breaks into downfalling arpeggios.

As SUGGESTED at its outset, the above structural analysis of the first volume of *Pride and Prejudice* is designed to show the degree to which that volume of fiction consists of five structural units whose proportions, "locale," and function are comparable to those of the five major sections of the first movement of K. 271. The bar and page numbers below show the degree to which the structural proportions within both the concerto movement and the novel volume are governed by the principles of balance and symmetry.[8]

Orchestral Exposition	1–62	Longbourn Exposition	5–24
Solo Exposition	63–155	Netherfield Exposition	24–53
Development	156–95	Collins-Meryton Development	53–74
Recapitulation	196–281	Longbourn-Netherfield Recapitulation	74–91
Coda	282–340	Collins Coda	91–114

It is indicative of the artistry of both Mozart and Austen that the symmetry of proportions that governs the component parts *within* the first movement and first volume will also govern the relations *among* the three movements and three volumes of each work as a whole.

A similar balance and symmetry governs the successive "locales" within the concerto movement and novel volume analyzed above. In its five successive sections, the first movement of K. 271 begins in the home key (E-flat major), modulates to the dominant (B-flat major), modulates further to a minor key (primarily F minor), returns to the home key, and remains in the home key. In its own five successive sections, the first volume of *Pride and Prejudice* begins at Longbourn, shifts to Netherfield, goes further afield to Meryton, returns to Longbourn and Netherfield, and remains at Longbourn. In each case the symmetrical pattern of home-away-home within the first movement or volume anticipates the pattern that will prevail for the work as a whole.

Finally, the major structural units of the concerto movement and the novel volume have functioned similarly with respect to the dynamics of equilibrium. In each case, the first exposition introduced a relatively stable world whose tendency was toward equilibrium. In each case, that equilibrium became richer but no less stable during the second exposition, was seriously threatened during the development section, was reestablished in the recapitulation, and was reaffirmed in the coda. Here too, in microcosm, is the pattern that will prevail for each work as a whole. Each work begins and ends with a volume or movement in which equilibrium prevails, these stable outer volumes and movements surrounding a central one in which equilibrium is deeply threatened.

In short, just as the opening bars of K. 271 and the opening sentence of *Pride and Prejudice* introduce "subjects" that will govern the entire first movement or volume, so then do the first movement and first volume themselves establish the structural principles—the balanced and symmetrical proportions, the home-away-home locales, the dynamics of equilibrium—that will govern the entire concerto and novel. Not only in structure but in spirit do the opening volume and movement contain the principles that will prevail throughout the whole.

As the following analysis shows, the balanced opposition between the "stately" and the "impertinent" is as important in the succeeding volumes and movements as it is in the opening ones. Likewise, the balanced opposition between the individual and the group will be deepened in the central volume and movement and will come to full fruition in the concluding ones. In this process of growth, neither the personality of Elizabeth nor that of the solo voice will be essentially changed from what it was in the opening volume or movement. But each will assuredly become deeper in experience—just as Elizabeth in chapter 17 of volume 1 and the solo voice in bar 196 of the opening Allegro are essentially unchanged yet deeper in experience after undergoing, respectively, the trials of the Meryton and the F-minor developments.

The Assimilation of the Other

So APT is Austen's description of *Pride and Prejudice* as "light, and bright, and sparkling" that it is often forgotten that she prefaced the phrase with the adverb *too*. Soon after the novel was published, she wrote her sister Cassandra that "the work is rather too light, and bright, and sparkling; it wants shade; it wants to be stretched out here and there with a long chapter of sense . . . or anything that would form a contrast, and bring the reader with increased delight to the playfulness and epigrammatism of the general style."[9] What the novel would appear to be lacking, in short, is the equivalent of the second movement of Mozart's K. 271.

The Andantino of Mozart's youthful E-flat-major Concerto is in C minor. It is full of "shade," shade that is elongated so as to form the sharpest possible contrast to the "playfulness and epigrammatism" not only of the first movement but of the third. Rather than playful and expansive, the musical material in this movement is compressed and constrained. The opening melody has a searching quality that is embodied in its wandering melodic line and intensified by its polyphonic and sometimes canonic self-reflexiveness. Compressed into sixteen bars, this melody seems to contain a world of sorrow. Its searching motion seems fated to discover only grief and remorse. The melody rises slowly, painfully, tentatively, again and again, only to fall back again in sighing, throbbing resignation. Repeated, restrained surges from *piano* to *forte* intensify the unspoken grief.

From these opening bars the melodic material for the rest of the movement is derived. This is one reason the movement as a whole seems, on first hearing, so restricted, hopeless, even claustrophobic. The intrinsic qualities of its musical material are further heightened by contrast with the "light, and bright, and sparkling" first movement. It would be no exaggeration to call the Andantino stark, dark, and melancholy.

To apply such a phrase to the second volume of *Pride and Prejudice* might seem an exaggeration—especially in view of Austen's feeling that the work as a whole is rather lacking in "shade." Yet the second volume provides ample contrast to the "playfulness and epigrammatism" that prevails not only in the first volume but in the third. Volume 2 begins in hopelessness and it ends in gloom. The middle of the volume—and the bulk of it—is neither more hopeful nor less gloomy. Because its stark, dark, and melancholy aspects have drawn much less notice than have those of the Andantino, the outer boundaries of its prevailing "shade" need to be briefly established before extended comparisons begin.

Volume 2 begins with a terse sentence: "Miss Bingley's letter arrived, and put an end to doubt." The second paragraph begins: "Hope was over, entirely over." The third begins: "Elizabeth, to whom Jane very soon communicated the chief of all this, heard it in silent indignation. Her heart was divided between concern for her sister, and resentment against all the others." Loss of hope, endured silently, continues throughout the volume. By the end of chapter 3, Jane's letter from London makes clear that all prospects for her match with Bingley have vanished. The months of January and February pass so slowly at Longbourn that Elizabeth imagines the atmosphere at the Collinses' "humble abode" could be no worse. On the way to Rosings in chapter 4, she briefly visits the Gardiners and Jane in London. This visit is one of the few pleasant episodes in the volume—pleasant partly because Mrs. Gardiner proposes a summertime trip to the lake country. Depressed now, Elizabeth at least can project future joy: "'My dear, dear aunt,' she rapturously cried, 'what delight! what felicity! You give me fresh life and vigour. Adieu to disappointment and spleen. What are men to rocks and mountains! Oh! what hours of transport we shall spend!" (p. 133). Before summer and the lakes, however, she must endure spring at Rosings. Chapters 5 through 15 are full of solitude and pain—though not always of the kind Elizabeth had anticipated.

Elizabeth's return from Rosings at the end of the volume features not so much the Gardiners and London as Lydia and the last leg of the journey. Jane has joined her in London; she is eager to share with Jane that part of her experience at Rosings she feels she can and should share. But the presence of Kitty and Lydia, who meet them at an inn with the Bennet carriage, makes meaningful speech impossible. The talk this time is not of fish won and fish lost but rather of "nasty freckled things" and of schemes to follow the Meryton officers to Brighton. Elizabeth's revelation to Jane of Darcy's proposal and his letter must be postponed until they are settled again at Longbourn.

At the beginning of chapter 17 she tells Jane of the proposal and of the part of his letter that relates to Wickham. "The tumult of Elizabeth's mind was allayed by this conversation" (p. 191). Yet she feels that she must conceal from Jane the portion of Darcy's letter that might falsely resurrect Jane's hopes for Bingley. The relief she feels for herself is therefore outweighed by the knowledge that "Jane was not happy" (p. 192). Similarly, chapter 18, in which Elizabeth has the pleasure of informing Wickham that she now thinks more highly of Darcy than before, is severely darkened by the behavior of her family. Lydia's plans for Brighton ("A little sea-bathing would set me up forever") fill Elizabeth with "shame," as does her mother's advocacy of them. Mr. Bennet's callous indifference to his worst daughter's "absurdity" is equally painful. After speaking with him, Elizabeth feels "disappointed and sorry" (p. 196).

Chapter 19, the last of volume 2, begins as unhappily as did the first: "Had Elizabeth's opinion been all drawn from her own family, she could not have formed a very pleasing picture of conjugal felicity or domestic comfort" (p. 199). The second paragraph begins: "Elizabeth . . . had never been blind to the impropriety of her father's behaviour as a husband. She had always seen it with pain." In the third paragraph, Elizabeth finds their "domestic circle" at Longbourn to be in "real gloom." "It was consequently necessary to name some other period for the commencement of actual felicity; to have some other point on which her wishes and hopes might be fixed, and by again enjoying the pleasure of anticipation, console herself for the present and prepare for another disappointment" (p. 200). The proposed tour of the lakes is the point upon which she fixes her wishes. Even when the destination is altered to Derbyshire, making possible, though highly unlikely, some painful chance encounter with Darcy, Elizabeth eagerly awaits her trip in the company of the Gardiners. The volume that begins in hopelessness and ends in gloom concludes with this sentence: "To Pemberly, therefore, they were to go" (p. 203).

IF THE OPENING and closing chapters at Longbourn that frame the central section of volume 2 are "stark, dark, and melancholy," the eleven chapters at Rosings are even more so. Elizabeth must endure Charlotte's marital "stalemate" for six weeks, from chapter 5 through chapter 15. In addition to Mr. Collins, she must endure nine dinners and two teas with Lady Catherine—by the count of Maria Lucas, whom she must also endure. She must also endure a proposal and a letter from Mr. Darcy. Preservation of her equilibrium in such circumstances requires long stretches of solitude and meditation, which Elizabeth secures both in her room and on the garden walks.

Soon after being received by the Collinses in chapter 5, she escapes to "the solitude of her chamber." By chapter 7 she has discovered "a favourite walk" where she feels secure from "Lady Catherine's curiosity." She is "by herself" at the beginning of chapter 9—until Darcy interrupts her writing of a letter to Jane in order to initiate what seems a strangely inconsequent conversation. When Colonel Fitzwilliam invades her privacy at the beginning of chapter 10, she is on another of her "solitary walks," dwelling this time on the depressed spirits of Jane's letters. After Fitzwilliam unknowingly informs her that it was Darcy who broke up Jane and Bingley's engagement, an agitated Elizabeth "shuts" herself "into her own room." After the traumatic scene in chapter 11 in which Darcy proposes to her, she again "hurries away to her own room"—after crying uncontrollably for half an hour while alone in the drawing room.

In chapter 12, Elizabeth is wandering alone out of doors when Darcy brings her the letter. In chapter 13, she wanders alone for hours as she tries to decipher its meaning and implications. Her outdoor vigil in chapter 13 is the heart and soul of the volume—and of the novel as well. This vigil is not only opposed to but perfectly balanced by the letter from Darcy that prompts it. Elizabeth is at once farther from home and closer to herself than she has ever been. The deep emotional and intellectual exchange that takes place between her and Darcy in chapters 12 and 13 matches the exchange between the piano and orchestra in the Andantino of K. 271. The intensity of emotion is comparable—as is the formal restraint with which grief is registered and communicated.

The deeply woven contrapuntal grief of the opening bars of the Andantino is archaic in style: it is reminiscent of Baroque polyphony and of recitatives in the *opera seria* manner. Its dense texture is seldom found in Mozart's later concertos, even after he "rediscovers" polyphony in the library of Baron von Sweiten. Not only its texture and style but also its emotion is exceptional. "As an expression of grief and despair," in Rosen's words, "this movement stands . . . almost alone among Mozart's concerto movements; not until the Andante con moto of Beethoven's G-major Concerto is the same tragic power recaptured" (p. 211). Girdlestone finds in the Andantino "that despairing sorrow of the very young, a sorrow that feeds on itself and refuses to admit the least ray of hope" (p. 98). Its self-reflexive emotion is expressed, most obviously, by the searching melodic lines, the densely contrapuntal texture, the halting tempo, and the C-minor tonality. What I wish to emphasize in the account that follows is the relationship between the orchestra and the solo throughout the movement—for there, too, much of its musical meaning is to be found.

If, as Rosen asserts, the "tragic power" of this slow movement is "the same" as that of Beethoven's Fourth Concerto, the method of expressing it is as different as can be, especially as regards the relationship between orchestra and solo. Both movements are "stark, dark, and melancholy." But in the Beethoven movement the orchestra and solo are starkly juxtaposed from the opening bars; the exchange between them proceeds through gruff opposition that is resolved only when the solo manages to overcome and to "tame" the orchestra. In the slow movement of K. 271 each principal is allowed to express itself at some length until a mutual understanding is reached—an understanding in which the solo willingly accepts the emotional burden offered by the orchestra.

The Andantino differs sharply from the first movement of K. 271 in mood, melody, tempo, tonality, and texture. Yet it has some important similarities in structure. It, too, is a sonata-allegro movement with a double exposition, the first by the orchestra, the second by the piano. Then come development, recapitulation, and coda-cum-cadenza. Here, as in the first movement, the solo shows increasing initiative as the music unfolds. In this movement, too, the solo introduces the recapitulation by playing for the first time the beginning of the orchestra's opening theme. The initiative it shows in doing so is even more significant than in the first movement, as the following analysis will show.

Not only the opening melody but the entire orchestral exposition of the second movement is compressed into the first sixteen bars. For the purposes of analysis, the opening melody may be divided into three major sections (to be labeled "a," "b," and "c"). But the impression when one first hears the melody is of one uninterrupted, searching flow of grief. (Figure 3 shows the melody in the first and second violins.)

The polyphonic and self-reflexive nature of the "a" part of the melody is immediately established by the manner in which the second violins answer and complete the searchings of the first violins in the opening bars (1–3). The complex texture that results could hardly contrast more strongly with the opening phrase of the first movement—which was sounded out by the entire orchestra in unison. The fact that the melody of the opening bar is repeated in sequence in bars 2 and 3, rising but a step each time, emphasizes the tentative, painful, searching quality of the music. So do the two A-flats on which the melody temporarily rests (bars 4 and 6), only to continue its wandering. A further deepening of texture is achieved when the horns and oboes, silent so far, announce the "b" part of the melody by playing a "fate" motif in bar 7 (not shown

Figure 3

in Figure 3). This "b" part of the opening theme (bars 7–11) features a melodic line that moves in a contrary direction between the first and second violins. In the "c" part of the melody (bars 11–16) the second violins again fill in the gaps in the melody left by the first violins. Rosen rightly calls attention to the "architecture" of the opening sixteen bars: "The whole phrase is like a great arch, its classical rise and fall controlling and mastering the span of tragic grief from the canonic beginning to the climax and then to the halting, almost stammering end" (p. 212). In this compact orchestral exposition, the piano does not intervene in the formulation of melody, as it did in the opening bars of the first movement.

When the piano begins its exposition in bar 16 it ignores the portentous opening notes of the "a" section (bars 1–3). It chooses, rather, to take up the "b" material (itself derived from the second half of the "a" material, bars 4–6), which it will elaborate upon during most of its exposition. The opening bars of the "a" section do not go unheard here. The violins repeat them in bars 17–19, as the solo continues to decorate the "b" material. But the strings reiterate their primary burden to no avail, for the solo remains with the "b" idea, finally taking it into brighter regions with a modulation to E-flat major, the "happy" key of the first movement. After the "fate" motif in the winds announces the formal arrival of the "b" idea in the strings (bar 32), the piano remains centered in the new key throughout the rest of its exposition (bars 33–53), which concludes finally with the "c" phrase of the opening melody, this time shared out between piano and orchestra. Although the modulation to the major key gives the bulk of the solo exposition a "happier" feeling than that of the orchestral exposition, the searching quality of the melodic line continues to intimate unrest: the melody always seems about to fall back into the minor at its next turn.

The solo exposition leads to a codetta which merges into a short development section. The orchestra introduces new material (bar 53) which is derived from the opening theme—and which the solo elaborates and decorates in the development (beginning at bar 60) with intimate collaboration from the oboes. This section of the Andantino is warmer, mellower, and more flowing than has yet been heard, but its primary function is to prepare for the inevitable return of the C-minor burden of the opening bars. An exquisitely painful chromatic retransition by the piano (bars 72–73) leads directly to the recapitulation (Figure 4). In Girdlestone's words, "two bars of dreamy and shimmering sadness, based on a descending scale of a minor seventh, fall back, discouraged, into the opening *melopoeia*" (p. 100). At this dramatic moment (bar 74), the piano takes up for the first time the phrase with which the orchestra had opened its exposition. When it stole the orchestral phrase to begin the recapitulation of the first movement, the piano seemed to be saying, "anything you can do, I can do better." Here it seems to be accepting, for the first time, the full burden of what the other has spoken.

The essential humility of the piano's response is emphasized by the fact that its sounding of the very beginning of the "a" part of the theme in bars 74 and 75 is, though respectful, incomplete. The answering part of the phrase (originally provided by the second violins) is not heard, as the piano seems unable to find the answer itself. As the right hand traces the broken melody that originally belonged to the first violins, the left is relegated to playing the repeated harmony notes originally played by the cellos and basses. But the answer to that broken melody is immediately provided by the first and second violins, which now resume the complete burden of the opening phrase themselves (bar 76; see Figure 4), just as they had at the beginning of the solo exposition. Although the piano now continues with the "b" material it had earlier taken refuge in, the effect is different. Whereas the solo had avoided the major burden earlier, it has this time announced and introduced it. The music in bars 76–78 is exactly that of bars 17–19, but the context, and therefore the

Figure 4

meaning, has changed. The solo has recognized and shared the orchestra's primary burden.

The recapitulation now continues to follow the pattern of the solo exposition very closely, including the modulation to E-flat major. But when the sounding of the "fate" motif in the winds (bar 92) announces the rearrival of the "b" part of the theme as it is stated by the strings and then further elaborated by the solo, there is a dramatic change. Bars 93–107 correspond almost exactly to bars 32–48 in the solo exposition— with the difference that they are now in C minor rather than E-flat major. The difference is stunning. The relatively bright and happy refuge for the piano in the solo exposition is now, when transformed into the minor key, an episode of grief-stricken despair. The grief increases when a painful rising chromatic scale (substituting for what was a "neutral" trill in the solo exposition) introduces the "c" material of the opening theme. Begun by the orchestra (bar 109), it is immediately taken up by the solo (bar 110). There follows the most intimate and deeply felt exchange of the movement, especially in bars 111–15, where the first violins seem to be answering the voice of the piano. It is, as Rosen has written, "a dialogue of great sadness . . . in which the speech rhythms inescapably evoke the sound of words" (p. 213).

Melodically, this intimate exchange is a canonic expansion of the "c" material as it was exposed in the orchestral and solo expositions (11–16 and 48–53). In texture, it is the equivalent of the canonic self-reflexiveness of the "a" material in bars 1–3, with the piano now included. With this eloquent dialogue over the "c" material, the deep emotion that was announced in three connected surges by the orchestra in bars 1–16 has now been fully accepted and assimilated by the solo. The recapitulation of the Andantino is melancholy in its C-minor tonality, its searching melodic lines, and its tight-knit structure, but it is exhilarating too. The sorrow, grief, and despair remain as deep as they were in the orchestral exposition, but now they are shared.[10]

As in the first movement, a coda with cadenza follows. Introduced with great economy by orchestra and piano, the cadenza begins with descending minor scales that are touched with unexpected chromatic alterations. The piano then ascends—only to land on the painful diminished-seventh chord. There follows another down falling surge of passage-work which changes to rising figures accompanied by trills marked *agitato*. After more preparation, including a new sounding of the "b" material (bar 133), the piano reaches the heart of the cadenza. There, in bars 136–41, the solo announces and further develops the "c" material. Playing the broken melody in the right hand, the piano accompanies itself with chords in the left hand (just as it had done with the "a" material at the beginning of the recapitulation). This chordal self-accompaniment does not rival the eloquence with which the strings responded to the solo's playing of the "c" material at the end of the recapitulation, but it does register the solo's ability to generate a new internal equilibrium with respect to this material.

The transition out of the heart of the cadenza (via suspended chords and descending scales) is as painful as the transition into it. But the pain now seems to have been assimilated, rather than flooding in anew with every note. The same is true of the transition out of the cadenza itself. The piano's measured trills (bar 147) and its series of paired sixteenth notes in the right hand answered by eighth notes in the left (bar 149–51) are painful, but they also express admirable composure (Alfred Brendel's recorded performance of this passage is particularly buoyant).

When the orchestra returns (bar 152), it is unmuted for the first time in the movement. It begins immediately with the "c" material. After one bar its burden is again taken up by the piano, which once again accompanies itself in the broken melody, allowing the orchestra to share only the final two-note C-minor cadence.

All the way to the end of the coda the musical materials of the Andantino have remained essentially what they were in the first sixteen bars. But what was originally announced by the orchestra has been increasingly shared with, and assimilated by, the solo. No less than in the first movement, but in an entirely different way, the orchestra has been opposed to the piano, and balanced perfectly by it.

THE LETTER Darcy delivers to Elizabeth in chapter 12 of volume 2 is as compressed and restrained as the orchestral exposition of the Andantino. It covers "two sheets of letter paper, written quite through, in a very close hand.—The envelope itself was likewise full" (p. 166). There are two paragraphs, one with three sentences, the other with ninety-four! The three-sentence first paragraph indicates the character of the letter—and of its sender.

> Be not alarmed, madam, on receiving this letter by the apprehension of its containing any repetition of those sentiments, or renewal of those offers, which were last night so disgusting to you. I write without any intention of paining you, or humbling myself, by dwelling on wishes, which, for the happiness of both, cannot be too soon forgotten; and the effort which the formation and perusal of this letter must occasion should have been spared, had not my character required it to be written and read. You must, therefore, pardon the freedom with which I demand your attention; your feelings, I know, will bestow it unwillingly, but I demand it of your justice. (p. 166)

In "tempo" this paragraph is deliberate and searching. In "mood" it is restrained. Its "texture" (the diction and syntax) is dense and archaic. Its "melodic line" (the step-by-step unfolding of thought and feeling) is intricate; to the considerable degree that the feelings of the sender and recipient are considered equally, it is also contrapuntal. The "tonality" is decidedly minor-key.

The ninety-four-sentence concluding paragraph is in the same scrupulous and deeply felt style. In it, Darcy addresses the two great offenses with which Elizabeth had charged him when rejecting his proposal the night before. In the "a" part of his defense, Darcy explains why he knowingly "detached Mr. Bingley" from Jane. In doing so, he necessarily dwells on the "repugnance" of the Bennet family's connections and actions. In the "b" part, which follows without a pause, Darcy defends himself against the accusation of "having injured Mr. Wickham." If the letter has any "c" part, it is the high regard which Darcy—in spite of everything—admits that he continues to feel for Elizabeth. This regard is most clearly evident in the last sentence, one of the few short ones in the letter: "I will only add, God bless you" (p. 173).

The architecture of Darcy's letter, like that of the orchestral exposition of the second movement, "masters" a "great span of grief." Its emotional burden is dense, its mode of expression archaic. Just as the Andantino of K. 271 adheres more to the formal conventions of the earlier *opera seria* than to those of Mozart's day, so does Darcy's letter adhere more to the conventions of the mid-eighteenth-century epistolary novel than to those of Austen's day (for the latter, we must wait for the short, impromptu letter Wentworth writes to Anne Elliot near the end of *Persuasion*). Occurring near the midpoint of the novel, Darcy's letter represents the maximum intensity of expression that has so far been achieved. Its intensity is matched and surpassed only by the genuine grief, remorse, and understanding with which Elizabeth silently responds in the following chapter.

In her first reading of the letter, Elizabeth is no more able to gather its true import than is the solo when first responding to the orchestral exposition of the Andantino. She ignores the main burden of the "a" part of Darcy's exposition as completely as the solo ignored that of the "a" part of the orchestra's opening melody. Because she feels his analysis of her family, Jane, and Bingley to be "all pride and insolence," she does not even register the train of thought that supports it. She is able to "read with somewhat closer attention" the "b" part of the letter: Darcy's explanation concerning Wickham. Here she registers much of what is written, but its truth does not yet hit her personally. Her assimilation of this part of the letter compares to the solo's assimilation of the "b" material during the solo exposition; she sees its painful shape, but can feel it only in the major key, not yet in the unadulterated minor. She hurries through the rest of the letter in a mood of unbelieving resistance, "scarcely knowing anything of the last page or two." She then "puts it hastily away, protesting that she would not regard it, that she would never look at it again" (pp. 173–74).

The first reading of the letter has excited in Elizabeth a "contrariety of emotion" (p. 173). It is comparable to the harmonic contrariety experienced by the solo during the solo exposition. As Rosen points out, a continuing "oscillation between E-flat major and minor" has the curious effect of retaining the minor-key mood "even in transposition," an effect that is "heightened by the dissonant major-minor clash" (p. 211). The clash between what Elizabeth has already understood and what remains for her to understand heightens for the reader the distress she already feels during the first reading.

After putting the letter aside and deciding she will never read it again, Elizabeth for a short while wanders rather aimlessly. This brief passage compares with the short development section of the Andantino as an attempt to postpone the inevitable. "In this perturbed state of mind, with thoughts that could rest on nothing, she walked on; but it would not do; in half a minute the letter was unfolded again, and collecting herself as well as she could, she again began the mortifying perusal of all that related to Wickham, and commanded herself so far as to examine the meaning of every sentence" (p. 174). The result of this thought process is a complete understanding not only of what Darcy had written with respect to Wickham but of its implications for herself. "She grew absolutely ashamed of herself. Of neither Darcy nor Wickham could she think without feeling that she had been blind, partial, prejudiced, absurd" (p. 176). She has now, in effect, "recapitulated" the "b" material of the letter in its proper minor key. "Till this moment I never knew myself" (p. 177).

Her "recapitulation" of the "a" material she had previously dismissed follows immediately upon her self-recognition.

> From herself to Jane—from Jane to Bingley, her thoughts were in a line which soon brought to her recollection that Mr. Darcy's explanation *there* had appeared very insufficient; and she read it again. Widely different was the effect of a second perusal.—How could she deny that credit to his assertions, in one instance, which she had been obliged to give in the other? . . . When she came to that part of the letter in which her family were mentioned, in terms of such mortifying, yet merited reproach, her sense of shame was severe. (p. 177)

Her "shame" in acknowledging the truth of the "a" material is soothed somewhat by her concomitant recognition of the "compliment to herself and her sister" in being exempted from the familial censure. This compliment "was not unfelt. It soothed, but it could not console her for the contempt which had been thus self-attracted by the rest of her family." So does the sad exchange between the piano and violins over the "c" material at the end of the recapitulation of the Andantino "soothe but not console." Elizabeth does register Darcy's compliment to her. Yet at the end of her "recapitulation" of his letter she feels "depressed beyond anything she had ever known before" (p. 177).

Before reexposing herself to the society of others, Elizabeth, having accepted the essential burden of Darcy's letter, sifts through its various implications alone.

> After wandering along the lane for two hours, giving way to every variety of thought, reconsidering events, determining probabilities, and reconciling herself as well as she could, to a change so sudden and so important, fatigue, and a recollection of her long absence, made her at length return home; and she entered the house with the wish of appearing cheerful as usual, and the resolution of repressing such reflections as must make her unfit for conversation. (pp. 177–78)

Though depressed at the end of this process, Elizabeth, no less than the solo during the transition out of the cadenza, is also strangely exhilarated: "She could only think of her letter" (p. 178). She has assimilated great pain, but in doing so she has shared Darcy's—and understood his right to feel it.

Elizabeth's return to society occurs in chapter 14 when, with Darcy gone, she endures numerous engagements with Lady Catherine and the Collinses during her last week at Rosings. Usually the consummate social animal, Elizabeth finds it almost impossible "to appear tolerably cheerful" (p. 181). Her need is not for society but for solitude; she is outdoors and alone as often as she can be. "Reflection must be reserved for solitary hours; whenever she was alone, she gave way to it as the greatest relief; and not a day went by without a solitary walk, in which she might indulge in all the delight of unpleasant recollections" (p. 180). So in the Andantino does the solo "indulge in all the delight of unpleasant recollections"—not only in the cadenza but in the final bars of the coda, where it again takes the painful "c" material from the orchestra into its own hands.

In the second volume and movement, both Elizabeth and the solo have shown an elasticity that is capable of assimilating great grief. Connoisseurs of the "light, and bright, and sparkling" in the opening volume and movement, both have shown themselves capable of experiencing as well that which is stark, dark, and melancholy. Each has continued to grow, not by initiating new action, but by continuing to respond with feeling and imagination to the initiatives of others. The deep elasticity of each crystallizes in a single moment: in Elizabeth's decision to reread the letter and in the solo's two-bar retransition to the recapitulation. Girdlestone finds not only "shimmering sadness" but "disillusioned grace" in the solo's painful, yet elegant retransition. Elizabeth's return to Darcy's letter reveals identical qualities. Girdlestone describes the two-bar retransition as "the musical acceptance of organized despair" (p. 100).

Elizabeth's rereading of two paragraphs is a comparable act of acceptance. In each moment the individual acknowledges the need of the "other"
in the deepest sense. The one moment is the heart of the Andantino—
and of the concerto. The other is the heart of the volume—and of the
novel.

HAVING EXAMINED in detail the affinities of mood and of emotional exchange between the second volume of *Pride and Prejudice* and the second
movement of K. 271, it remains to comment briefly upon the symmetry
and proportions of each—both internally and in relation to its predecessor. Comparison of the relations between the respective volumes and
movements will help to address curiously opposed problems in Austen
and Mozart scholarship. Because Mozart's multimovement instrumental
works generally do not carry the same thematic material from one
movement to another, it is often difficult to "prove" that a given slow
movement, for example, actually "belongs" with its preceding fast movement. With Austen the problem is reversed. Because the cast of characters generally remains unchanged from one volume to another, it is often
difficult to feel the force of the volumes as separate structural units. To
do so would be particularly difficult when reading the current Penguin
edition of *Pride and Prejudice*: the volume designations have been elimi-
nated.

In spite of the striking differences in mood, melody, tempo, texture,
and tonality, the second movement of K. 271 relates to its predecessor
in certain ways that have already been touched upon: in playing time
(twelve minutes compared to ten); in tonality (C minor is the relative
minor of E-flat major); in sonata-allegro form (double exposition, development, recapitulation, coda-cum-cadenza); and in relations between
solo and orchestra (the solo responding exclusively to the material introduced in the orchestral exposition, the solo beginning the recapitulation
by playing for the first time the beginning of the orchestra's opening
theme).

A further way in which the Andantino of K. 271 relates to its preceding Allegro is in the very severity of its contrast in mood, melody, tempo,
texture, and tonality. Just as Austen instinctively felt the need for strong
contrast in *Pride and Prejudice*, so did Mozart instinctively create powerful contrasts within individual works and even between successive ones.
The contrast between the playful first movement of K. 271 and its tragic
second movement could hardly be more severe—or more appropriate.
In Mozart's world, excess in one direction demands excess in another.
The perfect balance between opposing forces that is a ruling principle
in the opening bars of K. 271 applies not only to the rest of the concerto

but to the rest of Mozart's career. It applies not only to motifs and phrases but also to melodies, sections, movements, works, and even groups of works.[11]

Within the Andantino of K. 271, the principles of symmetry and balance are not as immediately obvious to the ear as they were in the first movement. As mentioned above, the movement itself, like its opening melody, seems on first hearing to unfold in one uninterrupted tragic span of grief. A degree of symmetry is enforced by the sonata-allegro form, but its internal proportions are in this case skewed by the relatively short orchestral exposition (16 bars) as compared to the solo exposition (37 bars). Yet in emotional force the orchestral exposition is certainly not disproportionate. The essential symmetry of the Andantino is to be found, not in numerical groupings of bar numbers, but in the distribution of the compact emotional burden of its orchestral exposition throughout the rest of the movement.

In texture, the polyphonic exchange between the first and second violins over the "a" material at the beginning of the orchestral exposition is matched by that between the piano and violins over the "c" material at the end of the recapitulation. The "a" material is emphatic the moment it is heard. The "b" material gets special emphasis during the solo exposition. Both the "a" and "b" material is reemphasized during the recapitulation, where the "c" material is strongly emphasized for the first time. The "c" material is then reemphasized in the cadenza and in the closing bars of the coda. Further contributing to the intrinsic symmetry of distribution is the fact that the three parts of the opening theme are intimately related to each other. As Rosen points out, the "c" phrase of the opening theme is "a free mirror version" of the first half of the "a" phrase, whereas the "b" phrase "clearly reflects" the last half of the "a" phrase (p. 212). Interrelated as they are, however, these three phrases are decidedly asymmetrical in shape. They span their original sixteen bars in arcs of 6½, 3½, and 5½ bars.

The second volume of *Pride and Prejudice* is also internally consistent in ways different from and similar to its first volume. Whereas the first volume is generally "light, and bright, and sparkling," the second is generally stark, dark, and melancholy. Whereas the first volume remains primarily "home" at Longbourn, the second remains primarily "away" at Rosings. Technically, however, the pattern is home-away-home in each volume. We have seen that volume 2 both begins and ends with three chapters at Longbourn. It turns out that these outer boundaries of the volume's prevailing "shade" are even more deeply related than in locale and mood. The hopelessness that pervaded the three opening chapters was owing to the inexplicable termination of Jane's and Bingley's romance. The gloom of the last three chapters is owing to the general irresponsibility of the Bennet family. As Darcy's letter in the middle of the volume reveals, the early hopelessness and the concluding gloom are intimately related: the irresponsibility of the Bennet family has provoked both.

The eleven central chapters at Rosings are balanced by transitional chapters via London on either side. Not only is the distribution of locales symmetrical but so are the distances involved. London is twenty-four miles from Longbourn. Rosings is another twenty-four miles from London. One curious parallel with volume 1 is that chapter 16 of each ends with a crowded carriage ride home dominated by the mindless chatter of Lydia. Consequently it is at the beginning of chapter 17 of each volume that Elizabeth is able to make a dramatic revelation to Jane concerning Darcy and Wickham. A more significant parallel between the two volumes is the manner in which Elizabeth's encounters with Darcy in volume 2 mirror in reverse her encounters with Collins in volume 1.

In volume 1, Elizabeth responds first to a letter from Collins, then to a proposal. In volume 2, she responds first to a proposal from Darcy, then to a letter. Whereas her response to Collins's letter in chapter 13 of volume 1 reveals her most delightfully playful side (she asks her father, "Can he be a sensible man, sir?"), her response to Darcy's letter in chapter 13 of volume 2 reveals her most elastically earnest side. Yet the opposite is true of her response to their respective proposals. Her response to Collins's impertinent proposal is stately. Her response to Darcy's proposal, itself stately, is not.

Darcy's proposal in chapter 11 of volume 2 begins with these words: "In vain have I struggled. It will not do. My feelings will not be repressed. You must allow me to tell you how ardently I admire and love you" (p. 161). The ardent proposal itself is summarized by the narrator in highly formal language. Elizabeth's response begins: "In such cases as this, it is, I believe, the established mode to express a sense of obligation for the sentiments avowed, however unequally they may be returned" (p. 161). This parody of Darcy's "stateliness" is followed moments later by a stupendously painful sentence that is the obverse of the tact and discretion with which she had deflected Mr. Collins. In form, Elizabeth's sentence is as "stately" as the ninety-seven-sentence letter Darcy will write the next morning. In feeling, it is impertinent, if not impudent (though, being so, it perfectly balances the unprovoked insult Elizabeth had received from Darcy the first time they had met, at the assembly in chapter 3 of volume 1).

> From the very beginning, from the first moment, I may almost say, of my acquaintance with you, your manners impressing me with the fullest belief of your arrogance, your conceit, and your selfish disdain of the feelings of others, were such as to form that groundwork of disapprobation on which succeeding events have built so immovable a dislike; and I had not known you a month before I felt that you were the last man in the world whom I could ever be prevailed on to marry. (p. 164)

If Darcy's impromptu proposal has, from his point of view, brought out the worst in Elizabeth, he has the character to deliberately compose the subsequent letter that will bring out the best. Collins's pompous proposal exposed the "stateliness" of the society at its worst; Darcy's heartfelt letter shows it at its best.

Whereas the encounters between Collins and Elizabeth in volume 1 are comic, though serious, those between Darcy and Elizabeth in volume 2 result in "recognition" very close to the tragic mode. The kind of realization Elizabeth makes is the kind that is often made too late. This change from the comic toward the tragic mode is reflected not only in the action but in the diction of volume 2. Chapter 6 does preserve some of the "playfulness and epigrammatism" of volume 1 when Lady Catherine's table is described as "superlatively stupid" (p. 142). But the verbal texture of this volume is more characteristically represented by Elizabeth's need in chapter 14 to "indulge in all the delight of unpleasant recollections." Here Austen uses the verbal technique that provides much of the novel's wit: she juxtaposes the heterogeneous. The purpose of "all of the delight" of the "unpleasant," however, is not to sparkle, but to cast shade.

Although editors and critics do not always distinguish among the respective volumes of *Pride and Prejudice*, its author certainly did. One sentence in a letter to Cassandra reveals Austen's consciousness of the shape, proportion, and texture of volume 2. "The second volume is shorter than I could wish, but the difference is not so much in reality as in look, there being a larger proportion of narrative [as opposed to dialogue] in that part."[12] Her sense of proportion, like that of Mozart, is not strictly arithmetic. She realizes that the smaller number of pages in volume 2 are somewhat offset by the denser texture. In the Signet edition, the respective volumes have 110, 89, and 132 pages. She could easily have approached arithmetic symmetry by moving what is now the first chapter of the third volume to the end of the second. The proportions would then have become 110, 102, and 120 pages. To have made such a change, however, would have ruined the emotional and narrative symmetry not only of volume 2 but of volume 3.

Another indication of the care Austen gave to her separate volumes is the ending she did give to volume 2: "To Pemberly, therefore, they were to go" (p. 203). This sentence is the verbal equivalent of the full cadence with which Mozart habitually ends his instrumental movements. It tells us the volume has ended as unmistakably as the final cadence of the Andantino tells us the movement has ended. Its anticipation of Pemberly also tells us that another volume is about to begin.

Home Free

AFTER the pervasive, restrained despair of volume 2, the third volume of *Pride and Prejudice* is animated and expansive from the beginning. From the moment Elizabeth lays eyes on Pemberly and its spacious grounds at the opening of chapter 1, the reader feels that she will some day become its mistress. And so it turns out to be. Certain threats must first be overcome, of course. She and Darcy must learn to speak with ease. Lydia's elopement and Lady Catherine's invasion of Longbourn must be endured. But overriding all episodes of pain and suspense in volume 3 is a momentum toward felicity that is simply too strong to be denied. Elizabeth's marriage to Darcy, combined with that of Jane to Bingley, resolves at the deepest level the implications of the novel's opening sentence.

The third movement of K. 271 is similarly animated and expansive from the beginning. The energy and verve with which the solo begins the Rondo restores at a stroke the lightness, brightness, and sparkle of the first movement. The liveliness of the opening refrain seems to guarantee that happiness will prevail—as it does. Threats do occur in the minor-key episodes that darken the first two returns of the refrain. But here, too, the momentum toward felicity overrides them. The "marriage" which the piano and orchestra achieve by the end of the third movement is a perfect resolution of the "balanced opposition" announced in the concerto's opening bars.

If the concluding movement and volume resemble the opening movement and volume in their happy and animated spirits, they differ from them in the distribution of initiative between the one and the many. Whereas the orchestra took the lead throughout the first movement, leaving the solo to "steal its subjects from the enemy" (which it did with alacrity and ease), the reverse is true of the last movement. Here the piano introduces all the major material. Even so, the orchestra manages to become an equal partner. One reason the marriage between the two forces is so balanced in the last movement is that it reverses the balance of the opening movement. The same may be said of *Pride and Prejudice* to the degree that Elizabeth, who essentially responded only to others in volume 1, takes much more initiative throughout the last volume (particularly with respect to Darcy, but not only Darcy).

The final movement and volume also differ from the opening movement and volume by being more relaxed in structure. The third movement of K. 271, as of most Mozart piano concertos, is in rondo form. Unlike the complex interrelations among the structural divisions of a sonata-allegro movement, the rondo structure is by definition episodic. In the third movement of K. 271, a refrain ("a") is introduced, and is followed by a "b" couplet. The "a" refrain returns, and is followed by a second couplet, "c". The "a" refrain then returns again, and is followed by a return of the first couplet, "b". A final return of the "a" refrain ends the movement. The relaxed nature of this particular rondo's structure is enhanced by the nature of the couplets themselves. The "b" couplet runs on with hardly a change from the animated spirits and spacious play of the opening refrain. The "c" couplet expands into a menuetto that becomes a theme with variations—a spaciousness unexpected even in the rondo form.

Volume 3 of *Pride and Prejudice* is similarly relaxed in structure as opposed to volume 1. Compared to the intricate relations among the five major structural divisions described above for volume 1, the treatment of action and locale in volume 3 is simple. Geographically, there are four chapters at Pemberly, then fourteen at Longbourn. Chapter 19 encompasses both locales. In action, the first four chapters of volume 3 are mainly concerned with the Elizabeth-Darcy romance. So are the last nine. This major concern is suspended for six chapters by the Lydia-Wickham affair. Similarly, there is one extended threat to the orderly progression of the Rondo. As we shall see, this sustained musical disruption parallels the Lydia-Wickham episode in the degree to which it abruptly but temporarily suspends the "apparatus of happiness."

The above phrase is from *Emma*, whose narrator applies it with delicious irony to the unpleasant Mrs. Elton. Without irony, it describes volume 3 of *Pride and Prejudice* and the finale of K. 271.

APPROPRIATELY, volume 3 begins not with a universal truth, not even with a letter from Miss Bingley to Jane, but with the word *Elizabeth*. Its opening three paragraphs are almost exclusively concerned with her feelings toward Pemberly and, by extension, Darcy (as are, in fact, the opening three chapters). The first paragraph of volume 3, like that of volume 1, is a single sentence: "Elizabeth, as they drove along, watched for the first appearance of Pemberly Woods with some perturbation, and when at length they turned in at the lodge, her spirits were in a high flutter." After the opening paragraph reveals the animated spirits that will prevail in volume 3, the second establishes a feeling of expansiveness: "The park was very large, and contained great variety of ground. They entered it in one of its lowest points, and drove for some time through a beautiful wood, stretching over a wide extent." The diction and syntax here are simple, even commonplace. But these two sentences, following the first two volumes of this particular novel, create a spacious sense of the out-of-doors.

In the third paragraph, the end of which anticipates the end of the novel, Elizabeth's animated spirits and her sense of expansiveness are further heightened.

> Elizabeth's mind was too full for conversation, but she saw and admired every remarkable spot and point of view. They gradually ascended for half a mile, and then found themselves at the top of a considerable eminence, where the wood ceased, and the eye was instantly caught by Pemberly House, situated on the opposite side of a valley into which the road with some abruptness wound. It was a large, handsome, stone building, standing well on rising ground, and backed by a ridge of high woody hills; and in front, a stream of some natural importance was swelled into greater, but without any artificial appearance. Its banks were neither formal nor falsely adorned. Elizabeth was delighted. She had never seen a place for which nature had done more, or where natural beauty had been so little counteracted by awkward taste. . . . At that moment she felt that to be mistress of Pemberly might be something!

On the first page of volume 3, Pemberly has already been described in more physical detail than Longbourn, Netherfield, and Rosings combined. In distance, this Derbyshire estate is farther from Longbourn than the novel has yet ventured. In description, it already rivals Longbourn as a new "home." The fact that Elizabeth is exploring it without Darcy's having invited her is one measure of her new initiative.

JUST AS the first page of volume 3 shows a rekindled animation and expansiveness in Elizabeth, so do the opening bars of the third movement express a fresh animation and expansiveness in the solo following the constrained despair of the second movement. In the first nine bars the solo announces and repeats the leading voice of the refrain ("a") that will mark the major divisions of this high-spirited Rondo. Its opening "melody" consists of two phrases, nearly identical, which run into each other without a break and which will be linked to the next section of the refrain with a barely noticeable pause (Figure 5). This repeated "melody" is nothing more than a succession of octaves in the left hand based on the E-flat-major triad. In this sense it is as commonplace as the words "The park was very large, and contained a great variety of ground." But its melodic and harmonic squareness is offset by its sharply defined rhythm, its *presto* tempo (hear the Kipnis recording), and the "high flutter" of spirits embodied by the non-stop arpeggios in the right hand.

Figure 5

This jaunty yet secure opening material is not designed for dissection. Rather it is designed to link up directly with more material of its own kind and to be easily recognized whenever it returns. It is followed by an even more animated melody group based on the E-flat-major scale, which through repetitions and extensions runs from bars 9 through 34.

THE EXPANSIVE opening chapter at Pemberly continues with a tour of the house itself, followed by a leisurely walk over the grounds. When Darcy, who was supposedly away from Pemberly, joins Elizabeth and the Gardiners not only once but twice in the course of their stroll, Elizabeth's already animated spirits flutter even higher than before. Their second conversation is gay and trouble-free for the first time in the novel. After their painful encounters at Rosings and the loneliness that has followed, this surprise reunion results in excitement almost ecstatic. Elizabeth is astonished that Darcy is so cordial as to invite them to dine at Pemberly the next day. That dinner, in chapter 2, is followed by another in chapter 3, the latter a result of Elizabeth's and Mrs. Gardiner's taking the initiative of repaying Georgiana Darcy's visit to them at Lambton.

After the first dinner, Elizabeth spends two sleepless nighttime hours trying to decide how she feels about Darcy. After determining that she does not "hate" him, she settles temporarily on "respect and esteem." She then moves on to "gratitude." She is grateful that he loves her enough to forgive her cruelty at Rosings. Sensing his still "ardent love," she wonders only how far to return it. At the second dinner, marred by the presence of Miss Bingley, she has very little opportunity to speak with him. Afterwards, however, she is so preoccupied with her feelings for Darcy and with his for her that she and Mrs. Gardiner discuss "the looks and behaviour of everybody . . . except of the person who had most engaged their attention" (p. 227). Here, as so often in the novel, restraint reveals deep emotion.

The next morning, at the beginning of chapter 4, the two letters arrive from Jane. The first had been "missent elsewhere" because "Jane had written the direction remarkably ill" (p. 227). Elizabeth sits down to "enjoy them in quiet," but the shocking news that Lydia and Wickham have run off to Scotland propels her from her chair—at the very moment Darcy arrives, unannounced, to pay a call. She bursts into tears before she can tell him the disgraceful news. He meanwhile waits in "wretched suspense." When she does find her tongue, Darcy is "shocked" and "grieved" by the news. Elizabeth is now more certain than ever that he would never wish to unite himself with her family. Ironically, "never had she so honestly felt that she could have loved him as now, when all love must be in vain" (p. 232).

In response to the crisis, Elizabeth's thoughts characteristically shift from herself and Darcy to Lydia and the family. "Self, though it would intrude, could not engross her" (p. 232). The last sentence of chapter 4 finds her and the Gardiners "seated in the carriage, and on the road to Longbourn." Lydia, though not physically present, dominates this painful carriage ride home as much as she did those in volumes 1 and 2. The growing momentum toward felicity in volume 3 has encountered a major—and seemingly insuperable—obstacle. The reader's one consolation is this: had Jane's first letter not been "missent," it would have arrived at Lambton before Elizabeth and the Gardiners had gone to Pemberly or seen Darcy, in which case the flutter and expansiveness which opens volume 3 would never have occurred.

THE PIANO's animated opening refrain (bars 1–34) is cordially answered by the orchestra (bars 35–82). First the instrumental group takes up the first part of the solo refrain (bars 35–43). Following the same melodic line, it varies the rhythm only enough to register its own inflection. The violins next introduce a descending four-note motif related to the second part of the solo refrain (bar 43). Played three times by the orchestra, it is answered three times by the piano. This explicit exchange of the four-note motif is comparable to the implicit exchange in Elizabeth's mind after the first dinner at Pemberly: Darcy's implicit "I love you still" answered by her recognition that "he loves me still." Such lively and equal collaboration of the piano and orchestra will dominate the spirit of the Rondo, even though this particular motif will not be heard again. A closing passage based on scales in the orchestra and passagework in the piano completes the refrain and leads to the first couplet, introduced by the piano.

The "b" couplet continues and even heightens the *moto perpetuo* drive of the refrain. It has even more energy, even less melody than the refrain itself. As it is dominated throughout by the solo, it has less exchange. The orchestra does manage to intervene at bar 147 long enough to establish a cadence on B-flat, from which the piano launches into a short cadenza. After the cadenza (of which Mozart left two versions), the piano returns, predictably, to the opening refrain (bar 150). Everything now seems as happy and in its place as when Elizabeth sits down to read her letters from Jane.

Just as the first half of Jane's "missent" letter "contained an account of all their little parties and engagements" and offered no cause for alarm, so does the return of the refrain begin comfortably and predictably. The piano plays its version of the refrain (bars 150–83) exactly as it did before. (The only hint of change is that the oboes are allowed quietly to accompany the last three bars.) The orchestra then follows, as before, with its individually inflected copy of the opening nine bars. But now the music betrays the kind of agitation evident in the second half of Jane's letter. In place of the four-note motif that had been lovingly answered by the piano, the orchestra breaks out with four bars of descending passagework which modulate quickly and severely into the keys of F minor, G minor, and C minor (bars 192–95). This unsettling passage concludes with four fateful reiterated B-flats in the first violins (B-flat now being the dissonant diminished seventh of the C-minor key rather than the stable dominant of E-flat major). The piano answers with a painful five-note phrase whose last two notes (a drop of the minor second) are repeated twice, after which the orchestra begins the whole episode again—this time a step higher in register and even deeper into the minor keys. This painful exchange between piano and orchestra is the first real threat to the momentum and equilibrium of the movement, and in this sense it corresponds to the painful exchange between Elizabeth and Darcy—to the "wretched suspense" and to the "shock" and "grief" over the news of Jane's letter.

By the end of bar 208 the crisis has enveloped both solo and orchestra. The piano looks for a way out through passagework, but finds none. The first violins search for composure by taking up the jaunty tune of the refrain (bar 220). Starting on G, they cannot get beyond the fourth note, so they merely repeat themselves, landing always on G. The piano begins the same process on A-flat (bar 224), and with the same result. The violins try again, this time on D-flat (the diminished seventh of E-flat). After four bars without progress (bars 228–31) they leap to D-flat an octave higher—from which the piano begins a menuetto seemingly unrelated to what has so far transpired. As abruptly as the Darcy-Elizabeth romance is suspended by Jane's letter and by Elizabeth's departure for Longbourn, so is the progress of the lively Rondo suspended by the minor-key episode and the solo's taking refuge in the interpolated menuetto.

IN CHAPTER 5 Elizabeth arrives home at Longbourn—again to discuss a serious matter concerning Wickham with her sister Jane. For the next five chapters, the progress of her relationship with Darcy is apparently suspended. Unaware of his actions or even whereabouts, she can only remain at Longbourn and await developments in the Lydia-Wickham affair. In chapter 6 the family receives the contrasting letters from Mr. Gardiner and Mr. Collins and welcomes Mr. Bennet back from London. In Chapter 7 a letter from Mr. Gardiner announces that the runaways may marry. In chapter 8 Elizabeth imagines that the marriage of Lydia to Wickham will make even more impossible a union between herself and Darcy, who, she now decides, in vain, "was exactly the man who, in disposition and talents, would most suit her" (p. 261). When the married lovers arrive at Longbourn in chapter 9, Lydia's unblushing lack of remorse and Mrs. Bennet's flawless lack of taste make the familial failings even more brutally apparent to Elizabeth than before. A casual remark dropped by Lydia, however, causes Elizabeth to "burn with curiosity" (p. 267): Darcy had met Wickham in London!

As Lydia was breaking a confidence in dropping this piece of news, Elizabeth does not press her for more information. But she does write immediately to Mrs. Gardiner, whose letter in chapter 10 acquaints Elizabeth with the central role Darcy had played in forcing (and financing) the marriage. Elizabeth reads with such rapt attention that she cannot tell at first whether "pleasure or pain bore the greatest share." But "her heart did whisper that he had done it for her" (p. 273). As she reads Mrs. Gardiner's letter, her romance with Darcy, her "high flutter of spirits" resumes in earnest. After the discussion with Wickham that concludes chapter 10, the Lydia-Wickham threat to her happiness has been outlasted. When Bingley and Darcy arrive at Longbourn in chapter 11, the central action of volume 3 resumes.

THE menuetto that is interpolated into the Rondo of K. 271 has a passive and anticipatory quality similar to that of the chapters in which Elizabeth must quietly wait out developments at Longbourn. The piano first generates a *cantabile* melody in A-flat major that is poised and composed (bars 233–43). The breadth of this melody establishes an immediate and total contrast with the breathless pace of the Rondo per se; its breadth then expands by becoming a theme with three variations followed by a coda. The solo remains in the lead during all three variations, being accompanied by the strings in the first two, the entire orchestra in the last. At the beginning of bar 290, the last variation reaches a painful, if restrained, climax on an F-flat played *forte* by piano, oboe, and first violins. Then the piano drops twice from a high F-flat to G. Even though it is played *piano*, this reiterated descent is intensely dramatic. After nearly sixty measures of studied A-flat composure, the muted shock of this surprising conclusion to the third variation rivals the shock Elizabeth feels when Lydia obliquely alludes to Darcy's involvement in London. But the subsequent coda has a calming, deeply soothing effect similar to that of Mrs. Gardiner's letter in chapter 10.

A one-bar transition leads to the gloriously chromatic coda, where soft arpeggios in the piano are warmly sustained by chords in the orchestra. Sweetly phrased in answering groups of three, the orchestral chords are extremely reassuring to the ear. They are heard again and again and again. Their effect is comparable to that of the implicit message Elizabeth receives from Mrs. Gardiner's letter, assuring her that "he loves me, he loves me" over and over again. By the end of the passage (bar 300), the solo regains enough control to sound out the lovely closing motif, answered perfectly by the strings, which had been exchanged at the end of the first two variations. The piano this time returns the orchestral answer, after which it launches into a short improvisation that leads through brilliant passagework to the return of the refrain in the home key of E-flat major. With the return of the refrain, the Rondo resumes its course almost as if the menuetto had never intervened.

ONCE the Lydia-Wickham affair has been waited out and resolved with the unanticipated aid of Darcy, progress toward equilibrium and felicity resumes at a brisk pace. Bingley and Darcy arrive at Longbourn in chapter 11 and once again in chapter 12. Bingley proposes to Jane in chapter 13, Darcy to Elizabeth in chapter 16. The first proposal is almost perfunctory, but the second occurs after some delay and adjustment. The splendid confrontation between Lady Catherine and Elizabeth in chapter 14 helps Elizabeth to feel that Darcy must love her still (their mutual reserve in chapters 11 and 12 had made her doubt again). The gossipy letter from Collins in chapter 15 seems to be further confirmation. But it is the initiative Elizabeth finally takes during their walk in chapter 16 that makes possible their joyous reconciliation.

As Kitty angles off to the Lucas estate, Elizabeth "boldly" decides to walk with Darcy alone. Acting on a "desperate resolution," she brings up those subjects dearest and nearest to them both (p. 306). Once their mutual fear is engaged, it quickly dissolves. After he proposes, they walk several miles in a leisurely but excited manner, recapitulating all that had occurred between them at Rosings and gaining each other's forgiveness. After the Bennet family is informed in chapter 17, Elizabeth and Darcy in the next chapter give voice to another recapitulation of their earlier relationship—this time from the first moment they laid eyes on each other. Chapter 19 is a fictional coda, divided between short summaries of the happiness that prevails within the domains of Longbourn, the old home of the novel, and Pemberly, its new one.

ONCE the "waiting period" of the menuetto has been outlasted, the Rondo proceeds to a harmonious conclusion with equal *brio*. When the piano returns with the opening of the refrain (bar 304) and the orchestra answers with its inflected version of the same (bar 312), it appears as if the movement is now home free in animated and expansive E-flat-major joy. But just as Jane and Bingley's nearly immediate pairing-off was offset by Elizabeth and Darcy's delay in speaking their feelings, so the Rondo is temporarily sidetracked by the return of the painful minor-key passage in the place of the pleasant four-note answering motif (bars 320–43). Now, however, the threat runs its course much sooner, for the piano is this time able to guide the resistant material back into the major key. The solo deftly couples this new resolution onto the original closing material from the orchestra's first version of the refrain (which has not been heard since the beginning of the movement). From there the "b" couplet returns in its original shape and blithe rapidity, now centered in the home key rather than the dominant (bars 356–416). A short pianistic transition leads to the coda—yet another return of the "a" refrain.

This time the opening "melody" of the refrain is announced not by the piano but by the winds. This exchange of roles, by which members of the orchestra finally introduce the opening "theme" for the first time late in the movement, reverses the dynamics of the first two movements (where the solo finally took the same initiative at the beginning of the respective recapitulations). The piano is content to trill on the dominant while the winds celebrate their theft, but it deftly cuts in to reclaim its second section of the opening refrain (bar 432). When this has run its course, the violins, as before, answer with their version of the opening part of the refrain, being doubled in octaves now by the piano rather than the winds (bar 458). But this time, just as at the end of the first and most treacherous minor-key passage, the violins cannot get beyond the first four notes of the phrase. In this case, however, the music is stuck on E-flat, the harmonic center of stability for the movement (and for the concerto). The once bouncy opening of the refrain is now stripped into even smaller components (F-D-E♭ in the piano and first violins, D-F-E♭ in the violas). It fades away in a decrescendo which leads to the triumphant two-note tonic cadence, *forte*.

THE NOVEL ends with a stately yet elastic sentence of which the Gardiners are the object: "Darcy, as well as Elizabeth, really loved them; and they were both ever sensible of the warmest gratitude towards the persons who, by bringing her into Derbyshire, had been the means of uniting them." Appearing rather seldom in the novel, the Gardiners are neither brilliant nor spectacular. They are, however, decent, good, and ever reliable. Austen, like Mozart, can afford an unspectacular ending because the various tensions—of which there have been many—have been assimilated into the body of the work not only during moments of stress but during those of resolution.

We have seen that Mozart's final cadence was immediately preceded by a benign version of the same four-note fragment of the refrain which earlier had expressed a hopeless stasis immediately following the major stress-point of the movement. So is Austen's closing paragraph immediately preceded by benign presentations of characters who had earlier provoked discord and pain. The chapter whose final paragraph is devoted to the Darcys and the Gardiners begins with a paragraph devoted to Mrs. Bennet. In between, paragraphs are devoted not only to Mr. Bennet and to Jane and Bingley, but also to Lydia and Wickham, to Miss Bingley, and to Lady Catherine. Austen's final pages, like Mozart's final bars, attain equilibrium by resolving, not overlooking, previously discordant elements. An especially vivid example of such dynamics toward the end of volume 3 is Lady Catherine's arrival at Longbourn in chapter 14, after the Lydia-Wickham affair had been waited out. Discordant as ever, she is this time, unknowingly, an agent of resolution. Comparable dynamics occur toward the end of the third movement with the brief irruption of the minor-key episode within the "happy" return of the refrain, following the waiting period of the menuetto.

The end of each work neatly resolves the tensions not only of the last volume or movement but of the earlier ones as well. The cadence in E-flat major which concludes the third movement reaffirms the E-flat-major cadence of the first movement at the same time that it resolves the C-minor cadence of the second movement. The last sentence of the last chapter of volume 3 (devoted to the Gardiners and the Darcys) resolves the first sentence of the last chapter of volume 2 (devoted to the Bennets): "Had Elizabeth's opinion been all drawn from her own family, she could not have formed a very pleasing picture of conjugal felicity or domestic comfort" (p. 199). No less so does the first sentence of the last chapter of volume 3—"Happy for all her maternal feelings was the day on which Mrs. Bennet got rid of her two most deserving daughters" (p. 323)—resolve the last sentence of the first chapter of volume 1: "The business of her life was to get her daughters married; its solace was visiting and news" (p. 7).

THE BALANCED OPPOSITION between the stately and the impertinent that is embedded throughout the fabric of both *Pride and Prejudice* and K. 271 is an excellent metaphor with which to perceive not only the dynamics of each work in itself but also each artist's implicit attitude toward the individual's ideal relationship with society. The splendid confrontation between Elizabeth and Lady Catherine in chapter 14 of volume 3 is the novel's final and most dramatic example of "the stately opposed to the impertinent, and balanced perfectly by it." Like Collins when proposing to Elizabeth in volume 1 and Elizabeth when rejecting Darcy in volume 2, Lady Catherine believes she is being stately when in fact she is being impertinent: "Do not expect to be noticed by his family and friends, if you willfully act against the inclinations of all. You will be censured, slighted, despised, by everyone connected with him. Your alliance will be a disgrace; your name will never even be mentioned by any of us." Elizabeth's indifference, which Lady Catherine takes as impertinence, is stately in both spirit and form: "These are heavy misfortunes. But the wife of Mr. Darcy must have such extraordinary sources of happiness necessarily attached to her situation that she could, upon the whole, have no cause to repine" (p. 298). Elizabeth's composure reflects her realization that Lady Catherine's intervention is not only impertinent in manner but nonpertinent in substance.

Readers who judge Austen to be a rigid social conservative, an unbending proponent of "whatever is, is right," tend to underestimate the force of such encounters, encounters in which the prevailing social values and forms are shown to be hollow when not animated by generous human spirit. The satirical portrayal of characters such as Lady Catherine and Mr. Collins is not only humorous but savage. The portrayal of Sir Walter Elliot in *Persuasion* is more savage still. In this sense, D. W. Harding is correct in finding such characters to be the target of Austen's "regulated hatred." The fact that each of them remains entrenched in his or her position at the end of the novel does not necessarily mean that there has been no revolution. Still, it is possible to exaggerate the savagery of Austen's—and Mozart's—attack upon conventional values.

Rosen concludes his extended analysis of Mozart's music with the assertion that "almost all art is subversive: it attacks established values, and replaces them with those of its own creation; it substitutes its own order for that of society." Finding Mozart's music to be "in many ways an assault upon the musical language that he helped to create," Rosen asserts that Mozart was "as unaccommodating as Beethoven," the only difference being that Mozart's assault is less "naked" because "masked" by the "sheer physical beauty, prettiness, even, of so much of what he composed" (p. 325). The assertion is undeniably true with respect to some of Mozart's later works. So is the assertion that Austen is a connoisseur of hatred. Yet I would suggest that these two artists, more than "attacking established values," tended to distill what was best in those values. Then, more than "replacing" established values with those of "their own creation," they chose to reanimate them with infusions of their own spirit and genius. As I see it, it remained for artists such as Beethoven and Emily Brontë to actually "subvert" and "replace" the established values they encountered and perceived.

Doubtless the "subversive" side of Mozart and Austen has recently been emphasized because both artists were for so long and to such a wide degree misunderstood by those who thought the one "tea-tablish" and the other tinkling. In a 1948 essay Hans Keller commented that Mozart and Benjamin Britten "are the only two composers I know who strongly and widely attract people who do not understand them."[13] Among prose masters of the English language, Austen belongs in the same category. Readers who are attracted to her without understanding her are so numerous that they have become known as "Janeites." (A Janeite is the kind of person who believes that Mrs. Bennet is a fine mother and that young Mr. Collins is a most polite and gracious gentleman.) Such wrong-headed response to either Austen or Mozart naturally prompts the connoisseur to embrace subversion. But to embrace it entirely is, in either case, to simplify a complex issue.

At the beginning of K. 271, the orchestra is not "replaced" or "subverted" by the piano but rather is "balanced perfectly by it." One might allow that a revolution occurs: the solo does turn the orchestra's opening phrase upside down (or, more precisely, downside up). Yet that revolution is a modest one at the same time that it is bold, and it is more playful than subversive. The same holds true for the perfect balance between solo and orchestra throughout the concerto—and throughout nearly all of Mozart's other piano concertos as well. Mozart's most subversive solo voices are often the most seemingly modest ones—as our discussion of

K. 595 will show. But for a solo voice that openly "subverts" or "replaces" the values established by the orchestra, I would point to the second movement of Beethoven's Fourth Concerto.

By the same token, one certainly can say of *Wuthering Heights* that Heathcliff "subverts" or "replaces" the established values of society. But one cannot say the same of *Pride and Prejudice*. Mr. Collins and Lady Catherine are two characters who represent the established values of society and whose stateliness richly deserves to be overturned. But Darcy is equally representative of the society's values, and his stateliness deserves to be cherished. During their confrontations with Elizabeth near the end of volume 1 and of volume 3, respectively, Mr. Collins and Lady Catherine do experience a revolution similar to the one experienced by the orchestra at the beginning of K. 271: their stateliness is turned upside down (or downside up) by Elizabeth. Yet neither is replaced nor subverted so much as found to be "nonpertinent" by the novel's end.

The most meaningful opposition between the stately and the impertinent in the novel is the evolving opposition between Darcy and Elizabeth. Darcy is as stately at the end of the novel as he was at the beginning, and Elizabeth is as impertinent (both words appear often in the text). But because they know themselves and each other better than before, this opposition now produces pleasure and vitality rather than anger and irritation. Elizabeth, at the beginning of the novel, interprets Darcy's stately air as expressive of insufferable pride. She retracts that accusation in volume 2 after showing considerable pride herself in her manner of rejecting his proposal—and after being humiliated by what she learns from his letter. Her retraction is owing not so much to a change in Darcy as to a change in herself, as she makes clear to Wickham in chapter 18. "In essentials, I believe, he is very much what he ever was. . . . When I said that he improved on acquaintance, I did not mean that either his mind or manners were in a state of improvement, but that from knowing him better, his disposition was better understood" (p. 198). In the "flutter of high spirits" that pervades Pemberly early in volume 3, Mrs. Gardiner has the final word on the stateliness of Darcy: "There *is* something a little stately in him to be sure, but it is confined to his air, and is not unbecoming" (p. 215). Because what is stately in Lady Catherine is confined to her "stateliness of money and rank," it *is* unbecoming (p. 138).

It is Darcy who has the final word as to Elizabeth's "impertinence." In chapter 16 of volume 3, when they recapitulate their painful encounter at Rosings, Darcy apologizes for his own "absurd and impertinent" interference in the romance of Bingley and Jane (p. 311). In chapter 18 of volume 3, when they review their earlier Netherfield encounters,

Elizabeth apologizes for her "impertinence" from the time she first knew him. Darcy brushes her apology aside by calling that very quality "the liveliness of your mind" (p. 319). The difference between Elizabeth's and Mr. Collins's and Lady Catherine's "impertinence" is the difference between liveliness, dullness, and selfishness of mind.

In Austen's world, as in Mozart's, qualities such as stateliness and impertinence are not good or bad per se. Such qualities may be subversive or tonic, enervating or enlivening; they are to be valued or disvalued according to the context in which they appear. (Imagine the result, for example, if the solo's "charming" impertinence in the opening bars of the first movement of K. 271 had invaded instead the opening bars of the second movement.) Darcy comes to value Elizabeth's impertinence because it is so consistently tasteful and lively—as is that of the solo in K. 271. Elizabeth comes to value Darcy's stateliness because it is flexible enough to incorporate her vitality and strong enough to ground it. The solo in K. 271 comes to value the stateliness of the orchestra for the same reasons. This shifting value of any given human quality according to the circumstances of context, timing, and taste is one reason why any broad generalization as to the degree of either Mozart's or Austen's subversiveness—or conventionality—is always in need of careful qualification.

Just as the lively opposition between the stately and impertinent in these two works reflects each artist's implicit attitude toward the opposition between individual and society, so does it reflect each artist's implicit attitude toward his or her own audience. The opening sentence of *Pride and Prejudice* is stately in tone and it seems to support the society's established values. At the same time, the ironies implicit in its syntax and diction are impertinent to the degree that they imply other truths quite contrary to those found on the surface. The opening sentence establishes not only a "subject" for the novel itself but a paradigm for Austen's relationship with her audience. It declares independence from, as well as dependence upon, the established values of her readers. The author is saying, in effect, "I am going to subvert your values, to the extent only that they are hollow or superficial, by working within their confines and by imbuing them with spirit. I will do so in such a manner that those of you who are not perceptive will enjoy what I am doing because it entertains you, whereas those of you with sharp eyes will enjoy it because it also enlightens and enlivens you."

This simultaneous challenge to and affirmation of the society's established values marks off the boundaries within which Austen will operate, the frame around her "two-and-a-half inches of ivory." Within those limits she shows how such values can be hollow or superficial (Collins, Mrs. Bennet, Lady Catherine) or imbued with spirit (Elizabeth, Darcy, the

Gardiners) or something in between (almost everyone else). In doing so, she shows that a "truth universally acknowledged"—and a society that propounds it—has human dignity only to the degree that the "truth" is made to apply with taste and elasticity to individual human beings. Still within these limits, she shows how one individual of taste, intelligence, and wit (and even a good dash of impertinence) can achieve full dignity and humanity within the established values that society proclaims. The individual can do so by opposing those individuals and societal assumptions that are inimical to human dignity and by embracing with imagination and humility those that are conducive to it.

In no subsequent novel does Austen achieve such a balance so harmoniously within the bounds of comedy and delight. Darker colors will invade her later works; her last novels are in no danger of being thought "too light, and bright, and sparkling." Even so, each of them finds its own balance between the imperatives of the individual and the society, balances that are equally harmonious even if embracing greater discord.

Just as Austen never again began a novel with so clearly articulated a statement of the boundaries of her fictional "subject," so did Mozart never again begin a concerto with the piano's interrupting the orchestra. It was as if the young composer (and soloist) was saying to the "stately" society for whom piano concertos were polite entertainment and nothing more, "I am here as a composer and as a pianist to divert you. That is what you pay me for, as you would any hired servant, so that is what I will do. But watch out. I will keep my place, yes. But not servilely. I will play only when you ask me to and my music will never be unpleasant and you can enjoy it without listening very carefully, if you wish. But I am, in fact, someone to be reckoned with, and as carefully as you listen, so richly will you be rewarded."

The opening bars of K. 271, then, express a balanced opposition not only between solo and orchestra but between the young composer and his society. As the rest of the movement and the rest of Mozart's career demonstrate, his brand of impertinence, like that of Elizabeth (and of Austen), was ever to remain "liveliness of mind." Likewise were he and his society, in the creative sense at least, to remain "perfectly balanced" by each other. Mozart never broke inextricably from that society or from the established forms of musical expression it held out to him to master. When he did finally break from the impertinent Archbishop of Salzburg, he took up with alacrity the society of Vienna, even to the extent of assuming the "stately" title of Imperial Court Composer, which position, unfortunately, was not imbued with a spirit commensurate with that of its holder. If some of Mozart's later works, like Austen's, became darker in tone, they remained balanced and harmonious nonetheless.

The occasional minor-key concerto or symphony or quintet that seems to turn the established values of his patrons upside down is in every case matched by numerous works in each form that embody, on the surface, the most manifest affirmations of those values. Typically, as we have seen, K. 271, one of the lightest, brightest, and most sparkling of all his works, also contains one of the starkest, darkest, and most melancholy movements he would ever compose. In his career, as in Austen's, the reconciliation of opposites reigns, in changing shapes, from beginning to end.

In Einstein's words, K. 271 is "one of Mozart's monumental works," which he "never surpassed" (p. 294). To Rosen it is Mozart's "first unequivocal masterpiece" (p. 59). So is *Pride and Prejudice* Austen's first monumental, unequivocal masterpiece. The two works, as we have seen, have much in common besides the parallel position in their creators' catalogues of great works. Each is "light, and bright, and sparkling," though not without profound emotional depth. Each is in three movements or volumes of comparable length whose respective "tempos" are fast-slow-fast and whose geographic or harmonic "locale" is home-away-home. Each begins with a clear opening statement that implies the structural and spiritual boundaries within which not only the first volume or movement but the entire work will be contained. Each dramatizes "the stately opposed to the impertinent, and balanced perfectly by it." Each features a brilliant and witty individual voice that by its presence throughout gives formal unity to the work and that by its ability to experience and to express deep emotion gives spiritual unity to the work. And each embodies the ideal by which the individual person or solo voice can achieve an expansive and elastic freedom within the limitations established by the social or orchestral world in which it functions.

As will be seen, some of the above parallels are found in other Austen novels and Mozart concertos; others are unique to these particular works. Significantly, the most perfect description I have encountered of the spiritual and formal essence of K. 271 is Tony Tanner's description of the spiritual and formal essence of *Pride and Prejudice*. According to Tanner, the novel "shows us energy and reason coming together, not so much as a reconciliation of opposites, but as a marriage of complementaries. Jane Austen makes it seem as if it is possible for playfulness and regulation—energy and boundaries—to be united in fruitful harmony, without the one being sacrificed to the other." Certainly to an equal degree does K. 271 reveal "playfulness and regulation . . . united in fruitful harmony." This "marriage of complementaries" compares closely with the union Rosen finds in K. 271 between what he calls "freedom" and "submission to rules" (p. 210). "Since," in Tanner's words, "to stress one at the expense of the other can either way mean loss, both to the self and to society, the picture of achieved congruence between them offered in *Pride and Prejudice* is of unfading relevance."[14] Of equal relevance is the "achieved congruence" of K. 271.

In one of the brief strobelight asides cited in the Introduction to this book, A. Walton Litz offered a general comparison between *Pride and Prejudice* and Mozart based upon "a sense of the union of opposites—without injury to the identity of either." Mozart's "Jeunehomme" Concerto gives very precise application to this intuition—as it does to Litz's accompanying suggestion that *Pride and Prejudice* achieves "a sense of complete fulfillment analogous to that which marks the end of some musical compositions." Even though some of Mozart's and Austen's later masterpieces are less overtly playful than these two early ones, all of them express in their relations between the one and the many a fruitful union between "energy" and "boundaries," between "freedom" and "submission to rules." In those cases where the energy and the freedom become less playful, a new kind of congruence, as we shall see, is the inevitable result.

Rosen writes that Mozart, in his piano concertos, "bound himself only by the rules he reset and reformulated anew for each work." Austen worked in the same spirit. Dismissing the idea that the concertos are merely "ingenious combinations" of certain musical forms available to Mozart, Rosen argues that they are, instead, "independent creations based on traditional expectations of the contrast between solo and orchestra reshaped with an eye to the dramatic possibilities of the genre." Change "solo and orchestra" to "heroine and society" and the statement applies verbatim to Austen's novels. Rosen concludes his overview of Mozart's concerto form by stressing that the concertos are "governed by the proportions and tensions—not the patterns—of the sonata style" (p. 210). So, to a considerable degree, are Austen's novels.

Chapter Five

EMMA AND
PIANO CONCERTO NO. 25 (K. 503)

P RIDE AND PREJUDICE and K. 271 are youthful masterpieces among the half-dozen novels and the two dozen concertos; *Emma* and K. 503 are seasoned masterpieces. Mozart's Concerto No. 25 was composed in 1786, nearly ten years after Concerto No. 9. *Emma* was published in 1816, only three years after *Pride and Prejudice*, but twenty years after the earlier novel was written in its first version. K. 503 and *Emma* differ from their youthful counterparts in spirit and form, just as in spirit and form they compare with each other.

Like the earlier works, *Emma* and K. 503 both consist of three volumes or movements. Yet the proportions and tensions among the structural units differ in these later works. As we have seen, both *Pride and Prejudice* and K. 271 achieve their maximum density of expression in the central volume or movement, the outer structural units being lighter and more playful. With *Emma* and K. 503 the density of expression is distributed more evenly and is actually stronger in the outer volumes and movements than in the central one. Their outer structural units are not only denser but longer than those of their predecessors. This results in works that are spacious and grave—as does the manner in which the "material" of each work is treated.

Among Austen's novels and Mozart's concertos, *Emma* and K. 503 are among the least loved by the general public and the most admired by connoisseurs. Many readers who prefer *Pride and Prejudice* consider *Emma* to be exceedingly dull, cold, and reserved. Many listeners who prefer K. 271 feel the same way about K. 503. Rosen's explanation of this attitude toward K. 503 applies to *Emma* with equal force:

> The Concerto in C major K. 503 has never been a favorite with the public. . . . It is a magnificent and—to many ears—a cold work. Yet it is the one that many musicians (historians and pianists alike) single out with special affection. The unattractiveness for the public comes from the almost neu-

tral character of the material; in the first movement in particular this material is not even sufficiently characterized to be called banal. . . . The splendor of the work and the delight it can inspire come entirely from the handling of the material. . . . Throughout this concerto, we are made to feel how much pressure the form itself can bring to bear even while using almost completely inexpressive ideas. (p. 251)

In Mozart's era, the primary "material" of music was its melodic themes. The "almost neutral character" of the melodic material of K. 503 is particularly evident when compared with that of K. 271.

In contrast to the sprightly, witty, and energetic theme immediately announced in the earlier concerto, K. 503 begins with a series of C-major chords. Melodically, an opening theme could hardly be more neutral. Indeed, it is less a theme in the melodic sense than it is the establishment of C major as the harmonic home. Whereas the first theme is more harmonic than melodic, the next one is more rhythmic than melodic. The five-note rhythm introduced in bar 18 pervades much of the movement. Yet on its first appearance it functions more as transitional bridging material than as a separately articulated theme. The first melodic theme in the movement arrives at bar 50: the simple little march tune that is to play such an important role in the development. Comparison with the smooth, mellow second theme of K. 271 highlights its patently neutral character. As for the closing group of the orchestral exposition of K. 503, it begins with conventional material highly reminiscent of the "Hallelujah" flourishes of Handel. The only material of the entire first movement that is strikingly attractive, original, or memorable per se is the pair of melodies reserved for the piano in the solo exposition, melodies that are heard again only briefly in the recapitulation.

The material of the second movement is no less neutral when compared with the earlier concerto. Corresponding to the richly interwoven and eloquent melody that opens the Andantino of K. 271 is what seems on first hearing to be a rather vapid and flat melody, which, if not wholly inexpressive, has great difficulty communicating what it has to say. Likewise, the refrain that begins the finale of K. 503 is subdued and constrained in comparison to the earlier refrain.

Most of the characters in *Emma*, like most of the melodies in K. 503, are neutral, unattractive, or banal. This is true even of the heroine, whose name begins the novel: "Emma Woodhouse, handsome, clever, and rich, with a comfortable home and happy disposition, seemed to unite some of the best blessings of existence; and had lived nearly twenty-one years in the world with very little to distress or vex her."[1] This description is seemingly as static and conventional as the C-major chords that begin K. 503. Unlike Elizabeth Bennet, Emma is not, even in the mind of her creator, "as delightful a creature as ever appeared in print." Austen did not expect her to be "a general favourite." She indicated in 1814, when beginning the novel, that "I am going to take a heroine whom no one but myself will much like."[2]

Nor are many of the other characters in *Emma* very attractive when compared with their counterparts in *Pride and Prejudice*. Mr. Woodhouse is a dear but insubstantial fool as compared to the clever—if finally over-clever—Mr. Bennet. Knightley is even more of a "stick" than Darcy to the kind of reader who can tolerate neither. Mr. Elton, the clergyman, is neither so entertaining nor so delightfully quotable as Mr. Collins, nor is the woman he marries—after the failure to land the heroine—half so easy to care for as even Charlotte Lucas. The commonplace Miss Bates, who would hardly have been allowed to wedge a single word into the lively texture of *Pride and Prejudice*, is allowed to run on and on in *Emma*, as is the unpleasant Mrs. Elton. As in K. 503, the "splendor of the work and the delight it can inspire" come much less from the material itself than from the way in which it is handled.

Emma and K. 503 are not "light, and bright, and sparkling," nor are they eager to please. The process of assimilating them is complex. *Pride and Prejudice* and K. 271 do richly repay reacquaintance. But continued encounters with those works essentially deepen and enrich patterns perceived in broad outline during the first reading or hearing, for much of the charm of each is brilliantly expressed in accessible surface details. By contrast, it would be an extraordinary reader or listener who would perceive the broader and deeper patterns of *Emma* or K. 503 during a first encounter; indeed, many of their most characteristic effects depend quite literally upon reading between the lines and listening between the staves. Austen's use of irony and Mozart's of counterpoint contribute mightily to the comparatively dense texture of these seasoned works—as well as to their splendid handling of commonplace material.

To read *Pride and Prejudice* and to follow what Elizabeth sees and understands is for the most part to experience the novel: the reader's enlightenment closely parallels that of Elizabeth herself. With *Emma*, as early as the opening chapter there is a severe gap between what Emma knows and experiences and what the attentive reader knows and experiences. The gap is created by dramatic irony—the difference between what the words say and what the author means. The reader who is to savor *Emma* must always keep at least two perspectives simultaneously in mind: that of Emma and that of the implied author. If contrapuntal music "consists of two or more melodic lines sounding simultaneously,"[3] then *Emma* may be considered a contrapuntal book. The reader who only sees and hears with Emma's eyes and ears is blind to the texture and deaf to the tone of the novel.

Dramatic irony was not lacking in Austen's ealier work. It operated with devastating effect on numerous minor characters—Mr. Collins, Mrs. Bennet, Lady Catherine—in *Pride and Prejudice*. But never before in Austen's fiction has dramatic irony been applied so unremittingly to the heroine herself as in *Emma*. Nor has it ever been such a primary structuring principle for an entire novel. In *Pride and Prejudice* most of the surface details conspire to let us know who is good and who is bad, when to laugh and when to empathize (though we and Elizabeth are misled as to Darcy's character). Most of the surface details in *Emma*, however, conspire to undermine the easy pleasure of ridiculing the foolish and of knowing one's own superiority. Even the attentive reader who perceives more than Emma does is likely to misread such characters as Frank, Jane, and Miss Bates. To the extent that this is so, Emma's growth and maturity become the reader's own.

Whereas the dramatic irony in *Pride and Prejudice* tended to be isolated and overt, in *Emma* it is pervasive and unobtrusive. The major irony of the earlier novel, Elizabeth's misperception of Darcy, could hardly be missed. It comes into acute focus in chapter 13 of volume 2, the emotional climax of the work. The major ironies of *Emma* are more subtle and are distributed throughout. The primary dramatic irony of volume 1 involves the commonplace trio of Emma, Mr. Elton, and Miss Harriet Smith. That of volume 2 involves Frank Churchill and Jane Fairfax, though the reader realizes this only in the retrospect of volume 3. In that volume, Emma, Harriet, and Mr. Knightley are the principals in irony. In each case, the reader must attend very closely to realize that irony—and a dense texture—is present.

The difference between the light, quick, sharply drawn surface of *Pride and Prejudice* and the neutral, slow, sometimes purposely blurred surface of *Emma* parallels the difference in musical surface between K. 271 and K. 503. And Mozart's use of counterpoint as an intensifying device in the one pair of works compares with Austen's use of irony in the other pair. The counterpoint of K. 271, like the irony of *Pride and Prejudice*, is restricted, striking, and overt. The contrapuntal effects in that concerto are concentrated in the self-reflexive Andantino, whose archaic density of texture contrasts with that of the two outer movements as sharply as Darcy's letter and Elizabeth's response contrast with the prevailing texture of *Pride and Prejudice*. In neither case does one need the eye or the ear of the connoisseur to realize that the texture is dense.

In K. 503, as in *Emma*, the density of texture is at once less overt and more pervasive. Here, too, the density is distributed throughout the outer structural units rather than concentrated in the central one. And here, too, it is applied to extremely commonplace material. In the first movement of K. 503 both the five-note rhythmic motif and the simple march melody receive contrapuntal treatment—the former in several places throughout the movement, the latter essentially in the development section. In the third movement of K. 503 it is a simple three-note motif from the second couplet that is subjected to a masterfully expansive polyphonic "development." Here, as in *Emma*, the listener must attend very closely in order to experience the rich, dense texture.

Another way in which these two seasoned masterpieces differ from their two youthful counterparts is in the character and distribution of emotion. With *Pride and Prejudice* and K. 271 it was meaningful to speak of the outer volumes and movements as essentially "light, and bright, and sparkling" and of the inner structural unit as "stark, dark, and melancholy." *Emma* and K. 503 cannot so easily be characterized. The majestic, buoyant first movement of K. 503 has a heavy undertow of sadness that periodically and memorably tugs at the prevailing high spirits. The second movement is difficult to characterize in the direction of either happiness or sadness. The third movement is unusually pensive for a classical rondo, and it contains an extended episode that is at once the most beautiful and the most melancholy of the entire concerto. In *Emma*, the most dramatic episodes tend to be comic and sad at the same time. The third volume has a patently "happy" ending, yet it contains numerous episodes of acute pain. The second volume is as difficult to categorize emotionally as is the second movement of K. 503. The first volume, in many ways so buoyant as Emma busily manages the lives of her Highbury neighbors, is at the same time full of ironic undercurrents and emotional back-eddies. These two seasoned masterpieces illustrate the tendency of late Austen and late Mozart to investigate more subtle kinds of emotion than was typical of their earlier works—a tendency that will be even stronger in *Persuasion* and K. 595.

Whereas the seamless blending of homophonic and polyphonic textures in K. 503 shows Mozart's increasing mastery over his musical materials, the subtle rendering of emotion shows his increasing penetration into the complexity of human experience. The emotional complexity and the transparent density of *Emma* likewise testify to Austen's increasing penetration and mastery. This is not to say that these later masterpieces are better than the youthful ones—only that they are different. And for all of the differences that have been pointed out in this introduction, there is one way in which K. 503 and *Emma* re-create the achievement of K. 271 and *Pride and Prejudice*. Each features a heroine or solo voice that achieves a "marriage of complementaries" with forces that seem at the outset to be in opposition to their brightest hopes and deepest needs. These later marriages, however, differ in kind. Emma Woodhouse and the solo voice of K. 503 differ from Elizabeth Bennet and the solo voice of K. 271 as strongly as they compare with each other. This heroine and this solo voice compare in their intrinsic qualities, in their pattern of relating with others, and in the experience they need in order to mature.

A Grandiose Ambiguity

VOLUME 1 of *Emma*, like volume 1 of *Pride and Prejudice*, features the absurd proposal of the clergyman to the heroine. When Mr. Collins proposes to Elizabeth it is he who is absurd. When Elizabeth eloquently and persistently refuses his offer, neither her opinion of herself nor ours of her is essentially altered by the comic, if earnest scene. When Mr. Elton proposes to Emma the absurdity of the proposal is similar, but the emotions expressed and aroused are more complex. Both Mr. Elton and Emma have contributed to the situation: he, like Mr. Collins, by being silly enough to think that a woman of some intelligence and taste would have him; Emma, unlike Elizabeth, for having contributed, though unknowingly, to the man's delusion. Adding to the emotional complexity of the proposal scene in *Emma* is the fact that it occurs during a claustrophobic carriage ride in the snow. The excruciating slowness of Mr. Woodhouse's carriage up ahead only prolongs the "swelling resentment and mutually deep mortification" experienced by Emma and Mr. Elton (p. 90). The sensory details of space, speed, and temperature (the confines of the carriage, the slow pace, the chill of the snow) contrast with the relatively abstract proposal scene between Mr. Collins and Elizabeth. That earlier episode, like so many important events in *Pride and Prejudice*, transpires in surroundings spatially, temporally, and meteorologically unspecified.

Mr. Elton's proposal and Emma's rejection of it take place in chapter 15 of volume 1. In the subsequent chapter, with the weather outside in the intermediate condition "between frost and thaw," Emma undergoes a vigil similar to the one Elizabeth experiences after receiving the letter from Darcy. She realizes for the first time in her life that her perceptions have been false and her actions immature. This realization by the heroine, nearer the tragic than the comic mode, helps give volume 1 of *Emma* a deeper center of gravity than its counterpart in *Pride and Prejudice*. Likewise, the delay of Knightley's "good" proposal until late in volume

3, after the heroine has been painfully prepared to receive it, helps to give the last volume of *Emma* more density than the corresponding volume of *Pride and Prejudice*.

Volume 1 of *Emma* is the longest opening volume in Austen's fiction. Volumes 2 and 3 are each longer still. This novel's peaks of emotional intensity are therefore spread out over increasingly long volumes rather than centered in a relatively short one, as they are in volume 2 of *Pride and Prejudice*.[4] But more important than *Emma*'s absolute length is its psychological length, or emotional tempo. Readers who dislike its commonplace characters, complex texture, and pervasive ironies find its measured pace akin to torture. Those who savor them find it exhilarating. A brief outline of the structure of volume 1 will help to show how the treatment is unique.

The eighteen chapters of volume 1 form symmetrical blocks of nine chapters each. The first nine chapters take place indoors—and almost exclusively within the doors of Hartfield, the Highbury estate where Emma and her father, Mr. Woodhouse, live. In the first four chapters, none of which has much dialogue, the reader is introduced, largely through narrative exposition, to Emma, Mr. Weston, Mr. Woodhouse, and Harriet Smith, respectively. When the reader encounters some extended dialogue in chapter 5, the speakers are Mrs. Weston and Mr. Knightley. The following chapters prepare for the comparatively long chapter 9, in which the three-way "charade" involving Mr. Elton, Emma, and Harriet—punctuated by Mr. Woodhouse—leads to a subdued climax which concludes an unusually homogenous and dense series of opening chapters.

The second block of nine chapters opens with the outdoors trip to the poor cottage at the beginning of chapter 10. A commonplace walk is felt to be a spacious and almost heroic occurrence because the previous action has transpired uninterruptedly inside. It changes the prevailing mood as clearly as does a dramatic modulation in a classical sonata or concerto. Yet this contrasting chapter is intimately related to its predecessor both geographically (being no more than a mile or two removed from Hartfield) and in plot (Harriet and Emma are joined by Mr. Elton in this outdoor chapter just as they were in the previous indoor one). This and subsequent chapters prepare for the dinner in chapter 14 at Randalls, the Westons' home—itself less than a mile from Hartfield. Emma's "mortifying" ride from Randalls to Hartfield with Mr. Elton in chapter 15 is followed by her vigil in chapter 16, plus the two chapters in which she confesses her mistake to Harriet and then regains her equilibrium.

As this summary suggests, the brief excursion to the poor cottage in chapter 10 is the only truly outdoors episode in the volume. And even that chapter has an "indoor" feeling, owing to Emma's scheming to get Harriet and Mr. Elton together. The indoor world of Randalls is a natural extension of the indoor world of Hartfield, and Emma's and Elton's carriage ride in the snow is both outdoors and not. The last three chapters of the volume anchor the action firmly within the indoor world of Hartfield where it began. That the limitation of space in *Emma* makes possible the "splendor" of treatment has been appreciated by Mary Lascelles: "When Highbury takes visible shape we understand why there is no real need for Emma to leave it; where definition is so sharp and scale so exactly kept the contrasts which it offers within itself are sufficient."[5]

The human limitations of Highbury are handled with a comparable sureness of touch. For a splendid instance of such handling, consider chapter 9 of volume 1. Its action can be summarized as follows. Mr. Elton, who has earlier delivered a painting to Hartfield, where Harriet Smith spends much time with Emma, deposits on a table a pretty "charade" (or riddle)—allegedly composed by a "friend"—whose message, deciphered after he leaves, informs its recipient of an interest in "courtship." Emma immediately interprets the message as applying to Harriet, for the benefit of whose slower apprehension she must spell it out in pompous and condescending language. Simple, good-hearted Harriet can neither find offense in Emma's overbearing manner nor cause in herself for Mr. Elton's loving her, but she sincerely allows herself to be persuaded that she is the object of the stricken clergyman's affection. The arrival of Mr. Woodhouse causes Emma to have to read and interpret the charade even more slowly and painstakingly than she has done before. She (and we and Harriet) must then listen to her father's unfair and inconsequent comments about Emma's sister Isabella, which are interrupted only by the return of the enraptured Mr. Elton, eager to see the effect of his clever courtship. After a somewhat muddled conversation, he leaves confused, with Emma repressing laughter and Harriet moved to tenderness.

On the surface, little has happened. Yet the chapter is a long one, in which every word counts. It is as entertaining and glorious as its contents are commonplace and worse. The secret lies in the treatment, a few details of which may now be touched upon.

Before Mr. Elton calls to deposit his riddle, the narrator devotes a page to informing the reader that Emma has been trying to improve Harriet's mind with reading projects. As of yet they have not got much beyond gathering gilt-edged riddles, collections of which "in this age of literature" are "not uncommon," even "on a very grand scale" (p. 46). The narrator then informs us of Mr. Woodhouse's gentle but undiscriminating interest in such riddles (preparing us for his intervention later) and of the fact that Emma had the day before requested that Mr. Elton try his own hand at writing one. His response is reported as follows: "'Oh, no! he had never written, hardly ever, anything of the kind in his life. The stupidest fellow! He was afraid not even Miss Woodhouse'—he stopt a moment—'or Miss Smith could inspire him'" (p. 47). Mr. Elton's momentary stop provides the key not only to this chapter but to everything that happens between him and Emma until his proposal in chapter 15. His hesitation correctly suggests that Miss Woodhouse, not Miss Smith, is his intended game. But Emma is too busy matchmaking to perceive it. She is certain in her dual pride that such a man as Mr. Elton would never aspire to court Emma Woodhouse, but that he might be the perfect one to save a slightly-better-than-common Miss Smith from the fate of marrying the wholly common Robert Martin (who might have been a perfect mate for a Miss Smith had not she the honor of counting Miss Woodhouse among her friends). So Emma, in her dual pride, fails to pick up this or other hints that Mr. Elton intends her as the object of his affection. The reader who *has* picked up such hints savors the maze of misunderstandings into which she unknowingly wanders.

When Elton presents the riddle, he says to Emma,

> "I do not offer it for Miss Smith's collection. . . . Being my friend's, I have no right to expose it in any degree to the public eye, but perhaps you may not dislike looking at it."
> The speech was more to Emma than to Harriet, which Emma could understand. There was a deep consciousness about him, and he found it easier to meet her eye than her friend's. He was gone the next moment:—after another moment's pause,
> "Take it," said Emma, smiling, and pushing the paper towards Harriet—"it is for you. Take your own." (p. 48)

What Emma thinks she understands is that Mr. Elton loves Harriet so much he had to present the riddle indirectly through Emma. The reader who understands otherwise has the ironic enjoyment of hearing not only Emma's interpretation of the riddle itself but her subsequent explanation of why a man like Mr. Elton can love a woman like Harriet. Ineffably boring and mundane to the reader who does not yet realize that Emma has it all wrong, the scene is delicious to the reader who has registered enough hints to be in the know. This is one of the many scenes in *Emma* with ironies so subtle they are likely to be missed on first reading.

Mr. Elton's return after the interlude with Mr. Woodhouse satisfies the formal symmetry of the chapter. He, looking into Emma's eyes for a return of his affection, seems "confused" when he sees that she has shared his riddle with Harriet. The broken syntax with which he struggles to say something acceptable compares with the stuttered rhythms Mozart often gives discomforted characters in his operas: "'I have no hesitation in saying,' replied Mr. Elton, though hesitating a good deal while he spoke, 'I have no hesitation in saying—at least if my friend feels at all as *I* do—I have not the smallest doubt that, could he see his little effusion honoured as *I* see it (looking at the book again, and replacing it on the table,) he would consider it as the proudest moment of his life'" (p. 56).

It might be expected that his overt confusion would suggest to Emma that his attentions had been directed to her, but such is not the case. Clearly, the human riddle buried in this chapter has been understood by none of the three principals. "After this speech he was gone as soon as possible. Emma could not think it too soon; for with all his good and agreeable qualities, there was a sort of parade in his speeches which was very apt to incline her to laugh. She ran away to indulge in the inclination, leaving the tender and the sublime of pleasure to Harriet's share" (p. 56). Even in chapter 10, when Emma deserts Harriet and Mr. Elton on the pretense of fixing a shoelace but with the intention of leaving them alone so that Mr. Elton can propose to Harriet, his failure to do so enlightens neither Emma (as to his interest in herself) nor Mr. Elton (as to her utter lack of interest in him). The revelation awaits them five chapters later during the carriage ride in the snow.

THE FIRST MOVEMENT of K. 503 is, as Girdlestone points out, the longest first movement in all of Mozart's instrumental music, including symphonies (p. 420). This Allegro maestoso of 432 bars in common time averages fifteen minutes in performance, as compared to ten minutes for the opening Allegro of K. 271. Although the absolute length contributes to the movement's spaciousness and gravity, the treatment contributes even more.

The spacious treatment begins (Figure 6) with the opening C-major chords, these being separated by generous rests that allow the opening bars to "breathe." (How different from the tight and close-knit phrase for orchestra and piano that opens K. 271.) The chords are followed by two bars (5–6) of unison notes in the bassoons, violas, cellos, and basses that march slowly from a low C to the higher C and then back down again. This solid, secure motion adds to the feeling of strength and space; it is followed by the delicacy of the oboes' inverted repetition of a short lyrical phrase introduced by the bassoons (bars 7–8). A leisurely repetition of the chord progression (somewhat altered), of the octave march from C to C and down again, and of the delicate figure in the winds (now extended to four bars) enhances the feeling of spacious and measured repose (bars 9–17).

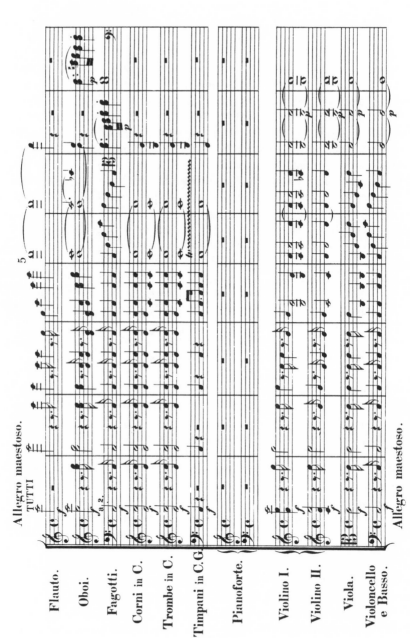

Figure 6

The transition to the unpretentious march theme (bars 18–50) is even more leisurely and spacious, allowing the five-note rhythmic motif (Figure 7a) to be introduced and to flex its supple muscles in a variety of postures. First appearing in the violins in measure 18, it is repeated in ascending sequence until taken over by bassoons and cellos in measure 26. It is present not only for most of the transition but for much of the movement. This five-note motif anticipates in rhythm the first five notes of the march theme (Figure 7b) that enters at measure 50. It also anticipates the four-note rhythmic motif (Figure 7c) that, first appearing with the closing group of the orchestral exposition, is also heard in much of the movement. The closing group itself concludes with an extremely

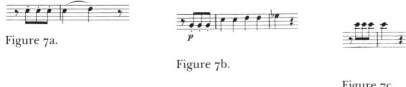

Figure 7a.

Figure 7b.

Figure 7c.

buoyant version of the five-note motif played in alternation between winds and strings.

In the solo exposition the five-note motif is heard in the strings during the transition to the piano's first melody (bars 129–35 and 143–46), is incorporated into the piano's first melody (both right and left hand, bars 151–59), and is prominent in the transition toward the closing group (strings from bar 187, piano and winds and basses from bar 214). The orchestra introduces the development section with a *forte* assertion of its four-note version (bars 226–27), which the piano answers *piano* and converts into the unpretentious march. As the simple march tune is developed by piano and winds, it becomes intertwined with both the four- and five-note versions of the rhythmic motif. During the recapitulation, the rhythmic motif, in addition to its earlier roles, helps escort the piano into the cadenza.

The continued reiteration and manipulation of this motif is unprecedented in Mozart's music. Less than a melody, it is more commonplace, neutral, and banal than the melodies the movement does have. Yet the ease, expansiveness, and assurance with which it is handled is one of the glories of instrumental music. (In both "material" and treatment it anticipates—especially in its four-note version—the "fate" motif of Beethoven's Fifth Symphony.) The bold yet subtle modulation and juxtaposition it undergoes in the development section is particularly exhilarating. As Girdlestone points out, "all this diversion, so transparent in performance, is really an eight-part counterpoint" of great subtlety (p. 429) that gives exquisite joy to the imaginative ear—as does the unspoken three-part counterpoint to those who hear it amidst the "diversion" of chapter 9 of *Emma*.

The length of the movement, the spacing of the opening chords, the leisurely transitions between sections, the expansive reiteration of the rhythmic motif—all contribute to the spaciousness of the Allegro maestoso. So, too, does the character of the solo voice. Unlike the solo in K. 271, which remained absorbed with the orchestra's musical material, deftly stealing its subjects from the enemy, the solo in K. 503 is wayward and dilatory. It tends to take its own time and to do what it pleases—as a short summary of its function in the first movement will indicate.

When the orchestra finishes its exposition and demands that the piano speak, the solo at first hesitates. After being coaxed once, twice, thrice, it then runs off with its own passagework, which becomes highly chromatic before the orchestra finally intervenes with a forceful reassertion of its opening chords (bar 112). After hearing out the opening chords and the two-bar one-octave ascent and descent, the solo covers the delicate bassoon-oboe exchange with descending arpeggios (bars 118–19). When the orchestra repeats its spacious chords, the piano now seems to mock them by inserting its own chords into the orchestra's rests. After covering the bassoon-oboe exchange once more, the piano then embarks upon an extremely long run of passagework leading to its two solo melodies, themselves connected by a spacious transition. These long pianistic transitions serve to isolate the solo's material from that of the orchestra. And the first transition tends to blur the orchestra's own transitional material based on the five-note motif. The piano does attach that motif to the end of its first solo theme, but it does so in its own time and in its own tonality. It omits the orchestra's march theme from its own exposition altogether. The solo also has very little to do with the orchestra's closing group, preferring displays of its own virtuosity through additional passagework.

Following the orchestra's insistent hammering of the four-note motif, the solo does acknowledge and repeat that motif (though *piano*) in order to begin the development section. And it does play the orchestra's march theme complete and in fragments during the development—though always in a remote key. In the retransition to the recapitulation, piano and winds cross each other in contrary motion to arrive at the C-major chord which brings the music home again (bar 289). As the orchestra restates its opening material, the solo is temporarily silent, allowing the bassoon-oboe exchange to be clearly heard. Then the solo for the first time takes the lead in the spacious chord progression, allowing the winds to fill in during the rests, as the solo had done before. The solo's subsequent arpeggios again blur first the lyrical woodwind exchange and then the orchestral lines in the extended transition section, but this time at least the solo does present its own thematic material in the tonic key. As before, it shows no subsequent interest in the orchestra's march theme (recapitulated gloriously in the winds) or closing group, saving itself instead for more brilliant passagework and for the cadenza, which unfortunately has not survived in Mozart's version. After the cadenza, the orchestra plays its closing group essentially as it was heard in the orchestral exposition.

Comparison with K. 271 highlights the wayward nature of this solo voice during the first movement. Whereas the earlier solo responded exclusively to the orchestra's material and had no separate theme of its own, this one responds only fleetingly to the orchestral material and in fact plays its own passagework or themes more often than it does the material of the other. The opposition between the piano and orchestra in the earlier concerto was both spirited and intimate, as reflected in the treatment of both the lively first theme and the mellow second theme. Here the opposition borders on irrelevance: the piano ignores or blurs the orchestral material as much as it acknowledges it. There *is* increased cooperation between the two forces as the movement progresses, but much less than in the earlier work. There is also an intimate sharing with the winds in the development section, but that quality does not carry over into the recapitulation as strongly as it did in K. 271.

The kind of togetherness that is achieved in the first movement of K. 503 involves melodic material less often than did the togetherness in the earlier concerto—and it often results in confusion more than in exchange. A prime example occurs at the end of the recapitulation of the opening group. While the oboe and bassoon exchange their lyrical melody for the last time and the strings enter into their glorious transition based on the rhythmic motif, the solo plays its ascending arpeggios and subsequent passagework. The principals are not sharing their material so much as they are tenaciously guarding their own prerogatives and managing to coexist. This passage must be heard many times (and performed with exquisite care) before it can be experienced as a kind of sharing and togetherness rather than a kind of apartness and obstruction. It demonstrates the importance in this work of hearing between the staves, for much of the sharing that does occur is vertical and complex rather than linear and direct—as it was in K. 271 from the opening bars.

The piano's rather headstrong isolation and its disinclination to connect often with the material expressed by the orchestra is comparable to

Emma's headstrong nature, particularly as she repeatedly ignores the firm warnings and advice given by Mr. Knightley. Likewise, the solo's relative apartness even when involved with orchestral material compares with Emma's apartness even when involved (and overinvolved) with others. Neither Emma nor the solo of K. 503 is easily able to achieve the flexible and close collaboration with other individuals or with the orchestra instinctively achieved by Elizabeth and by the solo of K. 271. If the later works are broader and more expansive in treatment it is partly because the individual and the group, being farther apart, need more space and time in order to reach a mutual accommodation. The wayward nature of the solo in K. 503 helps give its densely textured first movement the sense of being wide open and full of ease. One feels that anything can happen; one also feels that more is happening than one realizes. The same is true of Emma and of the first volume of her novel.

JUST AS THE ACTION of *Emma* remains unusually close to Hartfield, so does the harmony of K. 503 remain unusually close to its C-major home. Rosen speaks of the late Mozart's "economy of means" in the "renunciation of harmonic color" (p. 254). No movement shows this more clearly than the Allegro maestoso of K. 503. Just as the first volume of *Emma* lacks the equivalent of the extended and well-prepared excursion to Netherfield in the first volume of *Pride and Prejudice*, so does the first movement of K. 503 lack the equivalent of the extended and well-prepared modulation to the dominant in the solo exposition of K. 271. Instead, what Rosen calls a "simple alternation of major and minor" (p. 254) provides the necessary harmonic contrast—as does a simple alternation between Hartfield and "away" in the world of the novel.

The home key of K. 503 is at once more and less stable than that of K. 271. It is less stable in that modulations from it occur much sooner—as early as measures 17 and 18 of the orchestral exposition. It is more stable in that its most typical modulations are so abrupt and economical that, as Rosen puts it, they "leave the tonality unchanged" (p. 254). In measures 17 and 18 the oboe-bassoon passage is played in the tonic minor: C minor. In measure 50 the simple march tune is introduced in C minor rather than the expected C major—to which it quickly reverts. Because this simple "alternation of tonic major and minor is the dominant color of K. 503," the home key is at once stable and not. The result is "massive and yet disquieting" and it "is the key to this work's tranquil power" (p. 256). As Lascelles wrote of Austen's treatment of Highbury, "where definition is so sharp and scale so exactly kept the contrasts which it offers within itself are sufficient." The result in both works is, to use

Rosen's words for the concerto, "a grandiose ambiguity of stability and tension" (p. 256).

As Rosen goes on to point out, the simultaneous "opposition and synthesis of major and minor" also becomes "a prime element of the structure" of the concerto (pp. 254, 256). It results in a kind of emotional expression new to Mozart's music. "In general, the lyricism in Mozart's works lies in the details, and the larger structure is an organizing force; in K. 503, the details are largely conventional, and the most striking expressive force comes from the larger formal elements, even to the point of pervading a heavily symphonic style with melancholy and tenderness" (p. 257). In K. 271, tenderness and melancholy were expressed overtly in the melodic details of the second theme of the first movement and the first theme of the second. In K. 503 such emotion often "arises miraculously from the simplest of changes from major to minor, often leaving a tonic chord in root position: the resulting impression of tranquil power and lyricism is unique in music before Beethoven." If the resulting emotion "is less poignant than in some of the other concertos," its "combination of breadth and subtlety" is more grand (pp. 257–58).

In *Emma*, too, the emotions are less poignant but more pervasive than in some of the other novels, less the result of striking "details" and more the result of "the larger formal elements." In *Pride and Prejudice* the "melancholy" is centered in the dramatic exchange between Elizabeth and Darcy in the middle of volume 2, the "tenderness" found largely in the courtship between Jane and Bingley. The emotion in *Emma*, if less dramatic, is more comprehensive, and it springs miraculously from seemingly insignificant causes and characters. One example in volume 1 is the "melancholy" that poor Mr. Woodhouse feels whenever he must venture from home—even if to Randalls, only a mile away. Another is the "tenderness" Harriet feels for Mr. Elton in chapter 9—even if falsely inspired. Few such moments in *Emma* are strikingly expressive in themselves, yet the cumulative effect is massive. And the effect, like that of K. 503, can increase exponentially upon subsequent encounters with the work. During a first reading of chapter 9, for example, the reader might feel little or no "melancholy" or "tenderness" for Emma. On a second, third, or fourth reading, one might feel more and more and more, as one delves deeper into the "grandiose ambiguity of stability and tension" that pervades her world as much as it does that of K. 503.

BEFORE LEAVING the Allegro maestoso and volume 1, I wish to point briefly to one striking example of the perfection of detail and symmetry of expression in each. In the concerto, the lyrical motifs first exchanged by bassoons and oboes in measures 7–8 are immediately memorable because the one is the inverted image of the other. When they are repeated in bars 15–16 the material is the same but the treatment is delightfully reversed: the oboes speak their phrase first. This new order is repeated in measures 17–18, where the now familiar material is memorably transposed to C minor. The quiet one-bar motif (it is marked *piano*) is heard six times in the first eighteen bars in a way that is deeply memorable and expressive.

In the solo exposition and in the recapitulation the wind motifs are played exactly as they are in the orchestral exposition. Yet there is a difference. In the solo exposition, first the two-bar and then the four-bar passages are covered so thoroughly by the arpeggios in the piano that the beauty of the woodwind exchange would be blurred altogether had not the treatment of this simple material been so memorable in the opening bars. In the recapitulation, significantly, the piano allows the two-bar passage to be clearly heard. Its respectful silence seems to signal a growing cooperation with the winds, with which it had been so intimate in the development section. A few bars later, when the piano, after leading the chord progression for the first time itself, again covers the four-bar passage with arpeggios, the winds are more easily heard than during the solo exposition because of the solo's recent silence. In this context, the arpeggios this time may be heard as friendly decoration more than as competitive obstruction, though of course this depends on how the soloist plays them. The challenge presented by such a passage to soloist, orchestral members, and conductor is exquisite.

In all, the one-bar bassoon-oboe motif is heard in only 18 of the movement's 432 bars. Yet it contributes significantly to the otherwise sparse melodic material of the movement, to its short- and long-range alternations of major and minor, to its sense of sharing among the winds, and to the gradual process by which the headstrong solo voice begins to accommodate itself to the orchestral texture. Indeed, the three well-spaced appearances of the short exchange reflect the progress of the movement itself. In the orchestral exposition the oboe and bassoon are heard alone; in the solo exposition they are covered by the piano; in the recapitulation they are alone *and* covered. The last bar in which the motif appears (307) epitomizes the "vertical" kind of togetherness achieved in this movement: as the bassoons sound the last appearance of the lyrical motif, covered by the piano's beloved passagework, the first violins resume the five-note rhythmic motif (Figure 8).

Chapter 9 of *Emma*, described above, acquires symmetry because Mr. Elton's two visits to Hartfield are punctuated by the intervention of Mr. Woodhouse. But the appearance of Emma's father also has a symmetri-

Figure 8

cal function pointing back to chapter 8, which is the only early chapter that rivals chapter 9 in either bulk or density. In material as well as treatment it is closely related to its successor. As it opens, Emma wishes to tell Mr. Knightley of her plans to discourage Harriet Smith from marrying Robert Martin. As long as Mr. Woodhouse is present it is impossible to speak seriously. When Mr. Woodhouse decides to go for a walk, Emma and Knightley have the discussion that concludes the chapter. It is, for them, a heated one. Knightley, who knows the solid worth of Robert Martin, sees no reason why the young man should not be allowed to marry the Harriet he loves. Emma, of course, thinks that a friend of her own should marry someone better than a common farmer. As for Mr. Woodhouse, he is left outdoors.

The extended affair of the charade in chapter 9 occurs at an unspecified later time. Emma's attempts to set up Harriet with Mr. Elton show how little she has heeded Mr. Knightley's advice. And Mr. Woodhouse's arrival from out of doors in the middle of the chapter makes the careful reader wonder exactly how long the lovable hypochondriac has been wandering in the wilds of Highbury. Austen in *Emma*, like Mozart in K. 503, has created an artistic world in which the smallest detail contributes not only to symmetry but, through its place among the "larger formal elements," to tender and melancholy expression.

Homogeneous Contrast

VOLUME 2 of *Emma* lacks the geographical contrast of its counterpart in *Pride and Prejudice*: instead of moving to a far-off locale such as Rosings, this volume remains home in Highbury. Similarly, the Andante of K. 503 lacks the dramatic harmonic contrast found in the Andantino of K. 271: instead of being set in a related minor key (from E-flat major to C minor), this movement is set in a related major key (from C major to F major). As a result, the geographical and harmonic settings in these later works are relatively homogeneous. Yet here, as in the earlier masterpieces, it would be dangerous to emphasize either homogeneity or contrast without being aware of the presence of the opposite quality as well. The relative homogeneity among the inner and outer structural units of *Emma* and K. 503 no more deprives these works of balanced contrast than the relative heterogeneity among the respective units of *Pride and Prejudice* and K. 271 deprived those works of diversified unity.

In spite of its uniformity of setting, the second volume of *Emma* is no unvaried continuation of the first. Even within the physical confines of Highbury some diversity is gained by visits to the Coles and the Bateses. More important, however, is the fact that a new set of characters become pivots for the action: Jane Fairfax, Frank Churchill, Miss Bates, Mrs. Elton. With these characters Emma faces vexations different from the ones she had faced in the earlier volume. The unity provided by the identity of setting in the two volumes, then, is offset and enlivened by the contrast in human concerns—just as in *Pride and Prejudice* some of the diversity gained by Elizabeth's excursion to Rosings is offset by the fact that she engages there with characters she has known at Longbourn (Collins and Charlotte) and at Netherfield (Darcy) in addition to those she is meeting for the first time (Lady Catherine and Colonel Fitzwilliam).

Likewise, the Andante of K. 503, though closely related to the opening movement in key, differs from it in many other respects. In texture it is essentially homophonic, in contrast to the masterful polyphony in parts of the opening movement. In form it is deceptively simple, as compared to the overt complications of the Allegro maestoso. And in length it is relatively short—lasting eight minutes to the first movement's fifteen. In all of these ways it contrasts sharply with the slow movement of K. 271, which was dense, almost Baroque, in texture; unusually complex in form for a Mozart slow movement; and relatively long, lasting twelve minutes to the first movement's ten. Yet these two slow movements, antithetical as they are, have one thing in common: each is the complement of its predecessor. The playful and sparkling Allegro of K. 271 seems to demand the formal grief of its Andantino as surely as the massive and grandiose Allegro maestoso seems to demand its unpretentious Andante.

Without doubt, the central sections of *Emma* and K. 503 do lack the intensity of expression found in the corresponding sections of *Pride and Prejudice* and K. 271. Instead, each embodies a leisurely expansiveness that complements the denser breadth of the opening volume and movement. Both works save their maximum expressiveness for the third volume and movement, being content in the central ones to present commonplace material exempt from uncommon stress. These tendencies are present both in spirit and structure.

THE SECOND MOVEMENT of K. 503, like the first, follows the basic outlines of sonata-allegro form. Yet this Andante lacks the kind of pressure the form often engenders. It is a sonata-form movement without any great thematic contrast, without a dramatic development section, and without striking differences between the orchestral exposition, the solo exposition, and the recapitulation. Yet it is not wholly uneventful. Indeed, it is, as Girdlestone says, "one of Mozart's most original slow movements" (p. 435)—though its secrets and beauties are often unrevealed in performance.

The opening theme group is a slowly winding, somewhat diffuse melody in the orchestra that floats out over twelve measures, mostly on the breath of the winds. The second and third groups are short and are based on short motifs. This orchestral exposition extends only twenty-two bars—as compared to ninety in the first movement. Its "material" is even less striking than that of the Allegro maestoso, though it is extremely sonorous if played with imagination and listened to attentively. Like the first sixteen bars of the second movement of K. 271, this short exposition provides the essential material for the movement. As in the first movement of K. 503, the solo is allowed to introduce its own theme in its exposition; here too the solo theme is the most melodic of the movement. But the solo theme does not even return in the recapitulation of this Andante. Typically, one of the most expressive sections of the Andante of K. 503 is the nonthematic transitional passage that takes the place of the development section (bars 58–73). Particularly beautiful is the retransition itself (bars 66–73), which is as expansive and spacious and composed as the two-bar retransition of the earlier Andantino is compressed, intense, and painful.

This Andante is difficult to perform. Neither its shape nor its grace are easily transmitted—or received. As Girdlestone writes, the movement expresses "a deep feeling which has some difficulty in uttering itself" (p. 435). This is true even during a good performance. The conductor must find a tempo slow enough not to trivialize the musical material, at the same time giving continuity to stunted rhythms and melodies whose direction and pulse are not always clear. The soloist, too, must find a way to enliven the commonplace material. Many pianists have tried to "jazz up" this movement, to decorate it so as to cover up some of the bare spots.[6] But one pianist who has done so, Charles Rosen, now regrets it (p. 258). Without a doubt, the F-major Andante is a strange and elusive movement. Its emotional burden is as concealed and suspended as that of the C-minor Andantino is overt and impassioned. Yet in a successful performance (such as the recording by Friedrich Gulda, Claudio Abbado, and the Vienna Philharmonic) it can be deeply expressive. Much of its built-in expression depends upon the intimate interaction of solo and orchestra.

The second volume of *Emma*, like the second movement of K. 503, closely follows the overt structure of the opening volume. Again there are eighteen chapters. The first nine chapters build up to and conclude with the dinner at the Coles and its aftermath the next day. The second nine chapters build up to and conclude with the party at Hartfield. The action in volume 2 seems at first sight as mysterious and inconsequent as the themes of the Andante. Much of it ostensibly revolves around Jane Fairfax and Frank Churchill, but little is actually learned about them. The garrulous Miss Bates seems almost to be the central character early in the volume, with the vulgar Mrs. Elton taking over at the end: not until the third volume do we learn why so much time and space have been devoted to either one. Furthermore, Emma's own role in volume 2 is less striking than in the opening volume. Even so, Emma's interaction with others is of great interest here—as is that of the piano with the orchestra in the Andante.

The solo voice in the Andante is no longer the headstrong virtuoso of the Allegro maestoso. Here the solo closely follows the material of the orchestra, even though that material is designed to display the winds much more than the keyboard. At the beginning of the orchestral exposition (Figure 9), the short melodic arcs that dominate the first four bars are given in octaves to the flute, bassoons, and first violins (punctuated by the full orchestra in the second bar). In bars 5 and 7 the F-

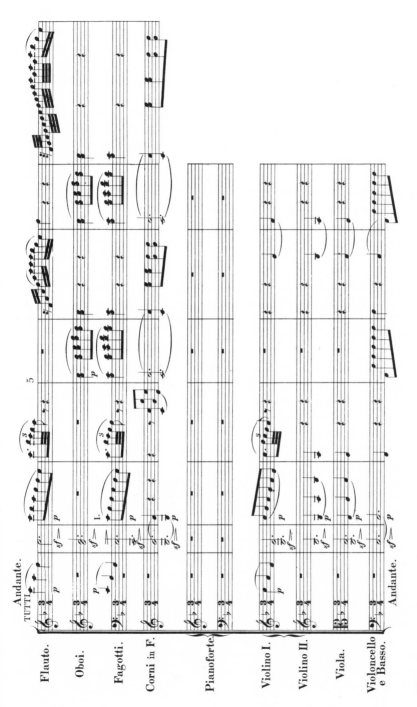

Figure 9

major harmony is securely established with a simple figure played by oboes, bassoons, horns, cellos, and basses; in bars 6 and 8 the harmony is further reiterated by simple passagework in the flute.

In the solo exposition (beginning bar 23), the piano, so independent in the first movement, follows the above pattern of the orchestra with extreme fidelity. It follows the melodic arcs of the first three-and-a-half bars note for note and it also duplicates the simple passagework played by the flute, the only difference being that it begins with the second, more rapid of the flute passages. This allows the piano to take its own second scale passage somewhat higher—all the way, in fact, to the high F that had previously been reached only by the flute on the last note of the orchestral exposition. In this modest but highly imaginative way, the piano makes its own contribution to the affirmation of the prevailing key.

The melodic pattern of the two expositions is repeated at the beginning of the recapitulation—with the important difference that now the horns and the piano share the first arc of the melody (bars 74–75). Here we have simultaneous note-for-note sharing of thematic material between piano and orchestra for the first time in the entire concerto. Yet the solo deftly manages to maintain some individuality by subdividing each quarter note into four sixteenth notes and distributing three of them an octave higher. These decorations, unlike those the solo made in the first movement, clarify rather than blur. Because they fully complement the melody, harmony, and rhythm of the familiar quarter notes held by the horns, they create an effect not of cross-purposes but of deepened harmony.

This harmonious sharing of the opening theme measures the progress of the movement itself. First played by the orchestra alone, then by the piano alone, the opening material is now shared by both. Although the horn-piano collaboration at the beginning of the recapitulation is the most obvious example of harmonious togetherness in the Andante, it is far from the only one. At the end of the solo exposition, the piano makes a somewhat extended improvisation on the orchestra's closing material that is then lovingly answered by the winds, both here and in the recapitulation. The retransition, mentioned earlier, is another example of intimate sharing. It begins (bar 66) with a short motif in the piano that is answered by the flute and that melts into suspended magic as airy arpeggios in the piano blend perfectly with held notes in the flute and horns, with simple stepwise motions in the oboes and bassoons, and with an occasional woodwind trill. The suspended magic ends only when the piano and horns descend from this sonic heaven with the opening melodic arc between them. The piano and winds, so often at odds in the first movement, now complement each other perfectly.

They do so again in the final bar (109) of the Andante (Figure 10). As

Figure 10

the winds slowly move a step down to arrive at the final F-major chord, the piano briskly ascends a step plus an octave while the basses quietly descend an octave. The notes the piano plays—a simple ascending scale, doubled in octaves—are exactly the notes with which the flute and bassoons had ended the orchestral exposition (bar 22). This is the final example in the movement of the solo's ability not only to follow the lead of the orchestra but to integrate its own movements within those of others. The result is one bar of music in which the vertical integration among a melodic fragment in the winds, passagework in the piano, and a rhythmic figure in the strings is harmonious and complete. It sums up the essence of the relationship among the instrumental forces in this movement as succinctly as the last bar of the bassoon-oboe melody (Figure 8) did for the first movement. The contrary motion is similar, but here the effect is wholly harmonious.

A final example of harmonious sharing in the Andante of K. 503 involves omission. As mentioned above, the most interesting melodic material in this movement, as in the previous one, is a new theme introduced by the piano in the solo exposition. In the Allegro maestoso, the piano reasserted its solo material in the recapitulation—at the same time that it showed only limited interest in the orchestra's material. In the Andante, the piano omits its own theme from the recapitulation and turns, instead, to the further sharing with which the movement concludes.

As in the Andantino of K. 271, the ending of this movement is exhilarating because the orchestra's original burden has been increasingly shared by the solo. Granted, the emotional burden and the melodic material of this movement are not nearly so dramatic or sharply defined; even so, the process of sharing is comparable. In each case, the solo, without losing its individuality, achieves a partnership with the orchestra different in kind from the one achieved in the opening movement.

Like the piano in the second movement, Emma is less headstrong in the second volume. Somewhat chastened after Mr. Elton's proposal to *her*, she is slightly less interested in managing the lives of others or in attracting unexpected attention to herself. Because of this, volume 2 lacks the kind of dramatic recognition that occurred in chapters 15 and 16 of volume 1. Instead, one feels that Emma is preparing and waiting for something unknown. She observes others more closely and with sympathy. The most interesting feelings in the volume belong not to her but to Harriet Smith and Jane Fairfax. Emma's growth, like that of the solo in the Andante, is measured by the delicacy and imagination with which she responds.

In chapter 3 Harriet is thrilled to learn of the "real feeling" still shown by Robert Martin and his sisters toward her. Emma hardly approves of Harriet's rekindled enthusiasm, but she does honor Harriet's response to the Martins' "interesting mixture of wounded affection and genuine delicacy" (p. 120). Emma does not know whether to "rejoice or be angry, ashamed or only amused" at Harriet's continuing susceptibility to Martin so soon after loving Mr. Elton, but she does now instinctively know that Harriet's feelings are worthy of sympathetic attention. When breaking the news to Harriet of Mr. Elton's abrupt decision to marry someone from out of town, Emma allows her still-wounded friend to talk herself "into all the sensations of curiosity, wonder and regret, pain and pleasure, as to this fortunate Miss Hawkins" (p. 121).

In chapter 8 Harriet makes her first public appearance after being mortified by Mr. Elton's decision to marry somebody else. As Harriet arrives at the Coles' party, Emma is able to register and to appreciate her simple composure. Emma

> could not only love the blooming sweetness and the artless manner, but could most heartily rejoice in that light, cheerful, unsentimental disposition which allowed [Harriet] so many alleviations of pleasure, in the midst of the pangs of disappointed affection. There she sat—and who would have guessed how many tears she had been lately shedding? To be in company, nicely dressed herself and seeing others nicely dressed, to sit and smile and look pretty, and say nothing, was enough for the happiness of the present hour. (p. 148)

Harriet's happiness is conventional and inexpressive; Emma's response to it is imaginative and full.

Of course Emma, at the Coles' party, is not satisfied with watching only Harriet. Soon she turns her attention to Jane Fairfax—and to her own suppositions about her. Before Jane arrives, Emma has been discussing her at length with Frank Churchill. Their conversation has revealed Emma to be in some ways unchanged from chapter 9 of volume 1. Responding to the news that Jane has mysteriously received a new square pianoforte from some unknown source, Emma has solved the riddle as quickly and as mistakenly as she solved Mr. Elton's charade. Her extended explanation to Frank Churchill that Mrs. Dixon, not the Campbells, as generally surmised, had certainly given the piano is, in view of the fact that Frank himself had actually given it, an irony as delicious as was her extended explanation to Harriet that Harriet was the object of Mr. Elton's riddle. Yet Emma, if wrong, is wrong partly because Churchill is willing to deceive her—and the rest of the village as well. Furthermore, she is this time wrong in a restrained rather than a meddlesome way. With some delicacy she refrains from asking Jane, when she enters, about the instrument. Instead she notes, from across the room, the "blush of consciousness" with which Jane responds to the pressing queries of others (p. 148). Emma, though equally curious, is sensitive enough to recognize that Jane would prefer to be speaking of something else.

Emma herself experiences two difficult moments at the party. The first is when Mrs. Weston suggests the probability of a match between Jane Fairfax and Mr. Knightley. Emma, who has no conscious interest in Mr. Knightley for herself, and who has been flattered by Churchill's attentions at the party, reacts rather violently. "Mr. Knightley and Jane Fairfax! . . . Dear Mrs. Weston, how could you think of such a thing?— Mr. Knightley!—Mr. Knightley must not marry!—You would not have little Henry cut out from Donwell?—Oh! no, no, Henry must have Donwell. I cannot at all consent to Mr. Knightley's marrying; and I am sure it is not at all likely" (p. 151). This impulsive outburst suggests that Emma cares for Mr. Knightley more deeply than she knows—or will know, until well into volume 3.

Her second difficult moment comes at the Coles' grand pianoforte, when both she and Jane are expected to perform. Emma knows that Jane has more talent and taste than she. Yet she manages to play, within her limits, most successfully. Accustomed to being the undisputed center of attention in Highbury, Emma has "mixed feelings" as Jane plays. Even so, she is able to acknowledge that Jane's "performance, both vocal and instrumental . . . was infinitely superior to her own" (p. 154). The next day, at the beginning of chapter 9, she does not so much resent the superiority of Jane's playing as regret the inferiority of her own. She impulsively sits down to practice for an hour and a half—until she is interrupted by Harriet, who offers sincere, if fawning, praise of Emma's playing the night before. Emma, showing a just appreciation not only of Jane's talent but of her own limitations, replies: "My playing is no more like her's, than a lamp is like sunshine" (p. 156). Her awareness of limitations and her appreciation of "the other" is new in this volume, and it corresponds to the growth of the solo in the Andante of K. 503.

At the beginning of chapter 10, Emma and Mrs. Weston enter the Bateses' sitting room. "The appearance of the little sitting-room as they entered, was tranquility itself" (p. 162). But in Austen's world, as in Mozart's, the appearance of tranquility often hides deep tensions straining to express themselves or to hold themselves back. Frank is sitting at a table. Jane is standing before her instrument. Although neither Emma nor the reader knows it, they have been arguing over his gift of the piano. They show no overt signs that this is so, but Emma, increasingly attuned to the feelings of others, senses that Jane is in a high state of nervousness strongly repressed. She sees that Jane is not "quite ready to sit down to the pianoforte again." Suspecting the hesitancy to "arise from the state of her nerves," Emma "could not but pity such feelings, whatever their origin" (pp. 162–63). In chapter 16 she finds occasion to be more actively sympathetic toward Jane and her unexpressed feelings.

On the morning of the dinner party at Hartfield, Jane Fairfax is observed to have gone to the post office even though it is raining. Neither the reader nor Emma knows why she has gone there, but both the reader and Emma can see that Jane is shaken by the manner in which she responds to Mr. John Knightley's polite commentary upon her morning excursion. One of his comments, in particular, was "kindly said, and very far from giving offence. A pleasant 'thank you' seemed meant to laugh it off, but a blush, a quivering lip, a tear in the eye, shewed that it was felt beyond a laugh" (pp. 199–200). Jane, whatever the reason for her agitation, must next shift her attention to the mindless urbanity of Mr. Woodhouse—and then to the mindless vulgarity of Mrs. Elton. In fact, she is forced to endure a veritable "theme and variations" on the subject of her trip to the post office.

This episode reveals all the poverty of conversation of which the assembled guests are capable and none of the further pain that Jane is no doubt experiencing. In such a situation, silence and restraint are the measures of taste, and these are qualities that Emma is now able to display. Though intensely curious herself, she refrains from entering in with her own questions. Chapter 16 of volume 2 ends with the kind of understated delicacy and togetherness with which the Andante of K. 503 ends. Emma "could have made an inquiry or two . . . —it was at her tongue's end—but she abstained. She was quite determined not to utter a word that should hurt Jane Fairfax's feelings; and they followed the other ladies out of the room, arm in arm, with an appearance of goodwill highly becoming to the beauty and grace of each" (p. 203). This moment of silent togetherness does not have the overt drama of Elizabeth's silent response to Darcy's letter in volume 2 of *Pride and Prejudice*, but it does reveal, in its own expressive way, striking growth in the heroine. Abstention, for Emma, is as heroic as acceptance of humiliation is for Elizabeth.

The social grace and true supportiveness of which Emma now is capable stands in eloquent contrast to the social vulgarity and false supportiveness displayed by Mrs. Elton in the last two chapters of the volume. The narrator does not call attention to Mrs. Elton's stupendous banality. Rather she invites such attention by the taste with which she allows tastelessness to be revealed. Inattentive readers will miss the impact of Mrs. Elton's speech, but the attentive will shudder from it, just as they will delight in the understated but powerful paragraph that ends volume 2 with the tight finality of a Mozartean cadence: "Mr. Knightley seemed to be trying not to smile; and succeeded without difficulty, upon Mrs. Elton's beginning to talk to him" (p. 213).

The Experience of Maturity

ONE MEASURE of the extent to which Austen "circled her domain with her first steps" is the similarity between the last volume of *Emma* and its counterpart in *Pride and Prejudice*. One measure of the extent to which she "progressed into the depths of her own soul" is the difference between the two volumes. Volume 3 of *Emma* is strikingly similar to its earlier counterpart in length, plot components, and overt structure. It is strikingly different in mood, internal dynamics, and breadth of treatment.

Each concluding volume consists of nineteen chapters. But the final volume of *Emma* is deeper in feeling and more spacious in treatment. In both novels, the final volume includes the heroine's first extended visit to the hero's estate, the heroine's first recognition that she loves him, a dramatic obstacle to that love, the overcoming of the obstacle, the successful proposal, and the marriage. But in *Emma* these events occur in a different order—and they have a different meaning. Volume 3 of each novel has a three-part structure resulting from the fact that the main love-match is seemingly suspended during the middle chapters. Yet in *Emma* the suspension of the match occurs before Emma knows that she loves Knightley. Moreover, it is caused by her own action, rather than that of others (i.e., Lydia's elopement with Wickham). As a result, these chapters during which the progress of her match with Knightley is suspended are also the chapters in which both she and the match are most dramatically growing. Because Emma's growth is both painful and self-reflexive, the "apparatus of happiness" of the third volume of *Emma* incorporates the kind of starkness, darkness, and melancholy that in *Pride and Prejudice* was centered in the second volume. Elizabeth Bennet grew in volume 2 and learned to wait in volume 3. Emma Woodhouse learned to wait in volume 2; she blossoms in volume 3.

THE EMMA WHO opens volume 3 of the novel is much altered from the Emma who opened volume 1. She is subdued, sensitive, introspective.

> A very little quiet reflection was enough to satisfy Emma as to the nature of her agitation on hearing this news of Frank Churchill. She was soon convinced that it was not for herself she was feeling at all apprehensive or embarrassed; it was for him. Her own attachment had really subsided into a mere nothing; it was not worth thinking of;—but if he, who had undoubtedly been always so much the most in love of the two, were to be returning with the same warmth of sentiment which he had taken away, it would be very distressing. If a separation of two months should not have cooled him, there were dangers and evils before her:—caution for him and for herself would be necessary. She did not mean to have her own affections entangled again, and it would be incumbent on her to avoid any encouragement of his. (pp. 213–14)

In addition to being subdued, sensitive, and introspective, Emma, of course, is wrong. If Frank is returning with "warmth of sentiment" it is for Jane, not for her, though there is no way she can know it. Eager to avoid the kind of mistake she made with Mr. Elton in volume 1, she is leaning too far backward. But she is leaning in the right direction, which is an important change.

Because the action moves so quickly in volume 3, Emma is able to learn from her mistakes and grow more rapidly than in the previous volumes. Here the large-group events, so evenly spaced in volumes 1 and 2, fall upon one another with a rapidity unique in Austen's fiction. The long-awaited ball at the Crown occurs in chapter 2. The narrator's presentation of the interrelations among a multitude of characters there is a perfect example of the mature Austen's ability to make the common-place exciting. It is also an example of the expressiveness (both short- and long-range) of the novel's structure. In its internal symmetry and in its progression from an edgy coexistence among the characters toward a more intimate harmony, chapter 2 of volume 3 is a microcosm of the novel itself. Its combination of breadth of treatment and economy of means rivals that of chapter 9 of volume 1, just as many of its events and complications have their source in that much earlier chapter.

The day of the ball is announced as arbitrarily as a new scene in an *opera buffa*: "The day approached, the day arrived." Emma at first is honored that Mr. Weston requested her to come early to the Crown. But she discovers that he asked everyone else to arrive early too, so there was no distinction in it. Frank Churchill thinks it won't be long before Mrs. Elton arrives. The next sentence reads: "A carriage was heard." The Eltons are in it. But they have forgotten to stop for Miss Bates and Jane Fairfax. "The carriage was sent for them now." "In a few minutes the carriage returned." Though as dry as a *secco recitative*, this narration is a pointed commentary on the Eltons' thoughtlessness—especially for the reader who remembers Mr. Knightley's thoughtfulness (noted by Emma) in chapter 8 of volume 2, when he went out of his way to bring the same Miss Bates and Miss Fairfax to the Coles' party.

There is conversation before the dancing. Mrs. Elton, after knowing Frank Churchill for a few minutes, praises him for not being a "puppy." Miss Bates enters with sixty-two lines of mindless and unanswerable chatter. Mrs. Elton breaks in. After praising her own clothes, she praises Frank Churchill again. Frank begins to talk "so vigorously" as to "drown the voices of the ladies," until "another suspension brought Mrs. Elton's tone distinctly forward." Now Mr. Elton adds his wit to the conversa-tion—until the dancing begins. Emma dances with Frank and enjoys it but is disturbed to see Mr. Knightley standing alone. The progress of the ball itself is summarized in these words: "Of very important, very recordable events, it was not more productive than such meetings usually are" (p. 222).

One event, however, is recorded. Emma, dancing, sees Mr. Elton "sauntering about" in the area of Harriet, who, like him, is not dancing. She sees and hears the clergyman purposely snub Harriet and then, after doing so, exchange "little smiles of high glee" with his wife. Emma is so angered "she would not look again. Her heart was in a glow, and she feared her face might be as hot." (Such language is as moving in Austen as it is rare.) But suddenly Emma sees that Mr. Knightley has asked Harriet to dance. "Never had she been more surprised, seldom more delighted, than at that instant. She was all pleasure and gratitude, both for Harriet and herself, and longed to be thanking him; and though too distant for speech, her countenance said much, as soon as she could catch his eye again" (p. 223). Knightley's action is doubly significant to the reader who remembers that he has previously shown little sympathy for either Harriet or dancing. This one "recordable event" concludes with Mrs. Elton's graciously hypocritical words: "Knightley has taken pity on poor little Miss Smith!—Very goodnatured, I declare."

Immediately the narrator's *secco recitative* marks a transition: "Supper was announced. The move began; and Miss Bates might be heard from that moment, without interruption, till her being seated at the table and taking up her spoon." Fifty lines later her monologue ends with these words: "Soup too! Bless me! I should not be helped so soon, but it smells most excellent, and I cannot help beginning" (p. 224). She lowers her spoon having spoken a monologue that, structurally, balances with perfect symmetry the equally inconsequent monologue she had uttered before the dancing began.

After supper Emma finds an opportunity to thank Mr. Knightley for his gallantry to Harriet. She also confesses to him the extent of her earlier meddling with Harriet and Mr. Elton. He praises her friend Harriet. This is the most pleasant conversation they have had in the course of the novel; when Mr. Weston interrupts, asking everybody to dance, it becomes even more pleasant.

> "I am ready," said Emma, "whenever I am wanted."
> "Whom are you going to dance with?" asked Mr. Knightley.
> She hesitated a moment, and then replied, "With you, if you will ask me."
> "Will you?" said he, offering his hand.
> "Indeed I will. You have shown that you can dance, and you know we are not really so much brother and sister as to make it at all improper."
> "Brother and sister! no indeed." (p. 225)

The main love match is finally under way. Quite a time remains, however, before either Emma or Knightley will acknowledge it.

After the commonplace but emotionally complex evening at the ball, Emma, at the beginning of chapter 3, is walking about on the lawn. She is mulling over the paradox that "the impertinence of the Eltons, which for a few mintues had threatened to ruin the rest of her evening, had been the occasion of some of its highest satisfactions." She is calm, she is happy, she has "arranged all these matters, looked them through, and put them all to rights," when Harriet appears on the arm of Frank Churchill. As soon as they are indoors, Emma sees Harriet sink into a chair and "faint away." Before informing the reader—or Emma—of Harriet's encounter with the gypsies, the narrator drily states that "a young lady who faints, must be recovered; questions must be answered, and surprises be explained. Such events are very interesting, but the suspense of them cannot last long. A few minutes made Emma acquainted with the whole" (p. 226). This episode recalls numerous moments in Mozart's operas and piano concertos in which a tranquil musical passage is briefly invaded by a theme in the minor mode that, though moving enough in itself, is not to be taken too seriously because it will be swiftly supplanted.

Soon after this brief crisis is over, a series of large-group events in chapters 5, 6, and 7 provide crises of emotion and situation that are less overt but more lasting. The alphabet game at Hartfield, the strawberry party at Donwell Abbey, and the excursion to Box Hill are full of intricate shiftings of understanding and of misunderstanding. During the indoors alphabet game, Emma, Frank, and Jane are as deceived and self-deceived as were Emma, Harriet, and Mr. Elton over the charade in volume 1. During the outdoors strawberry party, the splendid midsummer ambiance is darkened by the presence of Mrs. Elton, the absence of Frank Churchill, and the premature departure of Jane Fairfax. The equally splendid outdoor setting for the Box Hill excursion is marred not only by Emma's cruelty to Miss Bates but by the general lack of harmony among the entire party. Yet some of the emotions and sensations that stand out from these complex chapters are very simple: Emma's heartfelt declaration to Knightley at the end of chapter 5 that there can be nothing between Jane and Frank; Emma's simple enjoyment of the "delicious shade" at Knightley's estate; and Emma's deep remorse as she rides home from Box Hill after the discussion with Knightley over her cruelty to Miss Bates. Emma's remorse is so intense that it carries the novel onto a new—and simpler—plane.

Just as the scene at Donwell Abbey is one of the most pastoral in mood and luxuriant in sensory details in all of Austen's fiction, so is the subsequent outdoors scene at Box Hill one of the most cramped and claustrophobic. After Emma's warm response to a departing Jane Fairfax in chapter 6 shows her increasing ability to empathize with others, her casual coldness to Miss Bates in chapter 7 shows her need to continue to grow. No less than Mozart does Austen create an artistic world in which a single word, note, or phrase can have the effect of a crime or revolution, and no episode in her fiction shows this aspect of her art more clearly than the famous one at Box Hill.

Frank Churchill is flirting with Emma, who is responding with forced gaiety. No one else is helping much to keep the conversation going, and when Mrs. Elton or Miss Bates speak it is never to raise the tone of the exchange. Frank proposes a diversion.

> "Ladies and gentlemen—I am ordered by Miss Woodhouse to say, that she waives her right of knowing exactly what you may all be thinking of, and only requires something very entertaining from each of you, in a general way. Here are seven of you, besides myself . . . and she only demands from each of you either one thing very clever . . . —or two things moderately clever—or three things very dull indeed, and she engages to laugh heartily at them all."
>
> "Oh! very well," exclaimed Miss Bates, "then I need not be uneasy. 'Three things very dull indeed.' That will just do for me, you know. I shall be sure to say three dull things as soon as ever I open my mouth, shan't I?—(looking round with the most good-humoured dependence on every body's assent)—Do not you all think I shall?"
>
> Emma could not resist.
>
> "Ah! ma'am, but there may be a difficulty. Pardon me—but you will be limited as to number—only three at once." (pp. 253–54)

Emma, for whom it is heroic to abstain, here has not been able to. But her lapse does not become an issue until the end of the chapter, when Knightley rebukes her for it. She at first resents his criticism, and by the time she comes to feel the force of what she has done it is too late to let Knightley know. She is so "paralyzed" that she has "no tongue, no motion" (pp. 257–58). Knightley helps her into a carriage, but turns away before she can speak.

The carriage ride that closes chapter 7 is the one that carries the novel onto a new plane. "Time did not compose" Emma. As she rides silently in the company of Harriet, "extraordinary" and unchecked tears run down her cheeks "almost all the way home" (p. 258). Her mortification is as deep as it was during the carriage ride with Mr. Elton in volume 1, but there, at least, he had shared the responsibility for her acute discomfort. The current situation she has brought entirely upon herself. Abandoning herself to remorse, she experiences a "spontaneous overflow of powerful feelings" of the kind that Wordsworth felt to be the source of all poetry and truth. It will be some time before she will be able to recollect those feelings in tranquility.

At the beginning of chapter 8, Emma finds the events of the previous day fit only to be "abhorred in recollection" (p. 258). She visits the Bateses in order to act as generously as she can, but when she learns that Jane must soon leave town she feels even more remorse for not having been more of a friend to her. The mood brightens briefly in chapter 9 when she encounters Knightley upon her return from the Bateses. Emma sees, from his countenance, that he recognizes her remorse. He takes her hand and almost kisses it. But instead he departs abruptly for London. And Jane, to whom she wishes to be helpful, repulses her offers of goodwill.

In chapter 10 Emma is shocked by the news of Jane's engagement to Frank Churchill. This news doubles her remorse for her own conduct toward Jane and it reveals a new cause for sorrow: her realization that she has vainly encouraged Harriet to have hopes for Churchill. In chapter 11 she has the painful obligation of breaking the news to Harriet. But now she has a new shock. She discovers that in encouraging Harriet to love the unnamed Churchill she has actually encouraged Harriet's hopes for Knightley. What is worse, Emma discovers at the same moment that she herself loves Knightley. Remorseful for having encouraged Harriet and fearful of losing to her the man she now loves herself, Emma must listen with "much inward suffering" and "great outward patience" as Harriet explains why she has cause to believe that Knightley is in love with her (p. 281). This painful encounter ends only when Mr. Woodhouse interrupts. Emma's bruised yet lucid meditation at the end of the chapter is the emotional, moral, and intellectual equivalent of Elizabeth's meditation in chapter 13 of volume 2.

As with Elizabeth's first reaction to Darcy's letter, Emma's first response to the encounter with Harriet is to wish to forget it. "This was the spontaneous burst of Emma's feelings: 'Oh God! that I had never seen her!'" (p. 283). But Emma's deeper impulse, like that of Elizabeth, is to understand "the blunders, the blindness of her own head and heart!" She now reconsiders her actions "in every place, every posture": "she sat still, she walked about, she tried her own room, she tried the shrubbery." The result is a hard-won understanding not only of her own vanity and arrogance, of her own mistakes and mischief, but of her own love for Knightley—which she now realizes had always existed, even when thinking she cared for Frank Churchill. Recognition of that love, of course, only renders her the more miserable.

The dark mood carries over into chapter 12. A conversation with Mrs. Weston helps her to see that she must have "stabbed Jane Fairfax's peace in a thousand instances" whenever she, Jane, and Frank were together (p. 290). Emma grandly decides that she must in all conscience renounce the possibility of her own happiness. "The evening of this day was very long, and melancholy, at Hartfield." She is alone with her father and she resigns herself to being so for the rest of her life. As was the case during her recognition in volume 1 (the frost-bound meditation following the carriage ride with Mr. Elton), the weather at the end of chapter 12 is described in a way that closely parallels her emotional state. "A cold stormy rain set in, and nothing of July appeared but in the trees and shrubs, which the wind was despoiling, and the length of the day, which only made such cruel sights the longer visible" (p. 290). At the brink of chapter 13, her now-acknowledged love for Knightley corresponds to the something "of July" which the "wind" of her multiple misdeeds is "despoiling."

The transition to bliss in the state of the weather and of Emma's emotions is as deft, sudden, and sensuously rendered as such rapid yet lasting transitions often are in Mozart. Here are the first five sentences of chapter 13.

> The weather continued much the same all the following morning; and the same loneliness, and the same melancholy, seemed to reign at Hartfield—but in the afternoon it cleared; the wind changed into a softer quarter; the clouds were carried off; the sun appeared; it was summer again. With all the eagerness which such a transition gives, Emma resolved to be out of doors as soon as possible. Never had the exquisite sight, smell, sensation of nature, tranquil, warm, and brilliant after a storm, been more attractive to her. She longed for the serenity they might gradually introduce; and on Mr. Perry's coming in soon after dinner, with a disengaged hour to give her father, she lost no time hurrying into the shrubbery.— There, with spirits freshened, and thoughts a little relieved, she had taken a few turns, when she saw Mr. Knightley passing through the garden door, and coming towards her. (p. 291)

The change of weather is unequivocal: in the long-range architecture of the novel the exquisite sensations of summer balance and displace the December snow that had provided the backdrop for Mr. Elton's proposal in volume 1. Whether the sudden appearance of Mr. Knightley will balance and displace the sorrow and remorse that have chilled Emma to the core is a matter of some suspense. They take two turns through the shrubbery, and the first is far from providing the serenity she longs for. Fearing that he is about to tell her of his love for Harriet, she forbids his speaking; he, having suddenly been moved to declare his love for *her*, feels she does not want to hear him. On their second turn over the same ground, however, the obstacles that had blocked the enunciation of love evaporate as suddenly as had the previous day's summer shower. Their love is spoken, as it has been earned.

Six leisurely chapters are required to conclude the novel. Emma has experienced such an "exquisite flutter of happiness" that it takes a while for the "fever" to subside (pp. 298, 299). She and Knightley need time to share their new joy and to plan ways in which to protect the feelings of both Harriet and Mr. Woodhouse. The newest complications involving Frank and Jane must be considered and understood, and of course Mrs. Elton and Miss Bates must be heard. These minor obstacles are worthy of attention, but none of them are a threat. The novel ends with the September wedding of Harriet Smith and Robert Martin, the October wedding of Emma Woodhouse and George Knightley, and the anticipated November wedding of Jane Fairfax and Frank Churchill. Its concluding paragraph incorporates with uncommon ease dissonant notes that in another context might have been thoroughly disruptive.

> The wedding was very much like other weddings, where the parties have no taste for finery or parade; and Mrs. Elton, from the particulars detailed by her husband, thought it all extremely shabby, and very inferior to her own.—"Very little white satin, very few lace veils; a most pitiful business!—Selina would stare when she heard of it."—But, in spite of these deficiencies, the wishes, the hopes, the confidence, the predictions of the small band of true friends who witnessed the ceremony, were fully answered in the perfect happiness of the union. (pp. 334–35)

Mrs. Elton's off-key phrases no more detract from the harmony of the wedding than the abrupt C-minor departures in the first movement of K. 503 detract from its massive C-major harmony.

The final volume of *Emma*, then, gives to a novel whose first volume is less colorful than its counterpart in *Pride and Prejudice*, and whose second volume is less dramatically intense, a conclusion which makes absolute virtues out of what earlier might have seemed faults. Its ending is as "happy" as that of the earlier novel, but it incorporates greater discord. This is true not only of the last paragraph but of the last volume as a whole. Volume 3 of *Emma* is an "apparatus of happiness" that contains within it a "span of tragic grief" (to use Rosen's phrase for the Andantino of K. 271). That span reaches from chapter 7 to chapter 13. Within its "delicious shade" all of the latent growth that had been buried beneath the subtle ironies of volume 1 and the suspended mysteries of volume 2 comes to full fruition in the high summer of volume 3. The concluding volume of *Emma*, with its shapely organic form and its spontaneous overflow of feeling, turns a novel that might have been as commonplace and dull as its "material" into one of the maturest masterpieces of English fiction.

THE LAST MOVEMENT of K. 503 is to the last movement of K. 271 as the last volume of *Emma* is to the last volume of *Pride and Prejudice*. As with Austen's volumes, the similarities between the two movements measure the extent to which Mozart "circled his domain with his first steps"; the differences measure "progress into the depths of his own soul." The Allegretto of K. 503 is remarkably similar to its counterpart in K. 271 in length, balance among the forces, and overt structure. It is remarkably different in mood, distribution of balance, and internal dynamics.

The finale of each concerto is a rondo in a:b:a:c:a:b:a form that lasts ten to eleven minutes. But the Allegretto of K. 503 is more varied in feeling and more complex in texture. In each case the central episode (or "c" section) is so expansive that it has the effect of suspending the progress of the movement as a whole. But in K. 503 the episode that suspends the progress of the movement is also the one in which the movement (and the solo) grows most intensely. Each movement achieves a lively equilibrium between solo and orchestra that grounds the tensions of the earlier movements. But the attainment of equilibrium in K. 503 is less immediate, the internal threats to it more severe. Because of the nature of those threats, the last movement of K. 503 incorporates some of the starkness, darkness, and melancholy that in K. 271 was centered in the second movement. Both its emotional dynamics and its formal structure compare closely with those of volume 3 of *Emma*.

Just as the paragraph devoted to Emma that begins volume 3 is subdued and introspective compared to its counterpart in volume 1, so is the orchestral refrain that opens the Allegretto of K. 503 subdued and introspective compared to the majestic, spacious chords that opened the Allegro maestoso. Girdlestone observes that "the chief difference between this movement and the first is the absence of heroic accents" (p. 435). One hears this difference in the opening notes—just as one reads it in the opening words of volume 3. Indeed, volume 3 of *Emma* differs from volume 1 chiefly in the "absence of heroic accents" in the heroine.

As Girdlestone points out, the refrain and the episodes of this Allegretto "have nothing of the merry tone of the usual rondo." This is easily demonstrated by contrast with the finale of K. 271. The opening refrain of the earlier rondo had begun with thirty-four measures of exhilarating perpetual motion. The moment the solo had completed its opening sprint, the orchestra had responded in kind, and together the two forces had extended the continuous motion all the way to bar 82—where the solo had picked up the baton again and carried the breathless pace all the way through the first couplet to the pause on the dominant at bar 149. A "flutter of high spirits" had prevailed throughout. The Allegretto's opening refrain, by contrast, is more tentative than jaunty. It is more deliberate and compact. The refrain per se is compressed into twenty-three bars. These are divided into six distinct, though closely related, phrase groups, the first two in the strings, the next two in the winds, the last two led by the strings. A busy orchestral codetta (bars 24–32) concludes the refrain.

Whereas the opening refrain of the earlier work had run on in an unflagging and exhilarating E-flat major, this refrain contains a modulation to the tonic minor similar to the one found early in the first movement of K. 503. The opening phrase, from which the others derive, is solidly in the home key of C major (though it is colored by a C-sharp in measure four). The next four phrases are equally anchored in C major.

Figure 11

But the last phrase of the refrain per se, the one begun low in the basses and then extended by the higher strings and woodwinds, modulates strikingly to C minor (bars 16–23). The home key of C major is strongly reasserted in the codetta, but any listener familiar with Mozart's generally "merry" rondo refrains feels that this one is taking a new path. In Girdlestone's words, the opening refrain is "tinted with melancholy, serious, almost brooding, and full of languishing grace unexpected in a concerto finale" (p. 436).

The first couplet (the "b" section) is as expansive as the refrain was compact. The solo, assuming control from the start, introduces three well-spaced themes. The first is of the "personal" variety it had played in the earlier movements (bars 32–46), the second contains only the barest outline of a melody (bars 62–66), and the third, after some hesitation, turns into a rather flowing melody with a glancing relation to the opening of the refrain (bars 73–82). The latter melody draws out a lovely answer from the winds (bars 83–90), but apart from that the couplet is dominated by the solo, which makes as much of an impression with its flowing passagework as it does with the themes themselves. A long transition led by the piano (bars 91–113) leads to a return of the refrain, now played by the solo for the first time. This transition, which Girdlestone calls "the most sustained and perhaps the grandest in all Mozart," is "based entirely on a dominant pedal adorned by scales and fragments of arpeggios" (p. 436). None the less it is dramatic; it passes briefly into the minor and features a short but intense stretch of nonthematic sharing between piano and winds such as had occasionally been heard in the previous movements.

Until the response by the woodwind to the solo's third theme, the orchestra and piano have been equal but separate partners in the first two sections of this rondo. The one has dominated the refrain, the other the couplet, and very little material has actually been shared. The orchestra is firm, compact, self-contained. The solo is assured, expansive, self-reliant. They can interact, if need be—just as Emma and Knightley can dance together at the Crown, if circumstances suggest. But the solo and orchestra do not yet seem to need, or respond to, each other with the intensity of their counterparts in the opening section of K. 271—or of Elizabeth and Darcy at Pemberly. In the earlier rondo, the orchestra had immediately answered the animated phrase with which the piano had opened the refrain (bars 35–43). The piano had then lovingly duplicated the orchestra's extended treatment of the charming four-note descending motif (bars 46–65). Even the scales and passagework that concluded the refrain were intimately shared between the two forces (bars 66–82). By the time the piano had run off with the first couplet at bar 82 there had been nearly fifty bars of nonstop sharing. In the Allegretto of K. 503 there is no sharing in the first 82 bars. This difference is entirely in keeping with the dynamics of interaction in the respective first and second movements.

During the first movement of K. 271 the piano and orchestra had shared the lively first theme from the opening bars and had shared the mellow second theme in both the solo exposition and the recapitulation. After the deep, passionate communion between the two forces in the Andantino, it was fitting that solo and orchestra would be deeply responsive to each other at the beginning of the Rondo. During the first movement of K. 503 the piano and orchestra had kept much more to their own material and, apart from the development section, had made few allowances for the expression of the other. In the Andante there was togetherness, but not yet of an impassioned or deeply dramatic kind. In this concerto, a deep emotional togetherness remains to be forged in the third movement; it cannot be celebrated before it has been achieved. Nor has it been achieved in the opening refrain or the first couplet. The forces have remained essentially apart; they have maintained a cordial independence. The change occurs in the second couplet. Here, in Girdlestone's words, "the pensive grief of the refrain" and the "calm assurance of the first solo vanish before a sorrowful and passionate conflict which carries us for an instant into the world of the last concerto" (p. 437). In more ways than one, this conflict compares with Emma's sorrowful, passionate conflict in the middle of volume 3.

BEFORE DISCUSSING the musical and emotional transactions that occur during the central couplet (the "c" section of the rondo) it will be useful to lay out the basic outlines of its content and structure. The couplet grows directly out of the return of the refrain, announced this time by the piano. After the solo plays the first two phrases (its first direct response to the orchestra's material in this movement), the orchestra answers with all six phrases essentially as they were heard at the beginning of the movement, with the difference that the shift to the minor in the last phrase is not so pronounced. The basses remain in C major this time, rather than modulating to C minor, leaving the only minor-key expression to the higher strings and winds that briefly extend the phrase—this time in A minor. But before the orchestra can round off its last phrase, the piano intrudes with an A-minor transformation of the material with which it had begun the first couplet—then in C major. Before the refrain has ended, the couplet is underway.

The piano's A-minor material is relatively short and is repeated in somewhat altered form. After a one-bar burst from the orchestra transforms the key to F major, the solo introduces what Girdlestone rightly calls "one of Mozart's simplest and most personal tunes" (p. 437). After the melody is played by the solo, it is repeated by the oboes, which take the first half, and the flute, which takes the second. The piano, as if sustained by the woodwind support, spins out a further elaboration of the simple tune (bars 179–86) that is again answered perfectly by the oboes and then the flute, with the bassoons this time contributing as well. When the flute reaches the end of the new phrase it extends it, and, in doing so, leads the woodwinds through a modulation to C minor and into an intensely polyphonic development of fragments from the simple tune, all of the time accompanied by ever more passionate triplets in the piano. When the intensity finally abates, the solo, having regained the initiative, leads the music back to the open skies of C major and to the comforting strains of the opening refrain.

This central couplet, like the menuetto in K. 271, is extraordinary in a Mozart rondo for its length alone. It runs no less than eighty-four bars (144–228). Yet its force comes not from its length but from its internal dynamics. These are as different from those of the earlier menuetto (itself sixty-nine bars in length) as Emma's crisis in the middle of volume 3 is from that of Elizabeth. In the menuetto the solo undertook a graceful holding action which allowed it to wait out the crisis that was precipitated by the orchestra in the preceding refrain—just as Elizabeth gracefully returned from Pemberly to Longbourn to wait out the crisis provoked by Lydia and Wickham. In the central couplet of K. 503, the piano, like Emma, provokes the crisis itself. Also like Emma, the solo achieves its most passionate growing and sharing during the development of that crisis.

One of the most dramatic conflicts within the couplet is the one within the solo itself. There is an extraordinary difference between the aggressive, disturbing A-minor theme with which the solo interrupts the last strain of the refrain and the simple, melodious F-major theme it generates soon thereafter. These two themes express diametrically opposed sides of the solo's character—and all that separates them is one bar of orchestral music. Even so, the one theme follows from the other as convincingly as Emma on the carriage-ride home follows from Emma on Box Hill, separated only by her encounter with Knightley.

The A-minor theme that initiates the central episode is highly disturbing for a variety of reasons. Like Emma's comment to Miss Bates, the theme itself would not be intensely dramatic if heard in isolation. But it is heard in a context that makes it memorably expressive and aggressive. It is aggressive because of the abruptness with which it interrupts the end of the refrain. As mentioned before, the refrain per se included six separate phrases in its original twenty-three bars. Each phrase was allowed to end before the next would proceed. This established the musical equivalent of a gentleman's agreement during the opening refrain, an agreement that is honored when the refrain returns—until the solo, impatient at the end, enters two beats too soon. Given the context, the solo has violated the implicit rules of good breeding as surely as Emma has in being deliberately snippy to Miss Bates.

The A-minor tonality of the theme is also disturbing. A minor is the relative minor of C major; that is, the minor key with the same signature. It has been conspicuous by its absence thus far in the concerto, C minor having usurped the role of the contrasting minor key, with F major dominating the slow movement. If its earlier absence makes its appearance here more of a shock, so does the boldness with which the piano delivers the three accented notes that immediately define the key and the rhythm of the disturbing solo theme: A, C, E (bars 145–46). The rhythm says "One-Two-Three"; the harmony says "We're in the minor key"; and the melody says both things several times over. When the melody begins again, the A-C-E succession is given even more emphasis (bars 153–54), being accompanied this time by ascending grace notes in triplets that, in the context, are anything but gracious. The unpleasantness here is as insistent, deliberate, and technically polite as is Emma's pointed attack on Miss Bates.

A third disturbing quality about the A-minor theme is its derivation from the C-major theme with which the solo had graciously begun the first couplet. There the bold opening notes were on C, E, G. The rhythm said "One, Two, Three," the harmony "We're in the major key." The elaboration of the theme had included one of the most beautiful and tender moments in the entire concerto, a passage of four bars (40–43), all in the treble clef, in which the right hand played glorious flowing triplets over quarter notes in the left. The equivalent passage in the second couplet (bars 148–50) is one of the most painful in the concerto. Here the ascending figures are the opposite of glorious; each bruise of D-sharp against E (the sharpened fourth against the perfect fifth of the A-minor scale) brings palpable pain. Hearing material once so harmonious and sensitive turn so sharp and dissonant (see Figure 12) hurts as much as hearing a seemingly sensitized Emma turn deliberately cruel.

Figure 12

After the solo plays the A-minor material for the second time, it sounds the opening note, A, once again. But this time the orchestra takes over and, led by the flute, lifts the music not only to C and E but beyond to F. This orchestral intervention has the effect of changing the key from A minor (based on the A, C, E triad) to F major (based on F, A, C). Harmonically, the high F allows the earlier painful notes to be interpreted in a new context; technically, the high F undermines the earlier dissonance by becoming the root of the new key. As the flute reaches its high F, the piano, which has rested a beat, drops from its A to the lower F. From this harmonious base it launches the simple tune that provides the material for the rest of the couplet.

Because the solo's first melody note—the F—is covered by the sound of the orchestra (which played *forte* while the solo rested), the first distinct melody notes to be heard are a descending three-note motif: A, G, F (labeled x in Figure 13). These three notes are somehow infinitely

Figure 13

moving. They are as moving as Emma's tears. They fall again and again, as do those tears. And in doing so they carry the concerto onto a new emotional plane.

That this is so is easy to feel but difficult to explain. One can speak of Mozart's genius for melody. But that is to beg a most interesting question. One can agree with Girdlestone that in this case simplicity is not "ingenuousness," that somehow one "feels the experience of maturity" behind this simple tune (p. 437). But that, too, does not take one very far into the music itself. Following Leonard Meyer's example, one might attempt to analyze the "grammatical simplicity and relational richness" of this rich and simple melody.[7] But that would require more space than is available here—as well as requiring Leonard Meyer. So I will offer two explanations, one technical, one analogical, both contextual.

In the context of the third movement and of the concerto as a whole, the simple three-note motif has turned dissonance into harmony in more than a metaphorical way. The first note of the motif, A, is no longer the root of the relatively dissonant A-minor triad; it is now, instead, the major third of the more stable F-major key. This impression of stability is strengthened when the two falling eighth notes (A and G) are allowed to land solidly on the quarter note (F). To show that this new, more stable interpretation of A is no fluke, the A, G, F succession repeats itself. It is then taken a half-step higher (Bb, A, G), a form that further reaffirms the key of F major by beginning on B-flat, the note that distinguishes the key signature of F major from that of A minor or C major.

The second half of the melody (bars 167–70) repeats the beginning of the entire phrase one step higher. This time, however, the three-note motif makes a leap rather than a descent on its second appearance. It lands firmly on C, which in this context is no longer the painful minor third of A minor but rather the stable perfect fifth (the dominant) of the key of F major. In the context of the entire movement and concerto, of course, C is also the stable root of the home key itself. As the melody unfolds in the piano, the low strings sound out the "true" bass that is the foundation for the F-major harmony that now prevails. F major, of course, was also the prevailing harmony of the extremely sonorous second movement.

If the F-major melody is moving and reassuring in the technical harmonic context, it is also moving and reassuring in a more general way. Because the entire concerto has been so lacking in extended songlike melodies, this one is particularly welcome. It is also welcome coming from this particular solo voice. Intrinsically, the melody itself is warm, generous, heartfelt. But these qualities are strongly enhanced by the fact that they are generated by a solo voice that has expressed no comparable emotion in the course of the concerto. So it is with Emma's tears. They move us and reassure us not because they are tears but because they are Emma's.

From the moment it appears, this warm melody based on the eloquent three-note motif makes us feel that the headstrong, errant solo voice of the first movement has found a new equilibrium, that the subdued, restrained solo voice of the second movement has been moved beyond passive sympathy to an active outpouring of spontaneous emotion. This melody, like Emma's tears, distills much of what the solo has experienced throughout the work. When Girdlestone writes that "one feels the experience of maturity" in the melody, he seems to mean Mozart's maturity. Certainly the composer had to draw deeply upon his own human experience to compose such a melody, just as the author of Emma's carriage ride from Box Hill must have drawn deeply upon hers. But to claim that the solo's notes reveal Mozart's "experience of maturity" would be comparable to claiming that Emma's tears reveal Austen's maturity. They do. But primarily they reveal the maturity of Emma and of the solo.

The solo has not, of course, any more than Emma, achieved this emotional epiphany on its own. Just as Emma's remorse was provoked by Knightley's intervention and was implicitly supported by his deep concern for her, so the solo's melody is provoked by the orchestra's one-bar intervention and then supported by the "true" bass in the strings. In the space of a few bars, the central couplet has moved from the most disturbing melody in the entire concerto to the most profoundly satisfying. Now that the solo has spoken so eloquently, the winds are able to respond in kind. Here, even more than in the exchange between the piano and violins near the end of the Andantino of K. 271, "the speech rhythms inescapably evoke the sound of words." There, musical phrases the length of a few syllables were exchanged (bars 110–15); here they are the equivalent of compound sentences (bars 163–78). Whatever the solo's melodic "sentence" is saying (it has a sorrowful and confessional quality to my ear and heart), its message and rhythm are perfectly assimilated and returned by the winds.[8]

When the solo, buoyed up by the winds' response, spins out a new version of the melody, the three-note motif remains the basis of what is being said, but the emphasis is now different, as if to acknowledge the winds' response. In the first four bars (179–82), the pulse of the motif is the same, but its melodic shape and harmonic force have changed, for now its middle note dips down on a dissonant F-sharp that intensifies the emotion. In the second half of the phrase (bars 182–85), the three primary notes (A, G, F) do occur once in their original order, but they are now incorporated into a larger phrase structure that is taking them somewhere new. Again the solo melody is answered note for note by the oboes, then the flute (bars 187–93). Without a break, the flute then extends the melody and begins the passionate and vigorous development section of the couplet.

Whereas the loving and direct exchange of profound emotion during the extended dialogue between solo and winds is horizontal and sequential, the exchange of emotion in the development that concludes the central couplet is vertical and simultaneous. As the music modulates to C minor and the winds begin to have their own say with the solo's sorrowful motif, the piano is left with vigorous triplets in the bass. The vertical sharing that now occurs is the kind that has occurred in the previous movements of K. 503 whenever the winds have played melodic fragments that are accompanied by determined passagework on the part of the solo. But never has that texture been so intense and exhilarating as it is here. The emotion of the couplet—and of the entire concerto—is carried to yet a higher and deeper plane.

As Girdlestone points out, it is typical of Mozart that "the moment of the most poignant emotion is also that of the most complex and closely woven technique" (pp. 437–38). The primary material is simple enough. It is provided by the flute when it announces, in a new key, the first four notes (F-A-G-F) of the solo's original melody (bars 202–3). But the treatment becomes increasingly complex as this phrase is shared out in growing contrapuntal density among flute, bassoons, and oboes. Here is only part of Girdlestone's summary of the couplet's development.

> Like all very dramatic passages in Mozart this one is short, but in every respect it is the most significant moment in the finale. Never had Mozart used the canon to express such passionate feeling. The growing intensity is perceptible, not only in the extending to a fourth, then to an octave, of the leap in the original figure, but also in the length of the different episodes. . . . The overlapping phrases and episodes, the increase in length of periods and in numbers of parts, and the compression of the last episode, is exhilarating. No passage reveals more intimately the perfect union in Mozart between form and thought; in it we grasp admirably the manner in which one is at the service of the other, without either of them lording it. (p. 440)

There is also a perfect union here between the solo and the winds, though it might appear that the winds are in fact "lording it." As Girdlestone points out, "The lines of the design belong to [the woodwinds] but the task of evoking the atmosphere, the impressionistic function, is the piano's" (p. 441). Here the piano is in no way blurring the lines that belong to the winds, as it often tended to do in the first movement. Rather it is heightening the intensity and impact of what they have to say.

The short but intensely dramatic scene in chapter 11 of volume 3 in which Emma learns, almost simultaneously, of Harriet's and her own love for Knightley expresses a comparable poignance, intensity, overlapping, compression, and restrained balance among the forces. The entire novel comes immediately into focus for the first time, not with the formal gravity of chapters 12 and 13 of volume 2 of *Pride and Prejudice* or of the Andantino of K. 271, but rather with the sudden and simultaneous spontaneity of the crisis that concludes the central couplet of K. 503. Emma has never been so eloquent as when she represses her own "inward suffering" and, with "great outward patience," encourages Harriet's exposition of the mutual love between herself and Knightley. Harriet may have the "lines of the design" in this conversation, but it is Emma's expressive restraint that evokes the poignant and intensely dramatic atmosphere. The texture earlier in the novel was often contrapuntal because the reader and the heroine experienced the action on different planes. Here Emma herself is able to internalize such a double view: she is able to follow Harriet's line at the same time that she withholds her own. As during the canonic exchange in the couplet, form and thought are perfectly united.

The transition out of the crisis is as sudden and lasting in the concerto as is the passing of the summer storm in the novel. The intensity of the woodwind exchange abates, the accidentals disappear, the tension eases, and the solo suddenly finds itself alone on the path to happiness in the form of the opening refrain in its familiar C-major harmony. Before the melancholy C-minor section of the refrain is reached, the solo launches boldly into an abbreviated version of the first couplet (the "b" section of the rondo). When the opening refrain returns once more, the piano itself takes the lead in the modulation to C minor. But the resulting "tints of melancholy" are immediately counteracted by a long stretch of passagework in C major that includes a new motif for solo and winds to toss back and forth. The movement concludes with the solid C-major orchestral codetta as it was heard at the end of the original refrain.

THE FINAL a:b:a section of the Allegretto has provoked considerable critical controversy. Girdlestone is one of several admirers of the concerto as a whole who feel its conclusion to be rather perfunctory and uninspired; he even goes so far as to suggest that a cut of no less than eighty bars would do little damage (p. 442). He argues that the listener, after the drama and poignance of the central couplet, is no longer disposed to hear so much that is commonplace. But Joseph Kerman, in his notes to the Norton Critical Score of K. 503, suggests that a critic "should ask himself whether the relatively unadventurous structure at the end of the finale really results in impoverishment or whether it may serve a specific aesthetic purpose."[9] A few such purposes might briefly be suggested.

First, the expansive treatment of rather commonplace material that concludes the work does serve to anchor the concerto firmly in the home key. Moreover, the spacious treatment of neutral material has been a feature of the entire work. If the concluding section of the concerto is somewhat of a letdown from the intensity of what came just before, so are the last six chapters of *Emma*. Austen did not for that reason truncate volume 3. In chapter 14 she even calls explicit attention to the time needed for Emma's "fever" to subside. Emma may never again experience either the anguish of the carriage ride from Box Hill or the bliss of her second walk over the grounds with Knightley. But this does not lessen the worth of those heightened moments—or of the more prosaic ones that follow.

In addition, the expansive concluding material allows the solo and the orchestra to celebrate the deep emotional exchange that was consummated in the central couplet, in the same way that Emma and Knightley are allowed to celebrate in various rather mundane ways the emotional consummation that blossomed in the summer shrubs. As they do so, the piano shows self-restraint with regard to its own material at the same time that it responds imaginatively to that of the orchestra. Girdlestone objects that the piano omits its most attractive theme (the first one) from the return of the first couplet. So it does. But that was a theme that belonged to the solo alone. Its omission from the return of the "b" section parallels the solo's restraint in omitting its solo theme from the recapitulation of the second movement. (The omission here may also reflect the piano's renunciation of the A-minor aggression with which it had transformed this theme during the second couplet.) The third theme from the first couplet, the one that is exchanged with the winds, *is* heard at full length; it reaffirms, in its more commonplace way, the extraordinary exchange that has occurred in the central couplet. Moreover, the solo this time announces this theme on a high clear F, rather than the earlier C. The hesitant nature of the theme causes the high F to ring out six times before the melody itself actually gets underway (bars 267–69). The repetition is exceedingly welcome, for this is the very note that had concluded the sonorous togetherness of the second movement and that (an octave lower) had launched the sorrowful and passionate intimacy of the third.

Finally, the last two returns of the refrain are neither perfunctory nor unimaginative. The penultimate return is limited to the two opening phrases as played by the piano (which is yet to play the entire refrain) and then by the violins (which have not had any melodic material since before the central couplet). The last return of the refrain begins with the piano, jumps to the two short phrases in the winds, and concludes with the solo's version of the two concluding passages originally led by the strings. The piano not only takes over these two descending phrases for the first time: it decorates and fluidifies them, showing not only that it can now assimilate all of the orchestra's material but that it can do so with imagination. Its presentation of the last phrase, low in the bass, the phrase that had originally belonged to the low strings and that modulates to C minor, is particularly effective and memorable. This moment would not be so telling if the last part of the movement were not so spacious or if the piano had not been allowed its recent climb to the height of the keyboard—including the reiterated high F. Like Emma in the last six chapters of the novel, the solo demonstrates a new range and flexibility as it relates to familiar, even commonplace material with an ease and imagination it had been incapable of before.

It goes without saying that the variety of effects enumerated above will not salvage the spacious and somewhat commonplace conclusion to the Allegretto of K. 503 for those listeners who feel the need for something more exciting and compact. Perhaps those who admire even the end of K. 503 will take heart from the fact that the end of *Emma* has been similarly decried. George Whalley allows that "*Emma* is much admired, and rightly so; yet the closing chapter is the one place in all of Jane Austen's novels where I feel that she is writing a little perfunctorily, with less respect for her reader than is her use; as though it could be said for the author, rather than for the actors, that all passion is spent."[10]

To my mind, what finally has been spent, at the end of *Emma* as at the end of K. 503, is the "grandiose ambiguity of stability and tension" with which each work began. Suspended in volume 2 and in the Andante, it has been energized and grounded in the heartfelt experience of volume 3 and of the Allegretto. Emma Woodhouse and the solo voice *have* lost themselves in the commonplace; in so doing they have found brighter hopes and deeper needs—in the "other" as well as the self—than their earlier, more heroic selves could have known.

Our discussion of these two works, which some think "cold," began with reference to their commonplace materials. We are now in a position to understand Karl Kroeber's assertion that "were the characters in *Emma* . . . special or spectacular instead of 'normal,' a central meaning of the novel would be blurred."[11] So would a central meaning of K. 503 have been blurred had its primary melodic material been more special or spectacular—or had it been composed in other than the most commonplace of keys, C major.

A quick plot overview emphasizes the extent to which *Emma*, the longest of Austen's novels, is the one in which the least seems to happen. Emma meddles with Harriet, steering her away from Robert Martin and toward Mr. Elton, who loves Emma instead. Mr. Elton, unable to convert Emma into Mrs. Elton, so converts Augusta Hawkins. Emma and the rest of the town misjudge Jane Fairfax and Frank Churchill, whose act of deception works quite well. There is a ball at which Mr. Elton initiates the most recordable event and Miss Bates speaks the most quotable words. There is a strawberry party featuring Mrs. Elton's "apparatus of happiness" and a Box Hill party in which the verbal ridicule of a bore becomes a moral crisis. Then there is the long-awaited proposal by the right man to which the heroine replies with "just what she ought, of course. A lady always does" (p. 297).

Emma is a novel without dense letters of the kind Darcy wrote, or silly ones of the kind Collins wrote, or "missent" ones of the kind Jane Bennet wrote, one reason being that the action never moves from the seemingly static village of Highbury where it begins. The most highborn and eligible lady of that village marries the most highborn and eligible man after three fictional volumes whose commonplace events occur within the confines of that village and within the space of little more than a year. Yet this commonplace, even neutral material is treated in such a way as to make the predictable and the conventional not only dramatic but pulsing with human complexity.

Unlike Elizabeth Bennet, who achieves a richer complexity by the end of her novel, Emma moves toward a broader simplicity that makes her finally worthy to share the common ground of Donwell Abbey, which Knightley has been occupying all along. Here, as in *Pride and Prejudice*, the climax of the third volume pivots on a scene in the shrubbery. Chapter 14 of the earlier work featured Elizabeth's brilliant confrontation with Lady Catherine; chapter 13 of *Emma* features Emma's hesitant engagement to Knightley. Elizabeth's perfect assurance and ease are never more in evidence than during that final encounter with Lady Catherine, nor has Lady Catherine ever been more predictably herself. The encounter between Emma and Knightley is far less predictable. The joy they achieve by the end of their walk is earned by the anguish they feel during their first turn on the grounds. Elizabeth's polite demolition of Lady Catherine has something of the feeling of a virtuoso cadenza that concludes the rondo of a flashy and elastic concerto. It is a set-piece of the highest order. Emma's union with Knightley is a direct outgrowth of the dynamics of pleasure and pain that have alternated throughout the more resistant texture of her novel. It compares with the union achieved in the alternately painful and blissful central couplet of the finale of K. 503, which of all Mozart piano concertos is the closest in mood and achievement to *Emma*.

It is significant that K. 503 ends, not with a brilliant solo cadenza, but with the extended sharing of commonplace material by solo and orchestra—the kind of extended sharing that did not occur in any systematic way until well into the third and final movement. The Mozart concerto that begins with the opposing forces the farthest apart ends with them the closest together. As Einstein writes, "In no other concerto does the relation between the soloist and the orchestra vary so constantly and so unpredictably" (p. 312). The same is true of *Emma*. Emma herself is the most unpredictable of Austen heroines; her relations with society (and particularly with Knightley) are as varied and changeable as those of the solo with orchestra in K. 503.

As we have seen, the orchestra, in the first movement of the concerto, keeps watch over the errant solo in much the same way as Knightley watches over Emma in volume 1. In the Andante there is increasing mutual respect between the two instrumental forces, but little or no passionate engagement—just as Knightley and Emma are neither at odds nor in close collaboration during the bulk of volume 2. At the beginning of the third movement the piano and orchestra are cordially independent (bars 1–144). By the end they are most cordially *inter*dependent (bars 228–382), having experienced the crisis (bars 144–228) that threatened to suspend their cordial equality but that actually brings them closer than ever together. So in volume 3 are Emma and Knightley at first cordially independent (chapters 1–6). By the end (chapters 13–19) they, too, are most cordially interdependent, having experienced the sustained crisis that paradoxically unites them (chapters 7–13).

As the above chapter and bar numbers show, both the third volume and the third movement have an internally symmetrical three-part structure. The same was true of the third volume of *Pride and Prejudice* and the third movement of K. 271. We have seen, however, that the internal dynamics among those symmetrical parts in *Emma* and K. 503 are as different from those of their predecessors as they are similar to each other. The active, dynamic growth that occurs in the central episodes of the later works results in a concluding volume and movement whose organic filaments are more tightly knit.

In all four works the three-part symmetry of the concluding volume or movement corresponds to the larger three-part structure of the work as a whole. But again, the dynamics among the three volumes of *Emma* and the three movements of K. 503 are closer to those of each other than they are to those of their respective youthful predecessors. The sorrowful and spontaneous overflow of emotion that bursts forth in the middle of the Allegretto of K. 503 seems to gather into its spacious course all of the latent energies that were at cross purposes in the first movement and in suspended animation in the second. The same may be said of the central chapters of volume 3 of *Emma*.

Not only are those central chapters the setting for Emma's "experience of maturity"; they also take the novel outdoors in a way that is new in Austen. A splendid illusion of spaciousness is achieved at Donwell Abbey, at Box Hill, and in the stroll through the garden in which Knightley finally proposes. In setting alone, each of these outdoors scenes has a precursor in volume 3 of *Pride and Prejudice*: the tour of Pemberly, the garden scene with Lady Catherine, Darcy's ambulatory proposal. But the respective scenes in *Emma* are considerably richer in sensory details that bring out the full emotional force of the indoor-outdoor contrast— a force that will be even more strongly felt in *Persuasion*. Not only in sensory richness but in emotional complexity, the outdoors scenes in volume 3 of *Emma* contrast with their predecessors in *Pride and Prejudice* to the same degree that Mr. Elton's snowbound proposal scene contrasts with that of Mr. Collins.

Similarly, the transitions between home and away in *Emma*, though shorter in distance, are deeper in emotion. Consider the function of carriage rides in the two novels. In *Pride and Prejudice* they are transitions mainly in a geographical and structural sense. They move characters from one place to another and they help to establish symmetry within and among the individual volumes. The carriage rides in *Emma* are generally transitions in an emotional sense as well. Emma's returns from Randalls in volume 1 and Box Hill in volume 3 are moving, active examples of her capacity for feeling and growth. Elizabeth's carriage rides from Meryton, Rosings, and Lambton are static and anticipatory by comparison—as are the musical transitions in K. 271 when compared with those in K. 503.

The first "bridge" passage in K. 503, the one built on the rhythmic motif in the first movement, is as much a new theme as it is a transition. It is perhaps the most striking example in all Mozart of his deepened transition technique, yet this same concerto has other striking transitions entirely different in kind. In the Andante the glorious retransition out of the nonthematic development section is the most continuously expressive stretch of music in the entire movement. And the Allegretto features the extraordinary one-bar orchestral transition that transports the solo from its disturbing A-minor melody to its soulful F-major one.

These heightened musical transitions are one way in which a concerto whose harmonic and melodic contrasts are minimal gets maximum mileage out of its materials. Emma's heightened carriage rides have the same function for a novel whose geographical and human contrasts are minimal. The expressive transitions in both works illustrate Rosen's assertion (about the concerto) that "the most expressive force comes from the larger formal elements, even to the point of pervading a heavily symphonic style with melancholy and tenderness." This ability to make "transitional" passages central to the emotional meaning of a movement or volume is one measure of each artist's progress into the "depths of the soul."

Perhaps the most penetrating summary of *Emma*'s many excellencies is that of R. W. Chapman, who in the twentieth century has been to students of Austen what Alfred Einstein has been to students of Mozart. Chapman prefers *Emma* to *Pride and Prejudice*. Whether or not one shares the preference, one can marvel at the boldness and precision with which he captures the essence of Austen's most ambitious novel: "I find the supremacy of *Emma* in the matchless symmetry of its design, in the endless fascination of its technique, above all in the flow of the blood beneath the smooth polished skin: a flow of human sympathy and charity that beats with a steady pulse, rarely—but the more momentously—quickening to a throb that sets our own veins leaping in unison."[12] The above-named virtues of *Emma* are those of K. 503 as well. These two works stand among Austen's novels and Mozart's piano concertos as the most uncompromising examples of the manner in which the classical artist can create extraordinary beauty and truth out of the most ordinary material. To those who feel them, the rare but momentous throbs that quicken beneath their smooth polished skins are worth many bursts of volcanic, Romantic convulsion. The flow of human sympathy and charity that beats with a steady pulse in the rhythms of their words and notes moves those whose veins surge in unison as high as the leaping fountains and as low as the weeping mountains of sentimental *Angst*.

Chapter Six

PERSUASION AND
PIANO CONCERTO NO. 27 (K. 595)

USTEN'S LAST NOVEL and Mozart's last piano concerto are "autumnal" works, as each has often been called.[1] Concerto No. 27 was composed in January of 1791—five years after Concerto No. 25 and during the last year of Mozart's life. More than any of the others, K. 595 dramatizes the truth of Rosen's observation that K. 503, for all its "breadth and subtlety," for all its "tenderness and melancholy," is "less poignant than some of the other concertos." Mozart's last concerto is the most personal and poignant of them all—and not because of the biographical fact that he would never compose another.

Austen began *Persuasion* soon after she completed *Emma*. The "flow of human sympathy and charity" which throbbed beneath the surface of Emma Woodhouse's story finds full and open expression in that of Anne Elliot. Austen finished work on the new novel in January of 1817—the last year of her life. Published posthumously in 1818, *Persuasion* is her most personal and poignant fiction, not because she died soon after writing it, but because of what it contains.

Each of these autumnal works is pervaded by a stream of poignant emotions. Girdlestone rightly associates the emotions of K. 595 with those of the Clarinet Quintet (K. 581), which Mozart composed about the same time. He sums up the emotional ambiance of both compositions with the words "weariness, resignation, detachment, yearning, vigor, introspection." He suggests that the dominant mood of each might best be characterized as "wilting" (p. 470). *Persuasion* has a comparable mood. If Anne Elliot is not yet "wilting," she has, we are told again and again, "lost her bloom." Whalley suggests, without elaboration, that "if Jane Austen can be seen as Mozartean, it is in her character that *Persuasion* should be her Clarinet Quintet."[2] I agree, but find K. 595 even closer in spirit to *Persuasion*.

Girdlestone rightly notes that the "chief interest" of Mozart's last piano concerto, as of his Clarinet Quintet, "is its inspiration." His summary of that inspiration applies almost verbatim to Austen's last novel:

Before all, it is a *Tondichtung*, where the nature of the emotion is more important than the relations between protagonists. Its sorrow . . . is so strongly tempered by the spirit of resignation that one might take it at times for mere tearfulness. But its classical restraint hides a sorrow as sincere as that of more vehement music. And above all, this sentiment, which might have been so selfish, is fragrant with that spirit of kindness and love breathed by so much of Mozart's art. (pp. 478–80)

As Arthur Hutchings observes, the restraint with which K. 595 expresses its sorrow makes the concerto "seem confidential between the composer and listener."[3] *Persuasion* is similarly confidential owing to the restrained presentation of Anne Elliot's resigned but fragrant sorrow.

Girdlestone notes that the Mozart who created K. 595 is "no longer interested in structural problems" to the extent that he was in the great concertos that preceded it (p. 473). The same is true of the Austen who created *Persuasion*, a novel without the structural intricacies and excellencies of *Pride and Prejudice* or *Emma*.[4] Because structure per se is not as complex or primary in these later works, the comparisons below tend to stress spirit more than structure. Or, to put it another way, once the external structures are outlined, the emphasis shifts to the deeper, emotional structures.

K. 595 is like K. 271 and K. 503 in having three movements in a fast-slow-fast pattern. Its second and third movements, however, are both considerably shorter (in elapsed time) than the first movement. Whereas the first movement runs about thirteen minutes, the second and third run seven and nine, respectively. With *Persuasion* the proportions are comparable. Whereas *Pride and Prejudice* and *Emma* each consists of three volumes containing eighteen to twenty-three chapters apiece, *Persuasion* consists of two volumes of twelve chapters each. Its first volume rivals those of the other two novels in length (103 pages in the Signet edition), but the subsequent material is comparatively telescoped. Volume 2 of *Persuasion* runs 125 pages in the Signet edition, but it is also the last volume.

Not only the proportions but the treatment is comparable in these two "autumnal" works. Girdlestone notes that "virtuosity is almost entirely absent" from Mozart's last concerto (p. 478). It is equally lacking in *Persuasion*: Anne Elliot does not display the "virtuosity" exhibited in contrasting ways by Elizabeth Bennet and Emma Woodhouse. The resignation that pervades the last novel and the last concerto makes for less "action" than is found in their predecessors. The emphasis on emotion rather than on structure means that what action there is is often of a different kind. And the reduced interest in the "relations between protagonists" results, eventually, in more emphasis on the heroine and the solo voice.

Anne and the solo of K. 595 are more timid and restrained than their predecessors, but each, paradoxically, comes to dominate the work itself more completely. Each work progresses, as Anne and the solo progress, from resigned melancholy to lonely hope to profound joy.

Resigned Melancholy

ANNE ELLIOT's resigned melancholy is unbroken during the first six chapters of volume 1. It has two causes. The first is that her father and her two sisters are vain egotists who view Anne as a "nobody" and with whom it is impossible to have intellectual or emotional exchange. What is worse, neither Sir Walter nor Elizabeth nor Mary will ever change. "Vanity was the beginning and the end of Sir Walter Elliot's character; vanity of person and of situation."[5] Worse still, Anne has nowhere else to go: she must live either with Sir Walter and Elizabeth at Kellynch (and Bath) or with Mary and the Musgrove in-laws at Uppercross. The first cause, then, for her resigned melancholy is the necessity of living with family who are stupid, vain, and unfeeling and who may change their locale but never their character.

The second cause for Anne's resignation and her melancholy is the inverse of the first. The two people with whom she has had deep human exchange—her mother and Frederick Wentworth—are no longer present. Anne's mother was "of very superior character." She "had been an excellent woman, sensible and amiable; whose judgment and conduct, if they might be pardoned the youthful infatuation which made her Lady Elliot, had never required indulgence afterwards" (p. 10). She died when Anne was fourteen. When Anne was twenty, she refused to marry the one man she had loved, Frederick Wentworth. When the novel begins, Anne is twenty-seven.

The first indirect mention of Wentworth (whose name itself suggests something of value that is gone) comes at the end of the claustrophobic first three chapters, which have been dominated by Sir Walter and Elizabeth and by the fact that Sir Walter's vain ways and spendthrift habits have made necessary the renting out of Kellynch Lodge, the ancestral estate. An Admiral and Mrs. Croft are the prospective tenants, Mrs. Croft being the sister of Anne's Frederick Wentworth, who, like the Crofts, is just returned from six years on the open seas, concluding with the great naval victories over the French. Wentworth himself is introduced to the reader with great restraint in the last sentence of chapter 3. That chapter has been devoted to the efforts of the Elliots' lawyer, Shepherd, to persuade Sir Walter to accept the Crofts as tenants. "Mr. Shepherd was completely empowered to act; and no sooner had such an end been reached, than Anne, who had been a most attentive listener to the whole, left the room, to seek the comfort of cool air for her flushed cheeks; and as she walked along a favourite grove, said, with a gentle sigh, 'a few months more, and *he*, perhaps, may be walking here'" (p. 29, italics Austen's). This indirect, yet most direct manner of introducing the man Anne used to love—before the reader has even heard of that love—is one of the ways in which this novel "seems confidential between reader and novelist."

Chapter 4 transports the reader from the cold, heartless world of Sir Walter Elliot into the warm, heartfelt world of his best daughter. The chapter is tender but it is not "mere tearfulness." It begins with Anne's (and Austen's) characteristic restraint. "*He* was not Mr. Wentworth, the former curate of Monkford, however suspicious appearances may be, but a captain Frederick Wentworth, his brother" (p. 30). The reader now learns of the "exquisite felicity" Anne and Frederick Wentworth had enjoyed—until Anne allowed Lady Russell, her mother surrogate, to "persuade" her not to marry a man with "no fortune," a man "who had nothing but himself to recommend him" (pp. 31, 30). The chapter then reveals in Anne the emotions that pervade Mozart's last concerto. There is weariness:

> A few months had seen the beginning and the end of their acquaintance; but, not with a few months ended Anne's share of suffering from it. Her attachment and regrets had, for a long time, clouded every enjoyment of youth; and an early loss of bloom and spirits had been their lasting effect. (p. 32)

There is resignation and detachment:

> More than seven years were gone since this little history of sorrowful interest had reached its close; and time had softened down much, perhaps nearly all of peculiar attachment to him—but she had been too dependent on time alone; no aid had been given in change of place, . . . or in any novelty or enlargement of society.—No one had ever come within the Kellynch circle who could bear a comparison with Frederick Wentworth, as he stood in her memory. No second attachment, the only thoroughly natural, happy, and sufficient cure, at her time of life, had been possible to the nice tone of her mind, the fastidiousness of her taste, in the small limits of the society around them. (p. 32)

There is yearning:

How eloquent could Anne Elliot have been—how eloquent, at least, were her wishes on the side of early warm attachment, and a cheerful confidence in futurity, against that over-anxious caution which seems to insult exertion and distrust Providence! She had been forced into prudence in her youth, she learned romance as she grew older—the natural sequel of an unnatural beginning. (p. 33)

And there is vigor and introspection:

With all these circumstances, recollections and feelings, she could not hear that Captain Wentworth's sister was likely to live at Kellynch, without a revival of former pain; and many a stroll and many a sigh were necessary to dispel the agitation of the idea. She often told herself it was folly before she could harden her nerves sufficiently to feel the continual discussion of the Crofts and their business no evil. She was assisted, however, by that perfect indifference and apparent unconsciousness, among the only three of her own friends in the secret of the past, which seemed almost to deny any recollection of it. She could do justice to the superiority of Lady Russell's motives in this, over those of her father and Elizabeth; . . . but the general air of oblivion among them was highly important, from whatever it sprung. (p. 34)

By the end of chapter 4, two antithetical worlds are juxtaposed: the vain, public, conceited, superficial world of Sir Walter Elliot and the warm, private, introspective, spirited one of his daughter Anne. To a much greater degree than Elizabeth Bennet or Emma Woodhouse, Anne Elliot exists in a world blind to her best qualities.

Much of the special tone and texture of *Persuasion* derives from Anne's poignant and seemingly hopeless situation. Austen's last novel registers new subtleties and intensities of emotion because the ebb and flow of Anne's emotion is the essential action of the book. Its language is more metaphorical than that of its predecessors because many of Anne's ideas and feelings are incapable of conventional expression. This novel reveals a new kind of appreciation for the out of doors—even deeper than in *Emma*—because nature is often the only refuge, outlet, or counterpart for Anne's feelings.

Anne is as resigned to the limitations of her surrounding society as she is to the loss of the man she had loved. She does not complain, she does not hope. She does, however, cope—by making herself as useful as she can wherever she happens to be. As soon as arrangements are made to let Kellynch, it appears that she will have to move immediately with her father and Elizabeth to the "white glare of Bath." This necessity finds her "grieving to forego all the influence so sweet and so sad of the autumnal months in the country" (p. 36). But her plans change when it is determined that her sister Mary requires her at Uppercross, only three miles from Kellynch. Even so, Anne feels a "desolate tranquility" (p. 38) in chapter 5 during her last days at Kellynch Lodge with Lady Russell—days that are dominated by "solitariness and melancholy" (p. 39). Nor does the move to the bustling world of the Musgroves at Uppercross make her any less melancholy or desolate.

Early in chapter 6 Anne vows to make the best of her stay there. But the negative syntax in which she does so reveals her resignation. "She had no dread of these two months. Mary was not so repulsive and un-sisterly as Elizabeth, nor so inaccessible to all influence of hers; neither was there anything among the other component parts of the cottage inimical to comfort" (p. 45). Anne's main "comfort" at Uppercross is to listen patiently as Mary complains about the in-laws and the in-laws complain about Mary. Her next "comfort" is to obligingly play the piano at the Musgroves' request, though knowing they are not really listening. Anne's experience at the keyboard may well correspond to Austen's own (as the Appendixes to this book will suggest).

> She played a great deal better than either of the Miss Musgroves; but having no voice, no knowledge of the harp, and no fond parents to sit by and fancy themselves delighted, her performance was little thought of, only out of civility, or to refresh others, as she was well aware. She knew that when she played she was giving pleasure only to herself; but this was no new sensation: excepting one short period of her life, she had never, since the age of fourteen, never since the loss of her dear mother, known the happiness of being listened to, or encouraged by any just appreciation or real taste. In music she had been always used to feel alone in the world. (p. 48)

Anne's isolation at the keyboard, which could have made her selfish, is nevertheless fragrant with the "spirit of kindness." The Musgroves' "fond partiality for their own daughters' performance, and total indifference to any other person's, gave her much more pleasure for their sakes than mortification for her own" (pp. 48–49). She preserves an admirable equilibrium until the end of chapter 6, when certain references to the brothers Wentworth ruffle her studied composure.

When Mrs. Croft, who is visiting Uppercross, says to Anne, "It was you, and not your sister, I find, that my brother had the pleasure of being acquainted with, when he was in this country," Anne is "electrified" (p. 50). Her immediate fear is that Mrs. Croft has somehow learned of her romance with Frederick. But a quick turn in the conversation makes clear that the reference was to Edward, the curate. "The rest was all tranquillity; till just as they were [leaving], she heard the Admiral say to Mary, 'We are expecting a brother of Mrs. Croft's here soon; I dare say you know him by name.'" (p. 51). Anne is desperate to hear which brother it might be. But the Musgrove children prevent Admiral Croft from "finishing or recollecting what he had begun," and Anne is left suspended.

The suspense becomes all the more intense when the conversation at Uppercross that evening happens to center on "poor Richard" Musgrove, the recital of whose "pathetic piece of family history" causes Captain Frederick Wentworth's name to be mentioned over and over again (he being the man under whom Richard had served a brief stint in the Royal Navy). This is a "new sort of trial to Anne's nerves." She must, however, "inure herself" to it, for the Musgroves are intent on procuring a visit from their dead son's captain as soon as possible (p. 53). Whether or not Frederick was the brother referred to by Admiral Croft, Anne will soon have to endure the presence of the man she had rejected—and the dire agitation it is certain to provoke in her carefully composed emotional life.

K. 595 is in the key of B-flat major, the relative major of G minor. For this reason, as for others, Einstein finds Mozart's last piano concerto to be "a sort of a complement" to the great G-minor Symphony (K. 550), composed some two years earlier. As Einstein points out, each work expresses a profound—and resigned—melancholy. But in the concerto, as in the Clarinet Quintet, "the mood of resignation no longer expresses itself loudly or emphatically; every stirring of energy is rejected or suppressed; and this fact makes all the more uncanny the depths of sadness that are touched in the shadings and modulations of the harmony" (p. 314). This mood of resignation, neither loud nor emphatic, pervades the melodic material of the entire first movement. It also pervades the treatment of that material, including the relations between the solo and orchestra.

The mood of resigned melancholy is firmly established by the melody which opens this somber Allegro. The opening theme is given out by the first violins in three quiet phrases of four bars each that are separated by one-bar motifs in the winds (Figure 14). The first phrase establishes the mood for the theme itself and for the entire movement. In four bars, its simple melody moves slowly up the tonic triad (B♭, D, F), touches briefly on G, descends to D, and comes to a full cadence on the original B-flat. The phrase is *piano* throughout, it has moved less than an octave, and it comes to a full close. The next two phrases are equally quiet, restricted, and self-contained. Each begins on the same B-flat and

Figure 14

moves directly upward to D and to F, though not so slowly. The second comes to a half-cadence on D, the last to a full cadence on the same B-flat from which the melody has thrice begun. This quiet subdued motion within a narrow compass will characterize the concerto as a whole— and the first two movements in particular.

The woodwind motif that twice punctuates the opening melody defines its upper limits and confirms its prevailing key. Twice the motif descends, *forte*, from the B-flat an octave above the one from which the melody thrice ascends. Twice it drops directly to F and to D, the same notes of the triad to which each phrase of the melody rises. Separately and together, the string melody and the woodwind motif establish a musical world as limited and confined as the fictional world of Kellynch in the opening pages of *Persuasion*. The melancholy inertia with which K. 595 begins could hardly contrast more sharply with the sprightly opening melody of K. 271 or the majestic opening chords of K. 503.

The rest of the orchestral exposition is as rich in affecting melody as that of K. 503 was lacking in it. Yet there is little contrast of mood among the many themes. The second theme (bars 16–22), though brief, also unfolds in three rather static phrases that remain within the octave. Admirably designed to display the contrasting sonorities of the strings and the winds, its melody resembles the mellow second theme of K. 271—much compressed. The third theme (bars 29–38) pivots on the simplest of materials: a descending scale and a chirping repeated note. Yet this theme not only extends but intensifies the mood of subdued, resigned melancholy established by the earlier themes. In addition, it introduces both the sliding chromaticism and the lilting grace that will darken and lighten, often simultaneously, the music to come. Its special poignance is as indigenous to this particular concerto as Anne's is to the world of *Persuasion.*

Like the first melody, this one begins on B-flat (Figure 15). *Its* original B-flat, however, is an octave higher—the highest note that had been reached by the first melody. This melody, too, immediately rises to D.

Figure 15

But instead of moving higher, it immediately drops two octaves. This deliberate fall, in descending scales, is dramatic because the first two themes had moved so little. Its drama is intensified because its lowest and last notes, the E-flat and the D, are augmented and given a *mezzo forte* emphasis. Throbbing groups in the violas and second violins give added urgency to the descent. And the abrupt silence of these instruments gives special poignance to the succeeding chirps in the first violins that counteract the downward movement with their graceful resilience.

When this third melody group repeats itself (bar 33), the descending scale modulates into the minor by becoming intensely chromatic. The modulation causes the subdued melancholy to intensify greatly—an emotional shading that could hardly have been so striking had the essential material not been so simple as a scale. This time two series of chirps are necessary to counteract the downward motion, the second set gracing the high B-flat on which the entire melody had begun. This third theme does not come to a full close, but rather leads directly to the first (and most conventional) of several closing themes that double the length of the exposition (bars 39–80) and prolong its resigned melancholy until the solo voice is at last allowed to enter.

The solo enters by playing the orchestra's opening three-part melody exactly as the violins had given it, adding only the slightest decoration of its own. Its treatment of the short, mellow second theme is equally submissive: it modestly takes the part that had earlier belonged to the violins. After leading the transition to the third theme, the piano leaves the first descent to the strings. When the violins begin their second (and chromatic) descent, the solo doubles the downward motion and touchingly decorates it with broken octave scales. After playing the second set of resilient chirps, the solo then contents itself with decorating the orchestra's closing material. "Devoid of all personal ambition" even at the end of its own exposition, Girdlestone points out, this solo "does not undertake a bravura passage as in nearly all the other concertos; it confines itself to reproducing the unpretentious decorative passage which the strings had given out in the tutti" (p. 475).

The piano in its solo exposition is as submissive toward the orchestra and the material it has provided as Anne is to her immediate family and the opportunities they provide early in the novel. No less than Anne in chapter 3, the solo shows itself to have been "a most attentive listener to the whole." Its single sign of individuality in its own exposition is to introduce between the orchestra's first and second themes a sad and pensive theme of its own in F minor. As Girdlestone remarks, this melody "becomes almost poignant when the piano rises high into the treble and reiterates thrice a pathetic phrase against which the flute and later the [oboes] outline a restrained but expressive counterpoint" (p. 473). But the solo theme, like Anne's reminiscence in chapter 4, exists in its present context as a beautiful but incongruent memory; there seems to be no way for it to be incorporated into the world of the present. The excitement subsides, and the solo returns to the orchestral themes.

Girdlestone's comment on Mozart's treatment of the solo melody—

"Never had Mozart's moderation and reserve betrayed so heart-rending an emotion" (p. 473)—applies as well to Austen's treatment of Anne's recollection in chapter 4. Throughout both works, extreme emotion is presented with moderation and reserve. Austen had anticipated Anne's reminiscence in chapter 4 with the confidential *he* at the end of chapter 3. Mozart uses similar expressive restraint in bar 33 of the orchestral exposition, a split-second before the descending scale in the third theme turns painfully chromatic. The emotion about to be revealed is hinted at, but not expressed, by the accompaniment in the lower strings. Mention has already been made of the throbbing notes in the violas and second violins that accompany the descent. But there are also two notes in the cellos and basses in bar 33—a D and a D-flat.

Rosen's explanation of what these two notes add to the emotion is technical, but the parallel with Austen's restraint in the presentation of Anne's emotion will nevertheless be clear.

> In this same passage, the sweetness of Mozart's dissonance is at its most powerful: the clash in measure 33 between a D natural in the first violins and a D♭ three and four octaves below in the cellos and basses is one of the most painful in tonal music. The brutality of the clash is neatly sidestepped in the shortest possible time, and a more acceptable dissonance is substituted, yet our ear and our memory supply all the expressive force. . . . On the third beat of the measure there is the unplayed but audibly imagined harshness of a minor ninth (D-D♭) along with the major seventh (D♭-C), which gives the effect of the most dissonant and most expressive harmony without the harshness of actually playing it. Throughout the work the most painful dissonances are evoked and yet softened. This passage is an important moment in the concerto, the first appearance of the minor mode and of the chromaticism that plays such a crucial role, the first sign of the work's limitless melancholy. (p. 263)

In the development section of the first movement, as in chapters 7–9 of the first volume, the "unplayed but imagined dissonances" characteristic of each work become much more overt and dramatic.

THE DEVELOPMENT section plunges directly into the sliding chromaticism and minor-key anguish that had been obliquely touched upon earlier in the movement. The solo begins the development by playing the opening phrase of the first theme in the new key of B minor. Because the theme itself begins with a slowly ascending triad, this modulation, like all that follow in the development, is easy to follow and feel. As the solo and winds toss this modulating phrase from key to key, the kind of heart-rending exchange experienced only momentarily during the solo's F-minor theme now extends itself in overlapping waves of poignant emotion. This modulatory intensification of already melancholy material deepens, without changing, the mood that has prevailed throughout the movement. Finally, exhausted, the music drops back to the opening melody in the home key for the start of the recapitulation.

As Rosen points out, this development section, "where the key changes almost every two measures, carries classical tonality as far as it can go; the chromaticism becomes iridescent, and the orchestration and spacing transparent." Even so, the "emotion, for all its anguish, never disturbs the grace of the melodic line" (p. 263). So it is with Anne when Wentworth arrives at Uppercross in chapter 7. Her emotions are the same ones she has quietly harbored for seven years, but now they become iridescent, modulating wildly. In spite of her inner agitation, however, she retains her outward grace.

At first she avoids meeting him: she feels "the joy of the escape" from certain pain (p. 56). But soon they are in the same room. "A thousand feelings rushed on Anne, of which this was the most consoling, that it would soon be over" (p. 60). When Mary innocently reports to Anne what Wentworth had said—"You were so altered he should not have known you again"—Anne imagines the worst. She "fully submitted, in silent, deep mortification" (p. 61). In chapter 8 she manages to be with him in public and to maintain composure, but to do so is not easy. Being *with* him is worse than was being apart. "Now they were as strangers; nay, worse than strangers, for they could never become acquainted. It was a perpetual estrangement" (p. 64). As Wentworth is obviously interested in the two Musgrove girls, Louisa and Henrietta, Anne's role is to play the piano while he dances with the one or the other. "Anne offered her services, as usual, and though her eyes would sometimes fill with tears as she sat at the instrument, she was extremely glad to be employed, and desired nothing in return but to be unobserved" (p. 71). Here, surrounded by others, she experiences a sharper "solitariness and melancholy," a more "desolate tranquility," than during her last days at Kellynch.

In chapter 9 her studied composure is internally shattered once more, this time when Wentworth does her the simple kindness of lifting the Musgrove boy off her back (this passage is quoted at length in the "Sanity and Madness" section of Part 1). Her "most disordered feelings," her "varying, but very painful agitation," her need to leave the room and "arrange" her feelings before being able to attend to those of others, her "shame" at being "so nervous, so overcome by a trifle"—all of these sensations testify to the strength of the feelings she is struggling to suppress. As never before in an Austen novel, the heroine's feelings have become "iridescent." Yet Anne does manage to keep her anguish to herself. At the beginning of chapter 10 she appears as composed and resigned as ever, so much so that she is able to accompany Wentworth and the Miss Musgroves on a group outing without displaying any overt signs of her feelings. The celebrated autumn walk concludes her stay at Uppercross—and it crystallizes the emotions she has experienced throughout volume 1.

Anne's "autumnal months in the country" have turned out sadder than she could have imagined. She is more "perpetually estranged" from Wentworth in actuality than she had been in memory. The poignance of this condition is heightened by her having to observe his attentions to the Musgrove girls—and especially Louisa. As the party sets out on a November afternoon, she is resigned to the fact that her own pleasure in the walk "must arise from the exercise and the day, from the view of the last smiles of the year upon the tawny leaves and withered hedges" (p. 82). Composed and resigned she is, but it gives her great pain to overhear Wentworth praise Louisa Musgrove's "firmness of mind"—the quality he will never forgive Anne for having lacked when she allowed Lady Russell to persuade her not to marry him. She is momentarily alone, but "her spirits wanted the solitude and silence which only numbers could give" (p. 86).

As the party returns toward Uppercross, Anne rejoins the larger group with all the submission with which the solo in K. 595 characteristically loses itself in the material of the orchestra. Still, she cannot subdue her feelings entirely. When the Crofts' carriage draws near, Wentworth thoughtfully helps her in it. This trivial action affects her much as did his lifting of the child in the previous chapter. It causes such a rush of emotion that she is nearly overcome, and she speaks with the Crofts almost by rote for much of the trip home. She still does not have any hope for Wentworth—consciously. But his action is "proof of his own warm and amiable heart, which she could not contemplate without emotions so compounded of pleasure and pain that she knew not which prevailed" (p. 88).

Those mixed emotions pervade the last two chapters of volume 1, which begin with the trip to Lyme, which feature Louisa's disastrous fall, and which end with Anne, Wentworth, and Henrietta returning in a carriage to Uppercross to break the news to Louisa's parents. Anne is so rejuvenated by the view of the sea and the effect of its breezes that she attracts the "earnest admiration" of a passing gentleman, who it turns out is her cousin Mr. William Elliot. "She was looking remarkably well; her very regular, very pretty features, having the bloom and freshness of youth restored by the fine wind which had been blowing on her complexion, and by the animation of eye which it had also produced" (p. 100). Anne is also enlivened by the warmth and hospitality of Captain Wentworth's friends, the Harvilles and Captain Benwick. But Louisa's fall in chapter 12 dampens the spirits of the entire party, and Mary's idiotic self-centeredness means that Anne, rather than staying with the injured Louisa, where she could have done much good, must instead return to Uppercross in the carriage with Wentworth and Henrietta. The ride is mostly silent. Anne's only "pleasure" is in the fact that Wentworth once asks her advice. As soon as he speaks to the parents, he rides off to Lyme and Louisa. Anne is as alone at the end of volume 1 as she was at the beginning, if not more so.

JUST AS the acute agitation of Anne's first meetings with Wentworth at Uppercross eventually gave way to a more resigned melancholy, to a more "desolate tranquility," so does the iridescent agitation of the development section of the first movement give way to the resigned melancholy in which the movement began. As Girdlestone says, nothing could be "more static" than the "climate" of this recapitulation (p. 477). Neither the melancholy of the three main orchestral themes nor the wistfulness of the solo theme has been altered by the singleminded intensity of the development, and all four major themes are heard in the same order in which they appeared before. In both K. 271 and K. 503 the return of the first theme at the beginning of the recapitulation had inspired fresh collaboration between solo and orchestra, these forces in each case reversing the earlier roles in which they had shared the same material at the beginning of the solo exposition. Here the solo and orchestra remain as unadventuresome as they had been before. The violins give out all three phrases of the first theme exactly as they had at the beginning of the movement; the solo is not even heard until the transition to the solo theme. The second and third themes are shared out exactly as they were in the solo exposition, the only difference being their return to the home key (there they had been in F major, the dominant). At the end of the recapitulation, "when one expects the concluding solo which was not missing in any other concerto," the piano, as Girdlestone points out, "repeats an orchestral passage" (p. 478).

The cadenza that Mozart left for this movement, like Anne's rejuvenation at Lyme, is brief but vigorous. It shows that the solo, though submissive as ever, remains very much alive. It features, however, the least ambitious and the least "personal" melody of all—the second orchestral theme. After the cadenza, the solo is silent. The orchestra, after a brief *forte* flurry, concludes the movement as softly as it had begun, *piano*, with the same notes with which it had ended its own exposition. As much as

Anne in the first volume, and with the same melancholy resignation, the solo in the opening Allegro has experienced "the solitude and the silence which only numbers could give."

Passionate Tranquility

WE HAVE SAID that both *Persuasion* and K. 595 progress from resigned melancholy to lonely hope to profound joy. In both the first volume and the first movement the resigned melancholy has prevailed with a persistence and singlemindedness unique in a Mozart concerto or Austen novel. In the opening Allegro there was no bright, cheery, contrasting theme to counteract the quiet, limited, self-contained opening theme. Even the chirps of the third theme—the most striking element of lilting grace in the movement—were always linked to the melancholy descending scale that immediately preceded them. Nor was there a bright, cheery, contrasting suitor to counteract Anne's loss of the one man she has loved. Throughout volume 1 her qualities of lilting grace are perforce expressed in a context of restraint and renunciation, whether with regard to the society at large or to Wentworth, after his return. Even the most agitated sections of the Allegro and volume 1—the development section and Anne's early encounters with Wentworth at Uppercross—served not to alter or overcome the prevailing mood, but rather to deepen it and make it more "iridescent." The transition from resigned melancholy to lonely hope does not occur until the second movement of the concerto and the second volume of the novel.

The Larghetto of K. 595 and the first half of volume 2 of *Persuasion* each begin in melancholy and end in hope. The melancholy in which each begins, however, already differs from that in which the works themselves began. For here the emotion is generated by the solo and the heroine, not the orchestra and the society. By the end of the Larghetto and by the end of chapter 6 of volume 2, the solo and Anne each reach the threshold of joy. Paradoxically, each does so not by renouncing but by intensifying and further purifying the sweet sadness each has embodied in the opening movement and volume.

AT THE BEGINNING of volume 2, Anne is left alone at Uppercross when the Musgroves leave to retrieve Louisa from Lyme. She has "the solitary range of the house" and her thoughts and feelings become appropriately expansive, if nevertheless melancholy. Anne now has less reason than ever to expect happiness herself; her ability to imagine happiness for others, for once, becomes almost self-indulgent. "A few months hence, and the room now so deserted, occupied but by her silent, pensive self, might be filled again with all that was happy and gay, all that was glowing and bright in prosperous love, all that was most unlike Anne Elliot!" (p. 117). Near "mere tearfulness" here, Anne advances beyond it.

It is "a dark November day," with "a small thick rain almost blotting out the very few objects ever to be discerned from the windows." Before Lady Russell's carriage arrives to carry her alone to Kellynch Lodge, Anne has "an hour's complete leisure for such reflections as these." In the solitude of the carriage ride, she has even more such leisure. The ride itself is rendered not in terms of scenery or of miles but in terms of Anne's character. Her heart recollects pain, yet still treasures the "precious" and the "dear."

> Though desirous to be gone, she could not quit the Mansion House, or look an adieu to the Cottage . . . without a saddened heart.—Scenes had passed in Uppercross which made it precious. It stood the record of many sensations of pain, once severe, but now softened; and of some instances of relenting feeling, some breathings of friendship and reconciliation, which could never be looked for again, and which could never cease to be dear. She left it all behind her; all but the recollection that such things had been. (p. 117)

This poignant meditation stands to her recent experience at Uppercross exactly as the one in chapter 4 had stood to her early courtship. Just as in the former case "time had softened down much," so now does Anne dwell on "sensations of pain, once severe, but now softened." Here, as in K. 595, "the most painful dissonances are evoked and yet softened."

"Time softens down much," but so does Anne's resilient character. Her elasticity allows her not only to retain what was dear in the past but also to be receptive to the influx of the new. As she leaves Uppercross, dwelling on what she has lost, she registers the "black, dripping, and comfortless veranda" of the Cottage and even notices "through the misty glasses the last humble tenements of the village." Before she knows it, she finds herself not only at Kellynch Lodge but suddenly hoping "to be blessed with a second spring of youth and beauty" (p. 117).

On her first return to the family estate since it had been let out to the Crofts, Anne has two fears. One is that seeing others in possession of the place will bring severe pain to herself. The other is that seeing Frederick Wentworth, should he happen to visit his sister there, would bring severe pain to them both. But she is soon satisfied on both scores. The Crofts receive her with a graciousness and warmth of which her own family would have been incapable. They also announce that they plan soon to be away, thus precluding any visit from Frederick. "So ended all danger to Anne of meeting Captain Wentworth at Kellynch Hall. . . . Everything was safe enough and she smiled over the many anxious feelings she had wasted on the subject" (p. 122).

In chapter 2 Charles and Mary Musgrove arrive at Kellynch with the latest news from Lyme. Louisa is recovering and Captain Benwick can speak only of Anne, whose "elegance, sweetness, and beauty" he continually praises (p. 125). Anne takes many "strolls of solitary indulgence in her father's grounds." Each time she returns she hopes to encounter Captain Benwick, but she does not. After a Christmas visit to Uppercross, bustling as usual, Anne and Lady Russell arrive in Bath at the end of chapter 2. The rendering of their arrival is extremely sensory and subtle, being expressed at first through Lady Russell's enjoyment of the city's myriad winter noises. But Anne, confronted with "the first dim view of the extensive buildings, smoking in rain," does not share her friend's enjoyment. Instead, she looks back, "with fond regret, to the bustles of Uppercross and the seclusion of Kellynch" (p. 129).

In chapters 3 and 4 Anne is plunged again into the frigid world of Sir Walter and Elizabeth, this time at their new "home" at Camden Place in Bath. "They had no inclination to listen to her" (p. 130). "They could not listen to her description" (p. 133). More "earnest admiration" from Mr. William Elliot, the cousin glimpsed in Lyme, enlivens the atmosphere somewhat, but Anne tells a surprised Lady Russell that she could never marry him. To the further surprise of the family circle, Anne's main interest in Bath seems to be in a certain Mrs. Smith, a former friend, now a widow, who happens to be living there in reduced circumstances. Anne greatly admires her friend's buoyancy in the face of continued distress.

Anne's tribute to Mrs. Smith's resilience in chapter 5 recognizes that hers is

> not a case of fortitude or of resignation only.—A submissive spirit might be patient, a strong understanding would supply resolution, but here was something more; here was that elasticity of mind, that disposition to be comforted, that power of turning readily from evil to good, and of finding employment which carried her out of herself, which was from nature alone. It was the choicest gift of Heaven. (p. 147)

Such a gift, of course, is also Anne's. Her own "elasticity of mind" is as strong as that of Elizabeth Bennet or Emma Woodhouse, but it is of an entirely different tone. It is characterized exactly by "that disposition to be comforted, that power of turning readily from evil to good, and of finding employment which carried her out of herself." Her friendship with Mrs. Smith is just such employment. It is selfless in a manner that Emma's employment with her *Miss* Smith was not.

For all her admirable qualities, this same Mrs. Smith, by this stage of her life, "had seen too much of the world, to expect sudden or disinterested attachment anywhere" (p. 147). Anne cannot agree with this evaluation of life, nor can she agree with Mrs. Smith that "there is so little real friendship in the world" (p. 149). It might seem that Anne's own experience—past and present—would point in the same direction. But she remembers "sudden and disinterested attachments" she has witnessed on the part of the Hargraves at Lyme, the Crofts at Kellynch, and even Frederick Wentworth at Uppercross (picking the boy off her back, handing her into the carriage after the autumn walk, asking her advice on the return from Lyme). For Anne, the memory of evil no more blots out the memory of good than does the lapse of attention preclude its resumption. Remembering "sudden attachments" and "real friendships," she retains resilient if lonely hope about the possibilities of life.

Her hope becomes less lonely and more tangible in chapter 6, when the Crofts arrive in Bath. They deliver a letter from her sister Mary which informs her that Louisa Musgrove is to marry Captain Benwick! After enduring the inane and unfelt inquiries of her father and eldest sister about the letter and the Crofts, Anne is "at liberty" to go to her room and try to understand it all (p. 159). Typically, her first thoughts are for the friendship of captains Benwick and Wentworth, which she hopes has not been strained. She then tries to imagine Louisa and Captain Benwick, so different in temperament, in love. Having set these matters somewhat to rest, she approaches those thoughts nearest her own heart. "No, it was not regret which made Anne's heart beat in spite of herself, and brought the colour into her cheeks when she thought of Captain Wentworth unshackled and free. She had some feelings which she was ashamed to investigate. They were too much like joy, senseless joy!" (p. 160). Anne somehow manages to suppress her public curiosity until the time is right. When she twice meets the Crofts formally in the presence of her family and sees no recognition on their part when the name of Louisa or Captain Benwick is mentioned, she makes no inquiries of her own about Captain Wentworth. Her burning curiosity as to Wentworth's view of the engagement between his good friend and his own presumed "intended" must go unsatisfied for ten days more, until she has the "good fortune" to meet Admiral Croft outside the print-shop window.

The Admiral suggests they go for a walk, saying he has some news for her. The news, when he finally comes, in his digressive way, to tell it to her, is the news she already knows of Louisa's engagement to Captain Benwick, about which Captain Wentworth has now written him. Anne's only fear, her only hope, both of them unspoken, is that Wentworth has gotten over his attachment to Louisa and that there are no hard feelings between him and Benwick. As to the tone of the letter from Wentworth, the Admiral assures her that it contains "not an oath or a murmur from beginning to end." When Anne "looks down to hide her smile," the reader knows that she secretly hopes her "second spring of youth and beauty" is near at hand. She suppresses her further curiosity, however, and Admiral Croft is allowed to end their walk (and chapter 6) with his characteristically jaunty and expansive prescription for "poor" Wentworth's quick recovery.

> "Poor Frederick!" he said at last. "Now he must begin all over again with somebody else. I think we must get him to Bath. Sophy must write, and beg him to come to Bath. Here are pretty girls enough, I am sure. It would be of no use to go to Uppercross again, for that other Miss Musgrove, I find, is bespoke by her cousin, the young parson. Do you not think, Miss Elliot, we had better try to get him to Bath?" (p. 164)

JUST AS ANNE is alone at the beginning of the second volume, so is the solo voice unaccompanied at the beginning of the second movement. Just as the opening chapters of volume 2 essentially continue the mood of volume 1, so, in Girdlestone's words, does "the E-flat larghetto dwell in the same mood as the first movement." But here, as in the novel, the melancholy mood takes on a much more personal accent. Girdlestone suggests that the melody with which the solo opens the second movement "is like a farewell. It sings of an irrevocable parting" (p. 480). If he is right, this solo melody has a closer relation to Anne's solitary farewell to Uppercross at the beginning of volume 2 than the most avid comparer of the arts could desire. Before analyzing the Larghetto and its opening melody, it will be well to locate them within a special family of Mozart slow movements.

The Larghetto of K. 595 is not the first slow movement of a Mozart piano concerto to begin with the solo playing unaccompanied. It is, in fact, the fifth. The others are the Romance of K. 466, the Andante of K. 488, the Larghetto of K. 491, and the Larghetto of K. 537. Only in these five late concertos does Mozart arrange for the piano to speak apart and alone at the beginning of the slow movement. In each case, the solo melody expresses the solitude the sensitive individual needs, at times, for the reflection and meditation essential to an expansive and elastic emotional life. In this sense, such moments in Mozart are the equivalent of Elizabeth in the shrubbery at Rosings, escaping the importunities of Mr. Collins or Lady Catherine; of Emma pacing the lawn at Hartfield, sorting out her impressions from the ball the night before at the Crown; or of Anne having the "solitary range of the house" at Uppercross as she adjusts her "silent, pensive" self to the recent departures of Wentworth and the Musgroves and to the seemingly bleak future that, as always, confronts her.

It is not only the solitude of the solo voices but the tempo in which they move that suggests a comparison with the above heroines. In Italian, the term *andante* literally means "walking." This is the original meaning behind its use as an indication of the tempo (and character) of certain slow movements. The term *adagio* (at ease) means slower still, whereas *largo* (broadly) means slower yet. *Larghetto* indicates a pace slightly faster than *largo*, yet slower than *adagio*, and considerably slower than *andante*. Mozart was increasingly drawn to this tempo late in life—especially for slow movements that begin with a solo. The slow, deliberate tempos of the solo melodies that begin the Larghettos of K. 491, K. 537, and K. 595 (the clarinet melody that begins the Larghetto of K. 581 belongs to the same family) all suggest the pace of a slowly walking individual—just as the delicate, deliberate shape of each melody suggests a walking individual who is meditating. This deliberate pace is a second way in which the solo melody that opens the second movement of K. 595 compares with Anne Elliot's meditation at the beginning of volume 2—whether or not that melody can be said to "sing," like Anne's meditation, of "irrevocable parting."

Even stronger than the similarities of pace and solitude is the similarity of emotion between Anne's opening meditation and the solo's opening theme. Girdlestone, before analyzing Mozart's piano concertos one by one, groups their respective second movements according to character. Significantly, he places four of the five which begin with the solo in the same category: that of the "mature romances." He groups them thus not because the solo begins each movement (a fact he does not even note) but rather because of their comparable emotion. For Girdlestone, the Romance of K. 466 and the Larghettos of K. 491, K. 537, and K. 595 are the mature romances in which Mozart transcends the "colourless sweetness" of his earlier "fashionable romances." He finds that these later slow movements transcend their earlier counterparts because they combine a "more pungent feeling" with a "tone of passing sadness" in such a way that "the sweetness itself becomes more quivering" (p. 38). These late slow movements therefore give perfect expression to "that passionate tranquility" which is one of Mozart's "most personal traits"—and which reveals "depths of melancholy which his exuberant joy sometimes covers up but never fills" (p. 39). Among this special family of movements Girdlestone finds the last, the Larghetto of K. 595, to be the most melancholy: it is "one long farewell, poignant yet resigned" (p. 39).

It is the "passionate tranquility" of Anne Elliot's farewell at the beginning of volume 2, a pulsing tranquility at once "poignant yet resigned," that most significantly links her solitary situation with that of the solo at the beginning of the slow movement of K. 595. Before discussing the character of the opening melody and of the movement itself in some detail, it will be useful to briefly outline the structure of the movement.

THE Larghetto of K. 595 follows a simple a:b:a form. The piano plays an eight-bar melody (P^1) that is directly repeated by the orchestra (O^1). The piano then plays an eight-bar extension of the melody (P^{1a}), after which it gives an exact repeat of the melody itself (P^1). The orchestra then answers with an animated and "sighing" coda (O^2). This ends the "a" section of the movement, in which the opening melody has been heard three times (P^1, O^1, P^1).

The "b" section begins with a new melody in the piano. With orchestral accompaniment, the solo extends the melody, allowing the music to modulate, finally into the minor keys, where there is some intimate exchange between the solo and selected members of the group. The return to the "a" section is negotiated through trills in the piano. The solo again introduces the opening melody (P^1). This time the piano moves on directly to the extension (P^{1a}). When the piano now retuns to the opening melody it is accompanied in octaves by the flute and first violins ($P^1F^1V^1$). The orchestral coda (O^2) follows as before, with slight modifications to allow for the inclusion of the piano.

On the surface, this movement is all symmetry. The melodies that begin each section are as internally symmetrical as the sections themselves are, both internally and externally. The original "a" section, for example, unfolds in groups of 8, 8, 8, 8, and 16 bars. Its 48 bars (1–48) are balanced by the 49 bars (82–130) of the "a" section at the end, the two being separated by the 30 bars of the "b" section (49–78), plus a three-bar transition. This rigid, simple structure, combined with the uniformity of the melodic material throughout, would seem to assure a static character for the movement overall. And so it does—to a point. The entire movement is extremely homogeneous in both texture and material. But its very symmetries make possible certain deviations from the prevailing pattern that are extremely expressive and even dynamic. The subtle, pulsing inner life that dwells within its static framework is what gives this "poignant yet resigned" Larghetto its fragrant bloom. It is this modest a:b:a structure that transforms the melancholy of Mozart's last piano concerto into hope and that carries that hope even to the very threshold of joy.

GIRDLESTONE, as mentioned above, suggests that the opening refrain is "like a farewell. It sings of an irrevocable parting." This kind of statement is difficult to prove—as Girdlestone acknowledges.

> When a musician has not spoken it is always rash to attribute a precise meaning to any passage in his work; we naturally do not assert that Mozart felt himself, as he composed this refrain, in the mood which accompanies a painful separation; yet the likeness in melody and harmony between this theme and the beginning of Beethoven's *Farewell* sonata may allow us to think that our impression is not wholly unfounded. (p. 480)

The evidence from Beethoven, of course, is at best twice removed. It must be in the music itself that one finds the key to its character. And even if Mozart himself had claimed that the refrain "sings of an irrevocable parting" that would not establish its character very precisely. "Irrevocable partings" can range all the way from Anne Elliot's "silent, pensive" separation from Uppercross (and Wentworth) at the beginning of volume 2 to Catherine Earnshaw's sobbing, vehement separation from Heathcliff in chapter 9 of *Wuthering Heights*. Whether or not this melody can be said directly to express "parting" or "farewell," Anne's meditation compares to it, we have already suggested, in solitude, pace, and emotion. In a more literal way than Mozart's late romances, Anne Elliot's November farewell to Uppercross embodies a "passionate tranquility" that combines "pungent feeling" with a "tone of passing sadness" in such a way that the "sweetness becomes the more quivering."

Mozart's "passionate tranquility" is nowhere more quivering than in the two-part melody (P¹) with which the solo opens the Larghetto of K. 595 (Figure 16). Slow, deliberate, searching, the melody begins on E-flat, reaches the A-flat in bar 2, slowly falls to B-flat by bar 4, and climbs ever so gradually to the E-flat that begins bar 5. The original melodic line is now repeated—this time slightly truncated. The same A-flat is reached in bar 6, but the lower B-flat is achieved in bar 7. This allows the melody to close on the E-flat that begins bar 8.

The end of each phrase—in which the melody twice ascends from B-flat to E-flat—is of particular importance. In bar 4 the ascent is entirely chromatic. Five successive eighth notes climb to a half-note in deliberate half-steps: B♭-B♮-C-D♭-D-E♭. This flood of accidentals into an otherwise diatonic melody gives special poignance to this ascent, as does

Figure 16

its rhythmic and intervallic regularity. The effect, in the context, is of graceful courage bearing inward pain.

The ascent to E-flat at the end of bar 7 is dramatically different. It is diatonic: instead of the deliberate chromatic ascent the melody now leaps quickly from B-flat to C to D to E-flat. The rhythm here (a dotted eighth note followed by two thirty-seconds leading to an eighth) creates a lilting, marchlike motion that is heightened by the preceding rest, the only moment of silence in the entire melodic line. This quicker, trouble-free rise to E-flat anticipates, in ways that will be seen, the increased buoyancy that will be found at the end of the Larghetto itself.

Like the melancholy melody that began the first movement, this one is quiet, it moves less than an octave, and it gives a sense of restricted motion within narrow boundaries. In this sense it is equally resigned. But this melody is not broken into separate phrases by an external force (the winds). Its two phrases are linked by the solo itself, creating a more coherent and self-generated feeling. The courageous and lilting ascents at the end of its two phrases contrast with the resigned descents to or toward B-flat at the end of each phrase in the Allegro. Finally, the tonality of this solo melody, E-flat major, is typically a "brighter" key in Mozart than is B-flat major.

These and other differences between the resigned melody which opens the Larghetto and its counterpart in the Allegro contribute to the comparatively buoyant manner in which the second-movement melody bears its melancholy. The difference compares to the one in the novel between the "desolate tranquility" Anne feels at Kellynch early in volume 1 and the more "passionate tranquility" she embodies at Uppercross at the beginning of volume 2. This melody is undeniably sad—as is Anne's meditation. But it too possesses a resilience that carries its sorrow beyond mere tearfulness.

Because of the compression at the end of the solo melody, the horn call which precedes the orchestra's repetition of the entire melody fits into the last three beats of bar 8. The orchestral repetition itself (O^1) therefore begins on the first beat of bar 9 and ends on the first beat of bar 16. This leaves the rest of that bar for the transition in the strings that precedes the piano continuation (P^{1a}), which begins on the first beat of bar 17. Such subtle adjustment within a rigid framework typifies the entire movement. Even the orchestral repetition of the solo melody (O^1) contains such adjustments. Girdlestone notices a "trifling" difference in the second bar between the two versions: the solo plays the ascending motif in sixteenth notes, the orchestra in thirty-seconds (p. 480). What he does not notice is a more significant difference in the fourth bar: the orchestral version of the chromatic ascent, lacking the D-flat, is not nearly so pointedly poignant.

Although the two forces play the opening melody three times (P^1, O^1, P^1) in the "a" section that opens the Larghetto, they never play it at the same time, and this perhaps contributes to the feeling of separation that Girdlestone intuits in the music. Heard in this light, one could say that the solo generates the melody of "irrevocable parting" and that the orchestra answers directly, as if to verify that it is true. The piano, again alone, plays its eight-bar extension and its "parting" theme once more. The orchestra then concludes the "a" section with the coda (O^2), in which the solo has no involvement. Whether one cares to adopt Girdlestone's program or not, each protagonist has twenty-four of the forty-eight bars of the opening refrain. None of those bars has been shared.

The orchestral coda features a complex combination of moods and sonorities. Although some of its outward manifestations are more vehement than the previous part of the "a" section, based on the solo melody, it too combines the passionate and the tranquil. H. C. Robbins Landon has caught its character with skill and feeling. "The second tutti passage, at bars 32 ff, is one of the most exquisite and poignant Mozart ever wrote. But even the aching chromaticism of the strings and bassoon over the horns' pedal point (32–34), or the urgent, thrusting G flat trills of the second violin part in bar 35, have a certain emotional repose about them, an inward self-sufficiency."[6] This repose and self-sufficiency help give the coda, eventually, a soothing, benedictory effect.

The "aching chromaticism" with which it opens results from "sighing" half-step descents that seem to be recognizing the pain of the solo voice. The broken melody in the next eight bars in the violins resembles the piano extension of the opening melody (P^{1a}), but the busy, thrusting accompaniment in the lower strings creates a much denser mood and texture. The last five bars of the coda, however, lighten the mood considerably. At least three factors contribute: the almost jaunty motif that is repeated in the violins and flute, the lilting march rhythm that is outlined in the basses and cellos, and the drop to the tonic in the winds and strings in the final bar. This last descent is a sighing motif similar to the one that began the coda, but this one is not chromatic: the "ache" is gone. Melodically, it is also an extension of the "jaunty" motif in the violins and flute. These elements combine to give the coda, like the solo melody itself, an ending considerably more buoyant than its beginning, though in no way betraying the original emotion. When the "a" section returns at the end of the movement, the entire section becomes considerably more buoyant than before.

THE DISTRIBUTION of forces within the "a" section when it returns at the end of the Larghetto is as different as are the respective dynamics between Anne and society in the first and fifth chapters of volume 2: there is still the fact and the sense of separation but it is not nearly so irrevocable. Because the orchestra's direct answer of the opening melody is omitted this time, the solo is essentially alone for the first sixteen bars (P^1, P^{1a}). But in one sense there is already more togetherness, for now the graceful bar of transition in the strings (89) is no longer a transition from the whole orchestra to the unaccompanied solo but rather provides striking orchestral support of the solo's own continuation from the "parting" melody to its extension. Similarly, the transitional motif in the horns that had originally preceded the orchestral version of the theme now occurs in the middle of the piano's continuation phrase—and is now doubled by oboes and bassoons. This, too, has the effect of support for the piano, rather than of the earlier transition away from it. The woodwinds also contribute to the entirely new transition that leads to the final and most important return of the opening melody, in which the solo receives the full and complete support of the flute in unison and the violins an octave below ($P^1F^1V^1$).

In the context of an outwardly static movement, this melodic collaboration is a moment of high drama. Robbins Landon is but one of many critics who have marvelled at its "staggering orchestration in bare octaves" (p. 278)—without any support in the bass. Yet certainly the effect of the new distribution of forces is equally noteworthy. The solo, which has three times played the melody of "parting" entirely alone, now has splendid support. The orchestra, which had once answered the melody separately and as a massive group, now responds in concert and with selected members. As Girdlestone points out, the flute and violins preserve the "trifling difference" from the earlier orchestral version of the ascending motif in the second bar. But more important is the difference in the fourth bar that now disappears. Unlike the orchestra as a whole in the first "a" section, the flute and violins now give out the poignant chromatic ascent exactly as it is played by the piano.

This harmonious sharing of primary material compares with the effect achieved during the last return of the main theme in the Andantino of K. 271 and in the Andante of K. 503. Here, too, the emotion at the end of the movement, though the same as at the beginning, is nevertheless altered, because now it is shared. Such sharing did not occur in the Allegro of K. 595, whose recapitulation (unlike those of the earlier concertos) was in this sense so static. Such sharing of primary material corresponds to the direct sharing of emotion that Anne is able to achieve with Mrs. Smith in chapter 5 of volume 2, for which there was no equivalent in volume 1. She is as "irrevocably" apart from Wentworth as before, but at least she now knows true warmth and companionship, even if in sorrow. So, now, does the piano, in the last return of its most personal melody. In the words of Robbins Landon, the solo is "still more introverted" than before, as, "escorted on either side by flute and first violin, the melody floats, serene and unearthly, into the [coda]" (p. 278).

When the orchestral coda returns at the end of the Larghetto, its material is essentially the same. The difference is in the addition of the solo and the interpolation of four new bars of music. In the equivalent of bars 33 and 34 (bars 111 and 112), the solo follows the "aching chromaticism" of the winds and strings with ascending two-octave runs of tonic passage-work. This puts the ache in a more stable, bracing context. After the orchestra follows with six bars of the next eight-bar passage, the solo takes over the accompanying material from the strings—a theft that is celebrated by the winds and particularly the flute, which floats to a high F as part of its ethereal supporting line. Thus encouraged, the piano breaks out with a new melody (bar 122) that incorporates a motif that would have followed in the violins. It is then supported in its elaboration of this new motif as warmly as it was in the final return of its opening theme. The flute plays in unison and the violins double an octave below. In addition, the bassoons double the motif another octave below, and the lower strings provide their support too. This simultaneous togetherness is vertically richer than was the sharing during the final return of the opening theme, though it lasts for only two bars (124–25).

Following this new intimacy, the movement concludes with the last five bars from the first "a" section, both the same and different. What is the same is the jaunty motif in the violins and the lilting marchlike rhythm in the cellos and basses. What is different is the incorporation of the piano and the material of the flute. Rather than the jaunty motif, the flute now outlines the march rhythm, sharing it in alternation with the lower strings. The piano now outlines the new melody it has just introduced. These seemingly disparate elements all coalesce in the final bar, where the original sighing close in the violins, balanced two octaves below by the resolution of the march rhythm in the basses, is now balanced two octaves higher by a comparable ascending motif in the piano. With this simultaneous resolution on such widely spaced E-flats, the movement that began with its solo melody of "irrevocable parting" has ended with as much harmony and warm sonority as did the Andante of K. 503.

The tranquility with which the Larghetto ends is as passionate as that with which it began, but it is much less troubled. Like Anne as she enjoys her "snug walk" with Admiral Croft at the end of chapter 6, the solo here undulates in the wake of the new. Both have reached this blessed condition without straining after it, without forcing either the self or the other. When the solo melody returns for the last time, the solo is playing the same notes, expressing the same character, as at the beginning of the Larghetto: only the accompaniment has changed. The light, graceful touches by which the piano brightens the return of the coda with ascending passagework here, an accompaniment figure there, and that last delicate, quiet leap to the highest E-flat it has yet played—all these compare with the "hidden smile" by which Anne acknowledges, inwardly, that her "second spring" may in fact be at hand. That silent smile betrays a tranquility as passionate as, but much less troubled than, that embodied by her rain-blotted departure from Uppercross.

Within the formal and seemingly static symmetries of the outer "a" sections of the Larghetto, then, an amazing range of emotional dynamics have taken place. Built into the seeming symmetry of the original solo melody (P^1) has been a lilting buoyancy at the end of its second phrase that both eases and rewards the courageous chromaticism at the end of its first phrase. In the last return of the solo melody ($P^1F^1V^1$), a comparable buoyancy is added to the entire melody by the perfect support given by the flute and violins. The original coda (O^2) too achieved a buoyancy in its closing bars owing to its march rhythm, its jaunty motif, and its relaxed sigh. This quality is augmented, when the coda returns at the end of the movement, by the presence of the solo and by every detail of rescoring which accompanies it. And here we come to one of those felicities of detail that make the close study of Mozart's works so exhilarating. The lilting march rhythm that so enlivens the last bars of

Figure 17

the coda derives from the rhythm which ends the opening melody itself (Figure 17). Not only is the rhythm related: the ascending notes which it animates are identical (B♭, C, D, E♭). The buoyant ascending motion that graces the solo melody *and* the orchestral coda at the beginning of the Larghetto as well as the shared solo melody *and* the shared instrumental coda at the end of the movement derives from the same rhythm as it operates on the simple diatonic ascent that moves from B-flat, the harmonic root of the first movement, up to E-flat, the harmonic root of the second. This is Mozart's symmetry (both short- and long-range) at its most brilliant, pervasive, and unobtrusive.[7]

IN COMPARING and contrasting the outer "a" sections of the Larghetto, it has been necessary to temporarily ignore the inner "b" section. It compares with the dynamics of chapters 3 and 4 of volume 2 as clearly as the outer "a" sections compared to chapters 1 and 2 and to chapters 5 and 6 in their transition from resigned melancholy to animated hope.

In chapters 3 and 4 Anne returned to the world of the first three chapters of volume 1—the cold world of Sir Walter and Elizabeth. This time, however, she experienced that world in a new setting, Camden Place rather than Kellynch. In more ways than one, the "b" section of the Larghetto returns to the world of the first movement. Its opening melody, though given out by the solo, has striking affinities with the opening melody of the Allegro. It consists of two four-bar phrases in a very familiar pattern. Each of them starts on the same B-flat of the earlier melody, ascends an octave, and returns to the same B-flat. Here the phrases are separated, not by a motif in the winds, but by an entire bar of repeated B-flats in the piano (bar 54). Although each phrase begins in the key of E-flat major, the key of the second movement, each phrase ends in the key of B-flat major, the key of the first movement. In this sense, the "home" of this melody, like that of Sir Walter and Elizabeth, has changed only ostensibly from that of the first movement.

Once the key of B-flat major is again reached by the repeated phrase of the two-part melody, the extension of that melody introduces strong modulations, which, though not so extensive as those in the development section of the first movement, do finally settle memorably on the key of B-flat minor, briefly touched on earlier. This modulatory episode of twenty-two bars expresses more overt dissonance and pain than was found in the "a" section of the Larghetto, and the return out of it is negotiated in a manner that again shows Mozart's uncanny artistry. At bar 78 the modulatory activity of the "b" section comes to rest on three reiterated B-flats. (In the present context, B-flat is the root of the relatively painful key of B-flat minor.) In three bars that are dominated by successive ascending trills in the piano, the music manages both to modulate to E-flat major and to reach the E-flat on which the return of the "a" section can begin. It does so in a chromatic series of ascending trills: B♭-C♭-C-D♭-D-E♭. This ascending progression, on trilled whole and then half notes, is the same chromatic ascent that, in eighth notes, had courageously carried the original solo melody (P¹) back up to the E-flat from which its second phrase could begin (Figure 18).[8]

Figure 18

Now we can see the full degree to which the eight-bar solo melody that begins the Larghetto is a microcosm for the movement itself. The deliberate painful chromatic ascent by which the solo overcomes the first downward movement of the theme itself is the same ascent by which the solo even more deliberately overcomes the larger downward thrust of the "b" section, a section as stuck on a modulating but essentially unchanging B-flat as was the first movement itself. Whereas the chromatic ascent at the midpoint of the opening melody anticipates the "b" section of the Larghetto and the transition out of it, the diatonic ascent at the end of the melody anticipates the buoyant close of both the coda and the movement itself. The uplifting effect of the concluding bars of this Larghetto is particularly clear when compared with the Larghetto of the Clarinet Quintet, the work whose "inspiration" is generally so similar. The quintet movement's concluding bars are more, not less melancholy than its opening bars. One can fairly call them "wilting."

Rosen writes that the Larghetto of K. 595 "aspires and attains to a condition of absolute simplicity" and that its music "accepts the reduction to an almost perfect symmetry and triumphs over all its dangers" (p. 263). The opening melody itself is the clearest example of that "almost perfect symmetry." The compression at the end of its second phrase turns what would have been a perfectly symmetrical eight-bar melody into a nearly symmetrical melody of little more than seven bars at the same time that it transforms the deliberate chromatic ascent from B-flat to E-flat into a lilting diatonic ascent. This principle of variety within symmetry dominates the rest of the movement in matters large and small—as do the opposing but complementary ways of getting from B-flat to E-flat. From the lilting compression of the last bar of its opening melody to the augmented ease of the last bar of the movement itself, this Larghetto aspires to "absolute simplicity" exactly because its "almost perfect symmetry" is less than absolute.

JUST AS the solo melody that opens the Larghetto stands in microcosm for the movement itself, so does Anne's solo meditation at Uppercross stand in microcosm for the first six chapters of volume 2. After Anne overcomes her internal depression during the solitude of chapter 1, she is able to overcome the downward pull of Sir Walter and Elizabeth's world after being immersed in it in chapters 3 and 4. Her comparative buoyancy in chapters 5 and 6 radiates from the resilience with which she has transcended her own sorrow. This self-generated tranquility has brought Anne to the very threshold of joy—as has that of the solo. The process by which each has arrived there reveals their "personalities" to be amazingly similar, as a brief contrast with our earlier heroines and solo voices will make clear.

In the Andantino of K. 271 and the Andante of K. 503 the orchestra had introduced the opening material and the solo had learned to come to terms with it. In the Larghetto of K. 595 it is the solo that introduces the main burden of the movement and the orchestra that learns to respond with increasing sensitivity. But this solo voice, the one that seems to show the most initiative in its slow movement, is actually the one that changes the least. In the Andantino of K. 271, the bright, sparkling solo of the first movement learned to assimilate the orchestra's deep grief in the Andantino. In the Andante of K. 503, the proud, wayward solo of the first movement learned to respond to the orchestra with modesty and restraint in the Andante. But in the Larghetto of K. 595, the resigned, refined solo of the first movement essentially retains its earlier qualities. Now, however, these are self-generated—rather than being the sensitive response of a perfect listener to the initiatives of others. The result is not so much the development of a new side of the solo's personality (as it is in the above second movements) but rather the creation of a new context in which to savor qualities already there.

Anne Elliot contrasts in precisely the same way with our previous heroines. In the second volume of *Pride and Prejudice*, the bright, sparkling heroine learned for the first time to assimilate the grief of others. In the second volume of *Emma*, the proud, wayward heroine learned for the first time to respond to others with modesty and restraint. In the comparable portion of *Persuasion*, Anne is as resigned and refined as she was in the first volume. But we now see those qualities as self-generated and intrinsic—not as a submissive response to the initiatives of others. The result is not so much the development of a new side of her personality (as with Elizabeth or Emma) but rather the creation of a new context in which to savor the qualities already there. As with the solo voice, her "sweetness" is unchanged from that of volume 1: it is only the more "quivering."

The quiet yet passionate tranquility expressed so memorably by both Anne and the solo voice at the beginning of the second volume and second movement projects a complex and self-generated equilibrium not reached until a much later stage by the earlier heroines and solos. Neither Elizabeth Bennet nor the solo voice of K. 271 was able to initiate such equilibrium until the beginning of the third volume or movement. Only after Elizabeth had assimilated the burden of Darcy's letter was she able to generate the "flutter of high spirits" in which she approached Pemberly; only after the solo of K. 271 had assimilated the orchestra's burden in the Andantino was it able to initiate the infectious high spirits of the rondo with its first solo melody of the entire concerto. Neither Emma nor the solo voice of K. 503, of course, was able to reach such a self-generated equilibrium until well into the third volume or movement. Each had to experience the "sorrowful and passionate conflicts" initiated at Box Hill and at the beginning of the central couplet before being able to find profound relief in the "spontaneous overflow" of melodious emotion and genuine grief.

In these two pairs of earlier works, the heroines and solo voices achieve their "experience of maturity" within the course of the works themselves; Anne and the solo of K. 595 seem to have reached this stage before the work itself begins. No less than Anne Elliot does the solo voice of K. 595 seem already to have experienced and assimilated great grief. Each begins the work capable of expressing and embodying a rich and complex equilibrium. Yet in the course of the first volume and the first movement that capability could in either case be mistaken for a meek submissiveness that allows the individual to be overpersuaded by others—a quality by no means characteristic of our earlier heroines or solos. But that impression does not long survive the opening pages of volume 2 or the opening bars of the Larghetto. The "passionate tranquility" of Anne's solitary meditation and the solo's solitary melody immediately reveals the earlier restraint to have been the "absolute simplicity" of a "poignant yet resigned" character. Moreover, the essence of the character of both Anne and the solo voice is much deeper than resignation only, as the rest of the Larghetto and as Anne's discussions with Mrs. Smith reveal. The essence of the character of each is nothing less than "that choicest gift of Heaven" that Anne attributes to Mrs. Smith: "that elasticity of mind, that disposition to be comforted, that power of turning readily from evil to good, and of finding employment which carried her out of herself."

We have already suggested the degree to which the solo's opening melody and Anne's solo meditation contain in microcosm the dynamics of the Larghetto and of the first six chapters of volume 2. The next section will reveal the degree to which those quivering moments embody in microcosm the spirit and structure of the entire concerto and novel.

A Second Spring of Youth and Beauty

THE STRONG IMPETUS toward joy that dominates the concluding section of each work carries over directly from the buoyant ending of the previous section. Anne's "snug walk" with Admiral Croft at the end of chapter 6 is immediately followed by this paragraph, which opens chapter 7: "While Admiral Croft was taking this walk with Anne, and expressing his wish of getting Captain Wentworth to Bath, Captain Wentworth was already on his way thither. Before Mrs. Croft had written, he was arrived; and the very next time Anne walked out, she saw him" (p. 166). With equal dispatch, the lilting undulations of the last five bars of the Larghetto give way to the joyous melody with which the solo begins the finale. In neither case is a happy outcome in serious doubt. But in each case the path toward that outcome remains strewn with a series of hazards which, even after they are overcome, serve to qualify the prevailing joy that emphatically crowns each work.

Anne and Wentworth's first meeting in Bath in chapter 7 is filled with the mixed emotions that will alternate throughout the rest of the novel. Seeing him in the street, she is so excited that she loses her senses "for a few minutes" and has to "scold" them back (p. 167). When he enters the store into which she has taken refuge from the rain, he is "more obviously struck and confused by the sight of her than she had ever observed before; he looked quite red." Their brief, hesitant first meeting, seen largely through her eyes, combines "agitation, pain, pleasure, a something between delight and misery" (p. 167). Because she is with a group, and because arrangements had already been made for Mr. William Elliot to escort her home, she must refuse his offer to accompany her.

This "something between delight and misery" is further heightened at the concert a few days later in chapter 8. When Wentworth enters the already crowded Octagon Room, Anne steps forward to initiate a conversation. Their talk escalates with almost alarming speed from the generally mundane to the personally germane. The change is registered in their appearance as well as their words. "He stopped. A sudden recollection seemed to occur, and to give him some taste of that emotion which was reddening Anne's cheeks and fixing her eyes on the ground.—After clearing his throat, however, he proceeded" (p. 174). Ostensibly speaking of the regrettable ease with which Captain Benwick has transferred his affection from Fanny Harville, recently deceased, to Louisa Musgrove, Wentworth's voice betrays a more deeply personal emotion as he firmly denies that a man should be able to cast off a "devotion of the heart" to a woman who is "a very superior creature." And Anne reads him well.

> In spite of the agitated voice in which the latter part had been uttered, and in spite of all the various noises of the room, the almost ceaseless slam of the door, and ceaseless buzz of persons walking through, [she] had distinguished every word, was struck, gratified, confused, and beginning to breathe very quick, and feel a hundred things in a moment. (p. 175)

She steers the conversation to the earlier visit to Lyme. But suddenly "Lady Dalrymple, Lady Dalrymple" is announced. Anne must join her fawning father as he meets the patronizing dowager with "all the eagerness compatible with anxious elegance" (p. 176). After this familial duty has been performed and Anne turns to rejoin Wentworth, he is gone. She sees him moving into the concert room.

Though temporarily apart from him, Anne is all "felicity." As the Elliot party enters the room, her sister Elizabeth is equally happy. "Arm in arm with Miss Carteret, and looking on the broad back of the dowager Viscountess Dalrymple before her, [Elizabeth] had nothing to wish for which did not seem within her reach." Anne, on the other hand,

> saw nothing, thought nothing of the brilliancy of the room. Her happiness was from within. Her eyes were bright, and her cheeks glowed—but she knew nothing about it. She was thinking only of the last half-hour, and as they passed to their seats, her mind took a hasty range over it. . . . All, all declared that he had a heart returning to her at least; that anger, resentment, avoidance, were no more; and that they were succeeded, not merely by friendship and regard, but by the tenderness of the past; yes, some share of the tenderness of the past. She could not contemplate the change as implying less.—He must love her. (p. 177)

The rest of the evening, however, brings only pain and confusion. Wentworth, seeing her the object of Mr. Elliot's pressing attentions during the first intermission, does not approach her. Her "delightful emotions" give way to "agitation" during the next hour of music. At the next opportunity, Wentworth does approach her, though with some hesitation. He "looked grave, and seemed irresolute" (p. 181). The moment their conversation begins to thaw, Mr. Elliot calls upon Anne to translate the next Italian song for Miss Carteret. When she returns to Wentworth, he abruptly takes his leave. Left alone, Anne finally realizes that he is jealous of Mr. Elliot. "For a moment the gratification was exquisite" (p. 182). But she then realizes the extent to which appearances have deceived him—and the difficulty she may well have in finding the opportunity to undeceive him.

Chapter 9 is devoted to her long conversation the next morning with Mrs. Smith. In chapter 10 Anne goes to the White Hart Inn to call upon the Musgrove party, newly arrived from Uppercross. Here she meets Wentworth again. And again "delight and misery" are equally mixed. Because the group is large, they at first cannot speak privately. He finally manages to maneuver to her side. Again their talk quickly escalates to the personally germane. But—as in the Octagon Room—it is suddenly interrupted. First Henrietta Musgrove calls upon the entire party to get outdoors, before anyone else arrives. Before this can be done, Sir Walter and Elizabeth enter to chillingly dispense invitations to a gathering the next evening at Camden Place. Anne is deeply embarrassed by the "heartless elegance" of her father and sister, who leave as soon as they have "pointedly" given a card to Wentworth too. "The interruption had been short, though severe; and ease and animation returned to most of those they left, as the door shut them out, but not to Anne" (p. 215). Nor does ease return to Wentworth. He is clearly troubled by this appearance of those who had treated him with insolence in the days he had courted Anne: his "cheeks glow" and his mouth settles into a "momentary expression of contempt" (p. 215). Because the male and female parties immediately separate for the rest of the day, Anne has no opportunity to continue the conversation or to ask whether he will accept the invitation. Again unsure of him, she spends an evening at Camden Place in "broodings of . . . restless agitation" (p. 216).

Chapter 11 at the White Hart Inn reenacts the extended and acute emotional dynamics of chapter 8 at the concert, with the difference that the outcome is this time happiness and clarification rather than misery and confusion. Again, however, the suspense is intense. When Anne arrives, Mrs. Musgrove is speaking with Mrs. Croft, Captain Wentworth with Captain Harville. It is suggested that she wait for the return of Mary and Henrietta. "She had only to submit, sit down, be outwardly composed, and feel herself plunged at once in all the agitations which she had merely laid her account of tasting a little before the morning closed. There was no delay, no waste of time. She was deep in the happiness of such misery, or the misery of such happiness, instantly" (p. 218). After trying to piece together fragments from both conversations, she finally engages Captain Harville in the argument about male versus female constancy. This leads to Anne's heartfelt assertion—some time after Captain Wentworth has dropped the pen with which he is supposedly writing a letter to Captain Benwick—that women possess a capacity for "loving longest, when existence or when hope is gone." Having thus openly declared herself, "she could not immediately have uttered another sentence; her heart was too full, her breath too much oppressed" (p. 224). Wentworth is no better off. Abruptly leaving the room, he as abruptly returns. He then leaves again, after thrusting into Anne's hand a letter as "ill-addressed" as the one Elizabeth Bennet had received from Jane at Lambton.

The letter is as simple and direct in syntax as Darcy's to Elizabeth was tortured and convoluted. The first five sentences are indicative. "I can listen no longer in silence. I must speak to you by such means as are within my reach. You pierce my soul. I am half agony, half hope. Tell me not that I am too late, that such precious feelings are gone forever." Sixteen more sentences, whose main burden is "I have loved none but you," lead to the hasty postscript: "I must go, uncertain of my fate; but I shall return hither, or follow your party, as soon as possible. A word, a look will be enough to decide whether I enter your father's house this evening, or never" (pp. 225–26).

As much as Emma's tears during the carriage ride from Box Hill, Wentworth's words are a "spontaneous overflow of feeling." But Anne at first has insufficient tranquility in which to recollect them. "Half an hour's solitude and reflection might have tranquillized her; but the ten minutes only, which now passed before she was interrupted, with all the restraints of her situation, could do nothing towards tranquillity. Every moment rather brought fresh agitation. It was an overpowering happiness" (p. 226). As soon as she manages to escape the White Hart Inn and to meet Wentworth outdoors, the agitation is left behind and the "overpowering happiness" is shared.

Their long conversation on the gravel walk, which lasts an hour and which covers many pages, is one of the most moving "recapitulations" in fiction.

There they exchanged again those feelings and those promises which had once before seemed to secure everything, but which had been followed by so many, many years of division and estrangement. There they returned again into the past, more exquisitely happy, perhaps, in their reunion than when it had been first projected; more tender, more tried, more fixed in a knowledge of each other's character, truth, and attachment; more equal to act, more justified in acting. And there, as they slowly paced the gradual ascent, heedless of every group around them, seeing neither sauntering politicians, bustling housekeepers, flirting girls, nor nurserymaids and children, they could indulge in those retrospections and acknowledgments, and especially in those explanations of what had directly preceded the present moment, which were so poignant and so ceaseless in interest. All the little variations of the last week were gone through; and of yesterday and to-day there could scarcely be an end. (pp. 228–29)

When the report of their extended conversation ends several pages later, Anne finds herself "home" again—not so much home in the physical boundaries of Camden Place and in the proximity of her family, as home emotionally and psychologically. "At last Anne was home again, and happier than anyone in that house could have conceived. All the surprise and suspense, and every other painful part of the morning dissipated by this conversation, she re-entered the house so happy as to be obliged to find an alloy in some momentary apprehensions of its being impossible to last." No less than the exultant Othello when reunited with Desdemona on Cyprus does Anne feel too, too strongly blessed. Her response to these feelings is the one that is so often present in Mozart's music. "An interval of meditation, serious and grateful, was the best corrective of everything dangerous in such high-wrought felicity; and she went to her room, and grew steadfast and fearless in the thankfulness of her enjoyment" (p. 233). With Wordsworth, too, she can now recollect in tranquility.

At the party given by Sir Walter and Elizabeth that evening, Wentworth, of course, is emphatically present. For the first time, Anne is unannoyed by the "elegant stupidity" (p. 171) of the entertainment at Camden Place: she "had never found an evening shorter" (p. 233). Complete not only within herself but with her Wentworth, she can now take Mr. Elliot, the Wallises, Lady Dalrymple, Miss Carteret, and even Mrs. Clay in stride. And, more than ever, she can enjoy the company of the Musgroves, Captain Harville, Lady Russell, and Captain Wentworth. The conversation between Anne and Frederick which ends the chapter completes the recapitulation of their earlier joy.

It would be no stretching of a musical analogy to call the final chapter of the novel a coda. It begins with the question "Who can be in doubt of what followed?" and ends with Anne's becoming a "sailor's wife." All the loose ends of the plot (including Mr. Elliot's removing to London in the company of Miss Clay) are brought together here, as they are in Austen's other "happy" endings. Yet here there is a difference. Anne's happiness and joy, hard-earned and long-awaited as it is, is qualified in a way that Elizabeth's and Emma's were not in the concluding chapter of their respective novels. The fact that Anne had "no family to receive and estimate [her husband] properly . . . was a source of as lively pain as her mind could well be sensible of, under circumstances of otherwise strong felicity" (p. 239). More important, after we are told that Anne's "spring of felicity" was in the "warmth of her heart" and that she was "tenderness itself," we are told that Wentworth's "profession was all that could ever make her friends wish that tenderness less; the dread of a future war all that could dim her sunshine" (p. 240).

Anne Elliot has achieved that "second spring of youth and beauty" she had hoped for at the beginning of volume 2. She has regained "her bloom and her spirits" and has dissipated those cares that had "clouded every enjoyment of her youth." But the "dread of a future war" makes the joy of Anne Wentworth, if inwardly deeper than that of Elizabeth Darcy or of Emma Knightley, outwardly more precarious.

THE SWEET, sprightly melody that begins the finale of K. 595 is one of the few melodies in Mozart's concertos that can legitimately be linked to a specific nonmusical idea. Because Mozart used the same melody to begin a song he composed immediately after finishing the concerto, both the title of the song and the opening line of its lyrics have been taken by most commentators to indicate the spirit—and even the import—of the melody itself. The song's title is "Sehnsucht nach dem Frühlinge" (Yearning for spring). Its lyrics begin, "Komm, lieber Mai, und mache die Bäume wieder grün" (Come, sweet May, and make the trees green again). The parallel here with Anne's yearning for a "second spring of youth and beauty," a "spring of felicity" that she finally achieves, and that brings with it a return of her "bloom," is uncanny, to say the least. Even so, it is the spirit and structure of the third movement as a whole, not just the inspiration and import of its opening melody, that compares most strongly with the concluding section of *Persuasion*.

Patrick Piggott, the first musician to have written a book about Austen, argues that her work "at its best can only be likened to some of music's finest achievements, and that for anything comparable to the dénouement of *Persuasion* one must turn to Mozart." He supports this assertion by referring to "the sublime final act of *The Magic Flute*"—and by speaking of this "great masterpiece which, like Jane Austen's finest pages, combines simplicity and beauty of detail with absolute clarity of form and with the expression of deeply felt, but perfectly controlled emotion."[9] K. 595, too, is such a masterpiece. And its dénouement compares even more snugly with that of *Persuasion*.

The finale of K. 595, like those of K. 271 and K. 503, is a rondo in a:b:a:c:a:b:a form. Although joy and rejuvenation prevail in the end, its seven sections oscillate "between delight and misery" as acutely as do the last six chapters of the novel. From the moment Wentworth had arrived in Bath, it had seemed likely that he and Anne would be united. As Girdlestone writes, "If we knew nothing more of the finale [than its opening refrain], we would think it sang of joy." But each time Anne and Wentworth meet—near the shop, at the concert, twice at the White Hart Inn—their incipient joy turns to doubt. "But other passages express a different mood: . . . four times over the music turns from joy and, leaving sunlit avenues, passes into the shade of doubt. At such moments we encounter something like the sadness experienced in the allegro and larghetto." Anne's doubt drives her to "broodings of restless agitation," but she does not lapse into the weariness and resignation of volume 1. "The note of weariness, however, is absent; at no stage does the rondo belie the vigour of its beginning and as a result its minor passages are more dramatic than those of the first movement" (p. 488). The minor-key passages of this movement contrast with those of the first to the same degree that the dramatic doubts of the hopeful Anne contrast with the earlier melancholy of an Anne resigned.

The very first bar of the springlike rondo establishes the buoyant mood that will dominate the opening melody and the opening refrain—and that will prevail, despite obstacles, in the movement as a whole. The lilting, ascending four-note rhythm of bar 1 is repeated in bar 3 and its spirit animates the entire eight-bar melody (Figure 19). We have said

Figure 19

that this opening melody seems to have its source in the relaxed, expansive mood that blossomed at the end of the Larghetto. As it turns out, the melody is as closely related to the last bars of that movement as the opening paragraph of chapter 7 is to Anne's "snug walk" with Admiral Croft at the end of chapter 6. Furthermore, it bears a close relation to the melody of resigned melancholy that had opened the first movement.

The melody with which the solo begins the rondo, like the one with which the orchestra began the opening Allegro, begins on B-flat, ascends immediately to D and F, and eventually returns to B-flat after having risen no more than an octave. But this more expansive melody takes eight bars, rather than four, to reach its first full close on B-flat. And this more lilting melody reaches its highest point (the B-flat an octave higher) already in the first bar, rather than the tenth, as did the earlier melody at the beginning of its third phrase. Actually, the third phrase of that earlier melody, a melody of melancholy resignation, begins with the same four notes as this buoyant, even joyous melody. The difference is in the rhythm, as is shown in Figure 20. And the new rhythm that has given fresh animation to the earlier notes of weariness, that has allowed them to breathe and to leap, is itself derived from the lilting marchlike rhythm that had animated the closing bars of the Larghetto. It derives not only from the first half of the motif, which had alternated

Figure 20

there between the flute and basses (whose rhythm had in turn derived from the lilting diatonic ascent at the end of the Larghetto's opening melody), but also from its second half (the quarter notes separated by rests). As Figure 20 shows, the range of the marchlike second-movement figure is identical to that of the first- and third-movement passages: the ascent of an octave, from B-flat to B-flat. Within that one-octave range the primary melodies and rhythms of all three movements have found expression.

In the delightful melody that opens the rondo the misery to come is only hinted at most lightly. The only shadow in its eight-bar path is cast by the accidentals (B-natural and E-natural) that appear in bars 5 and 6 (motif a) of Figure 19. As Girdlestone points out, "this fragment is the only chromatic part in a diatonic tune and later on it turns out to be an important element in the movement" (p. 485). For now, it adds but a touch of shade to a most radiant solo melody.

That melody (P^1) is immediately repeated by the orchestra (O^1) and is then extended by the solo (P^{1a}). After the solo repeats the original melody again (P^1), the orchestra takes up the extension (O^{1a}). *Its* extension differs from that of the solo by allowing the oboes to incorporate two elements taken directly from the opening melody itself. In bars 43 and 44 they play the chromatic fragment (motif a) from bars 5 and 6. In bars 61 through 64 they play, and then repeat, the first two bars of the opening melody. Then the orchestral extension, which has also featured a firm, descending chromatic figure in the bassoons and lower strings, comes to a quiet close. This completes the opening refrain ("a") of the rondo.

In the first couplet (the "b" section of the rondo), the oscillation "between delight and misery" begins in earnest. After the solo introduces a rather inert, step-wise melody that begins on B-flat and then ascends an octave higher only to dissolve, the solo reaches a modified fragment of the original melody (P^1) that is destined for modulation (bar 78). Spurred on by a short motif in the winds, the piano takes this familiar material into F major, F minor, and G minor, in which the solo dwells with some piercing arpeggios and broken chords. At bar 94 the solo arrives at another figure derived from the rondo's opening theme, this one hovering undecided between major and minor—as is the support in the strings and winds that follows. Finally the mood eases. A bright, witty exchange between piano and flute carries the harmony to F major, the dominant. And the piano, at bar 107, introduces an eight-bar melody related to the opening melody by its nearly identical opening rhythm. Relaxed and trouble free, this melody is immediately repeated by the winds over flowing accompaniment figures in the piano. This is the first moment of relaxed and simultaneous exchange in the movement so far, for the "a" section, like that of the Larghetto, had moved in a strictly alternating pattern in which the two forces shared the same material, but never at the same time. Although this first couplet has ended as harmoniously as those of the rondos of K. 271 and K. 503, it had to negotiate forty bars of doubt before reaching the stable, shared theme in F major.

The transition back to the opening refrain ("a") is led by the piano through excited passagework that incorporates a short, brilliant cadenza. The solo offers its buoyant, radiant opening melody (P^1) exactly as before. And the orchestra begins the exact repeat (O^1). As soon as the orchestra reaches motif a, however, it hesitates, repeating the motif (this time in the oboes, not the strings), and suddenly the solo finds itself playing the chromatic fragment in B-flat minor, a "danger" key in the first two movements. This modulation introduces the extremely painful "development" episode ("c") of the rondo. For more than twenty bars (153–77) the solo plays intensely modulating scales and passagework which the orchestra tries to calm by reasserting the opening bars of the buoyant first melody. These "broodings of restless agitation" finally take the solo to a diminished-seventh chord (bar 177) which the orchestra sounds out three times. The solo, answering, resolves the harmony to E-flat major. And now, as if finally to regain equilibrium, the piano returns to the opening melody (P^1) again, this time in the new key. In this return of the opening refrain ("a"), however, the joy is even more quickly deflected to doubt. As soon as the solo reaches motif a, the winds and then the violins take over the chromatic fragment, and another painful bit of modulation sets in. The solo's two attempts to return to the joyous refrain have been undermined as suddenly as were Anne's attempted reconciliations with Wentworth at the concert hall (by Mr. Elliot) and at the White Hart Inn (by the arrival of Sir Walter and Elizabeth).

When the solo finally returns to the first couplet ("b") at bar 204, its opening melody is warmly supported by the winds and strings. But again the subsequent minor-key modulations and major-minor alternations (given new pungency through harmonic transpositions) delay the arrival of the sonorous concluding melody. The latter, transposed from its earlier F major to the "home" key of B-flat major, is now more closely related than before to the opening melody of the rondo. After it is shared again, and the solo then continues with its passagework, five strong orchestral bars (268–72) escort the piano to the cadenza. The doubt seems finally to have lifted.

As Girdlestone observes, this cadenza, the last Mozart has left us, is "one of the prettiest" (p. 487). It is also one of the strongest. It corresponds to nothing less than Anne's "overpowering happiness" when all the obstacles between her and Wentworth have finally been overcome. Beginning with the first four notes of the buoyant first melody (from bar 1), the solo plays them three more times in rising sequence, so that the fourth lilting octave leap is from E-flat to E-flat. From there the right hand launches into a powerful stream of brilliant passagework while the left hand boldly presents the same four notes in descending sequence in the bass, where they have not yet been heard. After carrying its buoyant joy quite literally to the top and the bottom of the keyboard, the solo then breaks into swells of passagework in both hands that subside just once, when they settle twice on the familiar chromatic motif (a) before sailing on. In this exhilarating context, the chromatic fragment is no longer a threat.

At last the spacious passagework carries the solo to two trills of the sort that often announce the end of a cadenza. But here the buoyant solo continues to play alone, gliding directly on to the opening melody (P^1) as it was heard at the beginning of the movement. This time the orchestra omits its repeat (just as it had in the Larghetto at the last return of the opening melody). Instead the piano continues with its own extension (P^{1a}), now receiving warm but restrained support from the strings. Only after the solo repeats its melody once more (P^1) does the orchestra enter with its own extension (O^{1a}).

This final return of the opening refrain ("a") is as deeply moving as is Anne's return to a "second spring." Having been harshly interrupted during its two previous returns, the joyous opening melody is once more intact. Its return to its "home" key and to its repeated completeness (P^1, P^1) is the more welcome after the modulatory pressure it (and its derivatives) experienced not only in the two returns but in all three episodes. The psychic satisfaction of this opening melody's pristine return is, for a rondo, unusually close to that of a sonata-allegro recapitulation following a particularly trying development section. (This movement is one of Mozart's finest examples of what has come to be called the rondo-sonata form.) This return of the joyous refrain is all the more moving because it is embodied in thirty bars of continuous melody from this particular solo voice (P^1, P^{1a}, P^1). Structurally, it is doubly delicious because the solo has gone beyond the cadenza (by beginning the melody of the refrain) while not yet leaving it (continuing to play alone).

When the orchestra finally returns in full force to play its own version of the extension (O^{1a}), it begins exactly as it had early in the movement. But before it can finish, the solo intervenes to begin the coda—cutting in with a brilliant burst of virtuosity just when the oboes are about to quote the opening measures of the first theme (bar 323). For the first time in the concerto, Girdlestone observes, "virtuosity is for a moment an end in itself" (p. 488); the solo, like Anne, is momentarily feeling the first flush of its full power after a long history of submission and resignation. After twenty bars of buoyant bravura (which balance in their exhilaration the solo's restless broodings in the "development" couplet), the piano comes to rest on a trill, twice repeats the first two bars of the opening melody (the very bars it had just stolen from the oboes), and then allows the oboes to play them at last, accompanied by playful farewell pianistic arpeggios. The *forte* close is left to the orchestra as, in Girdlestone's words, "the last bars cast off all morbidity and resound with a joyful unison fanfare in the orchestra, based on the first bar of the movement" (p. 487).

Just as Anne, after she is finally united with Wentworth, is able to listen to her father and sister and various sycophants and hangers-on without their weighing too heavily upon her, so is the solo now able to allow the orchestra, which has hardly been heard at full strength since back in the first movement, to speak as one and to have the last word. Having found its own full voice, and having found its own select society within the group, the solo, like Anne, is no longer inhibited by the force of the whole.

IN OVERT FORM, the finale of K. 595 has closely followed those of K. 271 and K. 503. But the internal dynamics within its a:b:a:c:a:b:a structure have differed memorably. Its buoyant opening refrain is more melodious than that of K. 271, less tinged with melancholy than that of K. 503. But the major difference is in the heart of the movement. In the earlier rondos, the only severe threat to the prevailing high spirits occurred in the central a:c:a section. Here severe modulatory and motivic stress invades the "b" episodes as well—and they are the longest episodes. Only the outer "a" sections of this rondo, less than thirty percent of the whole, are harmonically and melodically secure. The rest of the movement (the b:a:c:a:b portion) can best be characterized as "a something between delight and misery."

We have seen that the concluding section of *Persuasion* differs in the same way from its earlier counterparts. Volume 3 of *Emma* is more deeply tinged with melancholy than volume 3 of *Pride and Prejudice*, but in each case the only severe threat to the prevailing high spirits is limited to the middle third of the volume. In each case the misery in the middle is balanced by equivalent stretches of "delight" on either side. This is not so with the dénouement of *Persuasion*, which oscillates between "half agony, half hope" from the moment Wentworth arrives in Bath. Just as the delight which ends the novel is qualified by the "dread of a future war" (the only thing that could "dim Anne's sunshine"), so is the joyous ending of K. 595 qualified by the "shadows of doubt" that have pervasively spotted its sunlit course. Each work remains within the convention of the "happy ending," but neither is likely to be accused of being "too light, and bright, sparkling" or too lacking in "shade."

The rondo of K. 595 also differs from those of K. 271 and K. 503 in its lack of thematic variety. The opening melody not only dominates each return of the refrain: fragments derived from it play an important role in all three episodes. Such dependence on material from one theme is unusual in Mozart even in a sonata-allegro movement; it is almost unheard of in his rondos. Yet such a tendency was found in the earlier movements of K. 595 as well. The first movement, with its development section based almost exclusively on the first theme, with its lack of sharply contrasting subsequent themes, and with its submissive solo exposition and recapitulation, was also unusually homogeneous in its thematic material. So was the Larghetto, dominated by its own first melody and without a great deal of contrast in its "b" section. This overall lack of sharp thematic contrasts differentiates K. 595—both movement by movement and whole by whole—not only K. 271 and K. 503 but from virtually every other Mozart piano concerto.

So is *Persuasion* unusually monothematic and homogeneous for an Austen novel. The entire work is devoted to the love story of Anne and Wentworth. There is no subplot even marginally equivalent to those provided by Jane Bennet and Bingley or Jane Fairfax and Churchill. Indeed, there is hardly the equivalent of a Collins-Charlotte or a Harriet Smith–Robert Martin sub-subplot. From the confidential and italicized *he* at the end of the novel's third chapter, the love story of one woman and one man is all that we have or need. *Persuasion* is considerably shorter than either *Pride and Prejudice* or *Emma*, but its main love story is more extended. Whereas neither Elizabeth Bennet nor Emma Woodhouse realizes that she loves Darcy or Knightley until well into the third and last volume, Anne Elliot loves Wentworth throughout her novel's two volumes.

In Austen's last novel, the elegance, grace, and restraint with which the heroine casts her warm heart and discriminating mind over the losses of the past and the life of the present is made, as action, to suffice. In Mozart's last piano concerto, the elegant, graceful, and restrained melodies generated first by the orchestra, then by the solo, create a world equally subdued, pulsing, and complete. The emotional progression in each work pivots upon the quivering solo meditation that begins the second volume and the second movement. Each is

> Composed of pleasure and pain
> Of hurt urged to tranquility
> So that sweetness may prevail.[10]

OUR EXTENDED COMPARISON of *Persuasion* and K. 595 began with the statement, commonplace in the commentary on each, that the "inspiration" of these two "autumnal" works is of greater interest than their structures per se. We have therefore emphasized not so much the formal structure of each work as the emotional structure that has carried us, in each case, from resigned melancholy through lonely hope to profound joy. We may now pause briefly to examine a few of the formal subtleties and felicities each artist achieved while his or her main interest was seemingly with "inspiration."

The two volumes of *Persuasion* are masterfully symmetrical—though not merely in having twelve chapters each, which in itself is no great achievement. Chapter 1 of volume 2 effectively balances chapter 1 of volume 1 with its return to Kellynch and its contrast of the Crofts' occupancy with that of Sir Walter Elliot. Spatially, the first ten chapters of volume 1 (restricted to the three-mile radius connecting Kellynch and Uppercross) are balanced by the last ten chapters of volume 2 (restricted to Bath). All major transitions—from Uppercross to Lyme, from Lyme to Uppercross, from Uppercross to Kellynch, and from Kellynch to Bath— occur in the last two chapters of volume 1 and in the first two chapters of volume 2. But the most masterful symmetry between the two volumes is at once the simplest and the most disguised, the most pervasive and the most poignant.

As pointed out in the above discussion of volume 1, Wentworth is absent for the first six chapters and present for the last six. Significantly, the identical pattern is repeated in volume 2. The resulting symmetry is more than technical, for the structural identity between the two volumes throws into high relief the emotional progression from the one to the other. Anne's "desolate tranquility" in the absence of Wentworth in the first six chapters of volume 1 is balanced by her "passionate tranquility" in his absence in the first six chapters of volume 2. Her iridescent agitation in his presence in the last six chapters of volume 1 is balanced by her iridescent exhilaration in his presence in the last six chapters of volume 2. Her oscillating experience of "a something between delight and misery" while with him at Uppercross and Lyme in the last half of the first volume is resolved in the direction of misery. With him at Bath in the last half of the second volume, it is resolved in the direction of delight.

We may never know whether Austen consciously intended this symmetrical division of the novel into four six-chapter sections based on the presence or absence of Wentworth. But whether she intended it or not, she could hardly have delineated the moments of transition more clearly. We have already had occasion to quote the first sentence of chapter 7 of volume 2: "While Admiral Croft was taking this walk with Anne . . . Captain Wentworth was already on his way thither." Here is the first sentence of chapter 7 of volume 1: "A very few days more, and Captain Wentworth was known to be at Kellynch . . . " (p. 54). This, in turn, is a direct answer to Anne's impassioned surmise at Kellynch at the end of chapter 3 that "*he*, perhaps, may be walking here." Even the first six chapters of Wentworth's absence, then, are perfectly divided by the italicized *he* that ends chapter 3 and that also begins chapter 4.

The dividing point between the two volumes themselves is marked with equal clarity. We have already seen that volume 2 begins with Anne's solitary meditation at Uppercross. What we have not yet pointed out is that volume 1 ends with the words "he was off" (p. 112). Anne's farewell meditation to Uppercross and to Wentworth at the beginning of volume 2 at once looks back to the melancholy of volume 1 and ahead to the "second spring of youth and beauty" that will blossom in volume 2. As analyzed above, the melody that opens the Larghetto serves the identical function in K. 595.

Although our comparison of these two "autumnal" works has been structured according to their emotional progressions, the proportions among their respective "emotional" divisions turn out to be surprisingly alike. We noted earlier that volume 1, the volume of resigned melancholy, is shorter than volume 2 in the proportion of 103 pages to 125. Within volume 2, the six chapters of lonely hope (and Wentworth's absence) are shorter than the six chapters of deep joy (and Wentworth's presence) in the proportion of 50 pages to 75. In the concerto the movement of resigned melancholy lasts 13 minutes, that of lonely hope 7, that of deep joy 9. The comparable overall proportions are therefore 103 to 50 to 75 in the novel and 13 to 7 to 9 in the concerto.

In the above discussion of the respective movements of K. 595 there has already been occasion to mention many of the important links—of rhythm, of melody, of harmony, of mood—among them. In conclusion I wish briefly to discuss two structural links—a large one between the beginning of the second movement and the beginning of the third, and a small one between the end of the first movement and the end of the third.

We have seen that the Larghetto is in simple a:b:a form, the finale in a more complex a:b:a:c:a:b:a form. The one movement, slow, expresses lonely hope; the other, faster, is more joyous. But in spite of these and other differences, the opening "a" sections of each movement are nearly identical in structure. Each begins with an eight-bar melody given out by the piano alone (P^1). Each follows with an eight-bar repetition of the same melody by the orchestra (O^1). Next comes in each case an extension of the opening melody by the piano alone (P^{1a})—in one case lasting eight bars, in the other sixteen. Then follows the piano's eight-bar restatement of the opening melody (P^1). Each section then concludes with a passage by the orchestra alone—a sixteen-bar coda (O^2) in one case, a twenty-four-bar version of the piano extension (O^{1a}) in the other.

Because of Mozart's wealth of invention (he gives us so much else to notice and to feel), the structural identity between these two opening sections is no more likely to be perceived during a first encounter than is the one between the two volumes of *Persuasion* based on Wentworth's dual absence and return. Once heard, however, it too provides for those who perceive it an excellent framework in which to measure the emotional progression from the one movement to the other. That progression is found in the melodies, rhythms, and harmonies that animate the identical structures; it is also found in the relations between the solo and the orchestra when the "a" sections return at the end of their respective movements. The return at the end of the Larghetto features the sharing of the solo theme with the flute and violins ($P^1F^1V^1$); that at the end of the rondo features the solo's return from the cadenza with thirty bars of continuous buoyant melody (P^1, P^{1a}, P^1) in its own hands.

Just as the opening "a" section of the third movement has structural parallels with that of the second movement, so do the last three notes of the third movement compare with those of the first. In one way they differ dramatically: the first movement, the movement of resigned melancholy, ends in a hushed *pianissimo*, whereas the more joyous finale ends on a clamorous *forte*. But the rhythm of the respective note clusters is identical: three notes of equal duration spoken in unison by the entire orchestra and separated by rests. Likewise, as Figure 21 shows, the flute in the upper register and the cellos and basses in the lower register conclude the third movement with the identical succession of pitches with which they had concluded the first. In the weariness and resignation

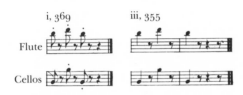

Figure 21

that end the first movement are the seeds of the joy of the last. And vice versa.

Persuasion ends in a similar manner. The joyous last paragraph of the novel hints at the sorrow which had ended volume 1: the "dread of a future war" both recalls and anticipates a time when "he was off."

OUR FIRST detailed comparison of individual works by Mozart and Austen began with the delightful opening bars of K. 271, bars in which the "stately is opposed to the impertinent, and balanced perfectly by it." As Rosen points out, the piano's answer to the orchestra is in perfect inverse symmetry—a symmetry that is "concealed, delicate, and full of charm." Our third detailed comparison of individual works has brought us to the longe-range but equally delicate symmetry of Wentworth's dual absence and return in *Persuasion*. This instinctive achievement of both short-range and long-range symmetry, inconspicuous yet pervasive, is one of the deepest affinities between Mozart's and Austen's art. Another is the striking degree to which such structural felicities inevitably serve the emotion of the work in which they occur. Rosen writes that in Mozart "the symmetry is a condition of grace" (p. 187). So is the symmetry of Austen.

Our selected comparisons of Mozart concertos and Austen novels have taken us in each case from the first unmistakable masterpiece to the last. We have seen the one artist take the piano concerto, the other the domestic novel, and transform each genre into one in which (to return to the words from *Northanger Abbey*) "the greatest powers of the mind are displayed, in which the most thorough knowledge of human nature, the happiest delineation of its varieties, the liveliest effusions of wit and humour are conveyed to the world in the best chosen language." Each has done so through "performances which have only genius, wit, and taste to recommend them."

All six performances analyzed above have remained within the domain each artist marked out with his or her "first steps." Each achieves its own perfect balance between "energy" and "boundaries," between "freedom" and "submission to rules." But in each successive pair of works the balance has been new. The three pairs of works have taken us from a youthfully idiosyncratic world to a maturely conventional one, to an autumnally poignant one. They have taken us from the kind of classical equilibrium that is "light, and bright, and sparkling" to the kind that is massive and expansive and grave, to the kind that, stylistically, anticipates Romanticism. Our two classical artists, without overstepping the original domain, have both circled deeper and deeper into the depths of the soul.

There is something very special about the tender gravity with which these two born humorists and classicists probe, in the last concerto and the last novel, into the world of Romantic sorrow and longing. Rosen finds it "fitting that Mozart, who perfected as he created the form of the classical concerto, should have made his last use of it so completely personal" (p. 263). The same may certainly be said of Austen's last use of the domestic novel. These two last works occupy a very special position not only in the traditions of the classical concerto and the neoclassical novel but also in the career and the life of each artist. Rosen calls K. 595 "a private statement: the form is never exploited for exterior effect, the tone is always one of intimacy" (p. 263). Because *Persuasion* is equally private and intimate, it, no less than K. 595, has provoked considerable biographical speculation. That speculation has in each case been so intense as to suggest that the change in style (from classical toward Romantic values) in fact reflects a change in the personality of the artist. Though delicate, the issue is a most appropriate one on which to conclude our comparison of Austen and Mozart.

We have already had occasion to note that the mood of a work of art does not necessarily reflect the mood of the person who created it. Students of Mozart have learned to be particularly careful in this regard because of his practice of composing simultaneously such emotionally polar works as the piano concertos in D minor and C major (K. 466 and K. 467) or the symphonies in G minor and C major (K. 550 and K. 551). Nor does the creation of an "autumnal" work mean that spring or summer is forever banished. Even within such works there may be, as we have seen, *second* springs. And there may be additional first ones—as Mozart's E-flat Quintet (K. 614) and Austen's opening draft of *Sanditon* (the novel that would have succeeded *Persuasion*) reveal.

Even so, K. 595 and *Persuasion* do appear to be "private statements" of a very special kind. Each does reflect a shift toward a more Romantic—as well as a more personal—mode of expression. Each was finished during the last January of its creator's life. Given these circumstances, biographical speculation is perhaps inevitable. That which follows here will be anchored to the internal dynamics of the two works themselves— particularly those of home and away, of clarity and ambiguity, and of individual and society.

NEITHER K. 595 nor *Persuasion* creates the unqualified sense of "home" and stability found in the two pairs of earlier works. One reason for this is the "inspiration" of each work. Each is dominated by its celebrated "autumnal" mood and reaches its "second spring" only after yearning for it during long periods of desolation. Another reason for this relative instability is to be found in the mechanics and subtleties of place and of key.

The geographic range of *Persuasion* is no more extensive than that of *Pride and Prejudice*. Uppercross is only three miles from Kellynch; Lyme is only seventeen miles from Uppercross. Nor is Bath itself terribly distant. But as Anne moves from the one place to the other there is no sense of a stable home to which she can return. Kellynch is shaky from the beginning; she does not really belong at Uppercross; Lyme is only temporary; and Bath, a new and apparently permanent home for Sir Walter and Elizabeth, is not so for Anne. Anne is not only without a stable home throughout the novel; she is without one at the end. We are not only uncertain as to whether Wentworth will someday be called off to war; we also are not told where he and Anne will live.

The treatment of home and away was entirely different in the earlier novels. When Elizabeth Bennet traveled to Rosings or to Pemberly, she always had the stable home of Longbourn to return to. The fact that she leaves Longbourn at the end of the novel induces no sense of homelessness, for Pemberly has been introduced at the beginning of volume 3 as a more spacious and pleasant home than Longbourn itself. Likewise, in *Emma*, all of whose action takes place in Highbury and its near environs, Emma's transition from the familial home (Hartfield) to the marital home (Donwell Abbey) has been carefully prepared by the presentation of the new, more perfect home during the strawberry party in volume 3.

Persuasion is the only Austen novel either to begin with the dissolution of a home or to end without the establishment of a new one. Its sense of home is not only less stable but also less tangible than in any of the other novels. The ultimate equilibrium to which this novel aspires is more intrinsic and internal. It is encompassed by Anne's character, without reference to the external frame of a house or the boundaries of an estate. We are told in the last chapter that Anne has "no Uppercross Hall, no landed estate" (p. 238); what she does have is the internal equilibrium that crystallized as she left Uppercross Hall in a carriage. This new kind of equilibrium is one measure of the shift in late Austen to more Romantic values.

In K. 595 the tonalities of the successive movements are as homogeneous as those of K. 503 and more homogeneous than those of K. 271. Yet the dynamics of home and away in this concerto are, paradoxically, more rootless. This is owing, of course, to the chromaticism that pervades Mozart's last piano concerto. The outer movements are in B-flat major and the central movement is in the related major key of E-flat, but the chromaticism and the modulations that invade this pattern are of such a nature as to render the harmonic home extremely vulnerable. Quite the opposite was the case in the earlier concertos.

In K. 271 the outer movements in E-flat major provided a strong sense of home from which the music dramatically departed during the second movement in C minor. The return home at the beginning of the third movement was as satisfying and complete as the departure at the beginning of the Andantino was disturbing. In K. 503 the C-major tonality was established so strongly in the opening bars and maintained so massively throughout the first movement that the abrupt shifts to C minor paradoxically strengthened one's sense of home. In the finale of K. 503 the strong sense of harmonic stability was temporarily invaded by the dramatic modulations of the passionate central episode, but this harmonic disruption was more than balanced by the 150 concluding bars that almost redundantly reaffirm the stability of the C-major home.

As we have seen, the home key of B-flat major is strongly established by the three-part opening melody of K. 595. Yet the first movement, in Rosen's words, "is gradually permeated by an expressive, even painful chromaticism that dominates everything by the beginning of the development section" (p. 260). This chromaticism, which is also characteristic of the second and third movements, gives the concerto much of its "wilting"—as well as its rootless—quality. Because the chromaticism of the third movement permeates a full two-thirds of its structure, the return to the home key in this finale is at once less stable and more poignant than in either of the earlier works. Indeed, in no Mozart concerto is the sense of a tonal home as vulnerable as in the last concerto. This is one important way in which K. 595 anticipates musical Romanticism.

Compared with their predecessors, then, K. 595 and *Persuasion* tend to eschew the stability, respectively, of a home key uninvaded by pervasive accidentals or of a physical home marked out by fixed boundaries. This tendency toward tonal or spatial instability causes each work in its quiet way to anticipate the world of Romanticism, in which ambiguity tends to become less a means of achieving a higher clarity than an expressive end in itself. As Rosen says of K. 595, the chromaticism in the development section of the first movement becomes so "iridescent" that it takes classical tonality "as far as it can go." As Stuart Tave says of *Persuasion*, Anne Elliot is constantly made to experience those "ambiguities of a something between" that were "treacherous ground" for Austen's earlier heroines. "Anne ever seeks these moments of ambiguity and never avoids them, but bears them all as she must until they can be brought to clarity. . . . It is her ability to sustain the buzz and the confusion and to hear distinctly what must be heard, to make the right distinctions under the agitation of pain, of pleasure, of mixed feelings, that makes her so lovely."[11]

In both works the moments of ambiguity are eventually brought to a kind of clarity. But in each case we are left less with clarity than with a heightened ability to "hear distinctly what must be heard" and to do so "under the agitation of pain, of pleasure, of mixed feelings." Certainly it is allowable to think of Tave's tribute as applying not only to Anne (and to the solo voice) but also to Austen (and to Mozart). Never had either artist explored such "treacherous ground" with such seeming assurance and ease. One can only wonder whether the poignant ambiguity of each autumnal work reflects, metaphorically, the artist's own recognition that his or her own earthly stay was becoming ever more temporary and transitory.

ANOTHER WAY in which these two works anticipate Romanticism and differ from their predecessors is in their increased emphasis upon individual expression. It is the quality of the emotion expressed by Anne and by the solo, more than the dynamics of their interaction with the larger group, that allows them finally to attain the joy for which they yearn. Given the character of these solo "personalities," it is not only paradoxical but natural that each finally attains deep personal joy within the context of the larger group in spite of being so submissive and re-signed in the opening volume and movement.

Anne, resigned and refined in volume 1, remains so in volume 2, yet her "passionate tranquility" endures to enable Wentworth finally to rec-ognize that he still loves her—and she him. Anne never compromises her quiet integrity to the demands of the larger society, even when self-lessly doing the bidding of her sisters or father. Instead, she holds out internally for the limited but deeper pleasure of a society of like souls, even during the lonely moments when it seems to be a society of one. In the end she finds herself to be the center of a considerable intimate society, all of whom lovingly embrace her unostentatious love and dig-nity—qualities now tolerated, if not lovingly embraced, by the larger society as well. This select society, even more than Emma's "small band of true friends" in the last paragraph of her novel, provides the only heartfelt support for Anne's "perfect union."

Similarly, the piano, so refined and resigned in the first movement, protecting its one private piece of individuality while politely doing the orchestra's bidding, has paradoxically taken the lead in the last two movements. It does so first by announcing its theme of "irrevocable parting" to begin the Larghetto, then by announcing its "yearning for spring" to begin the rondo. By the end of the second movement it has won the flute and first violins over to its side; by the end of the last movement it has brought the entire orchestra to its side in the clamorous close. But in the process of achieving this final and fruitful harmony it has achieved its closest intimacy, as has Anne, not with the "society" at large, but rather with solitary instruments, especially the woodwinds. The same tendency was present, though to a somewhat lesser degree, in K. 503. There, too, the solo is more intimate with individual members of the winds than with the strings or with the orchestra as a whole. In-deed, this tendency is found in most of Mozart's late concertos. Writing specifically of the great C-minor Piano Concerto (No. 23, K. 491), Eva and Paul Badura-Skoda find a distinct contrast between the use of "the strings, which have many players to a part and are therefore in a sense 'impersonal,' and the 'subjective' solo wind instruments."[12] The role of the "subjective" winds is to "occupy a middle position" between the solo and the larger group—a role they play to perfection in K. 595.

Corresponding to the role of the winds in K. 595 are the soulmates who become increasingly important to Anne in *Persuasion* (the Crofts, the Harvilles, Mrs. Smith). Corresponding to the "impersonal" strings, of course, are Sir Walter Elliot, his daughter Elizabeth, and the impersonal society they represent. These impersonal strings and beings provide the context in which the action of each work must take place, but they are not nearly as pertinent to the final outcome as were their counterparts in the earlier works. In K. 271 and *Pride and Prejudice* the dichotomy between the "subjective" and the "impersonal" was not nearly so acute. In those works the larger society and the instrumental whole were much more pervasive, prominent, and influential throughout, and the solo and the heroine interacted with a much broader range of individuals and instruments. In K. 595 and *Persuasion* it is significant that the "impersonal" forces which open each work are afterward not allowed to display their full "glory" until the final pages and final bars—until, that is, the humanly meaningful intimacy and exchange have already taken place.

K. 271 had initiated an intricate mating dance between a "stately" society and a brilliant composer-pianist whose "impertinence" never trespassed the boundaries of "liveliness of mind." Fourteen years and eighteen piano concertos later, K. 595 is the farewell of that pianist to a society whose "stateliness" had become nonpertinent to his human, spiritual, and economic survival—even though he had been named its imperial court-composer in 1787. As Mozart allegedly wrote on a tax return, Einstein tells us, the stipend he received for this largely honorary position was "too much for what I do; too little for what I could do!" (p. 58). One thing Mozart *did* do in the summer of 1788 was to write his last three symphonies (K. 543, 550, and 551) back to back. So far as we know, he never heard them performed, at court or anywhere else, during the three years that he continued to live and to compose. We do know of one performance of K. 595. As Einstein points out, Mozart "played it on 4 March 1791—but not in an 'academy' of his own, which the Viennese public would no longer support, but at a concert of the clarinetist Joseph Bähr" (p. 314).

According to Einstein, the piano concerto Mozart played that day was "the musical counterpart to the confession he made in his letters to the effect that life had lost attraction for him." But Mozart's last concerto—and especially its last two movements—pulses with life of a very special kind. I prefer to think of this concerto as reflecting the degree to which the universally acknowledged truths of society had lost attraction for him. Whereas K. 271 had embodied Mozart's dependence upon (as well as independence from) the acknowledged truths of the larger society, K. 595 reveals a terminal tilt in the direction of independence. The distance from the opening paragraph of *Pride and Prejudice* to the final one of *Persuasion* marks a comparable change.

Just as K. 595 begins and ends with an orchestral tutti that tends to preempt sensitive individual expression, so *Persuasion* begins and ends with the vanity of Sir Walter Elliot. Yet, though the heroine and solo have remained ostensibly submissive to the end, a revolution can be said to have occurred in each work. In each case an impersonal conventional world has been overturned by a single voice that does not rave or rant or even diverge, but holds to its own sweet integrity, its own "emotional repose," its own "inward self-sufficiency" until joy can be embraced even in the face of impersonality.

As Malcolm Bradbury argues, "the tension that Anne embodies" in *Persuasion* is "precisely that of a 'revolutionary' situation, or rather a situation of social transformation." The novel's action centers on the "accommodation of a new set of values," with Anne as the "necessary focus of that action."[13] These new values, of course, are embodied by the vitality and sensitivity of the Crofts and of Anne's other soulmates: it is no accident that Admiral Croft takes over Kellynch from the morally flaccid Sir Walter, whose spiritual death-knell is sounded in the opening paragraph of the book. Without overtly severing her ties with the social forms she has been brought up to adhere to, Anne perceives those forms to be nonpertinent to her own values to a much stronger degree than do either Elizabeth Bennet or Emma Woodhouse.

At the end of the earlier novels, Elizabeth Darcy assumes, and Emma Knightley retains, a leading position in that very world in which the Sir Walter Elliots have a secure place. Anne Wentworth leaves that world essentially behind her. In the company of her domesticated sailor husband and friends, she is about to explore the terra incognita of Romantic social transformation. She does not depart from the larger society and its traditional values as thoroughly as will the protagonists in the fiction of Emily Brontë or Edgar Allan Poe, but she is undoubtedly launched in that direction. In her unmoored marriage to Frederick Wentworth she is leaving behind not only the world of Kellynch Hall and of Camden Place but also the world of Longbourn and of Pemberly, of Hartfield and of Donwell Abbey. To a much greater degree than Elizabeth or Emma—and to a much greater degree than she herself was willing to hazard seven years earlier—Anne is undulating in the wake of the new.

K. 595 is quietly revolutionary in a similar manner. By pushing stable tonality toward its outermost classical limits, Mozart here threatens, as he often does in his most seemingly modest works, to unleash the forces of harmonic transformation. By divorcing the genre of the piano concerto from its primary function of providing brilliant entertainment for Vienna's fashionable salons, this resigned, personal, intimate concerto points, too, in the direction of social transformation. Attention has already been called to its "most painful dissonances that are evoked and yet softened" and to its "unplayed but audibly imagined harshness." These are the very forces that soon would erupt in Beethoven's far more overt impulse toward both musical and social transformation—and that would later become distilled, purified, and compressed into Chopin's solipsistic soloism. K. 595 clearly anticipates the world of Chopin's two piano concertos in spite of its relative lack of keyboard virtuosity. It is a world in which the solo voice, originally submissive, gradually takes the lead, even to the point of relegating the orchestra to the role of accompanist. It is a world in which the solo's most significant emotional exchange is not with the large body of instruments, perhaps not even with its chosen soulmates among the winds, but with itself.

Anne Elliot, no less than the solo of K. 595, bravely probes such a world of self-communion. One can only wonder whether the quivering solitude of each reflects, metaphorically, the experience of Mozart and of Austen themselves as each came to know the society and the self better—especially in the declining health and reduced circumstances that marked their last years.

THE MOVEMENT in *Persuasion* from neoclassical toward Romantic values, and from society's values toward those of the individual, is made unusually explicit in the polite debate between Anne and Lady Russell over Mr. William Elliot's character in volume 2. Lady Russell's praise of Mr. Elliot at the beginning of chapter 4 encompasses the neoclassical virtues that had been the touchstone of Austen's earlier fiction.

> Everything united in him: good understanding, correct opinions, knowledge of the world, and a warm heart. He had strong feelings of family-attachment and family-honour, without pride or weakness; he lived with the liberality of a man of fortune, without display; he judged for himself in everything essential, without defying public opinion in any point of worldly decorum. He was steady, observant, moderate, candid; never run away with by spirits or by selfishness, which fancied itself strong feeling; and yet, with a sensibility to what was amiable and lovely, and a value for all the felicities of domestic life, which characters of fancied enthusiasm and violent agitation seldom really possess. (pp. 139–40)

This would be a most convincing portrait were it not for Anne's reply at the end of chapter 5. She responds in words which seem to carry the unmistakable force of the author's own convictions.

> Mr. Elliot was rational, discreet, polished—but he was not open. There was never any burst of feeling, any warmth of indignation or delight, at the

evil or good of others. This, to Anne, was a decided imperfection. Her early impressions were incurable. She prized the frank, the open-hearted, the eager character beyond all others. Warmth and enthusiasm did captivate her still. She felt that she could so much more depend upon the sincerity of those who sometimes looked or said a careless or a hasty thing, than of those whose presence of mind never varied, whose tongue never slipped.

Mr. Elliot was too generally agreeable. Various as were the tempers in her father's house, he pleased them all. He endured too well—stood too well with everybody. (p. 153)

To invoke M. H. Abrams's metaphors, Mr. Elliot's classical mirrorlike qualities are undermined by his lack of Romantic lamplike qualities. In the opening chapter of this same volume 2, Admiral Croft finds the former dressing room of Sir Walter Elliot to be too mirrorlike: "Such a number of looking-glasses! Oh Lord! there was no getting away from oneself" (p. 121). In the concluding chapter, the narrator crowns Anne's happiness with a series of lamplike images: "the glow of her spirits," the "warmth of her heart," the light of Anne's "sunshine" (p. 240). The mirror that reflects a self-admiring society has become solipsistic. The lamp that projects an individual's warmth and sincerity has become the only guiding light.

GIRDLESTONE points out that a year before composing K. 595 Mozart had traveled to Frankfort and Munich, scenes of conquest during his youth. He speculates that the composer must have been poignantly struck by the contrast between his present condition and his earlier one.

He met old friends in both places . . . renewing acquaintances which went back to the great journey he had made to Mannheim and Paris thirteen years earlier. His letters give proof of the joy he felt in coming again into touch with these witnesses of a bygone period, yet such experience must have brought home more vividly and more sorrowfully to him the difference between past and present. The man of thirty-four, undermined by cares, beginning to suffer in body and spirit from the privations and disappointments of recent years, must have compared himself with bitterness with the stripling of twenty-one, sallying forth from Salzburg full of hope, on the threshold of his independent life. (p. 468)

Anne Elliot feels a comparable bitterness in volume 1, when the return of Frederick Wentworth revives all her deepest feelings of past joy and present privation. But neither Mozart's last concerto nor Austen's last novel gives in to such bitterness. Each is instead pervaded, as Girdlestone says of the concerto, by "a thirst, a yearning for beauty" (p. 469).

Each satisfies that thirst by accepting past and present pain as the only basis upon which to savor past and present joy—and thereby to transform them into eternal beauty.

A perfect paradigm for these dynamics in both works is found in Anne's response to Wentworth during their discussion of Lyme in the Octagon Room.

> "I should very much like to see Lyme again," said Anne.
> "Indeed! I should not have supposed that you could have found anything in Lyme to inspire such a feeling. The horror and distress you were involved in—the stretch of mind, the wear of spirits!—I should have thought your last impressions of Lyme must have been strong disgust."
> "The last few hours were certainly very painful," replied Anne: "but when pain is over, the remembrance of it often becomes a pleasure. One does not love a place the less for having suffered in it, unless it has been all suffering, nothing but suffering—which was by no means the case at Lyme. We were only in anxiety and distress during the last two hours; and, previously, there had been a great deal of enjoyment. So much novelty and beauty! I have travelled so little that every fresh place would be interesting to me—but there is real beauty at Lyme; and in short" (with a faint blush at some recollections) "altogether my impressions of the place are very agreeable." (pp. 175–76)

Substitute *life* for *Lyme* in this dialogue and one finds in Anne's words what I take to be the essence of both Austen's and Mozart's attitude toward life and toward art. If the spirit of either were to be interviewed on the subject of life on earth, I would expect either one to begin by saying "I should very much like to see life again" and to elaborate with Anne's argument embracing pain, pleasure, suffering, novelty, and real beauty.

To some degree, nearly all of Mozart's and Austen's works allow us to experience the truth that "when pain is over, the remembrance of it often becomes a pleasure." But perhaps none express it so pervasively or so purely as do K. 595 and *Persuasion*. Before Anne was able to communicate that truth to Wentworth in the exhilarating resurrection of their friendship in the Octagon Room, she had quietly, silently distilled it in the "passionate tranquility" of her farewell to Uppercross. ("She had left it all behind her; all but the memory that such things had been.") It is the generosity of Austen's and of Mozart's memory that fills these last works so full of life even at a moment when life itself, for the artist, is soon to be "left behind."

We have already suggested that Anne's farewell to Uppercross and the solo's "song of parting" at the beginning of the Larghetto stand in microcosm for the character and situation of Anne and of the solo throughout the entire novel and concerto. One might go a step further and suggest that each farewell moment stands in microcosm, too, for the character and situation of the novelist and the composer. In these two autumnal works, each artist's passionate tranquility in the face of an "irrevocable parting" is blessed, as the work of each always is at its best, with that classical restraint that turns tearfulness into sincerity and that allows a sentiment that might have been selfish to breathe with the fragrant spirit of kindness and love.

THE IDEA that pain may be transformed into pleasure in the retrospect of memory suggests that analogy of the mirror, which can make the lamp of pain tolerable by reflecting, purifying, even disembodying it. Even in Austen's and Mozart's most personal, poignant, and painful works, harmony and pleasure and equilibrium tend to be the ultimate goal—and achievement. In his discussion of K. 595, Girdlestone quotes Abbé Martinant de Préneuf, one of Mozart's "forgotten contemporaries": "This music, so harmonious and so lofty in inspiration, so pure, both soft and sorrowful . . . made me forget as I listened to it my past woes and those that the future held perhaps in store for me" (p. 480). Whereas many Romantic artists often choose to bring us into direct contact with the flame of pain (Berlioz's musical guillotine, Shelley's "I fall upon the thorns of life, I bleed"), classical artists such as Mozart and Austen tend, even at their most Romantic, to distance or frame that flame, thereby transforming it into timeless pleasure and joy. One might almost say of K. 595 and *Persuasion* that the depth of the sorrow in each work is to be measured by the extent to which the sorrow has been softened.

This framing of pain, this softening of sorrow, of course, does not mean that their transmutation into eternal beauty and joy is always unqualified or often unalloyed. Anne's noble tribute to the pleasures of Lyme, an oasis of spring water to the desert of Wentworth's fear, is interrupted by the sound of "Lady Dalrymple, Lady Dalrymple" before he can even begin to sip and savor it. Anne must join her fawning father; she must suspend and postpone the return to the intimacy that means more to her than anything in the world. She and Wentworth must wait out the first half of the concert, then the intermissions in which Mr. Elliot's interventions cause Wentworth's disheartened departure from the concert room, then the two encounters in the White Hart Inn, only the second of which finally leads to the spontaneous, hand-delivered declaration of love, returned by her on the street outdoors and savored by them both during their exhilarating stroll on the gravel walk.

As the narrator says in *Emma*, "perfect happiness, even in memory, is not common" (p. 156). Yet it does exist. And it is sometimes achieved not only in memory but in the present, as it is by Anne and Wentworth on the gravel walk. I would hope and expect each reader to have his or her own examples of such "perfect happiness" from the world of Mozart's piano concertos. As a counterpart to Anne Elliot's rare blending of past and present happiness during the extended recapitulation of her earlier joy near the end of *Persuasion*, I would offer the solo's gliding return from the cadenza to the original buoyant refrain, now more continuous than ever, near the end of K. 595.

Appendix One

JANE AUSTEN AT THE KEYBOARD

JANE AUSTEN was a devoted amateur pianist. In 1956 Mollie Sands was the first to describe her musical library, now preserved at Chawton. Finding it "a very fine one for an amateur," she went on to assert, though she did not elaborate, that Austen "followed the musical taste of her day with intelligence."[1] This view is correct, but it does need elaboration—especially in view of certain misunderstandings as to Austen's musical taste.

As late as 1969, W. A. Craik dismissed the question of Austen's relation to music in one sentence: "Jane Austen herself is not musical, so beyond the odd mention of Italian songs or Scotch Airs, there is no reflection of contemporary taste, or hint that this is the age when Beethoven and Schubert are writing, and Mozart is in vogue."[2] In 1979 Patrick Piggott began an entire book on Austen and music by asserting that "Jane Austen was musical: she played the pianoforte." Piggott goes on to discuss the role of music in her life and in her novels in more detail than anyone before him.[3] He concludes with two informative chapters on Austen's music books. But his judgments are occasionally marred by a certain impatience with his beloved novelist—perhaps because he is himself a professional pianist.

Discussing *Pride and Prejudice*, for example, Piggott cannot accept Austen's portrayal of Mary Bennet as "deep in the study of thorough bass and human nature." Missing the wit and the acuity of characterization, Piggott finds it "puzzling to find Jane Austen . . . sneering at a plain girl for studying a branch of musical theory. Why was Mary to be ridiculed for doing something so very well worth while?" (p. 54). He is equally shocked by what he feels are Austen's occasional lapses into musical "philistinism" in life—as when in Bath, after a concert including a work each by Haydn and Mozart, she mentioned in a letter only that "I wore my crepe sleeves to the concert" (p. 19). More important, Piggott is openly "disconcerted" by what he takes to be the generally undistinguished quality of the music Austen played herself. "It would be idle to pretend that many of the songs and piano pieces which Jane Austen copied with such care and labour into her books are of a good musical standard" (p. 153). Like Craik, he deplores the absence of Mozart and Beethoven (though he does admit that their works "were not easy to come by in the England of Jane Austen's time"). Though he applauds the presence of isolated works by Haydn, Handel, and Gluck, he finds too much of the music "third rate." Based on this evidence, he reluctantly accuses Austen of being "a little lacking" in musical "taste" (p. 153)—the very quality she derides Mary Bennet for lacking and praises Anne Elliot for possessing.

Piggott's judgment of Austen's musical taste, like Craik's, seems to have been reached by imposing the musicological standards of the 1960s and 1970s upon material of the 1790s as if it were material of the 1810s. The 1790s, not the 1810s, were Austen's formative decade at the piano. In England this was not the decade of Beethoven (who did not compose even the "Pathétique" Sonata in far-off Vienna until 1798). Nor was it the decade of Mozart (whose reputation at the time of his death in 1791 had already been eclipsed even in Vienna by names that today are only footnotes in musical history). In England, as in Vienna, the 1790s were the decade not only of Haydn but also of such musicians as Koželuch, Hoffmeister, Pleyel, Steibelt, and Sterkel. These were then leading representatives of what we now call the classical style in music; these are also leading names in Austen's music books.

What is unusual about Austen', musical taste is not that she played sonatas by these composers in the 1790s but that she seemed to find the taste of that decade satisfactory during the two additional decades in which she continued to live and to play. Musical taste did change considerably in those years, especially owing to the influence of Beethoven, whereas her own taste does not seem to have followed the trend. This, however, is in keeping with her literary taste, which was also resistant to infusions of vehement Romanticism. It is also in keeping, as Piggott allows in another context, with the tendency of many amateur pianists to remain with the music they first learned, music they are comfortable with.

Rather than generalizing about the music Austen did not play, therefore, the account that follows here will emphasize what she did play. After a brief biographical survey of her experience at the keyboard from the time she began *Pride and Prejudice* until the time she finished *Persuasion*, an analysis of the music she did play will allow a more accurate judgment of what her musical taste actually was. This analysis will deepen our awareness of Austen's artistic equipment; it will also suggest significant parallels with the fiction she wrote and with the concertos Mozart composed. This appendix is a review of the piano music she played; the next reviews the songs she sang.

In 1796, when Austen was twenty years old and already working on the first version of *Pride and Prejudice*, she was studying the pianoforte with William Chard, assistant organist at the Winchester Cathedral, who regularly visited the rectory at Steventon to give her lessons. In September she wrote her sister Cassandra, "I practise every day as much as I can—I wish it were more for his sake."[4] Three years later she writes Cassandra that she has been "writing music" for her sister-in-law Elizabeth, who is "very cruel" about her copying ability. Writing on a Tuesday, she also mentions "a complaint in my eye" which has kept her from reading or writing "since Friday." She allows humorously that "one advantage will be derived from it, for I shall be such a proficient in music by the time I have got rid of my cold, that I shall be perfectly qualified in *that* science at least to take Mr. Roope's office at Eastwell next summer" (1:48–50). When the family moved from Steventon in 1801, Jane recorded that the sale of her pianoforte brought her eight guineas, "about what I really expected" (1:126). Such an instrument, Constance Hill notes, was "a rare addition in those days to the furniture of a modest parsonage; but there was a genuine love of music in the Steventon household and the piano had been procured. Jane Austen has often ridiculed the *affected* love of music, but never its real appreciation."[5]

As soon as Austen moved into her next permanent home, at Chawton, in 1808, she acquired a new instrument. On December 27 the thirty-three-year-old author wrote to Cassandra: "Yes, yes, we *will* have a pianoforte, as good a one as can be got for thirty guineas, and I will practise country dances, that we might have some amusement for our nephews and nieces, when we have the pleasure of their company" (1:243–44). Piggott finds thirty guineas "quite a large sum to pay for a square piano in 1808," especially in view of the fact that "Jane's personal allowance never exceeded twenty pounds a year." Pointing out that "cheaper pianos were available," he is surprised that so much "could be spared for what was, after all, a luxury." He supports this view by reference to the "somewhat auntish" letter in which Austen disapproves of "the proposed purchase of a pianoforte for her recently married niece, Anna Lefroy" (p. 138): "I was rather sorry to hear that she *is* to have an Instrument; it seems throwing money away. They will wish the 24 Gs in the shape of Sheets & Towells six months hence." But he omits from the last sentence the clause, included in Chapman, that explains the disapproval: "and as to her playing, it can never be anything" (2:416). These words, like most that Austen wrote about music while living at Chawton, show no aversion to music or pianos; rather they show an aversion, based on taste, to the misuse or misapplication of either musical furniture or energy. She obviously considered her own instrument to be something other than a "luxury," her own playing to be something other than "nothing."

Letters from Chawton to two of her nieces, Fanny Knight and Caroline Austen, are particularly full of musical appreciation and concern. In October of 1815 young Caroline visits Chawton while Aunt Jane is away. She receives these instructions: "You will practise your Music of course, and I trust to you for taking care of my Instrument and not letting it be ill-used in any respect.—Do not allow anything to be put on it, but what is very light" (2:428). This same Caroline Austen has given us our fullest picture of Jane Austen at her keyboard during the years at Chawton in which she wrote and revised the great novels.

> Aunt Jane began her day with music—for which I conclude she had a natural taste; as she thus kept it up—tho' she had no one to teach; was never induced (as I have heard) to play in company; and none of her family cared much for it. I suppose, that she might not trouble them, she chose her practising time before breakfast—when she could have the room to herself—She practised regularly every morning—She played very pretty tunes, *I* thought—and I liked to stand by and listen to them.... Much that she played was manuscript, copied out by herself—and so neatly and correctly, that it was as easy to read as print—
>
> At 9 o'clock she made breakfast—that was her part of the household work.[6]

Appendix 1

A letter Austen wrote to Caroline in January of 1817, the month in which she finished work on *Persuasion*, gives us even more insight into the place of music in her life. Recovering from a long stretch of ill-health, Austen declares, "I feel myself getting stronger than I was half a year ago, and can perfectly well walk to Alton, *or* back again, without the slightest fatigue." Hopeful of being able to walk round-trip "when summer comes," she adds a postscript indicating that she has been putting some of her new energies into the keyboard. Using figurative language that is as rare in her letters as it is in her novels, she "personifies" her square piano; in doing so, she expresses her love for Caroline through her love for music: "The Piano Forté often talks of you; in various keys, tunes, and expressions I allow—but be it lesson or Country Dance, Sonata or Waltz, you are really its constant theme. I wish you c^d come and see us" (2:473). Subsequent letters during the last months of her life show attentive concern for Caroline's new grand pianoforte, for her "fingering," and for the imagined "pleasure of hearing you practice."

For Austen herself, playing the piano was clearly a regular part of her daily activity during her young adulthood at Steventon and during her maturity at Chawton—and perhaps even during the unsettled years in between.[7] At Chawton her expensive square piano was more than a luxurious piece of furniture, more than an instrument upon which to play dances for nieces and nephews. During the years in which she revised, wrote, and published the great novels, she got up every day to practice and play music before anyone else was up in the house. In was apparently her habit to work on her novels in the family "dining parlour" later in the day. Family legend has it that when the "creaking door" informed her someone was entering the room, she tucked her manuscripts away and stopped writing. Whether the legend is apocryphal or not, in the morning, before she prepared breakfast, she apparently did have the entire downstairs all to herself. She would have been able to write in complete privacy. The fact that she instead played her pianoforte suggests that the music she played must have meant something to her.

Piggott, having pondered this situation, rightly concludes that "one does not study an instrument, practise it daily and devote precious hours to music-copying without a very strong impulse from within." Yet because he judges these "solitary hours at the keyboard" to be "musically unadventurous," he surmises that they were valuable more "as a relaxation"—and therefore had very little to do with "*what* she played" (pp. 163–64). In other words, her "very strong impulse from within" was simply for digital calisthenics, for "innocent diversion." I will return to this question after examining the music itself.

THE MUSIC BOOKS at Chawton contain a great variety of music, both for solo piano and for voice with piano accompaniment. Austen's heartfelt 1817 postscript to Caroline had mentioned instrumental music only: "be it lesson or Country Dance, Sonata or Waltz." The fact that she made such music "talk" to Caroline suggests that it had emotional as well as calisthenic value for her. Because enough has already been made of the country dances and waltzes Austen played, the emphasis here will be on the sonatas and lessons (*lesson* being in the 1790s essen-

252

tially another term for *sonata*). Indeed, it is these latter and more serious forms of music that predominate in Austen's instrumental collection.

Three of the novelist's music books preserved at Chawton consist entirely of instrumental music. One is a collection compiled by Domenico Corri and published in Edinburgh. The book contains 164 oversize pages and is signed "Miss Jane Austen." In the table of contents listing some twenty-five works by sixteen composers (including Haydn and Handel), six items are marked for special attention. They include a Hoffmeister sonata, a Koželuch lesson, a Koželuch concerto, Schobert's two lessons ("March" and "July"), a Nardini minuet with variations, and Arne's "The Soldier tir'd."[8] Several of these keyboard compositions (and their composers) will be discussed after the instrumental music in Austen's other music books is briefly summarized.

A second volume of keyboard works is also signed "Miss Jane Austen." The table of contents is written in her hand, for the book contains four publications that were printed separately and that she has had bound together. The four publications are:

1. Fourteen Favorite Sonatinas for the Harpsichord or Piano Forte by Pleyel,
2. Pleyel's Celebrated Overture . . . Adapted for Piano Forte or Harpsichord by T. Haigh,
3. A Favorite Concerto for the Harpsichord or Piano Forte by William Evance,
4. The Battle of Prague: A Sonata for the Pianoforte or Harpsichord by Koczwara.

A third volume of keyboard works, also signed "Miss Jane Austen," consists of thirteen separate items she has gathered into one volume, inscribing the number from her own table of contents on the first page of each publication. Items of particular interest are:

1. Six Sonatas by Sterkel,
3. Deux Sonatas by Schobert,
10. Trois Sinfonies by Schobert.

Other works include six quartets by Davaux, arrangements for keyboard of six separate "Opera Overtures," and keyboard arrangements of Handel's "Hallelujah" Chorus and Coronation Anthem.

Just as there are three books signed by Austen consisting entirely of instrumental works, so are there three consisting entirely of songs. One is a bound collection of printed works, including twelve canzonets by William Jackson of Exeter. A second songbook, much larger, consists of some forty songs bound together. Most of these are in printed scores but some are copied out in Austen's own hand and inserted among the engraved songs (see Appendix 2). A third songbook is entirely in manuscript. Eighty pages long, it contains some thirty-six songs whose lyrics and keyboard accompaniments are all copied out in Austen's hand.

A second manuscript book entirely in her own hand—this one eighty-four pages long—contains both songs and instrumental works. The keyboard works include numerous waltzes, marches, and themes with variations. Among the larger

Appendix 1

instrumental works are sonatas by Sterkel and Mazzinghi and a *pot-pourri* by Steibelt. Piggott has discovered that one of the marches Austen copied into this book is by Mozart, though she would have had no way of knowing it. "The Duke of York's New March" is not new at all: it is a pirated version of "Non più andrai" from *The Marriage of Figaro*. As Piggott points out, this is the "only music by Mozart in the Chawton Collection" (p. 148).

Two other books preserved at Chawton did not originally belong to Austen, though she may have inherited them. One is a bound collection signed by Elizabeth Bridges Austen, who married Jane's brother Edward in 1791, complained of Jane's copying in 1799, and died in 1808. This book has the word CEMBALO on the cover and contains works by Schobert and Pleyel as well as sonatas by Ernesto Eichner, Adalbert Gyrowetz, Maria Hester Reynolds, and Koczwara (the "Battle of Prague"). The other book is a manuscript book not in Austen's hand. It may well have belonged to her parents, for the songs in it would have been long out of style by the time Austen began to study.

Two other books containing music likely to have belonged to Austen are currently in the possession of Henry Jenkyns, a direct descendant of James Austen, Jane's elder brother. One book consists of printed scores bound together; the pages are numbered consecutively by hand and run nearly 400 pages. Among the numerous keyboard works contained in this volume are six sonatas by J. C. Bach, Three Grand Sonatas by Pleyel, Cramer's sonata including "God Save the King," and Steibelt's Grand Concerto, Op. 33 (including the once-famous "Storm Rondo"). The other book contains various sonatas, waltzes, variations, and lessons for the keyboard, many copied out in a manuscript hand that appears to be Austen's. Among these works are a printed copy of Clementi's Sonata, Op. 26, and a manuscript copy of Haydn's Sonata in C major (Hob. XVI/35). These two books are signed not by Austen but by her sister Cassandra. Cassandra, however, is known to have been not at all musical; much of this music probably belonged to Jane and passed to Cassandra after her death.[9] In order to guarantee correct attribution, however, the following analysis of Austen's instrumental music will be restricted to the keyboard works at Chawton that we are certain belonged to her.

WITH ONE EXCEPTION (to be mentioned later), nearly all of Austen's instrumental music preserved at Chawton seems to have been purchased or copied out by her while living at Steventon in the 1790s.[10] In the context of that decade, one must agree with Sands that the young novelist-to-be "followed the musical taste of the day with intelligence" and that her library was "a very fine one for an amateur." As mentioned above, the keyboard works not only of Beethoven but of Mozart were essentially unknown in England at the time; it would be another decade before sonatas by either composer would begin to appear in stray English editions.[11] The keyboard works that Austen did play, however, are very much a part of the "classical" Viennese tradition in which Mozart and the early Beethoven composed—a fact that can be easily established even without recourse to Haydn's C-major Sonata in one of the "Cassandra" books. Examination of the spirit and structure of works she played by such composers as Schobert, Koželuch, Pleyel,

Jane Austen at the Keyboard

Sterkel, Hoffmeister, and Steibelt will show why they, at the time, were thought to be leading representatives of the "classical" style that today we know primarily through the works of Haydn and Mozart. My examination of the music itself will be supplemented by musicological authorities, especially by William S. Newman's *Sonata in the Classic Era*.[12]

Both limitations of space and similarities of general musical style make it necessary to examine only representative examples of the lessons and sonatas which Austen made to "talk" on her square pianoforte at Chawton. Of the six works that she (or her teacher) singled out for special attention in the volume of keyboard music edited by Corri, those by Koželuch, Schobert, and Hoffmeister are of particular interest.

Leopold Anton Koželuch (1747–1818) succeeded Mozart in 1792 as official court composer of Vienna. In 1795 he, and not Mozart, was called "the most celebrated [composer] in all of Musical Europe during the past ten years or so." In his own day his music was admired for its compounding of "liveliness and grace, of the noblest melody with the purest harmony, and of the most agreeable organization in respect to rhythm and modulation." In our own day, Newman points out that Koželuch's music "flows on essentially untroubled by deeper feelings and with no obstacles for the ready sight-reader." Even so, Newman allows that Koželuch's sonatas "might indeed be called models of Classic perfection in form, line, and fluency. No skill is lacking, not even that of true 'development.' . . . In fact, Koželuch's writing might be called the ideal of the high-Classic style, provided one limits the word classic to mean a perfect balance and coordination of the means, and a 'moderation in all things'" (SCE, pp. 557–58).

The two works Austen played by Koželuch are both sonatas under different titles. Each was written for the keyboard with an optional string accompaniment—a common practice of the day. Koželuch's "A Lesson" is a sonata in three movements that match the fast-slow-fast pattern of Mozart's K. 595: Allegro, Larghetto, Rondo. Koželuch's "Concerto" is also a sonata in three movements: Allegro spiritoso, Rondo, and Allegretto. The opening page of each work (which is all that I have been able to examine in any detail) shows the "form, line, and fluency" of which Newman writes.[13]

Johann Schobert (?–1767), an "early-Classic" composer, in Newman's classification, wrote four books of keyboard sonatas with optional string accompaniments. Young Mozart was so impressed with Schobert's music when he encountered it in Paris that he arranged one of Schobert's sonata movements as a movement in an early keyboard concerto (K. 39). Einstein favorably compares Schobert's "more passionate soul" with that of Johann Christian Bach as an early influence on Mozart. In addition to "taste in figuration" and "grace in melodic invention," Einstein finds "true passion" in Schobert's music (pp. 115, 121). Newman maintains that Schobert's sonatas anticipate the "classic" style in the sonata-allegro drive present in many of his first movements. Of the slow movements he says that "clear opening ideas cast in equally clear phrase-and-period structures are not wanting, but these often seem somewhat weak and ungraceful" (SCE, p. 633).

As Newman reports, Schobert published a series of five sonatas in Paris in 1764, "each named for the month of issue." Two of these are the "March" and

255

Appendix 1

"July" lessons marked for special attention in the table of contents of Austen's keyboard collection edited by Corri. Austen must have preferred the "July" lesson, for that one is also marked for special attention on the score itself. It is a three-movement sonata of considerable interest.

The first movement, Andante pastorale, has a nicely balanced opening theme that is repeated in sequence in the opening bars; the exposition is given an exact repeat. A development section modulates and takes the opening theme to foreign keys. A recapitulation returns to the opening material in the home key, beginning with the first theme. The subsidiary material is then presented in somewhat altered order, as it often is in a Mozart recapitulation. In the shape of its opening theme and in its spacious, calm mood, this movement anticipates Beethoven's "Pastoral" Sonata, Op. 28—as my colleague Ted Diaconoff has demonstrated to me at the piano.

The second movement, Minuetto-Trio, is a delightful example of the minuet form that Haydn and Mozart were soon to put to such good use. Structurally, this movement could have been composed by either; in melodic and rhythmic shape the minuetto, especially, is suggestive of Mozart.

The third movement, Allegro molto, even more than the first movement, has the sonata-allegro drive of which Newman speaks. The exposition begins with a balanced and clearly articulated phrase that anticipates the opening phrase of the Vivace of Beethoven's Sonata, Op. 79. After the exposition is repeated there is development by modulation and motivic play, after which the recapitulation returns directly to the material of the exposition.

Schobert's "July" Lesson is a sonata with spiritual and musical depth. Austen must have enjoyed playing it, for she acquired the scores for Schobert's *Deux Sonatas* (Op. 3) and *Trois Sinfonies* (Op. 9) for one of her bound volumes. These latter five works are all keyboard sonatas of some interest. One is in four movements; the others have three. All five sonatas begin with an Allegro movement followed by an Andante; each concludes with a fast movement. All of these sonatas consistently reflect the "grace in melodic invention" and "taste in figuration" which Einstein attributes to Schobert. The composer is no slouch; neither is the amateur musician of the 1790s who was drawn to his music.

Franz Anton Hoffmeister (1754–1812) is best known today for having published works by Haydn, Mozart, and Beethoven. He also published works by himself. According to Newman, he is "among the most prolific composers of all time." Grove estimated that Hoffmeister wrote some 350 works for the flute. The current count of the piano compositions indicates 20–26 sonatas, as many as Mozart composed for solo piano. Hoffmeister's piano style is so close to that of those we now call the Viennese classical masters that three of his sonatas were mistakenly published as works by Haydn in 1934. Newman explains that the "Göttweiger" sonatas were understandably attributed to Haydn because of "their harmonic surprises, wide modulations in the development sections, fresh, wide-spaced themes, ornamental pulsations in the repetitions of themes, melodic sighs in alternation with accompaniment chords, and frequent melodic interest in the bass." Examining three other sonatas by Hoffmeister, Newman finds "the ideas to be trite, the piano figuration to be brilliant, and the craftsmanship to be both sure and experienced" (SCE, pp. 550–51).

The Hoffmeister Sonata for Piano Forte that Austen marked for special attention is in three movements which match the pattern of Mozart's K. 503 both in tempo (*allegro, andante, allegretto*) and tonality (C major, F major, C major). The first movement, in sonata-allegro form, is based on a two-bar phrase (bars 1–2) that is repeated at the outset (bars 5–6), contrasted with a second theme in the bass, and modulated and given considerable motivic play in the development section. A return to the opening theme as originally announced clearly begins the recapitulation, which includes the second theme again in the bass. In structure as well as in clarity of articulation, this movement is undoubtedly in the style of Haydn and Mozart. The idea in the movement, however, seems to be as trite as in the sonatas examined by Newman.

The second movement, Romance (*andante sostenuto*), opens with a flowing decorated theme typical of Mozart's "fashionable romances." The form is not as regular as that of the first movement. It follows an a:b:a pattern overall, but the "a" section is in two parts, the second of which is an ornamented and modulated "free" variation of the opening material. After a rather long "b" section, which ends in a short cadenza, as does the second part of the "a" section, the movement ends with a return to the first half only of the "a" section. The melody itself is charming, though to my ears the "b" section is overlong.

The finale—Rondo (*allegretto*)—begins with a sprightly balanced phrase such as Haydn or Mozart might have written. The first episode, after beginning in C major, the key of the refrain, modulates. It contains some quite brilliant passagework. After the refrain is heard again there follows a long episode that begins in E-flat major and modulates to the minor keys, after which the refrain is heard again. The form is a:b:a:c:a. It is a delightful, if slight, example of the rondo form that Haydn and Mozart perfected.

Ignaz Joseph Pleyel (1757–1831) studied composition with Haydn. Like Hoffmeister he was extremely prolific. In addition, he once showed extraordinary talent. Mozart, who was far from lavish in his praise of other musicians, wrote these words to his father a year before composing K. 503: "Some quartets have been published recently by a certain Pleyel, a pupil of Haydn's. If you do not know them yet, try to get them; you will find them worth the trouble. They are very well written and most pleasing. You will also see at once who is his master. 'Twill be a happy thing for music if Pleyel is some day able to replace Haydn for us!"[14] Pleyel did not live up to his great promise as a composer; he eventually became better known for his piano factory. Still, his sonatas were "published and republished by all the best known publishers of the day." According to Newman, "the style and quality may be generalized as high-Classic, light, regularly phrased, skillful, fluent, melodious, and extremely watery, only the earliest works showing any spark of individuality" (SCE, p. 551).

The Fourteen Sonatinas that Austen acquired appear to be from a relatively early period in Pleyel's career. I have had occasion to examine the fourteenth, a theme and variations in C major. The theme, *andante*, begins with an eight-bar phrase that is repeated. It concludes with another eight-bar phrase given an exact repeat. Internally as well as externally, the buoyant theme could hardly be more symmetrical with regard to phrasing, balance, and proportion. The first eight-bar phrase itself consists of two four-bar phrases that are nearly identical. The second eight-bar phrase is similarly constituted, its first four-bar phrase introducing new material and modulating, the second being in key and melody a near repeat of the opening four-bar phrase.

So clearly articulated, this theme is clearly recognizable in the five variations that follow. These have the expected contrasts of mood, tempo, and texture, some being tender, some brilliant. Dynamic markings range from *p* to *f* to *pp*, rising to *ff* in the concluding Presto. This work gives the fingers an excellent workout; it is pianistically respectable. Though not musically profound, it is most charming. Typical of the themes and variations of Austen's day, it makes a fascinating contrast with those Emily Brontë would play a few decades later. The latter feature consistently more vehement dynamics, and consistently more radical transformations.[15]

The adaptation of Pleyel's "Celebrated Overture" follows the Fourteen Sonatinas in the volume Austen bound together. Piggott notes that it is "really a symphony" in five movements and "is quite difficult for an amateur. . . . If Jane Austen played the 'overture' creditably she must have had more technical proficiency than one had supposed" (p. 144).

Johann Franz Xaver Sterkel (1750–1817) was a composer and a piano virtuoso. Mozart criticized his playing in 1777; Beethoven praised it in 1791. He wrote some eighty sonatas for the keyboard, most with optional string accompaniment. According to Newman, "Sterkel's earlier sonatas are mostly in three movements (F-S-F), the later ones in two. . . . The harmony and modulations are technically well handled but are not used especially to achieve expressive effects or relationships. . . . The forms are clear and well-balanced, with undeveloped 'development' sections and incomplete 'recapitulations' being the chief shortcomings from the standpoint of textbook 'sonata form'" (SCE, p. 577).

Of the Six Sonatas by Sterkel in one of Austen's bound volumes, I have been able to study the third, which has been marked with an *x*. (Markings have also been written into the score, apparently in Austen's hand.) The sonata is in two movements. The first, an Allegro in F major, is in sonata-allegro form. After a sprightly theme is announced in the opening bars, a transitional passage leads to a contrasting theme. After a repeat of the exposition, the development begins, ornamented by additional trills Austen has written into the score. There are slight changes in register and harmony for both the first and second themes, and it is difficult to clearly differentiate between development and recapitulation.

The second movement, also in F major, is a rondo in ⁶⁄₈ time. The form is a:b:a:c:a and the "c" episode is a *mineur*. The opening refrain has a sectional and perfectly balanced opening melody of six bars in which bars 3–4 repeat bars 1–2 and bar 6 repeats bar 5. The opening phrase returns again in bars 8–9 and bars 10–11, still in the treble clef, but lower in register. Such a clearly articulated melody is, of course, easy to recognize when it returns after each of the episodes.

Its return after the agitation of the *mineur* episode brings a welcome sense of relief.

In Austen's manuscript book containing both songs and keyboard music the sonata by Sterkel is in three movements. The first is an Andante grazioso in sonata-allegro form. Its opening theme consists of two four-bar phrases, each of which is restated. The development, preceded by a bar of rests, varies the first theme by modulating, changing the register, and introducing quickly changing dynamics in the *pp*, *p*, and *mf* range. (The exposition had been *dolce* throughout, with a crescendo in the bar before the rest.) The development slows to *adagio* in its last bar, after which the opening theme returns in its original shape, harmony, and tempo. The closing material in the recapitulation is shortened.

Following the second movement, a minuetto in the classical style, the sonata concludes with a rondo, marked *presto*. This movement resembles the rondo-sonata form developed by Mozart (and exemplified in the finale of K. 595), for the middle ("c") section features motivic development based originally on material from the opening refrain. Austen's manuscript copy of the Sonata in F major is one of her finest, though it does not rival the visual beauty of one of the last works she copied into this manuscript book, Steibelt's *18th Pot-pourri*.

Daniel Gottlieb Steibelt (1765–1823) flourished in Paris, according to Newman, from 1790 to 1796. Some 150 keyboard sonatas appeared between 1788 and 1808. He is the one classical composer well-represented in Austen's music books whom Newman also terms "pre-Romantic" (SCE, p. 5). After analyzing numerous Steibelt sonatas, Newman finds that "lyrical, rather neutral themes" prevail and that "Mozart comes to mind when the idea is chromatic and ends in a feminine rhythm." Despite the lack of dynamic drive and structural solidity, Newman finds "a youthful, early-Romantic bloom and a degree of elegance, grace, and refinement in the nicely shaped melodies."[16] Examination of the *pot-pourri* Austen copied with such a flourish into her manuscript book reveals why Newman puts this composer more on the pre-Romantic than on the purely classical side of the history of the sonata. It also reveals, more than any of the music we have so far examined, the pre-Romantic side to Austen's generally classical music collection.

Steibelt's *18th Pot-pourri* (the title itself is something one might have expected Austen to have abhorred) is actually a theme and variations in C major. As in the Pleyel sonatina examined above, the theme is announced in a highly regular Andante of 32 bars that is the basis for the five variations that follow. (In Steibelt's theme, bars 9–16 are a near but not exact repeat of bars 1–8, as are bars 25–32. Bars 17–24 introduce the contrasting material.) The variations themselves are clear, witty, and increasingly brilliant—the last concluding with conventional but quite demanding chromatic passagework. Stylistically, the main difference between this work and the Pleyel is the Allegro brillante introduction of some eighty bars that precedes the announcement of the theme. This Allegro is *brillante*: it ranges widely through all the registers of the keyboard, it has major changes of tempo, it includes many indications for pedalling, and it contains a brilliant chromatic ascent of the kind not normally found in Austen's music. Its aura of improvisation and mood-setting anticipates Romantic keyboard practice, and Piggott is probably correct in dating this work after 1808, when Austen was already living at Chawton.[17] This is one work which clearly suggests that her "musical intelligence" extended beyond, though it may not have dwelt for long beyond, her formative musical decade of the 1790s.

ALTHOUGH the music summarized above is by no means "first-rate" to late-twentieth-century ears nurtured on the best of Mozart and Beethoven, it is not "third-rate" either. By the standards of Austen's own day, habitation, and status (the 1790s, the English provinces, amateur), it is respectable indeed. In learning to play the lessons and sonatas described above (as well as others that have not been discussed), Austen mastered the basic proportions and dynamics of the three-movement sonata form. The sense of development in a sonata-allegro opening movement, creating tensions that are eased by the return of the recapitulation; the contrasting second movement, in a new key and tempo; the concluding finale, often light-hearted and in the more episodic rondo form—these patterns so central to the style of Haydn and Mozart are central to the music Austen played, the music of their direct predecessors, contemporaries, and, in some cases, successors.[18]

In nearly all of the sonatas Austen played, the main themes are balanced, clearly articulated, and announced at the outset of the movement. The dynamic range between *forte* and *piano* is enough to attain a feeling of contrast, when needed, yet controlled in such a way that changes are seldom abrupt or disconcerting. There are few strong or long crescendos (especially by later Romantic standards) and there are hardly any *sforzandos*, which at any rate would be difficult to sound very impressively on the small instruments she played. As most of Austen's music was composed for harpsichord or pianoforte interchangeably (as was Mozart's K. 271), there are seldom marks for pedalling. Nearly all of her multimovement sonatas are set in a major key and even the contrasting central movements are seldom in the minor. Key changes not only between movements but within them are consistently smooth and well-prepared.

In short, the classical and neoclassical values of balance, equilibrium, proportion, symmetry, clarity, restraint, wit, and elegance that are typical of Austen's novels and of Mozart's piano concertos are typical as well of the music that Austen played on her square piano. Whether the "classical equilibrium" of the music she played influenced or only paralleled that of the fiction she wrote is perhaps impossible to know. But the stylistic similarity certainly suggests that "*what* she played" was important to her—perhaps as important as "what she read." There can be no doubt that her playing contributed, as did her reading, to her cultural and artistic experience—and equipment.

Piggott, following a hint from Jane Aiken Hodge, concludes his speculation about the importance of music for Austen by suggesting that her "solitary hours at the keyboard . . . may have acted as some kind of 'trigger' for her imagination, helping her to organize and plan her material before committing it to paper" (p. 164). But still he implies that *what* she played did not matter. Hodge is the only critic who has suggested that Austen's playing may in some direct way be linked to her literary creativity. She surmises that, in an unmusical family, Austen's morning hours at the keyboard may have been her only way of achieving the privacy needed in order to create. She suggests that Austen's relatives are not to be depended upon for a thorough understanding of the artist or the woman: "They will simply tell us that Aunt Jane played the piano before breakfast—and rather easy tunes at that. [But] while she sat there, every inch the maiden aunt, she was doubtless wrestling, like every other artist who has created something that endures, with her vision of the universe."[19] Hodge, however, does not suggest that the actual music Austen played contributed to her vision of the universe or to her art. She seems to view it, rather, as a benign opiate. "I suspect that Jane Austen planned her day's [writing], peacefully, at the piano before breakfast, while her hands found their way round the familiar notes" (p. 133). This may well be true, and in this purely mechanical sense Piggott perhaps correctly values the act of playing rather than the music itself. But the music is likely to have had value too.

In making those notes "familiar" during some twenty years of playing, Austen had assimilated the principles of what we now call the classical style in music. As Rosen stresses again and again in his study of that musical style, it is the proportions and tensions of the sonata form, not the textbook description of its component parts, that are essential in understanding its aesthetic. We saw in Chapter 4 the uncanny degree to which Mozart's Piano Concerto No. 9, the first work Rosen uses to illustrate those proportions and tensions in detail, matches the proportions and tensions of *Pride and Prejudice*. Austen wrote the first version of that novel at Steventon in the 1790s, the decade in which she herself had begun to assimilate the principles of the sonata form in music. The proportions and tensions of *Pride and Prejudice* are much closer to those of Mozart's three-movement concerto (or even to those of the three-movement sonatas Austen played both at Steventon and Chawton) than they are to those of the more obvious literary analogues for the neoclassical vision it so elegantly expresses (i.e., Johnson's criticism, Pope's poetry, even Fielding's fiction).

In its broadest outlines, the extended comparison made between *Pride and Prejudice* and K. 271 in Chapter 4 would apply to any number of three-movement sonatas that Austen herself played. The "light, and bright, and sparkling" texture of the opening movement and volume; the clear articulation and phrasing of the opening theme and sentence; the well-prepared excursions to and returns from related harmonic and geographic locales; the calculated contrast of mood and locale in the second movement and volume; the return to the spirit and locale of the opening movement and volume in the third and concluding one; the looser episodic structure of the third volume and movement, in which at least one disruptive episode (Lydia's elopement, an episode in the minor key) temporarily suspends the momentum toward felicity but is soon dispelled; the restraint, symmetry, and balance with which expressive and structural components both large and small are handled—all these components of artistic form are as central to the sonatas Austen played by Koželuch, Schobert, Hoffmeister, Pleyel, and Sterkel as they are to either *Pride and Prejudice* or Mozart's K. 271.

At a deeper spiritual and emotional level, of course, our most important comparisons between Austen's early novel and Mozart's early concerto cannot be extended to the keyboard music that Austen played. The exquisite balance between Elizabeth and the society, on the one hand, and between the solo and the orchestra, on the other, has no equivalent in the solo works for piano found in Austen's library (the few "concertos" in her music books are in effect solo sonatas). Nor is there often the equivalent of the exquisite wit and agility that distinguish Elizabeth Bennet and the solo voice of K. 271 from most other fictional heroines and keyboard solos. Nor, of course, does one find in the keyboard sonatas that Austen played the equivalent of the "experience of maturity" that both Elizabeth and the solo achieve in the course of their engagement with the world of the "other." Sources for these deeper spiritual, artistic, and emotional affinities between Austen and Mozart cannot by any stretch of the imagination be found in the music she played: they must remain, at least in these pages, mysteries to be celebrated rather than explicated.

As LITERARY HISTORIANS continue to emphasize, Austen remained true to neoclassical values in English letters at a time when the Romantic revolution was invading both poetry and prose. Her satire of "Romantic" and "sentimental" values in *Northanger Abbey* and *Sense and Sensibility* makes clear that she was aware of the new literary trends, as does her heartfelt and tender incorporation of such values into *Persuasion*. By choice and by instinct she preserved neoclassical values in the face of the powerful Romantic currents that were transforming literary taste in general and that altered, finally, even her own. When she did incorporate more overtly Romantic expression into her last novel, she did so nearly two decades after Wordsworth's "Preface to the *Lyrical Ballads*" (1798).

We have seen that when Austen began to study the piano in a serious way in the 1790s, the music she played represented contemporary developments in the "classical" style as it would have been available to an amateur pianist in provincial England. Yet she continued to play such music, and it seems *only* such music (with the delightful exception of the Steibelt *Pot-pourri*), until her death in 1817. Even though Beethoven and such pre-Romantic composers as Clementi and Dussek had begun to transform the kind of music available even to amateurs, Austen avoided the volcanic and eruptive forces of musical Romanticism as thoroughly as she did those of literary Romanticism.[20] Whether she did so knowingly or unknowingly is perhaps impossible to say: her music books are empty of Beethoven and his influence, but so are her novels and letters. A few of the piano pieces she played do show a "pre-Romantic" bloom of a nonvolcanic variety similar to that which finally found a place in her fiction. But the bloom in her music that corresponds most closely to the areas of experience explored in *Persuasion* is found in her songs, as Appendix 2 will make clear.

Writing in 1867, her niece Caroline indicated that the "pretty tunes" her aunt played for her in the 1810s "would now be thought disgracefully easy."[21] We do not know whether she is referring specifically to the three-movement lessons and sonatas that Austen played, though the phrasing of the 1817 postscript—"be it lesson or Country Dance, Sonata or Waltz"—suggests that those were among the works Caroline had heard. Even if it applies to sonatas, however, Caroline's evaluation speaks for her era as well as herself. By 1867 the powerful and vehement music not only of Beethoven but of such Romantic successors as Berlioz, Schumann, and Liszt had, in most people's minds, rendered "disgracefully easy" the music not only of the "classical" composers Austen had played but even that of Haydn and Mozart themselves. Such an attitude would remain widespread throughout the rest of the nineteenth century: it is epitomized in the condescending treatment that Haydn and Mozart receive in Grove's *Beethoven and His Nine Symphonies* (1898).

So far I have located only one comment which reflects Austen's own awareness of changing fashions in music. Significantly, it shows her preference for music she had encountered in the 1790s. In 1817 she wrote to thank Fanny Knight for sending her some music: "Much obliged for the *Quadrilles*, which I am grown to think pretty enough, though of course they are very inferior to the Cotillions of my own day" (Chapman, 2:48). One can only wonder what might have happened had Fanny sent her instead copies of one of Beethoven's more powerful sonatas—say, the "Pathétique" (1798) or the "Appassionata" (1805). Most likely, Aunt Jane would have objected not only to the titles but to the works as well. For authority she might well have quoted, had she known it, Mozart's now-celebrated statement that "passions, whether violent or not, must never be expressed in such a way to excite disgust"; that "music, even in the most terrible situations, must never offend the ear, but must please the hearer, or in other words must never cease to be *music*." To illustrate her point, she might well have offered a lesson by Koželuch or Schobert, a sonata by Hoffmeister, Sterkel, or Pleyel.

Speculation aside, we are left with the fact that Austen played music on her own pianoforte from the time of her earliest attempts to write serious fiction at Steventon in the 1790s through the time of her mature writing and publishing at Chawton in the 1810s. In phrasing, balance, restraint, structure, and elegance, the instrumental music she played consistently displays a "classical equilibrium" closely comparable to that of the fiction she wrote. I believe it impossible to determine the degree to which that music might have influenced the actual structure and spirit of her novels. But the evidence does strongly suggest that these two artistic activities, carried on side by side during Austen's most active years as a writer, were, if not mutually influential, at least mutually reinforcing. No less than Mary Bennet (though in a different spirit, to be sure) was Jane Austen herself, during much of her adult life, "deep in the study of thorough bass and human nature."

Appendix Two

PERSUASION AND JANE AUSTEN'S LOVE SONGS

THE POIGNANT pre-Romantic literary style of *Persuasion* has long intrigued students of Austen's art; the unblushing romance of the story itself has intrigued students of her life. In the words of A. Walton Litz, the eighteenth-century values that permeated Austen's earlier novels—"sense, taste, genius, judgment, understanding"—are here supplanted by an emphasis upon "the loss and return of 'bloom.'" The stylistic shift has caused many to feel that Anne Elliot's love for Wentworth is a fictional representation of Austen's own putative "broken romance," even though the details of that romance remain, as Litz says, "hopelessly obscure."[1] A most intriguing series of love songs that Austen inserted into one of her songbooks now at Chawton speaks directly to the stylistic issues raised by *Persuasion*—and glancingly to the biographical ones.

When examining Austen's musical library, I happened upon a group of manuscript love songs within a bound volume of mostly engraved songs that Austen probably inherited from her parents. The book had been neglected by previous scholars because the date 1778 appears on the title page above the hand-written table of contents. As Austen was only three years old in that year, it had naturally been assumed that the music inside did not belong to her. But in a space left blank under item 23 in the contents, the signature "Miss Jane Austen" appears. In addition to her signature, this 1778 songbook contains sixteen manuscript songs, mostly about parted lovers, that have been glued or pasted into the volume itself. Some are inserted at places indicated in the table of contents by the words "manuscripts" or "manuscript songs." Others are not indicated in the contents at all. Most, if not all, of these manuscripts are in Austen's own hand.[2] After briefly describing the love songs, I will comment on the stylistic and biographical significance they may have had for the woman who wrote *Persuasion*.

IN THE TABLE of contents of the 1778 songbook, item 8 ("How imperfect is expression") is followed by item 9 ("A flaxen headed Ploughboy"). Following item 8 in the book itself is a manuscript song entitled "Susan." The lovers in this song are apart. The man, William, is a sailor. The first stanza reads:

> Oh Susan, Susan lovely dear,
> My vows shall ever true remain
> Let me kiss off this falling tear
> We only part to meet again
> Change as ye list ye Winds   my heart shall be
> The constant compass that shall point to thee.

Immediately following "Susan" is another manuscript, a "Song" whose first stanza asks:

> Why tarries my Love! Where does he rove?
> My Love is long absent from me
> Hither my Dove, I'll write to my Love,
> And send him a letter by Thee
> And send him a letter by Thee.[3]

Both songs contain additional stanzas that Austen copied out below the musical staves.

Also omitted from the table of contents are two manuscript songs inserted after item 9. The first, Sheridan's "Song from the Stranger" (with music by the Duchess of Devonshire), is marked "Plaintive."

> I have a silent sorrow here,
> a Grief I'll ne'er impart;
> It breathes no Sigh, it sheds no tear,
> But it consumes my heart;
> this cherish'd woe   this lov'd despair,
> my lot for ever be
> So my Soul's Lord   the Pangs I bear
> be never known by thee.

The condition is imagined as lasting life long:

> And when pale Characters of Death
> Shall mark this alter'd cheek
> When my poor wasted, trembling Breath
> My life's last hope would speak
> I shall not raise my eyes to Heav'n
> Nor mercy ask for me
> My soul despairs to be forgiven
> Unpardoned Love by Thee.

The second song, from Philidor's *La Feì Urgele* ("Ah! que l'amour est chose jolie"), begins with a six-bar introduction for the piano. The lyrics are dominated by this refrain: "avec l'amour toute la vie, toute la vie / Passe comme un Jour."

Of the love songs indicated by the word *manuscript* but not by title in Austen's table of contents, Krumpholtz's "Whither Love thy beauties bring" is the first and one of the most beautiful. The words comprise a shepherd's plea for his love to return in all her "bloom of charm." The yearning is particularly strong in the music itself, marked *andante con expressione*. The words of the first stanza, as copied by Austen, read:

> Whither Love thy beauties bring,
> sweeter than the blossom'd Spring,
> Vernal beauty decks the plain
> bring thy smiles again.
> Come in all thy bloom of charm
> Come and bless thy Shepherd's arms
> Come and bless thy Shepherd's arms.

After a one-bar cadenza for the piano, it concludes:

> Gentle Virgin come and dwell
> happy in our native Vale
> Brightest joys I then shall prove
> Blest with thee and love.

Curiously, another song set to the same Krumpholtz melody during the 1790s expresses, instead of hopeful yearning, absolute despair.

> In this sad and silent gloom
> Lost Louisa pines unknown
> Shrouded in a living tomb
> Doom'd to pine alone.
> Midst the silent shades of woe
> Tears of fond regret shall flow.
> Tell soft lute in plaintive tone
> Sad Louisa's hapless moan
> Midst the silent shades of woe
> Still the tears must flow.[4]

The striking difference in lyrics is not so surprising when one hears the melody itself, for it hovers in the same bittersweet world of pleasure and pain that pervades Mozart's last piano concerto and Austen's last novel.

Johann Baptist Krumpholtz (1745–90) died one year before Mozart. His numerous sonatas for piano compare in style with those of the composers discussed in Appendix 1.[5] His song "Whither Love thy beauties bring" is moving, tender, and, in Austen's copy, beautifully rendered on the page. Indeed, she has marked its dynamic levels not only lovingly but redundantly, the indications for *p, mf, p, f*, and *mf* in the eight-bar piano introduction being written both below and above the treble clef—a procedure most unusual in her manuscripts (and in musical notation generally).

Immediately following "Whither Love thy beauties bring" is a manuscript copy of "Ellen, the Richmond Primrose Girl"; it is not about parted lovers. Whereas these two manuscripts follow item 17 ("Donna Della") in the songbook, the next group follows item 19, as the table of contents indicates. The lyrics of "The Egyptian Love Song" are full of spring, warmth, and sweetness.

Sweet doth blush the rosy morning,
Sweet doth beam the glistening Dew
Sweeter still the day adorning
Thy dear smile transport my view
Midst the blossoms fragrance flowing
Why delights the Honied Bee?
Sweeter breaths thyself bestowing
One kind kiss on me on me
One kind kiss on me.

After "The Prayer of the Sicilian Mariners," a "Duet in the Siege of Belgrade" returns to the theme of parting that has run through most of the manuscript songs. Stanza one concludes: "And we take our leave forever / Never more again to meet / Never more / Never more / Never more / Never more." This group concludes with another "Song from the Siege of Belgrade," an Andante in which a soldier assures his love that he is safe, though in battle.

The final set of manuscript love songs do not appear after item 21 (as indicated in the table of contents) but rather *before* item 21. After another song from "The Siege of Belgrade" comes an untitled song with a four-bar introduction for the keyboard:

Since then I'm doom'd this sad reverse to prove,
to quit each object of my infant care,
torn from an honor'd parents tender love,
and driv'n the keenest keenest storms of Fate to bear;
Ah! but forgive me   pitied let me part;
Ah! but forgive me   pitied let me part;
Your frowns too sure, would break my sinking heart;
Your frowns too sure w'd break my sinking heart
Sinking heart.

The next manuscript song, "As I was Walking," is also about parted lovers. The speaker's heart is "wearie" because the one "nearest my heart" is farthest "from me." Following on the same page, so that it almost seems to be part of the same song, is another copy of the first stanza (and music) of "Susan." The next song, in French, is "Pauvre Jacques"; its music is marked *affetuoso*. A final manuscript song, without a title, has the following lyrics:

Sure t'would make a dismal story,
If when honour leads him on
Love should slight his cause of glory
or disdain its wounded son.
If his Country's rights defending
he should some disasters prove
Pity with my passion blending
will but more increase my love . . .

The last four lines are repeated.

In all, some sixteen manuscript songs are inserted among the twenty-seven items listed in the table of contents of the 1778 songbook. Nearly all are about parted or parting lovers. The music tends to be "plaintive," "*affetuoso*," and "*con expressione*" whether these indications have been marked in the score or not. Had Austen compiled a table of contents for these inserted songs, it would have read about as follows:

1. Susan ("We only part to meet again")
2. Song ("Why tarries my Love!")
3. Song from "The Stranger" ("I have a silent sorrow here") (plaintive)
4. Song in *La Feì Urgele* ("Ah! que l'amour est chose jolie")
5. "Whither Love thy beauties bring" (*andante con expressione*)
6. Ellen, the Richmond Primrose Girl (*affetuoso*)
7. The Egyptian Love Song
8. The Prayer of the Sicilian Mariners
9. Duet in the Siege of Belgrade ("never more")
10. A Song from the Siege of Belgrade (*andante con moto*)
11. Song in the Siege of Belgrade ("The Sapling")
12. "Since then I'm doom'd this sad reverse to prove"
13. "As I was Walking"
14. Susan ("We only part to meet again")
15. Pauvre Jacques (*affetuoso*)
16. "Sure would make a dismal story"

Before commenting on the significance these songs may have had for Austen, I wish to refer briefly to two songs that are listed in the actual table of contents.

As mentioned above, when Austen signed the table of contents she wrote her name into the space that was left blank under item 23. It happens that item 23 is one of the world's great songs about parted lovers: Gluck's "Che farò senza Euridice?" Without the accompanying music, the plaintive lyrics of this famous song have much in common with the manuscript songs Austen copied into the volume that contains it. Here are the opening words as she knew them in English:

> What alas shall Orpheus do
> Whither go without his Love
> Whither go   whither go
> What alas shall Orpheus do
> Whither go without his Love
> Euridice   Euridice
> Cruel stars O answer me
> O answer me
> I have lost my darling Dove
> I have lost my darling Dove
> my Darling Dove
> What alas shall Orpheus do
> Whither go without his Love . . .

None of Austen's manuscript songs rival the music Gluck provided for these lyrics, yet they are all more moving and less sentimental in performance than their lyrics alone would lead one to expect.[6]

As mentioned above, the first two manuscript love songs are inserted into the songbook following item 8, "How imperfect is expression." This song, too, is in manuscript, even though nearly all of the other songs in the table of contents are printed scores. A fifty-five-bar keyboard introduction, with added fingerings that also seem to be in Austen's hand, precedes the lyrics. The words of the first stanza suggest a reason for the long pianistic introduction.

> How imperfect is expression
> Some Emotions to impart
> When we swear a soft confession
> Direct to hiding heart
> When our bosoms all complying
> With delitious tumults swell
> With what broken faultring dying Language
> would but cannot tell.

What "Language would but cannot tell," the song seems to imply, can be expressed by music. It would be difficult to imagine a more appropriate introduction to a series of manuscript songs accompanied by the keyboard which sing of the inexpressible joys and sorrows of those who love but are apart. Such joys and sorrows Austen finally expressed in *Persuasion*. They bloom in a heroine who, more than any other Austen heroine, finds "broken faultring dying Language" insufficient to the task of expressing—or stilling—the tumult of her heart.

Taken together, all of the manuscript songs in the 1778 songbook show that Austen—to the extent that she knew and loved these songs—was musically familiar with the moods and situations she would later dramatize so movingly in *Persuasion*. The long series of separated lovers, the first of whom is a sailor; the plaintive musical moods; the lyrics with the return of "bloom"; the emphasis on "silent" sorrow and grief; the poignant situations of "never more"; the second copy of the song about Susan and her sailor William: all indicate portions of her musical experience that parallel the fictional experience she would create in *Persuasion*. Two Austen manuscripts from another songbook are also of interest in this regard.

One of the songs that Austen copied into her all-manuscript songbook, now at Chawton, is Charles Dibdin's "A Soldier's Adieu."[7] As Piggott points out, Austen intentionally altered its lyrics. After transcribing the opening lines correctly—

> Adieu, Adieu my only life
> My honour calls me from thee—
> Remember thou'st a Soldier's wife
> These tears but ill become thee.

—she struck "Soldier's" from line 3 and substituted "Sailor's." Piggott finds this change by the author of *Persuasion* and *Mansfield Park* to be "amusing." But in the context of "Susan" and the love songs that follow it in the 1778 songbook one must wonder whether the alteration had personal meaning for Austen. Curiously, her transcription of the second stanza of "Susan" also contains an un-characteristic alteration: she first wrote "constant" where she intended "present" in the last line ("For thou are present where so e'er I go").

In the same manuscript song book as "A Soldier's Adieu" is Austen's copy of "William," with music by Haydn. Piggott dismisses the song as a "comic ditty" (p. 154), but the music and lyrics are worthy of attention. The music, transposed to F major, is taken from the first movement of the C-major Haydn sonata that is found in one of the "Cassandra" books. Austen has given loving attention to the dynamic markings throughout her copy; when the music modulates briefly to a minor key over the words "I drop the tear of sad despair" she indicates *con expressione* and *legato*. The lyrics reveal a familiar situation: a woman awaiting the return of the sailor she loves.

> Ye cliffs I from your airy steep,
> Look down with hope and fear
> To gaze on this extensive deep,
> And watch if William's there.

After "sad months" of "soft and constant pray'r," the "tear of sad despair" is answered by "a swelling sail in view." Her "timid doubts" now overcome, William's lady concludes with a rhetorical question fully appropriate to Anne's re-union with Wentworth on the gravel walk: "What was your pain ye terrors past, / To this dear hour of joy, / To this dear hour of joy." Susan's reiterated wish in the 1778 songbook—that "we only part to meet again"—has here been answered by William's return.

"THE INTENSITY with which readers have explored the 'personal' element in *Persuasion*," A. Walton Litz points out, "comes from the fiction, not from curiosity about the writer's life." It comes from Anne Elliot's own loss of "bloom," attention to which he finds "idiosyncratic and almost obsessive." Even so, Litz allows that "Virginia Woolf was probably justified in her belief that *Persuasion* confirms 'the biographical fact that Jane Austen had loved.'"[8] One certainly cannot make such a large biographical claim for Austen's manuscript love songs—songs valuable primarily for their own intensities and for their relation to like intensities in *Persuasion*. But certain circumstances surrounding these songs naturally lead to "curiosity about the writer's life."

We have seen that the sixteen manuscript love songs inserted into the 1778 volume are particularly insistent on parted lovers (who make no such dense appearance in Austen's other songbooks, including the one containing "A Soldier's Adieu" and "William"). We have seen that her manuscript copies in this volume have contained errors ("Susan") and redundancies ("Whither Love thy beauties bring") not typical of her other musical manuscripts (except in the telling case of "A Soldier's Adieu," where the alteration to "Sailor's" is obviously intentional). We have seen that four of the manuscript songs in the 1778 volume are hidden entirely, with no acknowledgment of any kind in the table of contents (a situation unprecedented in her other music books). We have seen that those four songs in particular are introduced by the manuscript song entitled "How imperfect is expression," a song whose appropriateness for introducing the hidden songs is matched only by the appropriateness of "Che farò senza Euridice?" as the title under which Austen wrote her name into the table of contents (after a false start elsewhere, after item 7). Finally, we have seen the degree to which a great number of these songs anticipate her most personal novel, both in mood and situation.

All of this evidence, all of it circumstantial, raises certain questions. Do these love songs reflect a love of her own? Did she purposely hide some of those songs in a volume where they were not likely to be found, a volume where even her own signature is half-hidden in the table of contents and where even those manuscripts indicated in the contents do not always appear where indicated? Did her uncharacteristic errors, redundancies, and alterations when transcribing certain of these love songs represent her own conscious or unconscious intensities of feeling (by analogy with Jane Bennet's letter that was "ill-addressed")? Did her copying, playing, and singing of these songs (to herself, if to no one else) stem, as her writing of *Persuasion* is thought by many to have stemmed, from a "broken romance" of her own?

The circumstances surrounding the love songs described above raise these questions but do not go far in answering them. All available evidence points to the 1790s as the period in which Austen would have copied out the manuscript songs that were inserted into the 1778 song book. She was sixteen years old in 1791, the year in which Storace's *Siege of Belgrade* opened in London; the presence of several songs from this opera suggests this period of her life as the time when she appropriated the 1778 book for her personal use. Most likely, it was her first songbook. As she copied out new songs, she glued them in between pages of the engraved songs, continuing the practice until she acquired the volumes specifically designed for manuscripts into which she copied all her subsequent transcriptions of both songs and keyboard works. According to this scenario, the songs in the 1778 book would have no special meaning as a group, being simply the first songs she copied.

But the manuscript songs do differ considerably in skill of transcription. This fact suggests that the book may possibly have been a repository for selected songs acquired over several years.[9] If this was so, the likelihood would be increased that they in some way reflected Austen's own experience in love. In 1796 she is known to have begun a mild flirtation with her cousin Tom Lefroy from Ireland, which seems to have lasted a year or more. But neither this affair, nor the mysterious one with the man from Sidmouth in 1801, is thought by most Austen scholars to be her great "broken romance," which remains a mystery to this day.[10] These songs might suggest that the man she loved—if they refer to that love—was a sailor. But sailor songs were in vogue; furthermore, the sailor songs she copied and recopied and even altered from soldier's songs could just as well be expressing her love for her brothers Francis and Charles. The manuscript love songs may deepen our interest in the biographical question of the putative "broken romance," but they in no way help to answer it.

What these songs do show with certainty is that Austen, probably in the 1790s, was copying and playing and presumably singing (she was said to have a small but sweet voice) music that anticipates *Persuasion* in both mood and situation. I believe it likely that these songs were as much a part of her artistic experience as the keyboard music analyzed in Appendix 1, and that this experience contributed to the human and artistic growth that later achieved its verbal bloom in her last novel. The sure value of these songs is in the emotional intensities they reveal in her musical experience long before she wrote the novel, whatever her reasons may have been for copying and playing and singing just those songs.

That said, I can only add that if Austen's spirit were to be brought back for that interview about life, it would be tempting to ask whether these manuscript songs about parted lovers were among the music she played before breakfast, alone, during the years in which she was writing and revising *Persuasion* at Chawton. If the answer were affirmative and the look in the eye inviting enough, one might then ask whether these songs had any particular meaning for her. The woman who wrote that "in music" Anne Elliot "had been always used to feel alone in the world" may have felt so herself more deeply than we have imagined.

Notes

INTRODUCTION

1. Leonard Meyer, *Explaining Music: Essays and Explorations* (Berkeley and Los Angeles: University of California Press, 1973), p. 105.
2. David Cecil, *A Portrait of Jane Austen* (London: Constable, 1978), p. 8.
3. Mark Schorer, Introduction to *Northanger Abbey* (New York: Dell, 1959), p. 10.
4. George Whalley, "Jane Austen: The Poet," in *Jane Austen's Achievement: Papers Delivered at the Jane Austen Bicentennial Conference at the University of Alberta*, ed. Juliet McMaster (London: Macmillan, 1976), p. 120.
5. Richard Church, Introduction to *Emma* (London: Folio Society, 1962), p. 7.
6. A. Walton Litz, *Jane Austen: A Study of Her Artistic Development* (London: Chatto and Windus, 1965), p. 102.
7. From Lionel Trilling's essay on *Emma*, reprinted in *Jane Austen: Sense and Sensibility, Pride and Prejudice, and Mansfield Park, a Casebook*, ed. B. C. Southam (London: Macmillan, 1976), p. 220.
8. Brigid Brophy, "A Remorseless Realist," in ibid., pp. 191–93.
9. Quoted in Andrew Wright, "*Persuasion*," from *Jane Austen's Novels: A Study in Structure*, reprinted in *Jane Austen: A Collection of Critical Essays*, ed. Ian Watt (Englewood Cliffs, N.J.: Prentice-Hall, 1963), p. 145.
10. Margaret Kennedy, *Jane Austen*, 2d ed. (London: Arthur Barker, 1966), pp. 104–5.
11. See *Rebecca West: A Celebration*, ed. Samuel Hynes (New York: Viking, 1977), p. 696; and Virginia Woolf, *A Room of One's Own* (New York: Harcourt, Brace, Jovanovich, 1929), p. 84.
12. Anthony Burgess is one writer who has contemplated a large-scale comparison of Austen and Mozart. Late in 1980 Burgess announced, "I'm going to try writing a Jane Austen novel in the form of a Mozart symphony." See Rhoda Koenig, "The Unearthly Powers of Anthony Burgess," *Saturday Review*, December 1980, p. 37.
13. In a 1976 dissertation entitled "Inter-Art Relations and the Novels of Jane Austen" (University of Wisconsin—Madison) Merike Tamm finds that "it *is* somewhat curious that the common comparison between Austen and Mozart has been taken for granted by critics and has rarely been examined

even in general terms." Tamm is surprised that critics have not investigated the general stylistic similarities between these two "classical" artists more thoroughly, but is not surprised that "there are no thorough, careful comparisons of individual works by Austen and Mozart," finding it "difficult to imagine how a detailed analysis of a musical composition by Mozart could help one in making a detailed analysis of an Austen novel" (p. 52).

14. See Joseph Kerman, "How We Got into Analysis, and How to Get Out," *Critical Inquiry* 7 (Winter 1980): 311–31.

15. Karl Kroeber, *Styles in Fictional Structure: The Art of Jane Austen, Charlotte Brontë, George Eliot* (Princeton: Princeton University Press, 1971), p. 171.

16. The best overview of the relations between the two arts is still Calvin S. Brown's *Music and Literature: A Comparison of the Arts* (Athens: University of Georgia Press, 1948).

17. Stuart Gilbert was one of the first to address Joyce's attempts to imitate musical effects. Harold Basilius's essay "Thomas Mann's Use of Musical Structure and Technique in *Tonio Kröger*," *Germanic Review* 19 (1944): 284–308, remains a model of its kind. Jean-Pierre Barricelli's fine analysis of the "Dante" Symphony ("Liszt's Journey through Dante's Hereafter") is found in the Literature, Arts, and Religion issue of *Bucknell Review* 26 (1982):149–66. Accounts of Berlioz's use of literary models, of course, abound. An excellent introduction to this complicated issue in the interchapter entitled "Program Music and the Unicorn" in Jacques Barzun's *Berlioz and the Romantic Century*, 3d ed. (New York: Columbia University Press, 1969), 1:169–98.

18. A recent book edited by Nancy Anne Cluck, *Literature and Music: Essays on Form* (Provo: Brigham Young University, 1981), does include several studies of unintentional parallels. One of them is my essay entitled "'The Murders in the Rue Morgue' and Sonata-Allegro Form," from *Journal of Aesthetics and Art Criticism* 35 (Summer 1977): 457–63.

19. H. D. F. Kitto, *Greek Tragedy* (New York: Doubleday, 1954), p. vii.

20. Leonard Meyer's extended essay is a study of the Trio of Mozart's G-minor Symphony (K. 550). See "Grammatical Simplicity and Relational Richness," *Critical Inquiry* 2 (Summer 1976): 693–761. His attempt to trace the "implicative" relationships in the music parallels some forms of literary analysis. Although part of Kroeber's stylistic analysis is concerned with quantitative matters that can be approached with the aid of a computer, he also explores the need for the investigation of the "essential" structures and forms of fiction.

21. E. M. Forster, *Aspects of the Novel* (New York: Harcourt, Brace, and World, 1929), p. 168.

22. In recent years a variety of books have appeared that attempt to relate fiction and music in one way or another. Among them are Vernon A. Chamberlin's *Galdós and Beethoven* (London: Gant and Cutler, 1977); William Freedman's *Laurence Sterne and the Origin of the Musical Novel* (Athens: University of Georgia Press, 1978); Alex Aronson's *Music and the Novel: A Study in Twentieth-Century Fiction* (Totowa: Rowman and Littlefield, 1979); James Guetti's *Word-Music: The Aesthetic Aspect of Narrative Fiction* (New Brunswick:

Notes

Rutgers University Press, 1980); Peter Conrad's *Romantic Opera and Literary Form* (Berkeley and Los Angeles: University of California Press, 1977); and Patrick Piggott's *Innocent Diversion: Music in the Life and Writing of Jane Austen* (London: Douglas Cleverdon, 1979). These works share no common methodology; nor is there any sustained attempt (even in Piggott's book on Austen) to address the issues or to employ the methods that are central to this study.

23. For an excellent recent example see Lilian Furst's *Counterparts: The Dynamics of Franco-German Literary Relationships, 1770–1895* (Detroit: Wayne State, 1977). This study attempts to document and then to explain the fifty-year lag between the advent of literary Romanticism in Germany and its appearance in France.

24. René Wellek, "German and English Romanticism: A Confrontation," in *Confrontations* (Princeton: Princeton University Press, 1965), p. 33.

25. Samuel Johnson's famous judgment is delivered in the essay on Abraham Cowley in *Lives of the English Poets.*

26. Jane Austen, *Pride and Prejudice* (New York: New American Library, 1961), p. 322. All further citations from the novel are from this edition and are incorporated within the text.

Part One

1. Wellek has brilliantly outlined the difficulties of determining the meaning of the term *classical* as applied to the literature of any single nation—not to mention its application among several literary traditions. See "The Term and Concept of 'Classicism' in Literary History," in *Aspects of the Eighteenth Century*, ed. Earl R. Wasserman (Baltimore: Johns Hopkins, 1965), pp. 105–28. Rosenblum's *Transformations in Late Eighteenth-Century Art* (Princeton: Princeton University Press, 1967) reveals some of the ways in which a simpleminded reliance on grandiose period concepts has blurred our vision of the actual development of painterly styles.

2. Charles Rosen, *The Classical Style: Haydn, Mozart, and Beethoven* (New York: W. W. Norton, 1972). Because Rosen's book will be referred to many times throughout this study, subsequent citations will be incorporated within the text.

3. Robert Schumann, *On Music and Musicians*, ed. Konrad Wolff (New York: W. W. Norton, 1946), p. 60.

4. Monroe Beardsley makes a similar point in "The Concept of Economy in Art," *Journal of Aesthetics and Art Criticism* 14 (1956): 370–75.

5. Paul Henry Lang, *Music in Western Civilization* (New York: W. W. Norton, 1941), p. 740.

6. Gilbert Phelps, *Short History of English Literature* (London: Folio Society, 1962), p. 124.

7. Volume 7 of the journal *Wordsworth Circle* contains an excellent series of essays on Austen's relationship to English Romanticism.

8. M. H. Abrams's *Mirror and the Lamp* is subtitled *Romantic Theory and the Critical Tradition* (New York: Oxford University Press, 1953). Although Abrams does not apply his two metaphors to English fiction, they could be used very nicely to illuminate the central differences between *Pride and Prejudice* and *Wuthering Heights*. An earlier work dealing with the same transition in critical and poetic thought is Walter Jackson Bate's *From Classic to Romantic: Premises of Taste in Eighteenth-Century England* (New York: Harper and Row, 1946).

9. Applied to painting and poetry, the term *neoclassical* often has a more precise denotative meaning than when applied to fiction. Whereas the neoclassical poet or painter often incorporates direct allusions to the ancient classical heritage into his work (i.e., Pope, Poussin), Austen's novels are as empty of direct allusions to a classical past as are Mozart's instrumental compositions. The work of each is therefore "classical" in a broadly connotative sense rather than "neoclassical" in a denotative sense. Applied to instrumental music, the term *neoclassical* generally refers to twentieth-century compositions (such as Stravinsky's) which purposely returned to the principles that animated the classical style of Haydn and Mozart.

CHAPTER 1

1. For general comparison of musical and literary terminology see the appropriate chapters of Brown's *Music and Literature*. See also G. P. Springer, "Language and Music: Parallels and Divergencies," in *For R. Jakobson: Essays on the Occasion of his Sixtieth Birthday*, ed. Morris Halle (The Hague: 1956), pp. 504–13.

2. Bernstein's Norton Poetry Lectures have been published in book form under the title *The Unanswered Question* (Cambridge: Harvard University Press, 1976).

3. Ruth Subotnik outlines and evaluates some recent developments in "The Cultural Message of Musical Semiology: Some Thoughts on Music, Language, and Criticism since the Enlightenment," *Critical Inquiry* 4 (1978): 741–68.

4. Mary Alice Burgan, "A Study of the Proposal Scenes in Jane Austen's Major Novels," in *The English Novel in the Nineteenth Century*, ed. George Goodin (Urbana: University of Illinois Press, 1972), pp. 31, 40.

5. Arthur Hutchings, "The Keyboard Music," in *The Mozart Companion*, ed. H. C. Robbins Landon and Donald Mitchell (London: Faber and Faber, 1956), p. 46.

6. Joseph Wiesenfarth, "*Emma*: Point Counterpoint," in *Jane Austen: Bicentenary Essays*, ed. John Halperin (Cambridge: Cambridge University Press, 1975), pp. 221–34.

7. Hugh Ottaway, "The Enlightenment and the Revolution," in *The Pelican History of Music*, vol. 3, *Classical and Romantic* (London: Penguin, 1968), p. 17.

8. Edgar Allan Poe, "Ligeia," in *Selected Writings of Edgar Allan Poe*, ed. Edward H. Davidson (Boston: Houghton Mifflin, 1956), pp. 81–82.

9. Pivotal books in this regard are Alfred Einstein's *Mozart: His Character, His Work*, trans. Arthur Mendel and Nathan Broder (New York: Oxford, 1945)

and Cuthbert Girdlestone's *Mozart and His Piano Concertos* (London: Cassell and Company, 1948; rpt. Dover, 1964). Citations from each of these works will be incorporated within the text.

10. In 1978 the excellent National Public Radio station in Cincinnati, WGUC, published a "Top Forty" of classical music as chosen by subscribers. Two of Rachmaninoff's five works for piano and orchestra were on the list. Of Mozart's twenty-seven piano concertos, there were none!

11. Quoted by Bate, *From Classic to Romantic*, p. 129.

12. Rosen, *Classical Style*, p. 307, sets this famous quote in context and suggests that Mozart was trying to use words to disguise a bold modulation. It is true that his modulations, so tame to most twentieth-century ears, were often considered daring by his contemporaries. Even so, the idea so eloquently stated in the letter—that music must ever please and must never offend the ear—is central to Mozart's aesthetic and his practice.

13. Philip Barford, "The Piano Sonatas—II," in *The Beethoven Companion*, ed. Denis Arnold and Nigel Fortune (London: Faber and Faber, 1971), p. 161.

14. This letter of December 28, 1782, is quoted in Einstein's *Mozart*, p. 112.

15. The phrase is from Rey M. Longyear, "Beethoven and Romantic Irony," in *The Creative World of Beethoven*, ed. Paul Henry Lang (New York: W. W. Norton, 1970), pp. 145–62. Longyear finds the violent "juxtaposition of the prosaic and the poetic" to be particularly prevalent in the music Beethoven composed after 1810. He finds that "playfulness" prevails in Beethoven's early period.

16. George Kubler, *The Shape of Time: Remarks on the History of Things* (New Haven: Yale University Press, 1962).

17. E. H. Gombrich, *Art and Illusion: A Study in the Psychology of Pictorial Representation* (Princeton: Princeton University Press, 1960).

CHAPTER 2

1. For Suzanne K. Langer's excellent discussions of this controversial subject, see "On the Significance of Music," in *Philosophy in a New Key* (New York: New American Library, 1948) and "The Musical Matrix," in *Feeling and Form* (New York: Scribner's, 1953).

2. J. W. N. Sullivan, *Beethoven's Spiritual Development* (New York: New American Library, 1927), p. 33.

3. Hector Berlioz, "On Imitation in Music," reprinted in *Fantastic Symphony*, Norton Critical Score, ed. Edward T. Cone (New York: W. W. Norton, 1971), p. 43.

4. Jacques Barzun, "The Meaning of Meaning in Music: Berlioz Once More," *Musical Quarterly* 66 (January 1980): 20. This passage continues: "And both are programmatic in the same sense of following inner experience while adapting material to set forms and sometimes giving, by association, reminders of the objective world."

5. Donald Francis Tovey, *Essays in Musical Analysis*, vol. 3, *Concertos* (London: Oxford University Press, 1936), p. 74.

6. The increasing imperative toward solo expression is but one of many expla-

nations for the relative dearth of Romantic piano concertos. In perfecting the piano concerto as a form, Mozart to some degree exhausted its best possibilities—as Beethoven was later to do with the symphony and the piano sonata. (Kubler's discussion of "sequence" in *The Shape of Time*, though not applied to music, is highly relevant here.) Even so, Mozart's perfection of the concerto form seems less to have intimidated his successors than to have been largely irrelevant to them. Whereas Beethoven's nine symphonies and thirty-two sonatas did intimidate every nineteenth-century composer who took up either form, Mozart's twenty-seven concertos were largely ignored until the mid-twentieth century.

7. Margaret Homans, "Repression and the Sublimation of Nature in *Wuthering Heights*," *PMLA* 93 (January 1978): 9–19.

8. Mark Schorer's oft-reprinted essay "Fiction and the 'Analogical Matrix'" contrasts the use of metaphor in Austen's *Persuasion* with that in *Wuthering Heights* and in George Eliot's *Middlemarch*.

9. Eric Blom, *Classics: Major and Minor* (New York: Da Capo Press, 1972), p. 29.

10. Alan Walker, "Chopin and Musical Structure: An Analytical Approach," in *The Chopin Companion* (New York, W. W. Norton, 1966), p. 247.

11. Jane Austen, *Persuasion* (New York: New American Library, 1964), pp. 78–79.

12. Just as Anne's "disturbance" combines elements both of disorder and order (the invasion of random impressions into the long fourth sentence, yet the solidity with which each is registered), so does the G-minor episode of K. 466. Its disorder is evident in the abruptness with which it invades the prevailing calm of the movement. Disturbing as it is, however, its form (like that of the fourth sentence) is, though unusual, perfectly orderly: 8 bars plus repeat, 10 bars plus repeat, and 11 bars of transition to the opening material of the movement. The Austen sentence itself concludes with a marked transition: "till enabled by the entrance of Mary and the Miss Musgroves to make over her little patient to their cares, and leave the room."

13. One reason that K. 466 is an exception among Mozart's concertos—and is often considered Romantic—is that the kind of disturbance that breaks out briefly in the second movement dominates both the opening and closing movements.

14. See Edward T. Cone, "Schumann Amplified: An Analysis," in *Fantastic Symphony*, Norton Critical Score, pp. 249–77.

15. This is true even of one of Mozart's most disquieting passages: the celebrated introduction to the "Dissonant" Quartet in C major (K. 465). Rosen points out that "if we stop the famous chromatic introduction . . . at any point and play the chord of C major, we find that not only have Mozart's complex and weirdly disquieting progressions established the key from the outset without once actually sounding the tonic chord, but they never leave the key: the chord of C major will appear always as the stable point around which every chord in these measures resolves. The opening of a work by

Mozart is always solidly based, no matter how ambiguous and disturbing its expressive significance" (p. 186).

16. Emily Brontë, *Wuthering Heights*, Revised Norton Critical Edition (New York: W. W. Norton, 1972), p. 107.

17. Edgar Allan Poe, "The Masque of the Red Death," in *Selected Writings*, pp. 174–75.

18. Jane Austen, *Emma*, Norton Critical Edition (New York: W. W. Norton, 1972), p. 266.

19. Poe, *Selected Writings*, p. 320.

CHAPTER 3

1. Herman Melville, *Billy Budd and Other Tales* (New York: New American Library, 1961), p. 61.

2. Barzun, *Berlioz and the Romantic Century*, 1:383.

3. The quasi-scientific criticism of our age has become wary of the unquantifiable concept of the *Zeitgeist* (which, admittedly, has been loosely used on occasion). Yet Robert Schumann, for example, surely knew what he meant when he wrote of "the mind of the times" and of "a *Zeitgeist* that tolerates a burlesque of the *Dies irae*" (in his splendid analysis of the *Symphonie fantastique*). He wrote of a *Zeitgeist* different from that of Mozart or Austen. See "A Symphony by Berlioz," reprinted in *Fantastic Symphony*, p. 248.

4. *Letters of Wolfgang Amadeus Mozart*, ed. Hans Mersmann (New York: Dover, 1972), pp. 19, 233.

5. Quoted in Romain Rolland, *Beethoven, the Creator*, trans. Ernest Newman (New York: Dover, 1964), p. 15.

6. See her letter to her nephew Edward reprinted in the Norton Critical Edition of *Pride and Prejudice*, p. 284.

7. Paul Henry Lang, Introduction to *The Creative World of Mozart* (New York: W. W. Norton, 1963), p. 11.

Part Two

1. Girdlestone in *Mozart and His Piano Concertos* uses a numbering system according to which Mozart's K. 271 is his fifth piano concerto, not his ninth. To avoid any confusion, my analysis generally refers to each concerto by its Köchel number.

2. Tovey, *Essays in Musical Analysis*, vol. 3, *Concertos*, pp. 6–7.

3. Jane Austen, *Northanger Abbey* (New York: Dell Publications, 1959), p. 55.

CHAPTER 4

1. The letters to Cassandra were written from Chawton on January 29 and February 4, 1813, shortly after the novel was published. They are reprinted in the Norton Critical Edition of *Pride and Prejudice*, pp. 280–81.

2. Robbins Landon, "The Concertos: (2) Their Musical Origin and Development," in *The Mozart Companion*, p. 253.

3. Dorothy van Ghent, "On *Pride and Prejudice*," from *The English Novel, Form and Function* (1953), reprinted in the Norton Critical Edition of *Pride and Prejudice*, p. 368.

4. Bar numbers throughout are from the Eulenberg edition.

5. Often the orchestral exposition of a Mozart concerto is seen as introducing all of the instruments minus one—the solo instrument. In this sense, K. 271, with its "premature" entry by the piano, is an exception. But some scholars, basing their reasoning on the evidence of the scores themselves, believe that Mozart intended the keyboard to be used not only as a solo but as a continuo instrument. Accordingly, the keyboard customarily *is* heard in the orchestral exposition. "In such cases as this," Eva and Paul Badura-Skoda have argued, "the piano must blend with the orchestral tutti so that the listener does not even notice it as a separate element in the overall sound. Thus in Mozart's piano concertos the piano has two quite distinct and contrasting functions; that of a solo instrument, which opposes the orchestra in a 'concertante' way, and that of a versatile orchestral instrument, which here and there has to support and enrich the texture." See *Interpreting Mozart on the Keyboard*, trans. Leo Black (London: Barrie and Rockliff, 1962), p. 203. For a thoughtful argument against the playing of the continuo passages, see Rosen, *Classical Style*, pp. 189–96.

6. The earlier preparation for the modulation to distant harmonies and for the transition to Meryton is in each case even more careful and subtle than is suggested above. Not only were Meryton and the more distant harmonies alluded to but not pursued at the very beginning of the Netherfield and the solo expositions; each was even more subtly alluded to during the Longbourn and the orchestral expositions. As Rosen points out, D-flat, the unstable diminished seventh of the scale of E-flat major, is finally reached in bar 45 at a pivotal point in the orchestral exposition. The strongest moment of harmonic tension in the exposition, this harmonic suspension lightly foreshadows the emphatic modulation to dissonant keys that is briefly anticipated in the solo exposition before finally breaking forth in the development. Similarly, the strongest moment of tension in the Longbourn exposition comes at the ball in chapter 3, when Darcy rudely offends Elizabeth. The location of the ball is unspecified at the time, but in chapter 5 the attentive reader is quietly informed that the ball had occurred in Meryton. This, too, lightly foreshadows the transition to Meryton that is anticipated at the beginning of the Netherfield exposition and that finally occurs during the Meryton "development." Just as the modulation to F minor and the transition to Meryton represent the high point of tension in the first movement and the first volume as a whole, so does the light foreshadowing of each in the middle of the orchestral and the Longbourn expositions represent the high point of tension within those structural units.

7. As the art of classical improvisation is lost, it is fortunate that Mozart wrote

out cadenzas for many of his concertos and that many of these—including those for K. 271—have been preserved. (He seems to have transcribed these cadenzas as learning devices for his piano students, who would later learn to improvise on their own.) The *Neue Ausgabe sämtlicher Werke* prints two cadenzas for the first movement of K. 271. My discussion is of its Cadenza "B"—the one that is printed in the Eulenberg score.

8. The general proportions summarized here for K. 271 are typical of Mozart's first-movement concerto form (though in few of the other concertos are the respective sections so perfectly symmetrical or so clearly announced in each case by a restatement of the opening theme). I know of no other Austen novel (nor of any novel by any one else) whose first-volume structure compares in detail to the one presented here for *Pride and Prejudice*.

9. Letter of February 4, 1813, reprinted in the Norton Critical Edition of *Pride and Prejudice*, p. 281.

10. While responding to my argument as presented in an early draft of this chapter, Jeffrey Siegel, the concert pianist (and a fine interpreter of K. 271), questioned whether there is any "exhilaration" at the end of the Andantino. For him, the movement expresses unadulterated sadness and despair. I understand his point, but agree with Girdlestone that those emotions are not only expressed but transcended. For Girdlestone, the Andantino of K. 271 is the first of Mozart's "tragic andantes." He finds that "the sadness is so transfigured in them that they leave no feeling of depression or disheartenment, but rather comfort and strengthen us as much as his most exuberant allegros. The beauty first glimpsed, then reached, through tears, is of such brightness that the listener is spell-bound and forgets the bitterness, forgets the suffering whence the movement sprang" (p. 41). I believe that the piano's imaginative acceptance of the orchestra's full burden during the recapitulation has much to do with what Girdlestone intuits as the transfiguration of sadness into comfort and strength. "First glimpsed" by the piano during the solo exposition, the beauty and the truth of the emotion is "then reached, through tears" in the recapitulation.

11. The most tragic first movement among Mozart's piano concertos, for example, is that of K. 466 (in D minor, No. 20). It is followed by one of the most serene of his second movements—until the Romance is itself invaded by the tempestuous G-minor presto. The most disturbing of all Mozart concertos, K. 466 is immediately followed by one of the most buoyant, K. 467 (in C major, No. 21). Other celebrated contrasting paired works by Mozart include the quintets in C major (K. 515) and G minor (K. 516), the symphonies in G minor (K. 550) and C major (K. 551, the "Jupiter"), and, among the operas, *The Marriage of Figaro* (1786) and *Don Giovanni* (1787).

12. Letter of January 29, 1813, reprinted in the Norton Critical Edition of *Pride and Prejudice*, p. 280.

13. Hans Keller, "Britten and Mozart," *Music and Letters* 29 (1948): 20.

14. Tony Tanner, Introduction to *Pride and Prejudice* (London: Penguin, 1972), p. 46.

Notes

CHAPTER 5

1. Jane Austen, *Emma*, Norton Critical Edition, ed. Stephen M. Parrish (New York: W. W. Norton, 1972), p. 1. All further citations from the novel are from this edition and are incorporated within the text.
2. J. E. Austen-Leigh, *A Memoir of Jane Austen*, ed. R. W. Chapman (1926), p. 157.
3. *Harvard Brief Dictionary of Music.*
4. As printed in the format of the Norton Critical Editions, *Emma* measures 335 pages as opposed to the earlier novel's 268. Its three volumes consist of 101, 111, and 122 pages, as compared to 92, 74, and 102 for *Pride and Prejudice*.
5. Mary Lascelles, "The Narrator and His Reader," reprinted in the Norton Critical Edition of *Emma*, p. 392.
6. The precedent for such decorations is strong—though the results often are not. Mozart himself expected some of his slow melodies to be ornamented in various ways not indicated in the score. As early as 1801 Philipp Karl Hoffmann published "A Decorated Version of the Andante" of K. 503 for just that purpose. But Hoffmann's version (reproduced in the Norton Critical Score of K. 503) is not necessarily reliable, and today it is impossible to re-create exactly how Mozart might have expected the ornaments to sound.
7. Meyer's essay (on the trio of Mozart's K. 550) was cited in the Introduction.
8. This melody, more than almost any instrumental music I know, seems to demand translation into words. In hazarding a translation here, of course, I am attempting to follow, not to confine, the melody. To me, the three-note motif says, "I'm sor-ry." The solo's reiterated rhythms therefore say, "I'm sor-ry, I'm sor-ry, I'm sor-ry; I'm sor-ry, I'm sor-ry, I'm sor-ry." These words correspond to the confessional quality I feel is inherent in the melody. But the same rhythms could just as well be confessing, "I love you, I love you, I love you; I love you, I love you, I love you." At times the music seems to be confessing both messages at once—especially when the winds, after returning the solo's original message and its melodic extension, subject the three-note motif to contrapuntal development. Girdlestone calls the central couplet "sorrowful and passionate." It is both, whether one is moved to attach verbal meaning to its "speech rhythms" or not. In one sense, the emotion exchanged between piano and winds corresponds to the emotion exchanged between two sisters, during a reconciliation, in Ingmar Bergman's film *Cries and Whispers*. The viewer *sees* two women exchanging words of remorse and consolation; the viewer *hears* the "speech rhythms" of a cello playing unaccompanied Bach. Their emotion is beyond their words. So, to take the idea full circle, is Emma's emotion once she feels true remorse. She does not tell Miss Bates she is sorry in so many words; rather she acts in such a way that allows Miss Bates to perceive and to register that emotion. Similarly, when Emma sees Mr. Knightley after visiting the Bateses, she has no opportunity to voice her remorse. But her countenance shows it, and her friend registers it.
9. Wolfgang Amadeus Mozart, *Piano Concerto in C major, K. 503*, Norton Criti-

cal Score, ed. Joseph Kerman (New York: W. W. Norton, 1970), p. 173, n. 16.

10. Whalley, "Jane Austen: The Poet," p. 130.
11. Kroeber, *Studies in Fictional Structure*, p. 23.
12. Chapman's appraisal is quoted in the preface to the Norton Critical Edition of *Emma*, pp. vii–viii.

CHAPTER 6

1. Arthur Hutchings, for example, finds that K. 595 is "full of the gracious wisdom of a man reaching his autumn," rather than the mere thirty-five years "alloted" to Mozart. Valerie Shaw, writing in 1975, argues that so many critics have commented on the "autumnal mood" in *Persuasion* that it has been overemphasized. See Hutchings, *A Companion to Mozart's Piano Concertos*, 2d ed. (London: Oxford University Press, 1948), p. 190; and Shaw, "Jane Austen's Subdued Heroines," *Nineteenth-Century Fiction* 30 (December 1975): 220.
2. Whalley, "Jane Austen: The Poet," p. 131.
3. Hutchings, *Companion*, p. 190.
4. One much discussed structural flaw in the novel is the long and dramatically superfluous conversation between Anne and Mrs. Smith which occupies all of chapter 9 of volume 2. Some critics surmise that this and other technical imperfections might have been overcome had the author lived to see the book through to publication.
5. Jane Austen, *Persuasion* (New York: New American Library, 1964), p. 10. All citations from the novel will be from this edition.
6. Robbins Landon, *The Mozart Companion*, p. 278.
7. Mozart's preparation for this rhythm has been even subtler still. The first anticipation of this rhythmic pulse occurs in the ascending motif in bar 2 of the solo melody (the bar in which Girdlestone notes the "trifling" difference between the solo and orchestral versions). The same ascending motif is repeated in bar 6, therefore twice preparing within the melody itself for the lilting, graceful ascent from bar 7 to 8. The exact rhythmic pulse found in bars 2 and 6 is also found in related motifs in the solo extension of the melody (P^{1a}) and in the violins' broken melody in the orchestral coda (O^2). This pulse is exactly the one that the solo incorporates as part of its "new" melody in bars 123 and 125 at the return of the coda. Its being sounded jointly by flute, bassoons, piano, and violins in bar 125 prepares for its reappearance (in the form of the earlier ascending marchlike rhythm) in the flute and cellos in the last five bars. One reason the piano only sketches the first half of its new melody in the closing bars is that the marchlike motif now alternating between the flute and cellos contains the rhythmic pulse of the second half of its "new" theme.
8. The second note of the progression—the C-flat—is simply a different "spelling" for the B-natural of the earlier chromatic ascent.
9. Piggott, *The Innocent Diversion*, p. 130. The words quoted conclude Piggott's

283

discussion of Austen's fiction. In a brief aside when discussing *Pride and Prejudice*, he imagines "the 'quartet' in Lady Catherine's drawing-room as part of some ideal but impossible operatic comedy, with a libretto by, perhaps, Hofmannstahl, and music, of course, by Mozart" (p. 62).

10. These lines are from a poem I wrote in response to a performance of K. 581, Mozart's Clarinet Quintet.
11. Stuart Tave, *Some Words of Jane Austen* (Chicago: University of Chicago Press, 1975), pp. 276–77.
12. Badura-Skoda, *Interpreting Mozart on the Keyboard*, p. 269.
13. Malcolm Bradbury, "*Persuasion* Again," *Essays in Criticism* 18 (1968): 388–89.

APPENDIX 1

1. Mollie Sands, "Jane Austen and Her Music Books," *Jane Austen Society Reports*, 1956, pp. 13–15.
2. W. A. Craik, *Jane Austen in Her Time* (London: Thomas Nelson and Sons, 1969), p. 60. A much earlier critic who also underestimated Jane Austen's relation to music is Elisabeth Lockwood, "Jane Austen and Some Drawing-Room Music of Her Time," *Music and Letters* 15 (1934): 112–19. According to Lockwood, "Music was simply a social amenity for her and chiefly by its association with dancing."
3. Piggott, *The Innocent Diversion*, p. 1. Subsequent citations will be indicated parenthetically in the text. For a delightful earlier summary of the role of music in the novels see Norman Cameron, "Jane Austen and Music," *Chesterian* 19 (1937–38): 33–38. Cameron finds that "the details" of the piano performances of Austen's heroines are "so frequently and interestedly chronicled that one suspects music to have played an important part in the life of the authoress itself." Sensitive to Austen's awareness of her own musical limitations, however, and unaware of her own extensive musical library, he does not develop those "suspicions." Harold Babbs utilizes the "piano scenes" in successive novels to trace changes in Austen's fictional technique. See *Jane Austen's Novels: The Fabric of Dialogue* (Columbus: Ohio State University, 1962), pp. 132–44.
4. R. W. Chapman, *Jane Austen's Letters to Her Sister Cassandra and Others* (Oxford: The Clarendon Press, 1932), 1:10. Subsequent citations will be indicated parenthetically in the text.
5. Constance Hill, *Jane Austen: Her Homes and Her Friends* (London: John Lane, 1902), pp. 84–86.
6. Caroline Austen-Leigh, *My Aunt Jane Austen: A Memoir* (London: Spottiswoode, Ballantyne and Co., 1952), pp. 6–7.
7. Until very recently it has been assumed that Austen was without a pianoforte from 1801 to 1807, when living first at Bath, then at Southampton. In a 1980 essay, however, Piggott produces evidence suggesting that she rented a pianoforte in Southampton, causing him to rate Austen's devotion to the piano somewhat more highly than in his book-length study. See "Jane Austen's Southampton Piano," *Jane Austen Society Reports*, 1980, pp. 6–9. He now

concludes that "music-making seems to have remained an unbroken thread in her pattern of daily life"; he also speaks of her playing as "having been a solace and perhaps an inspiration to her at Steventon and Chawton." The reference to solace and inspiration strikes a tone entirely missing from *The Innocent Diversion* and is unaccounted for in the rest of the essay. It may be a silent allusion to my essay "Jane Austen's Neglected Song Book" in the previous year's *Reports* (see Appendix 2).

8. Piggott's summary of the pieces marked for special attention in this book omits one of the two Koželuch works and leaves out the Nardini altogether. As my own analysis of the music books is based on separate visits to Chawton in 1977 and 1979, before *The Innocent Diversion* was published, our conclusions are based on independent study of the material.

9. Piggott presents an excellent summary of these and the other books now in the possession of Henry Jenkyns in his chapter "The Second Collection." His arguments that the "Cassandra" books are likely to have previously belonged to Jane are strong. My independent (though necessarily hasty) study of these books in 1977 had also led to the conclusion that many of the manuscripts—and especially those of the Haydn sonata and the overture to *La Buona Figliuola*—were in Austen's own hand. Piggott reports that the latter overture is signed "Mrs. Austen." My notes, which I have not been able to verify, indicate that this work was originally signed "Jane Austen" and then covered over. If this is so, we have even stronger evidence for her ownership of some, if not all, of the music in the two books that now have Cassandra's signature.

10. In the essay on the Southampton piano, Piggott speculates that Austen may have rented an instrument in Bath too, though as of yet there is no evidence that this is so. He then surmises that she may have acquired some of her keyboard music in the music shops of Bath during the years she lived there, but I did not notice any internal evidence in the Chawton collection of musical scores acquired after the 1790s.

11. The extensive music collection of the British Museum shows relatively few Beethoven or Mozart piano sonatas in print during Austen's lifetime, with no keyboard works by either composer available in the 1790s. Although Mozart had died in 1791, the first English editions of scattered sonatas do not seem to have begun appearing until 1802 at the earliest; most of his sonatas did not even appear in Austen's lifetime. The first London edition given for Beethoven's "Pathétique" is ca. 1807; his previous sonata, the delightful Opus 10, No. 3 (one that would certainly have been more to Austen's taste) is not represented in the British Museum collection until the Cocks edition of the complete sonatas in the 1880s.

12. William S. Newman, *The Sonata in the Classic Era*, 2d ed. (New York: W. W. Norton, 1972). Subsequent references to this invaluable study will be incorporated in the text following the abbreviation SCE.

13. When I returned to reexamine this book at Chawton in the summer of 1979 it had—for the moment at least—disappeared from the collection.

14. *Letters of Wolfgang Amadeus Mozart*, p. 220.

15. The stylistic change is apparent even in so slight a theme and variations as the one R. Andrews composed on the theme of "Jennies Bawbee," which Emily Brontë first played in the 1830s. The unmistakable influence of Beethoven is strongly felt in the opening introduction, which, judging from the rest of the work, Andrews probably lifted piecemeal from the master himself. My cassette recording entitled "A Musical Evening with Jane Austen and Emily Brontë" and published by the Jeffrey Norton Publishers (1981) includes the Pleyel theme and variations and the introduction to the Andrews, as played by Ted Diaconoff; also heard is the minuet from Schobert's "July" Lesson.

16. William S. Newman, *The Sonata since Beethoven*, 2d ed. (New York: W. W. Norton, 1972), pp. 468–69.

17. Piggott bases his determination of the likely date of composition (post-1808) on the chronology of Steibelt's residency in Russia. Both the internal evidence of the music itself and its position at the very end of one of Austen's manuscript books would tend to corroborate this dating. So would the beauty and assurance of the manuscript copy itself.

18. The sonata by Joseph Mazzinghi (1765–1844) that she copied into one of her manuscript books consists of movements marked Spiritoso, Larghetto, and Vivace. Many of the manuscripts that appear to be in her hand in one of the "Cassandra" books also follow the three-movement sonata form: the Haydn C-major Sonata (Allegro con brio, Adagio, Allegro); a sonata whose composer is unlisted (Allegro, Andante, Allegretto); and even the overture to *La Buona Figliuola* (Spiritoso, Andante, Presto).

19. Jane Aiken Hodge, *Only a Novel: The Double Life of Jane Austen* (New York: Coward, McGann, and Geoghegan, 1972), pp. 13–14.

20. The Clementi sonata found in one of the "Cassandra" books lacks the pre-Romantic power that, in some of Clementi's works, influenced the young Beethoven. Opus 26 is, in Piggott's words, "unfortunately one of that composer's weakest effusions" (p. 158). One somewhat vehement pre-Romantic work in the other Cassandra book is Steibelt's Opus 33, which, as noted above, contains the once-celebrated "Storm Rondo." More typical of the musical style in the book, however, are the "pre-Classical" Six Sonatas by J. C. Bach, a composer who strongly influenced the young Mozart.

21. Austen-Leigh, *My Aunt Jane Austen*, p. 7.

APPENDIX 2

1. A. Walton Litz, "*Persuasion*: Forms of Estrangement," in *Jane Austen: Bicentenary Essays*, pp. 223–24.

2. See my "Jane Austen's Neglected Song Book," *Jane Austen Society Reports*, 1979, pp. 7–12. Piggott is the only other writer to speculate that Austen may have had some hand in assembling the 1778 songbook. In *The Innocent Diversion* he notes that the songs from Storace's *The Siege of Belgrade*, which premiered in London in 1791, are more likely to have been copied out by Austen than by her parents. But he remains deterred by the 1778 date and, more importantly, by the fact that he does not note the signature of "Miss Jane Austen" on the contents page. He also fails to notice the manuscript

songs that have been inserted into the book without being indicated in the table of contents.

3. Although Austen titled this work "Song," it is known by its first line ("Why tarries my Love!") in a version harmonized for four voices that is preserved in the Library of Congress. The composer of the original melody is listed as Thomas Welsh.

4. The second song is "Louisa's Complaint, from Mrs. Robinson's Novel of Nancrenza, the music by Krumpholtz," published by G. Gilbert in New York, ca. 1794. A copy is preserved in the Library of Congress.

5. According to Newman, Krumpholtz studied composition with Haydn as a member of Prince Esterhazy's orchestra and published "some 32 sonatas" in Paris or London between 1775 and 1789. The one sonata Newman comments on is a "fluent, melodious, three-movement work with considerable Alberti bass and a tendency reminiscent of Haydn to develop each idea as it is stated" (SCE, p. 663).

6. The cassette recording "A Musical Evening with Jane Austen and Emily Brontë" (mentioned in the notes to Appendix 1) includes Gayle Sheard's performances of the following songs: "Susan," "Why tarries my love," "I have a silent sorrow here," "Whither Love thy beauties bring," "Che farò senza Euridice," and "William."

7. Dibdin, a popular English composer of the day, is well represented in Austen's songbooks. His signature is found on the printed scores of two of his works in the 1778 songbook: item 16 ("Sound Argument") and item 22 ("Bachelor's Ball").

8. Litz, "Persuasion" pp. 223–24.

9. So far as I can tell, all of the musical manuscripts in the 1778 songbook, including item 8 ("How imperfect is expression"), are in Austen's own hand, as is the table of contents. Yet some of the musical and verbal notation (especially that of item 8 and the contents) is cruder than that of the most polished songs, of which Austen's copy of Krumpholtz's "Whither Love thy beauties bring" is the most splendid example. Although the hand seems to be the same one, it seems likely that the Krumpholtz was transcribed later than some of the other songs, though how much later is impossible to say. At Chawton I compared the Krumpholtz manuscript with those in the books entirely in Austen's manuscript hand; there is no doubt that the hand is hers and that it is approximately in the same stage of development. Professional handwriting analysis might help in dating the songs and keyboard works that Austen transcribed, though judging from when most of her music was composed and was popular, the 1790s at Steventon seems to be the most likely decade.

10. These two romantic episodes in Austen's life are briefly summarized, among other places, in Cecil's A Portrait of Jane Austen, pp. 74–76, 96–97. Cecil concludes his brief discussion of Austen's relation to music with these words: "Her nephew Edward was to remember her playing and singing traditional songs with spirit and sweetness. Anyway, if she did not enjoy music at all, why did she bother to get up early in order to practise?" (p. 133).

Index

Index

Index

Index

Evance, William, A Favorite
Concerto, 253

Fielding, Henry, 7, 8, 261
Forster, E. M., *Aspects of the Novel*, 6
Freedman, William, 274 (n. 22)
Furst, Lilian, 275 (n. 23)

Gandhi, Mahatma, 73
Gilbert, Stuart, 274 (n. 17)
Girdlestone, Cuthbert: on Mozart's
piano concertos, 81–82, 208–
9; on *K. 271*, 79, 84, 88, 99,
105, 108, 114, 281 (n. 10); on
K. 503, 147–48, 155, 156, 172,
173, 175, 178, 179, 180–81,
182, 183; on *K. 595*, 189, 190,
198, 202, 207, 208–9, 210,
212, 214, 226, 227–28, 229,
230, 244, 246; *Mozart and His
Piano Concertos*, 24, 79, 81–82,
277 (n. 9)
Gluck, Christoph Willibald, 249; "Che
farò senza Euridice?" 268, 271,
287 (n. 6)
Goethe, Johann Wolfgang von,
Werther, 79
Gombrich, E. H., 35
Goya, Francisco, 73
Grieg, Edvard, 42
Grove, Sir Charles, *Beethoven and His
Nine Symphonies*, 24, 263
Guetti, James, 274 (n. 22)
Gulda, Friedrich, 156
Gyrowetz, Adalbert, 254

Handel, George Frideric, 137, 249,
253
Harding, D. W., 75, 129
Hawthorne, Nathaniel, 59, 61; *The
Scarlet Letter*, 64
Haydn, Franz Joseph, 13, 81, 249,
250, 253, 256, 270, 287 (n. 5);
and Mozart, 8, 24, 31, 33, 34,
36, 45, 64, 74, 255, 257, 260,
263; Sonata in C major, 254,
270, 286 (n. 18)

Hill, Constance, 251
Hodge, Jane Aiken, 260, 261
Hoffmann, Philipp Karl, 282 (n. 6)
Hoffmeister, Franz Anton, 250, 253,
255, 256–57, 261, 263; Sonata
for Piano Forte, 257
Homans, Margaret, 44
Homer, *Odyssey*, 46
"How imperfect is expression," 264,
269, 271
Hume, David, 25
Hutchings, Arthur, 18, 190, 283 (n. 1)

"I have a silent sorrow here" (Duchess
of Devonshire), 265, 268, 289
Irving, Washington, 59

Jackson, William, 253
Jenkyns, Henry, 254
Jesus Christ, 73
Jeunehomme, Mlle, 79
Johnson, Samuel, 7, 8, 9, 31, 261
Joyce, James, 5, 35; *Finnegan's Wake*,
35; *Ulysses*, 35

Keats, John, 16
Keller, Hans, 130
Kennedy, Margaret, 3
Kerman, Joseph, 3, 182
Kipnis, Igor, 83
Kitto, H. D. F., *Greek Tragedy*, 6
Knight, Fanny, 251, 263
Koczwara, František, "Battle of
Prague," 253, 254
Koželuch, Leopold Anton, 250, 253,
254, 255, 261, 263; "Concerto,"
253, 255; "A Lesson," 255
Kroeber, Karl, 4, 5, 184; *Styles in
Fictional Structure*, 6
Kronenberger, Louis, 3
Krumpholtz, Johann Baptist, 266;
"Whither Love thy beauties
bring," 265, 268, 270, 287 (nn.
6, 9)
Kubler, George, 34

Index